C000179831

Working with Others

Helping

and

Human Relations

Advice, Guidance, Counselling

by
Bryce Taylor

Taylor, Bryce
Working with Others
1 Human Relations
2 Helping
3 Counselling
4 Psychology
5 Education

ISBN1 1 871992 51 6

Published by
Oasis Press
Hall Mews
Clifford Road
Boston Spa
Wetherby
West Yorkshire
LS23 6DT

Tel: 01937 541700
Fax: 01937 541800
Email: books@oasisschool.org.co.uk

**To all those who
appreciate the value of
'ordinary caring'**

Contents

Acknowledgements   1

Introduction   2

Section I The World of Helping

Chapter 1   The Good Samaritan   7
Chapter 2   An Overview of Helping   15
Chapter 3   Helping Agencies & Helping Roles   28
Chapter 4   Practitioner Preparation & Experience   35

Section II The Helping Spectrum: Advice, Guidance & Counselling

Chapter 5   A Helping Framework   43
Chapter 6   Advisory Methods   51
Chapter 7   Guidance Methods   58
Chapter 8   Counselling & Support Methods   75

Section III The Helping Context: Careers and Conditions

Chapter 9   The Upstream Helper   87
Chapter 10   Helping as a 'Profession'   91
Chapter 11   Being a Professional Practitioner   100
Chapter 12   The Altruistic Practitioner?   108
Chapter 13   Practitioner Survival and Support   113

Section IV The Helping Conversation

Chapter 14 The Helping Conversation   119

Section V The Core of Helping: Listening & Responding

Chapter 15   Listening   141
Chapter 16   Between Listening & Responding   159
Chapter 17   The Importance of Rapport   172
Chapter 18   Responding   179

Section VI Practitioner Resources

Chapter 19   The Transition from 'Helper' into Practitioner   197
Chapter 20   Working with a Plan   213
Chapter 21   Approaching Problems   224

Section VII The Seven Stage Model of Human Relations

Chapter 22   The Seven Stage Model: An Overview   237
Chapter 23   The Seven Stage Model   246

Section VIII Deeper Issues

Chapter 24   Moving Towards Deeper Issues   313
Chapter 25   Working at Depth   317
Chapter 26   The Self as Instrument   331

References & Bibliography   343

Index   345

Acknowledgement

Working with Others owes a lot to a lot of people: colleagues who developed it; writers who contributed to the thinking behind it; individuals who adapted it for their own special use; and the literally thousands of people who have encountered the model and been given an opportunity to review their helping approach through the perspective it offers. My thanks to all.

Introduction

From life in the 1980s as an A4 collection of handouts illustrating some of the key ideas about helping and counselling skills, *Working with Others* is now in its sixth edition. It began life as a supplement to the work on short and then longer programmes developed at Oasis. As a result, the book is designed to complement practical experience and so is largely written in a conversational style.

The Seven Stage Model evolved from a variety of influences and arose out of the need to find a descriptive account of how we attempt to understand how it is that we come to be where we are. More than anything else, it seems to me, there is the need for individuals to find coherence in their account of themselves and this is something that is too often lacking in so much of modern life. The disorientation that accompanies the speed of change can leave people with little to hold on to by way of meaning and therefore open to being told what 'they need' if they aren't careful. Restoring the opportunity for self-direction through grasping our personal history seems one of the fundamental elements to any subsequent help that might be offered.

Few of us get a chance to tell 'our' story; all too often we are telling the story we think others want to hear, or the one we believe we *should* tell, or we are desperately seeking a space to say anything, let alone tell our story. The idea of helping being a means for someone to gain a sense of coherence over their own experience, through the listening and gentle exploration of another, stands at the heart of *Working with Others*.

Formulating the sequential progress of a helping relationship, now it is down on paper, looks straightforward enough, and is, but it has taken much reflection and testing out to get it there.

The model is more sophisticated and complex now, as a result not only of the thinking and reflection that has gone into it but also the way it has been tested in practice by literally thousands of people from any number of occupations, in a great many workplaces and settings. It has always held up as a useful way of 'mapping' interaction between people whether in the workplace, the counselling session, the work group or the interview room. Not only that, the model allows individuals to select those 'parts' that make most sense of their own particular circumstances and helping activities. In this way the model is not a text to be slavishly adhered to, it is simply a way of describing what happens in effective helping relationships. The real value of the model, however, is for those moments when the practitioner is wondering, 'What next?' or, 'Where next?' At such a time, having a model to refer to can provide an important source of support for the work of any practitioner, however experienced.

Working with Others, however, is more than the model; it is also a consideration of the major features of helping and human relations that affect a wide range of practitioners.

The first section, *The World of Helping,* highlights many key aspects of helping, helpers/practitioners[1] and the world of helping, and introduces the reader to the concept of 'ordinary caring' as the foundation for all other forms of help.

The second section, *The Helping Spectrum,* is an in-depth exploration of helper roles on a broad spectrum from advice, through guidance to support and counselling. Relevant situations, styles of operating, skills and approaches for each of the eight strategies in the spectrum are all clearly given. In the third section, *The Helping Context,* issues that influence the conditions practitioners work within and the need for involvement and understanding beyond the individual coming for help are all explored.

This leads into a section entitled *The Helping Conversation.* Here, the fundamental importance of the 'self as the instrument' through which help may be offered is described and discussed. The centrality of relationship, of being willing to be with the other person and of being willing to be real in that relationship all begin to be examined in some detail. The implications that this style of relating has for the training of helping practitioners and counsellors are also explored.

From here, in *Section Five: The Core of Helping: Listening and Responding,* there is an in-depth exploration of the key conditions that need to be present if a helping relationship is to be effective. The core conditions of helping, the development and maintenance of rapport, helpful – and unhelpful – responses, and the intricacies of effective listening are all examined.

In the next two sections, *Practitioner Resources* and *The Seven Stage Model of Human Relations,* we discover models of helping, look at matters relevant to a helping practice and issues that are important for practitioners, the clients they work with, as well as the agencies that are often involved. There is exceptionally useful and detailed information concerning the life of a helping relationship and the range of skills, interventions and strategies that are relevant and important to each stage.

All of the preceding work is relevant and applicable to anybody who finds themselves in any form of helping relationship; the following section begins to take the helping relationship to a greater depth. In order to do this, the importance and place of models and theories and the impact they have upon how people work with others, as counsellors, helpers or practitioners, is debated in *Section Eight: Deeper Issues.*

---

[1] 'Practitioner' is the term, one of many possibilities, chosen for use throughout this book to describe the person who is putting themselves at the service of the other in any helping situation – helpers, counsellors, helping practitioners, mentors, guides, therapists and many more all thus fall within its ambit. In its widest sense, a practitioner is someone who practises i.e. has an applied role and that might be in an official capacity or in a more informal ad hoc situation.

SECTION I

THE WORLD OF HELPING

Chapter 1
The Good Samaritan

Working with Others is about help – in its many forms and appearances – and what we mean by helping and the risks and temptations. Whilst the underlying view of the book and its author is that help is not something confined to experts or necessarily mysterious, it is nevertheless not something that can be left to happen by itself. If help is to be both effective and freeing to the person receiving it, then it needs consideration. In an important regard, help is not accidental.

The contention that this book sets out to argue and demonstrate is that *effective help is an educational process*. When help works, people learn; when they learn they are able to take that learning and apply it to other places and times in their lives. At its best, help enables the learner to generate even better ways of operating in the world because they learn how to develop their initial learning through the experiences and reflections they make as they go. That is the presupposition which this book applies to help of all kinds. Such a view is often spoken of as 'empowering the other'.

Admitting that we require help is not easy for many of us. It leaves us open for others to take advantage of our situation. Standing in need of help makes a person dependent upon the good will and intentions of the other. The relationship is no longer one of equality. There is imbalance and debt involved. However much the practitioner sets the debt owed aside, it is nevertheless felt strongly by the person in need of help. It may at some later point turn from indebtedness to resentment if the person in need begins to feel they have been in some way exploited.

Offering to help is momentarily to have a degree of power over another – even if it is only the power of withholding the offer as in 'I could help you but you will have to wait until…' – something many parents find themselves having to say when there are too many competing demands for their assistance. The practitioner is in the position of being needed: a strong position of power. It is possible for the practitioner to take advantage of this by withholding the help they can offer or by exploiting their position and manipulating the client. They may find it uncomfortable or a source of satisfaction but the power is undeniable and has to be taken into account.

For many, the very appeal of being a helper is itself a socially acceptable way of avoiding the fact that we have needs of our own. Helping then becomes a convenient means of disguising that I am a lot more like the other than I often allow myself to recognise. Indeed, the other person's need and my meeting it then becomes a way of creating the appearance that I am other than I am and they are not as I am. Being armed with the belief that the other needs help and that I can give it can make for a very perverse or very condescending form of help, if we are not careful. It is also a form of help from which it is hard to disentangle and escape. This matter of power and the awareness of how it is used lies at the heart of helping in all forms. Helping requires the exercise of power with care.

The other element in all forms of effective help is the care given by the practitioner to offer enough and no more; to offer what is required and no more and to leave the other person in a better place at the end of the exchange than they were at the beginning. *The Good Samaritan is frequently quoted as our culture's over-riding example of help.* It is a model that is exceedingly difficult to do well, though it is simple enough to describe. But to do enough, to do no more and to be sure that the other is more able, or at least no more un-able, to go on their way at the end of the exchange is often not as straightforward to assess as we might think.

Just what does the story of the *Good Samaritan* illustrate about helping? The first point to bear in mind is that the Good Samaritan was a Samaritan – he was not only different from the one he helped but his kind were in hostile dispute with the group to which the person who received his help belonged. The story centres upon an unexpected and risky act of selfless generosity from one stranger to another – one person reaching across a cultural divide to another. Here we have someone who has every reason *not to help* but does.

It is also the story of someone who, though a stranger, is not an unknown quantity. The Samaritan and his 'client' – as he would be titled in our day – are from the same region and share a recognised understanding of their situation. They hold common expectations of their view of one another and live amongst an understood system of considerations. The Samaritan does not come out of the blue from nowhere – Samaria is a land neighbouring Judea, the country where the injured person came from, and part of the Holy Land.

The Good Samaritan clearly makes a calculated act: he does what is *not* expected. To do that he must first know what is expected and decide it is more worthwhile to do the unexpected – at least for his purposes. He has to know the expectations in order to ignore them and do something else. In order to do that something else, he has to *choose* and take responsibility for his choices knowing they will have consequences not just for the injured man but for himself too. His act will have a ripple effect around his own circle of life.

The second thing to note here is that, in order to help, the Good Samaritan has to stand out and make himself 'visible'. He has to risk the disapproval of his fellows for showing such interest in someone who is not 'of us'. His actions are not without considerable risk and yet he goes ahead and acts.

The moral of the story, at one level, is that help helps. But the Good Samaritan does more than simply help. He sees it through. He *checks* that his work will be completed and that his own contribution is sufficient before he leaves. He clearly *cares for a result* and is not simply interested in storing up merit for himself by his actions. He wants his actions to make a *difference*.

The Good Samaritan may do no more acts of kindness of this kind during the rest of his life, but in this one act he does something that is irrevocable. He does something that changes things forever not simply between himself and the injured person he assists but for us all. He steps outside the accepted view of the world and in so doing he changes the world, in however small a way. Despite all ethnic claims to the contrary, cultural rules that forbid him and political arrangements that make it dangerous and positively taboo, he steps across these divisions, the barriers of separation, and responds to the other as a fellow citizen of the human community.

The Good Samaritan is not a missionary. He does not regard the other as one more recruit to his cause, another voice to add to the swelling choir praising his own religiosity. He does not regard the other as a demonstration of his own virtue in disguise or the other's thanks as a seal of approval on the arrogance his own humility disguised as self-sacrifice.

These are all important elements in any helping equation. But perhaps what is most important is that the *Good Samaritan, although he is a stranger, is not remote*. He chooses to be *'one with the other' rather than 'one at a distance from the other'*. He, in some way, is willing to identify with the suffering of the other without getting lost in that suffering. If he becomes lost in the suffering of the other, he is no longer able to do anything effective about it. Nor is he only able to respond to the suffering of the other as if it is of no concern to him. He allows himself to become 'engaged'. He is willing to know and, to a degree, be known in his act of assistance. His act reveals something unique and personal about himself – he discloses himself in his act of helping.

Once he has acted he becomes more than he was; the act is a growth in being. The challenge in the world is to act in freedom rather than out of convention and/or the expectations of others. The act is not, therefore, one of politeness or care in the usual sense, it is an act that asserts humanity in the world. In that sense, he acts for all in his singular personal act. He does not merely hold a view. He lives it out and expresses himself in a way that will distinguish him – not necessarily in a positive light. He is prepared to be responsible for himself.

Ordinary Caring

Another important feature of his offer is that it is an act of what Bishop David Jenkins calls 'ordinary caring'. The Good Samaritan does not 'refer' his 'client', does not put him through some interview process to assess whether he is qualified enough in his injuries to be worthy of the Samaritan's help. The injured person is not 'treated' with a technique or subjected to a method but given a strong dose of ordinary caring. At first the Good Samaritan unilaterally decides what is needed but as the injured person improves he will gradually take up his own role and contribute once more to his own welfare. His gratitude to the Good Samaritan will not be based on the amount of training or the level of qualifications the Samaritan possesses but on the Samaritan's demonstrable capacity and his decision in choosing to care.

Seen in this way, helping is a wholly human activity. It is also a profound activity for both parties involved. It takes place throughout all human cultures and across the span of human history. Such helping is about 'ordinary caring' and ordinary caring is the standard that needs to apply before we start looking for specialist help. Too often, in our times, ordinary caring does not so much break down as is never offered in the first place before experts and specialists are invited to take over.

Such dependence upon specialists and experts of all kinds undermines the belief in the capabilities of citizens and neighbours, friends and parents to take action themselves with a sense of competence. The resulting withdrawal of social engagement is then further compounded and a vicious circle ensues. It is less expected for the 'ordinary' individual to consider helping, therefore individuals think less and less about helping. As fewer opportunities to help arise in the routine of modern urban life so it isn't long before people are easily able to pass by another in deep distress, clearly noticing but unable to know whether to act, or what to do if they do act – and feeling it is nothing to do with them.

Since help, on any but the most routine of occasions, is almost always more complex, full of ambiguities and points of choice where things *could* be done differently, than often appears at the time, there is indeed every reason to be cautious about just what help we do give when we are prepared to act. But this should not discourage us from acting nevertheless. It should not lead to our abandoning the effort, leaving it to some white-coated 'specialist' to tell us what is needed.

A little reflection and we quickly recognise that someone else might have done something at a different point than we did, might have said something other than we said or approached the whole matter from a very different perspective. In fact, almost all helping situations are full of opportunities for opinions and views to differ widely about what *should* happen or, retrospectively, what *should have* happened. Such disputes, about how help should be offered and who should provide it, add to the reluctance of even professional practitioners to get involved in difficult situations. They may also lead to their wanting to retreat the moment a situation begins to show signs of complexity. The ever-growing culture of litigation, the need to find someone to blame and the increasing demands for liability, all contribute towards the urge to retreat from difficult or novel situations.

Practitioners and helping have therefore become much more protective. This is known as adopting 'defensive routines'. These routines are then used to minimise risk to the practitioner and the organisation rather than putting the needs of the client first. This is well summed up in F C Cornford's common quote, "just because something can be done, it is no good reason that it should be done". In other words, it is about CYA[2] before doing anything else. All this, whilst understandable, is lamentable.

Helping is an important element of social cohesion and is too important to leave to the highly qualified specialist. And though complex, it should not be left until we all possess the knowledge of the professional expert. Ordinary helping is complex enough, challenging enough and needed enough to merit description and comment.

---

[2] CYA is an acronym to describe 'cover your ass'.

Ordinary helping is in need of restoration or it may soon disappear in a world in which individuals are increasingly separated from one another[3]. This, then, is part of the background against which any ordinary caring and ordinary helping is being offered. The most uncertain help is likely to arise when practitioner and client stand worlds apart with little real understanding of each other – the situation that faces most experts and the clients they deal with.

Such lack of interest has a corrosive effect upon healthy human relations. The 'bystander society' means that we watch unsure of what to do and, rather than risk making a mistake, we are likely to leave the situation 'for someone else to sort out'. All this is understandable, especially when you take into account all the issues around liability already mentioned, and, certainly, if you don't have sufficient interest to understand then it is far better to do nothing.

Whilst our lives are infinitely more complicated and sophisticated in a technical sense than the days of the Good Samaritan, the enduring questions of, 'What do we owe to one another?' and, 'How shall we stand in relation to another's need?' have not changed.

So when we say, 'Isn't it the natural condition for people to help one another?' the answer is both 'Yes' and 'No'. And which side you lean towards seems to depend upon your beliefs about the ultimate purpose of human life. It seems to depend upon whether you view other people as a *means* to *your* ends or whether other people are unique, whole, ends in themselves and not a means to anyone else's ends.

The more you take the first view, that people are a means to your ends, the more you will be willing to decide in advance *for others, what they need, how it is to be provided and how they are to be as a result of your generosity.* You will, at the same time, always be careful to ensure you exempt yourself from becoming the means to someone else's ends! You will make a fundamental distinction that other people are a means to your ends but you will never allow yourself to be a means to anyone else's ends, if you can help it. This leads to a world based on power and control in which people are calculating how far they are able to limit the manipulation or exploitation of others.

- How do I stop you making me simply a tool for your purposes?
- How do I get my purposes accomplished if you are out to counter my intentions?

Even if you take the second view, that people are ends in themselves, unique and entire unto themselves, you still have to be careful to ensure that you don't inadvertently (or otherwise) end up exploiting others for your own ends.

---

[3] One third of all adults now live alone and the percentage is increasing. Car ownership means people travel separately from one another. Out of town shopping means we are moving less and less amongst others we know and spending less time with people who are familiar. The intimate stranger is increasingly the norm. It brings with it a lack of depth to civility and willingness to be personally responsive to situations that we see occurring around us. All this is in marked contrast to the community dimension of life in the past. This also emphasises the importance of one's physical environment.

Wider Influences

As a result of issues like these, helping and human relations soon ensure we enter the land of *ambivalence* with its perplexing and unstable terrain of *motivation*. It is, even between you and I, never so straightforward as we like to pretend. Because, however much you and I are free to work things out with one another and however much I believe this is an act of unquestioned spontaneous generosity and compassion when I assist you, together we are surrounded by a horizon of possibilities, a set of circumstances and a whole assembly of conditions, i.e. a *context* that is influencing how we go about what we do and how we do it.

One of the first things to note is that help is not neutral. Help is not simply the expression of boundless and unthinking generosity of spirit. For one person (you) to be in a position to help another there are questions to be answered about:

- How come you are there?
- How come the other is where they are?

Then there is the altogether more challenging issue of:

- How can you begin to think you know what someone else needs?

Do you happen to be there by:

- Chance?
- Destiny?
- The accidental result of social policy?
- Benefit of education?
- Social class advantage?

These are just a few influences and explanations. There are many, many more as we all know. Human relations and helping never take place outside such influences and constraints. That's why the further you are from those you are helping in social background, experience and other forms of 'distance', the more likely you are to end up in the complex land of *unintended consequences*. It may be true that we can never *know* what effects our actions may eventually have, but if we are working within a world that we know something about we have greater understanding of what is likely to follow from our actions.

Contrary to common belief, it is not easy to solve a problem from a distance because the further we are from the situation, the more the solution appears obvious and easy to apply. Yet what we all know to be the case is that when we do understand a situation it is often more difficult to know how best to act since we are much, much more aware of the nuances that mean a simple obvious answer is actually not going to work. This is likely to make us more restrained, more humble in our ambition.

It takes only a large measure of ignorance and the conceit to believe that your view is the self-evidently valid one that requires you to act in favour of the uneducated, the dispossessed, the… You provide the label that disempowers the other or some minority group, whilst at the same time you are assembling the justification for your being *obliged* to act.

Invasions of nations no less than individuals are often initiated on just such logic. It is not difficult to feel that the very logic of the argument compels you to intervene in order to demonstrate the purity of your own credentials. Whether it is requested seems not to matter. Whatever the long-term effect, again, seems not to be part of the equation.

This kind of 'helping' based on 'sincerity' is a dangerous form of helping indeed. Virtually every intervention made is claimed to be an act of untainted sincerity, yet sincerity is no guide to the wisdom of the act, only the feelings harboured by the actor. Sincerity is merely a cloak to disguise the real motives of the actor because they themselves are more important to the whole enterprise than those they are claiming 'to save'.

The other person is merely an opportunity for the sincere practitioner to demonstrate they are 'caring', or 'protective', or whatever term they apply to themselves that creates a circular logic from which there is no escape. 'I sincerely believe you need help. I act in the sincere belief you need help. The sincere act of my help is therefore appropriate.' On and on we go. Appraisal of the situation, appropriateness of the deed, suitability of response, all matter less than the sincerity of the actor's motive. Questions about the strength and ability of the individual or group thus saved to contribute to their own salvation are rarely weighed. They are, by definition, below the horizon of consideration. Such forms of help are dangerous and such practitioners are on a crusade to remake the world in the image of their chosen form of dogma. It has more than a whiff of the fundamentalist view about it.

This is a form of *human relating and helping* we are witnessing in large measure about us at the moment, not only in our social world but also in our international relations, with some unforeseeable consequences ahead. All this makes helping and human relations not just a utilitarian requirement, not just something required because… but also a political and even spiritual activity.

Implicit in all this is the element of power: where it lies, with whom and how it is used or abused. This discussion is not to suggest that people should not help but that regardless of what calls them to be helpers, they need, above all, to be *reflective* and aware of their own complex, interlinked motives. Sometimes we offer help with the best of intentions but, as we get deeper into the circumstances, we know there is more involved than we thought and that the requirements may go some way beyond our resources or our understanding. Some of us, in our effort to demonstrate just how well meaning we are, jump in to solve the problem before we can be sure we know what it is! Motives play a much larger part in the way people help one another, or not, than we are often willing to acknowledge or admit. Unrealised or unacknowledged motives on the part of the practitioner can distort the helping relationship and lead to the client being manipulated.

Helping is also big business[4]. As the State has withdrawn from many of its social and welfare activities, it has been left to voluntary agencies and private individuals to offer themselves as practitioners of one kind or another – the growth in helping agencies and the provision of counselling services being perhaps the most obvious. This has meant a proliferation of training programmes, the explosion of qualifications and an obsession with accreditation procedures, all of which stand to obscure the fact that it is the right of members of a free society to share in offering help to one another.

Helping, therefore, is important enough to do well, to explore closely and to explain clearly in order to encourage all of us to be willing to undertake our proper share for the common good. The starting point is to develop some overview of the world that makes up helping and to outline how the variety in styles of helping and the contributions they may make connect together.

[4] These issues are taken up in a later chapter, *The Upstream Helper*, because they have an increasing effect upon the work and long-term career prospects of practitioners in a way that has changed in the last 15 years or so.

Chapter 2
An Overview of Helping

What Do We Mean By Helping?

Strangely enough, many individuals are not altogether sure what they really mean by 'helping'. They also often find it difficult to know beyond any doubt if they have made any difference. There are occasions when we cannot be entirely sure that the person we think we helped actually experienced the help we gave in the way intended. And, if someone says they were 'helped', the person who received the help may well have difficulty in stating quite what the practitioner did that made the difference, or why that particular contribution should have been so significant in bringing about a change. In some situations, it may not be necessary to be aware of all this. However, people who regularly find themselves in a helping role need to have ways of reflecting upon their practice, assessing the effectiveness of their strategies and be able to describe their practice.

Over the last decade or so, professions not readily thought of as agencies of help have begun to make claims to be just that. Campaigns to 'put the customer first' and the growth of Customer Service Departments illustrate the growing attention that service organisations have learned to pay to those who receive their services. Banks — institutions not traditionally noted as philanthropic ventures — are an example of a whole industry that has changed its emphasis in recent years towards encouraging customers to believe that they are there to assist, when their real motive is to make money through 'helping'. We live in a society where everyone wants to claim that what he or she does is 'helpful'. Such a widespread use of the word only serves to disguise the essence of help, thereby making it difficult to get at the heart of what helping really is and how it really works.

Stopping to help a fellow motorist change a tyre may be an everyday example of one person helping another but it is not typical. Individuals rarely meet situations so appealingly straightforward. Arriving at a situation of difficulty, knowing what is needed, providing it and then seeing a stranger drive away with a smile and a wave, may be an example of helping that is more ideal than the day-to-day uncertainties many individuals face. A situation that on the face of it appears straightforward enough, a child complaining that the group will not let them make a contribution, for example, can become alarmingly messy once a teacher or other adult gets involved in 'sorting it out'.

Even those individuals in real and evident difficulty, who have sought help, can often become resistant to the best efforts the practitioner offers. In order to accept help, the client has to recognise their own part in the difficulty and that there is also a need to take some responsibility to bring about change. The client may well be clinging to the emotional advantage of playing 'victim'. When a practitioner meets such a situation, the relationship all too frequently gets into competition. This can reach the stage where every suggestion is felt by the client to be yet another example of what 'won't work' and every solution the practitioner offers is rejected. The practitioner ends up frustrated that the client won't be 'helped'; the client won't accept help and yet is saying they do not like the circumstances they are in. This is not a healthy or helpful position for either person in the relationship.

Changing Priorities

We live in times of growing confusion about what importance to attach to which social issues. Many past rituals and initiations no longer exist or they hold little importance in our lives.

> "And whilst counselling cannot create rituals, patterns and moments of ceremony for the individual in their wider life, it can help individuals to uncover and recover some of the meaning of events by enabling them to construct those kinds of boundaries and markers which in the past society has ensured were there for individuals to make sense of what happens." J. Hillman, 1980.

There is greater uncertainty and we are confused about how to respond to many issues – refugees, health care accountability, crime, drugs, and GM crops – both institutionally and individually. We are confused about what role we think service and help should take in the life of the citizen. We have no shared view of the participation expected of ourselves as citizens when decisions so often require complex assessments that frequently rely upon contributions from specialist experts. We are also unclear about how far our responsibilities and obligations to one another should rightfully extend.

> Is it a good thing that an incontinent and handicapped young woman who has survived into her thirties, thanks to medical improvements, is still looked after at home by her mother who is now seventy – especially when there is no possibility of the mother finding anyone to help give respite care?

Such an example, which can be read in so many ways, forcefully confronts us with questions about the wider social responsibilities we have towards one another and how to fulfil them.

Without the innovations of modern medicine, it is unlikely that the young woman described above would have survived beyond adolescence. From birth, her mother made a commitment to care for her daughter for the rest of her life. The daughter is now thirty-seven and the mother seventy; how feasible is it for the mother to manage? What kind of life has it been for her, as she shuffles into old age looking after a daughter who cannot look after herself? Yet the bond of love and commitment remains.

The situation they are dealing with was not envisaged at the time of her birth. Only now do we face the consequences of the medical revolution. People who would have died of their ailments and injuries in the past, now live on with greater and greater expectation of a longer life.

Such situations will become more commonplace as we move further into the twenty-first century and they pose important moral dilemmas. Many of us tend to hold to the hope that if only we could identify whose job it is to look after these messy, human issues, life would be altogether more comfortable. In a society as complex, specialised, fenced-off and parcelled-out as ours, we know that everyone cannot do everything for everyone, so it must be somebody's job: a social worker, a nurse, a health visitor. 'That's what they are paid for, after all, isn't it? If they cannot do it, with all the training they get, what good could I do?'

Such responses cannot be dismissed simply as examples of a mean-spirited wish to displace social obligations. It is too easy to claim it is an example of the 'I'm-alright-sod-you' approach. To one degree or another, we have all experienced something of the same realisation, that same sense of numbed withdrawal when faced with the difficulty of not knowing how best to respond.

Complexities of Helping

Much of the help that is offered on a day-to-day basis is informal, incidental and taken for granted. Many people do what they do without thinking much about how helpful they are and yet they can be indispensable – a postman/woman for instance. Equally, there are currently many individuals and organisations claiming to be helpful, yet the help they offer is dubious – banks again provide a good example of this. There are also people in many occupations who only recognise their helping role when pushed into thinking about it.

There are also those who occupy ambiguous roles when it comes to helping. Take the police officer for example; a help when she gives me directions in a strange place and a pain in the neck when he stops me for violating a traffic law! The more ambiguous the role, the more difficult the relationship will be with those people to whom the practitioner has to respond. Not knowing whether you are really here to help me or whether you are going to offer some sanction may make the first exchanges, or even a lasting aspect of the relationship, suffer.

Many people who have a helping role are, in fact, in this position. They are clearly not there to serve the interests of those they meet indefinitely. Conditions of some kind will surround what they are contracted to offer and how long they offer it. In addition, they have the right to be treated with civility and to look after themselves in the process – the abused practitioner is a far from rare creature.

Good preparation largely enables practitioners to begin to explore some of the dilemmas and uncertainties that go along with certain helping roles. Some go with the uniform, the police, for example. Some are part of the complex task involved in the actual work itself, such as social workers. Some are part of the particular aspirations of the agency and its messages to its service users of just what it can deliver. There are many features of the helping role that need to be separated out when it comes to looking at the effectiveness of the help offered.

Well, it certainly wasn't always like this. At simpler stages of social life the roles people played might have been more clearly defined, but the overlap of duties and responsibilities meant that many people could feel legitimate and rightful interest in offering help. No longer. Our society is much more differentiated with roles that are much more specialised. This differentiation leads to a range of individuals: from psychotherapists, who are highly focused in their work and who have very rigorous conditions surrounding their practice, through to first-in-line individuals who might be involved in the work of a housing agency; from care workers through to social workers and mental health practitioners. Such folk, even when they have relatively clear roles, offer them in a variety of ways to the different people they meet.

The helping role is not something straightforward nor can it be easily assigned to a range of particular people who can have their 'bit' and the whole matter be left at that. In many *arenas* (places where helping may be taking place) there is likely to be a range of practitioners, more or less co-operating with one another to the benefit or otherwise of the client. The client, however, may be getting either consistent advice or a lot of conflicting suggestions. For many clients, this plethora of advice and suggestions becomes an additional problem to the one they had when they started, because they cannot figure out which help to accept when it comes in so many guises and in so many conflicting forms.

In addition, practitioners under pressure and under scrutiny may well be out to colonise the client group – to make them a part of their legitimate population and defend them from the predatory embraces of competing practitioners from other agencies. Put like this, the whole enterprise may sound crude but many practitioners know that the situation is at times like this.

There is an increasing level of competition amongst helping agencies to retain a role in the lives of those they assist. At the same time, they also have to provide increasing evidence of their effectiveness if they are to continue to receive funding. It is not so much that helping professionals are under threat but that helping itself is undergoing a major redefinition. This is not because the pattern of human misery is changing and requires new forms of compassion or new skills in diagnosing the causes of human unhappiness – far from it. It is due to a combination of influences:

- A diminishing share of resources.
- The reluctance of people in modern societies to surrender so much of their income, via taxation, to provide services on the scale of the past.
- The crisis in our understanding of just what and who qualifies for what kind of help.
- The unmanageable complexities of some of those who seek help.
- Increasing medical knowledge. The kind of medical conditions that today can be successfully treated, like the example of the young woman given earlier, means people live who once would have died and the cost of their treatment is lifelong.
- Demographic changes mean there is less money available to meet the burden of need.

All these, and other factors too, combine to place the world of official and semi-official helping under pressure to 'deliver', to 'meet targets' and to operate more and more like a 'proper' business. Such a business model of the task of helping is a long way from the world of the Good Samaritan. All this makes the helping practitioner's world particularly volatile.

How Do We Help?

As a result of these changing priorities and social conditions, answering the question, 'What do we mean by helping?' is not as simple and clear in practice as it seems at first. An easier place to begin might be to ask, 'How do people help?' and look at the answers people give.

This book takes the view that helping is a fundamental and integral part of ordinary social life. It does not inevitably or always require experts (though it sometimes does). It does not take years of practice (though it can be beneficial). It does not need to be separated from the rest of social life (though it has some special aspects that are useful to highlight). It is about making a difference and enhancing the well-being, not only of those who are helped but also the community in which we all live. In our present culture, with all its stresses, changes, pressures, breakdown of communities and extended families, we need more help, not less. But above all we need good help rather than poor help and bad help is worse than no help.

Bad or poor helping happens when those involved are unclear about what they are doing at best, or are attempting to deceive the other at worst. If one simple way of looking at help is *that it is a way of someone attempting to make a positive difference to the circumstances, opportunities, conditions or potential of another* then it seems to follow that help is more likely to be effective if:

- Both parties know what they are doing and know their role in the enterprise.
- They have the time available to accomplish what they set out to do and that this is estimated from the outset.
- The resources that might be required are available and one or both know where and how to obtain them.
- Once it is over, each party takes stock of how it happened and what difference they each have made to the equation.

The aim behind such suggestions is to raise to consciousness the intention of those involved in the act of helping, to make helping less and less a mystery, to make it more of a collaborative endeavour and to make it more and more something that we can articulate and discuss. In this way the whole process becomes much more transparent.

It is also to make sure, as far as possible, that help remains an 'ordinary activity' unless there are overwhelming reasons to prevent it. The drift into specialised and increasingly professional forms of help is one of the great calamities of modern societies. Unwittingly, as a consequence, we begin to ration out compassion, marginalise those in need and leave the resulting 'problems' to the attention of those paid to 'mop up the mess'. In short, it reduces the humanity of our society.

This is not to say that conscious, aware helping and professional help are anything other than vital. Indeed, it always needs as much consciousness as those who are involved can bring to the helping relationship and there certainly is the need for the intervention of skilled professionals at the right time. But professional intervention must not occur to the exclusion of individuals involving themselves in what is taking place all around them, only then to find that they have surrendered all sense of social responsibility. Behind the idea of helping is one of the founding drives of society itself – that together we can do better than we can alone.

What Helps?

These kinds of concerns are more and more likely to emerge in any helping relationship where those involved don't spend time working out how they are going to operate at the outset. This is especially so if both practitioner and client do not explore together:

> **1. What they are doing:** have an agreed definition of the purpose of their work.

> **2. How they are each going to contribute:** recognise there are two parties to make contributions and outline something of the nature of each contribution.

> **3. How they might review matters as they proceed:** that they will only know if they are getting somewhere usefully if they stop from time to time and think back over how they have got to where they are and what they can learn from that review.

By taking these simple steps the nature of the helping relationship begins to become *demystified* and starts to be recognised as having a structure and a way of operating that is neither mysterious nor reliant on the magic of the practitioner. Demystifying the helping relationship can be as important as the helping itself. Time spent creating a shared approach is always time well spent.

Crisis/Remedial/Therapeutic or Developmental?

An important initial question when looking at how we help is, 'What stance do we – the practitioners – take to our work?'

> Are we largely working with people in *crisis*? If so, the work is likely to be short-term.

> Is our aim to *remedy* some shortcoming that arises out of lack of experience or limitation as a result of some trauma that has occurred, where essentially we are aiming to restore someone to a former position (even though this might not actually be possible)?

> Are we working with the *therapeutic* difficulties of a person's life experience, enabling them to integrate what has happened and make themselves more whole?

> Are we taking a *developmental perspective* in which we see the person as capable, no matter what current concerns and difficulties, of contributing centrally to their own welfare and future possibilities?

How we view the work we do holds a critical influence upon how we approach it and the people who come our way. Whatever stance, or combination of stances, we take, it should have as its aim *the promotion of a working alliance*.

The traditional model of helping always sees an imbalance between the dependent needs of the client upon the greater expertise of the practitioner and it is the nature of this power imbalance that we are investigating here. The perspective of this book, and the work the author and his colleagues engage in, are undertaken as a *developmental relationship*. This places much more emphasis upon helping as a form of *collaborative endeavour* between practitioner and client. The relationship is regarded as central to the enterprise — far more important than the technical resources the practitioner may be able to call upon.

Promoting a Working Alliance

Whatever we decide the aim of help should be is going to drive our actions. If it is based upon a need to 'rescue' poor deluded souls then we will find there are plenty of poor deluded souls who need rescuing. If, on the other hand, we subscribe to the tenet that all of us have been victimised in some way and that it is important to 'be alongside the client' (identify with them and affirm them in their chosen view of reality), then we will find a lot of victims heading our way. Victims need 'persecutors', and there will be plenty of those too. We cannot escape from the fact that our purposes for helping contribute to the world that appears around us. Just as the way we perceive the world around us justifies why we offer the help we do for the reasons we do.

If the aim of help is to 'empower the client', to enable them to act as self-responsible individuals, capable of self-direction and choice, the practitioner needs to be aware that, in some circumstances, it may not be possible to achieve such an outcome. Where a client is suffering from declining functioning is perhaps the most obvious of examples. In these cases, minimising the acceleration of dependency and positively enhancing a person's capacity to maintain self-direction[5] for as long as possible would be the chosen aim.

Such an aim, i.e. to empower the client, ensures that the practitioner is never free of self-examination and careful reflection, and it invites them to keep in view such questions as:

- How do I enable the other to be more free than they were?
- How do I increase my freedom beyond what it was?

Enlarging freedom, awareness, action and engagement with others becomes a programme for continuous self-development that underpins the practitioner's constructive actions with those they help. It may well come as something of a challenge for the practitioner to enter into constructive and inquiry-based dialogue with the

---

[5] Many people may remember Christopher Reeve, the actor who played 'Superman' until he had a serious accident. He is a remarkable example of someone who, using all the material resources he had to hand, lives a relatively self-directed life despite awesome physical difficulties.

world and the social conditions surrounding them. For many, adopting a helping role is a move away from the uncertainties and complexities of being a member of the organisational world. Traditionally, practitioners have viewed engaging with the wider concerns, even intellectually, as having little place in how to act with *this* person *here, now,* about *these concerns.* It is often set aside as 'playing politics'. But an increasing number of 'problems' that people seek help or are referred with have socio-economic, political or social aspects and considerations to them that require practitioners to have an aware sense of the current issues.

Substance use and drug issues are obvious cases in point; immigration and asylum are others. At a time when society itself has a very confused understanding of where it positions itself about these matters, the effective practitioner needs to be aware of the spectrum of opinions and where they fit within it. They also need to ensure that they are not in a position of assisting someone as a disguised way of attempting to fulfil their own agenda about such matters – using their position neither to excuse or encourage, nor to persuade or to condemn.

In an important regard, the practitioner offers themselves as a model of a process that they should at least more than notionally apply to themselves. Help then never becomes something that one person *does* to another. Unlike the traditional model, the author takes the view that it is never an activity that marks out those who need it from those who offer it.

Help is never an excuse to limit the other or to collude with a view that they can do 'no better'. Offering help is not an opportunity to use such explanations as a means of elevating oneself above the client's limitations. It is instead a call to a shared world in which there is a time and a place where I, too, stand in the same relation to someone else at times as you do to me now. Practitioner and client are best seen as *temporary roles* occupied by all of us from time to time on the journey toward increasing self-responsibility and greater wholeness.

Working Assumptions

Working out what assumptions are in force in any social context or meeting is a helpful way of getting at 'what is going on'. This approach takes as its assumptions:

- The more collaborative the help, the better.
- The more conscious the work that is being attempted, the better.
- The clearer the roles, the better.
- The more explicit the power relationships between those involved, the better.
- The more the implications or consequences of the work for both parties are considered, the better.
- The more the person being helped is assisted to work out for themselves, not only what to do and how to do it, but also how to generalise so they may take the learning elsewhere and to other situations, the better.
- That both take on a shared responsibility for the relationship they need in place for each to play their part.

Concerns within Helping

When somebody does get help and it starts to be effective, it raises certain issues and concerns for the individual who started out with a 'problem'. It is one thing having a problem and quite another to find there is a solution to it, or at least a suggestion that might make a difference. The person then moves from 'can't' to … They have to move into some form of change and that requires overcoming all the inhibitors and fears that may be as important in their having their problem as the problem itself. It is not that people often don't know what to do about the situations and the circumstances that limit them, it is that they have to find a way to mobilise their will over a sufficiently long period to innovate and then maintain the changes they wish to have in their lives.

Practitioners at the early stages of their careers (see practitioner naïvety in *Practitioner Resources*) often forget all this. In the eager rush to prove how helpful they are, they are busy making all kinds of sensible and even suitable suggestions whilst overlooking the fact that there is more to a problem than a 'solution' or even a plan to implement the said solution. It is this aspect that makes so many politically appealing solutions fail to have the impact that their proponents hope. Bringing about change is a much slower process than people realise. Having said that, the right intervention at the right time, when the person is open to change, can make the process effortless – or nearly so. But that is much more unusual than having to work patiently.

There are many issues that can arise for the client, both in the way they view themselves and in the way they view and respond to the practitioner. These issues all hold the potential to have a fundamental impact upon how help is received and perceived. Some of the most common are described below.

The client's personal concerns

What other dilemmas or problems will I need to face? This difficulty I know well; solving it will only surface others more intractable. The work won't stop with this one step but there will be other changes too.

If this works, and I put this much effort into it, does this mean I have to put this amount of effort into the rest of my life? Sometimes having the solution and knowing how to implement it only reveals that being 'proactive' is something that cannot be confined to occasional bursts but is a quality to bring to life as a whole. Am I ready for that?

If this works, I will have to think of myself differently. My self-image is bound up with my circumstances and being able to change them will inevitably mean I come to see myself a little differently. I may usually see myself as pretty hopeless and have to reconsider that. I may see my difficulties as the result of other people's failings and will have to think about that more, and so on.

If this works, I'll be pleased until… On the face of it, the idea of solving the difficulty is really appealing but then again... How far do I really want that solution? Can I find a good reason not to quite accept that suggestion and hang on to my pet problem a little longer?

How the client views their practitioner

If you solve my problem, will you now solve the next one? Having someone take this much interest in my life circumstances suggests that you may be more available for more help from here on. Here the client extends an indefinite, and often unspoken, expectation to the practitioner.

If you solve my problem, it shows you are a friend. Having shown this much interest in me, I am now hoping this is an indication that we can become much more in contact with one another. After all, 'You wouldn't show this kind of interest towards just anyone would you?'

If you solve my problem, it shows how clever you are and how dumb I am. Your being so clever and finding an answer that eluded me is a matter for furious but suppressed resentment and my future aim is to ensure that you are exposed for being the clever know-all you think you are.

If you have solved this one, I will find one you cannot solve. Because you think you are so smart in solving other people's problems (and I bet you have some of your own), my purpose is now to ensure that you are brought down a peg or two and that you are seen not to be the all-wise all-knowing guru that you pretend.

Now you've solved this one, am I supposed to find another? Am I simply one of a caseload who then has to keep coming up with new difficulties to maintain your interest?

Now you've solved this one, how come I don't feel any better? I thought reducing or eliminating the problem altogether would change the way I feel but it hasn't. I suspect that's something to do with the solution being yours and my simply being someone trying out your pet theories and ideas rather than working toward my own answer.

These are all strategies people employ to take advantage of help without making good use of it. They are also all qualifications to the desire to be helped that someone is unaware of at the point of distress. The equation of: problem = hurt = need help = suggestion = action = solution, misses a lot of steps out, steps that we consider throughout this book. All of the above concerns can also contribute to a naïve client finding it easy to see a practitioner as any of the following:

- Magician.
- Life guide.
- Personal saviour.
- Friend, as we've already mentioned.
- All-purpose rescuer.
- Someone who, at all costs, they must not let go of.

It is out of concerns and considerations such as these that clients often look for ways to perpetuate their relationship with the practitioner or come to feel resentful at the lack of interest the practitioner shows back to them.

These kinds of remarks highlight once again that wanting help, getting it and making use of it are not straightforward. Having a problem and getting it solved isn't either. Many of us want to hang on to our problems – at least for a little while longer. After all, we spent a long time acquiring them and we give a good deal of attention to cultivating them. Better not to be rid of them too soon.

'Problems' in this sense can be thought of like old familiar friends. 'Hello, lateness again.' Or, 'Ah ha, I see my desire to be thought of as superman is at work and undermining my efforts'. Well, we don't usually look upon them with such an amused, ironic sense of affection (a pity, though, because it would reduce the pain they engender if we could be a little more amused and a little less fierce in our responses when they appear) because they do so much damage to our personal well-being and our relationships. But many of our 'problems' are very well known acquaintances and we are not going to part with them until... And that is often what effective help has to uncover – the underlying forces at work in our lives that keep self-defeating behaviours and thoughts in place, or the way in which, despite having all the information we need, we nevertheless still don't make the decision we say we want to make.

Specialness & Shyness

Many clients want more than anything to be 'special' before they want to be 'helped'. The interest and attention of someone who cares is a powerful experience for many who have had far too little of it earlier in their lives.

The attention a practitioner can give, even for a short period, can generate so profound a sense of being made to feel important it soon overshadows the original reason for the meeting. For the client, the problem then becomes simply something that they need in order to ensure the practitioner remains interested in them so that they can go on meeting. As a result, the client emphasises the specialness of the relationship and begins to think they have a line of access or a depth of involvement that is exclusive to them. They want to be the 'best client' or the 'favourite person you see' and to know that this very special kind of attention is not something that is available to others.

The more the practitioner wants to be thought of as special, too, the more this kind of *'folie à deux'*[6], as it is termed, can arise. The *folie à deux* is the increasingly shared world of idealisation and exclusivity that the practitioner and client pretend to one another they are in. It may be that the practitioner does not want to upset the client and so goes along with the growing hints and suggestions of this deepening bond between them. It may be that the practitioner has never experienced the strength of interest someone is showing in them and indeed finds it is something 'special' too and begins to encourage it – all without realising it in the beginning. But at some point the resulting emotional entanglement has upsetting effects. People who need help can easily become fond of their practitioner. The practitioner can easily unwittingly suggest to the client that they have a personal interest in them that implies a stronger connection than the interest and care that arises out of the time they spend together.

There are others, too, who have the reverse experience. Subjected to so much focused attention on themselves, they feel the need to shrink into themselves. They find the whole helping situation one that is perhaps even more excruciating than the problem they have to manage.

Most people seeking help for the first time (the inexperienced client), however, are neither of these. They desperately want *approval* and believe it is up to them to show the 'right signs' of improving. Believing that the practitioner has the solutions (and many practitioners do act as if they have, and even believe they have) then they patiently await the solution, do their best to implement it when they get it and return to report back what happens, expecting to be given a rating of approval for their efforts. The idea that the solution lives in the person who has the problem and not outside in the practitioner is a foreign notion to many people and is a huge element in the learning. This is not surprising since so many requests for help are of what we could term an *instrumental kind*. This is where there is a stated need that once it has been identified, it can be met by someone else: broken pipe, plumber arrives and the solution is soon in hand.

---

[6] *Folie à deux*; a delusion shared by two persons (The Concise Oxford Dictionary).

There is also another concept that seems to be alien to many people. This is the idea that the task of the client is to learn how to make sense of their own world and take the benefit of the practitioner's detachment (from the problem, hopefully, not from the clients themselves) and evaluate how far the observations and suggestions that they receive apply to them and their own understanding of the world they inhabit.

However, not knowing any of this and following the socially accepted model of conformity learned in the past when it comes to getting help from any expert, most people dutifully fall into some version of compliance and blame themselves when they don't deliver the goods they believe the practitioner expects.

But many forms of help need something in addition to the notion of instrumental help, and, however expert the practitioner, they need more than just a set of circumstances to work with. *They work with the person with the problem.* A refugee support worker, for example, may be able to provide material assistance of certain kinds but they need to have a much wider range of knowledge and understanding than that the people they are helping are cold and haven't enough blankets!

Most present-day problems of helping are not straightforward and the solution, at least in part, is related to the person who has the problem. Where this is not the case and the matter is as straightforward as a plumbing job, then we can all give thanks that there are moments when life is not so complicated. For the rest of the time…

Chapter 3
Helping Agencies & Helping Roles

Whilst the emphasis in this book falls strongly on the one-to-one relationship – the focus of interaction between those involved in almost all forms of help – we must at the same time remember there is more to what happens than the actions and aspirations of the two parties involved, in almost all cases. So, for the moment we will focus upon the helping agency, its concerns and the relationship between the agency and its practitioners.

There is usually some 'agency'[7] that assists the person being helped and that employs or at least gives a licence to, the practitioner. The agency is the link between the need and its being met. The agency is the structure that brings the resources and the people together for the work to be undertaken. The agency has needs and requirements of its own and a range of commitments that it, too, has to meet if it is to remain viable.

There are literally hundreds of different helping organisations around us and, depending upon how far you extend the spectrum, they could cover almost every aspect of our contemporary life. Insurance companies, banks, medical centres and mail order companies of all kinds all depend upon people helping those making enquiries. Even if we keep the idea of helping to a relatively narrow definition and think of it in traditional terms, there has been an explosion of agencies and organisations on hand to assist.

Helping agencies are unlike other organisations in two significant ways: there is no product and, perhaps more importantly, they usually depend upon individuals to represent their whole activity. For example, the practitioner in a women's centre stands in place of the organisation but few people confuse the garage attendant with Shell Petroleum, say. The attendant may reflect the views or the working practices of the franchisee or proprietor but they do not hold a role in promoting the oil company as a whole – though even that is changing as many organisations realise that those who have a face to face role are invaluable in their capacity for influencing customers.

In helping agencies, however, this link is very much stronger. The reputation of the agency depends upon each practitioner and each contact they have. The only reason for the organisation's life is to continue to meet the needs of those it serves and it must do that via the response the practitioner makes. There is nothing else to fall back on. This puts the stability and strength of the organisation on a very fragile basis. One misguided contact, one poor connection, one seriously misunderstood client and the reputation of the organisation may be placed in jeopardy.

When a newcomer to the agency meets the practitioner for the first time, the practitioner represents the whole set up: the work, the aims of the organisation and

---

[7] In this context, the term 'agency' is used synonymously with a helping organisation of whatever kind. The organisation is the agent that brings the client and the practitioner together.

the purpose for which it exists. This has major consequences in the preparation of staff, the work of the agency, the roles people occupy and the use of referral practices.

The practitioner, for example, is engaged to respond within a range of parameters and with a range of interventions or they risk misrepresenting the work of the agency, stepping outside its stated world of practice and operating in an unregulated and unlicensed way.

The practitioner, however free they are to respond to the client's needs, does so only within the agreed framework of the agency. They cannot respond to what they like or to what appeals to them and must assess the needs of the client according to the work of the agency and the role they perform. Help, in this sense, is anything but personal and does require the individual practitioner to work with self-discipline and to respect the alignment between the needs the agency is meeting and their own interests and skills. This is something that sounds straightforward but is far from easy in practice for many practitioners.

There are a number of contributory factors involved and not all (one would hope) will come together in one place or the result would be a major disaster! There is some overlap in these factors for practitioners and agencies since each will look at issues from their own particular and unique perspective, with their own agenda and needs. Whilst acknowledging these differing agendas and needs, there will need to be sufficient commonality too or the practitioner is unlikely to be happy working in that agency and the agency is likely to have difficulties with the practitioner.

Influences upon Practitioners

Mismatch in Ability
Interest is insufficient if the mode of response of the agency is far removed from the abilities of the practitioner.

The Crusading Newcomer
A crusading newcomer, who sees the work needing to go in a different direction, can cause major upheaval in an agency that has carefully worked out its remit and struggled hard to gain recognition in the community.

Practitioner Influences

The 'Lone Ranger'
The practitioner, who now 'knows better' than the agency because of new training, or experience etc, extends their practice without anyone else knowing what is happening. This is a way of using their position to redefine the organisation's response.

Expectations
Practitioners, well trained in their work with clients, often do not know how to manage the 'real world' survival needs of the agency. Their expectations about the levels of service to be offered can create major challenges to an agency that is struggling to survive.

Influences upon Agencies

Balancing Interests
Agencies have to balance the interests of their practitioners with their overall aims and mission. They have to be open to learning from practitioners about how services can be improved and yet hold firm to the boundaries the agency has agreed to meet.

Career Pathways
Many agencies have a role for first-in-line providers of services and one or two specialists on hand (not usually full time), but opportunities for practitioners to become specialists are not likely to appear as often as practitioners would like.

Influences on Agencies

Expectations and Reality
Practitioners show great enthusiasm to gain experience, only to want to 'move on' and take on more complex and more sophisticated caseloads. Agencies can rarely provide such enriching opportunities. These expectations are soon moderated by actual experience and maintaining motivation and interest can be a major issue. This is particularly acute in helping agencies.

External Influences
Agencies also have to manage the external and extended influences upon how they operate and the restraints they face. One such influence is often the need to respond to the demands of funders or donors. Those who provide funding are able to make certain stipulations to which the agency needs to respond – or risk losing the funding.

As a result of pressures like these, managers may find themselves attempting to hold together an increasingly critical and disgruntled workforce who are continually reminding the organisation of the complex needs it is apparently doing little or nothing to meet. The role of the manager can then end up as little more than the perpetual appeaser of the staff rather than as the developer of the organisation.

Helping Roles in Organisations & Agencies

The issue of 'practitioners' in organisations and agencies is complex. Some agencies may have one or two specialists on hand but this is not common because it is expensive. Many agencies, however, run entirely on volunteer first-in-line providers and have a referral system to call on others who have a proven record in the required area. There is a whole other aspect, too, supervision, whether the agency consists of largely volunteers or staff with particular skills, is an important contribution to monitoring and reflecting upon practice.

Because so few roles are clear-cut and simple and because few are offered unambiguously and without the possibility of misunderstanding, the work of most practitioners is open to misreading by those they help. This is explored in more detail later but for the moment we shall look at the major roles practitioners take up in most helping organisations. However, at the outset we need to remember that there are innumerable roles individuals occupy that in some way are recognised as having a helping component.

Some people have a helping role that is exclusively their area of practice, such as nurses, social workers and so on, yet there is much more besides direct helping even in such helping roles. Some individuals, whilst having a helping role, such as teachers, might well differentiate 'helping' as referring to pastoral duties rather than the task of teaching itself. Still others offer help 'incidentally', as part of some other role they perform – a good manager or a thoughtful forecourt attendant. *Helping is not something that is distinguished by where it happens, to whom it happens or who performs it.*

Helping roles vary according to the degree that overt helping is a consciously described aspect of the work undertaken and how far practitioners are accountable for the helping activities they undertake. Four key roles are described in more depth below.

1. First-in-line Practitioners/ Providers. There are two main aspects within the concept of first-in-line provision. Firstly, *first-in-line practitioners* are those who do the majority of their work in a helping agency, and have a formal role and job description/title which reflects this. Examples would be Housing Support workers, voluntary counsellors and other, similar fields of work. The first-in-line practitioner may then choose to refer the person in difficulty to a specialist or continue the work themselves, bearing in mind all the restraints and influences already described.

Secondly, *'first-in-line provider'* describes anyone who offers help at a point of need, regardless of job, role or 'helping expertise'. If we take organisations as an example, frequently, it is the case that the individual with first-in-line responsibility for staff in an organisation – the supervisor, the foreman, the teacher, the ward manager – will be the first-in-line point of contact for a member of staff meeting difficulties. This raises immediate problems. Most staff with first-in-line responsibilities have a contrasting role to that of 'helper' to their staff: they are also *boundary managers*. They have a function in setting and maintaining clear boundaries of action and conduct. It is often felt that these two aspects of the role are in conflict – as indeed they are – and therefore incompatible, which need not be the case.

Such *role conflict* is not unique to managers but it can be an acute problem for them. It will often be the case that an individual who needs help will be performing below their usual level of competence and may well be presenting problems of attendance or discipline as a symptom of their current difficulties. This places both the manager and the first-in-line practitioner in something of a dilemma.

Whenever such role relationships exist, the nature of the meeting needs to be set out from the beginning and so leave the other person with no room for uncertainty about its purpose. If the meeting is a fact-finding exploratory discussion, this should be made clear and it should stay in that territory. If it is really a means to challenge individuals to improve their performance, this should equally be made clear. If it is to offer people a genuine opportunity to begin to unburden themselves of the concerns that are influencing their performance, this again should be made clear.

2. Specialists. Some organisations have already convinced themselves of the need to have specialist practitioners on hand. They don't view them as 'a non-productive use of resources' but as valuable contributors to maintaining the overall effectiveness and morale of the staff. Clearly, if the tasks of the first-in-line provider are to be performed skilfully, there will be a need for some form of support. This is an important role for specialists, who may themselves not have direct contact with clients throughout their working time but who may act in a consultancy advisory and support role to first-in-line providers and undertake a proportion of internal referrals.

Such specialists are also in key positions to negotiate, not only across the internal boundaries of the organisation in which they work but also across external boundaries with other agencies. This makes them well placed for co-ordinating helping activities within their organisation and between their organisation and relevant referral agencies.

3. EAP (Employee Assistance Programme) Schemes. Increasingly, organisations recognise they have a responsibility to support their staff during stressful periods, whether these are caused by events in the workplace or their wider life situation. Such provision gives staff impartial support offered by a specialist provider and often enables the individual staff members to manage their way through a crisis that might otherwise lead to a potentially long absence. Organisations offering such a service almost always find them a cost effective way of ensuring that specialist support, when required, is available. EAP Schemes offer a variety of provision and are a support to the practitioners, both first-in-line and specialist, inside the organisation, hence the reason they are include here.

4. Key Roles & Key Workers. Because the helping world can be extremely labyrinthine and complex, many agencies that have a substantial role in the lives of their clients have adopted a version of the key worker principle. Essentially, a key worker is a named individual practitioner linked to a particular client and they are teamed up for most purposes. It is not mandatory for the client to use their key worker for each and every need but, in most cases, the key worker would follow the journey of their client throughout their stay with the agency.

In systems where this works well, both agencies and clients stand to gain from the arrangement. Clients gain because they have someone who begins to know their circumstances and concerns well, and agencies gain because there is a point of contact for the delivery of the services they are offering.

Unless such a system is well defined, attentively managed, strongly supported and regularly reviewed, it is likely that the agency is only paying lip service to it. Like anything else, a system that is ineffective is worse than no system at all. In agencies where this is the case, everyone will lose out. Key workers may well have little direction in the focus and the aims of the help they are offering, and clients may have little opportunity to change their key worker if they are not getting the kind of attention they have a right to expect.

Such a system is difficult to evaluate since the clarity of the provision is not well expressed or described. It is hard to know what might be accomplished and how far it might go. Often key working becomes little more than an agency's way of ensuring that someone is keeping an eye on particular individuals rather than it being a strong and conscious element in the helping process.

A Note on Referral

It is usual for us to expect that it will be first-in-line practitioners who have most interest in and concern about the use of referral points. After all, they are the people who meet whoever comes through the door – although this is not strictly speaking true. In fact it is often the *receptionist* who meets people coming through the door and often it is useful for a helping organisation to brief the receptionist in how to act as an internal referral agent at the very least.

There are some caveats about this though. Receptionists are just that; they are not employed to screen out unwanted or unsuitable clients, unless they are well prepared in how to handle such situations. In practice, of course, they are often used in just this way or they evolve into just this role. They are the ones who are meeting the complexities of response that come through the door, helping people to shape their 'story' into something that can be assessed before they can be pointed in the direction of the 'right' practitioner within the agency.

Receptionists often see the over-burdened practitioners of an agency and in their understandable desire to 'rescue' them, make evaluations and covert judgements about which clients get through to see which practitioners. Surgery receptionists in GP practices have often performed this function – acting as gatekeepers to keep the pressure off the over-burdened doctor. Such informal referral practices need to be vigilantly observed since they can lead to receptionists making decisions quite outside their expertise and over-stepping their role boundaries.

On the other hand, there are very many helping agencies that are blessed by the competent receptionist who seems to have an unerring understanding of just who to recommend the clients to and can forestall problems by making valuable responses to the over-wrought seeker of help.

For those paid to respond or prepared to respond, it is usually first-in-line practitioners that have to adjudicate the referral decision. 'Is this someone I can reasonably respond to or is this someone whose need extends beyond my role?' If it does extend beyond my role, 'Who is best placed to respond and where are they?' Referring someone in trouble is never straightforward. Which agency is most suitable? Will the client accept being sent on to another agency and having to repeat the story yet again to another stranger? Isn't the client likely to feel like a parcel and an unwanted one at that? First-in-line-practitioners know these problems only too well. One temptation is to attempt to stay involved with the client but then find it would really have been better to make a referral earlier. The question then is, 'How do you end it now or suggest at a late stage what would have been valuable weeks ago?' Regular reflection and support helps the inexperienced practitioner realise these are not unique issues applicable only to them but that they are part of the learning that goes with being a practitioner in any agency or organisation.

When any practitioner reaches the limit of their capability, referral becomes a serious proposition. This may be to someone outside the host agency and to another kind of expert altogether – the staff member of a housing agency seeking medical help for a frail individual who has fallen, for example, or a query that has come into a family centre that is more substance-related and needs greater expertise in that area than is held at the initial point of contact.

Most practitioners recognise these kinds of potential referrals without difficulty. In addition, they are often required to help the client make a case or assemble information to supply to other agencies – to seek a benefit or other entitlement, for example (advocacy). They may also be involved in negotiating provision for the person concerned, or supporting them through a difficult meeting. They may be offering a lengthy commitment that involves a range of different roles and types of help.

In such cases, how is the practitioner to know at the outset what might be needed and how far they can go? In part, it is the responsibility of the agency, through its induction process and in its monitoring and review process, to ensure that the practitioner is both prepared and enabled to reflect upon their experience and to manage difficult situations more effectively. In part, the awareness of how far the practitioner might be able to go comes with experience and in the level of interest the practitioner has in the work and, especially, in the client. Most practitioners have their own range of interests and this quite understandably affects the profile of their work.

Chapter 4
Practitioner Preparation
& Experience

Practitioner Preparation

An important element in the preparation of all practitioners should be reflection upon how they stand in relation to receiving help themselves. It may be that the clients you are assisting do not respond in the way you do nor do they experience life's challenges in the way you do. However, a full measure of shared human ordinariness about what it is like to be in need of help, and to have to seek it, is a huge aspect of what makes help effective. One reason why many people have greater difficulties than they might is that they find the idea of approaching someone or an agency for help beyond them until they reach a level of desperation.

In the daily rhythm of the work, it is all too easy to forget, that for the client, arriving at the door of an agency and seeking help for the first time represents a struggle. It is a struggle not only with a problem getting too difficult to bear alone, but also a struggle that has reached the point where the person has had to admit 'this is now beyond my resources to cope'. Our self-esteem often takes a knock when we get to the point of admitting we need help. At such a time many of us have an additional burden of expectation – that we will somehow be made to pay for the acknowledgment that we can no longer manage.

Punishment is often the condition of gaining help in the wider world and many potential clients feel that is what they will receive when they approach an organisation for help. Either that, or they will be condescended to and patronised by people who have plenty of overt concern but who do not really understand, because they ensure they hold themselves remote from ever having to face the prospect of seeking help themselves. Indeed, their own contribution to the world of helping may well be a disguised form of keeping their own difficulties at bay.

Help of this kind is *exploitative* just as is the help of the first kind – that dispenses punishment, however subtly. Neither has a place in effective help. Both are pernicious in their different ways. Since all of us have to work out just how much we 'feel sorry' for people or resent them and how far that influences how we work with them, it is in preparing our selves to work with clients that we need to begin to explore our own view of people who need help and examine what we feel about ourselves as clients.

It is not too much to suggest that the preoccupation, which has taken over the helping world in recent years, with all forms of qualifications, accreditation and the paraphernalia of professionalisation is, in part, an attempt by practitioners to distinguish themselves from those they assist. In other walks of life the practitioner and the helped are clearly distinguished. White-coated experts in hospitals are clearly separate from patients. Individuals walking round with equipment visibly on display, such as a stethoscope or a bag of tools, provide another illustration to the world at large that they are here doing the work and not, in this situation, the ones in need of help!

Practitioners of all kinds develop self-protective mechanisms for distinguishing themselves from those they serve as a means of managing the anxiety that being in need generates. Positioning of chairs, tables, clocks and so on are all ways practitioners create distance between themselves and their clients. The more formal a system, the more those in it like to create clear signals to others of the roles they perform – to eliminate any confusion about who is in need and who is providing it. Understandable though much of this is, unless we are very aware of the creeping signs of our efforts to maintain separation and role distance, as it is termed, from those we help, it leads to cold compassion and mechanical assistance offered to individuals in distress.

The 'Naïve' Practitioner

The work of most practitioners is far from straightforward, however much this book attempts to describe it clearly. In practice, practitioners are confronted on a daily basis with complexities of choice and decision about how far to go, what to suggest and how far their influence should go before it is experienced as interfering.

The more inexperienced the client or the practitioner, the more likely it is that these concerns will arise. In the attempt to secure the best result for the client many practitioners can be tempted to stray outside the boundaries of their legitimate work and into areas that are less manageable and for which they are not accountable. Of course, once they do that they are 'on their own' and should anything go wrong (as it may well), or if it gets 'messy', there is little support to fall back on.

The inexperienced practitioner often takes a straightforward view of a situation and believes that the problem has a really obvious remedy and they know what it is. It just happens to lie a little outside their competence to suggest it, or, equally, it lies beyond their experience to manage the impact. There can be few practitioners who have not had this kind of experience at some point in their career. Usually it is one from which they learn: but that learning can come at a great cost.

This is, as much as any reason, why a space for *reflection* and support to consider their work is so important for the development of any would-be effective practitioner. Initial preparation is insufficient for a practitioner to field all the expectations and ambiguities that are likely to come their way. These issues are taken up further in this book.

Many practitioners also know that the range of interventions they might offer is much more a matter of some largely unconscious process than anything worked out with clarity and a rationale: and what has worked in the past is what tends to be offered more and more. Practitioners only work at this level when they have not conducted an exploration into the nature of self, the agency and the nature of helping. As a result, individual practitioners often end up with a relatively restricted repertoire of styles and strategies that leave a great deal of potential untapped in the situation and in each of the contributors. In large measure, good preparation helps to avoid these restrictions of practice and helps to open practitioners up to reconsider how else and what else they might do to increase the scope for their response and their potential effectiveness.

Practitioner Context

Practitioners must have a *sense of purpose* about what they do and a realistic framework within which to understand what informs their practice. Help is never straightforward, as we have already pointed out, and all practitioners need to be able to articulate how they do what they do and why they choose to do what they do in *that way*. What practitioners do choose needs to make sense of:

- The work they undertake in their particular context.
- The roles in which they meet.
- The setting.
- The boundaries.
- The clients.
- Their own capabilities.
- The time available.

The work. How a person comes to be offering help is often work-related: it is part of the job or accompanies the duties that go along with a role. It is usually limited in some way. Few work roles give free licence for a practitioner to offer unlimited help to anyone about anything. Being clear what the limits are of the work you are doing is a prerequisite for not offering too much too soon or for not remaining involved for too long. On those occasions when the practitioner has not been clear with themselves or the client at the outset, the help can soon become less and less useful as the practitioner becomes more and more riddled with anxieties about how long it might go on for and what the organisation might have to say about it.

The roles in which client and practitioner meet. Helping has expanded in the last twenty five years. There is now an over-abundance of terms to describe increasingly smaller and smaller divisions within the spectrum of help. This is both a reaction to the professionalisation of helping and a manifestation of it.

How people meet creates expectations about what will take place. However, when people seek help it is often the first time they have done so, so their expectations are anything but clear. Or their need is so great that they either have unrealistic hopes or believe no one can help. These kinds of influences have a serious effect upon what happens unless the practitioner is alert and responsive to the person in difficulty.

What titles people have offers some clue to their contribution, or does it? No one is under any illusions about what to expect when they go and see a GP or call at the dentist and yet... Some roles are well-embedded in our social life and they provide newcomers and those unfamiliar in practice with at least some sort of orientation.

Some helping agencies are focused upon a single clearly identifiable client group, a young people's counselling service for example, or respond to anyone who has a generic concern related to the topic, such as a drugs agency. But helping agencies have proliferated and may well offer a variety of responses under one umbrella name. They may be largely interested in advocacy and campaigning for the rights of those they represent yet also in providing direct services, such as 'Mind'[8] for example. Some may offer a largely information-based service, associations that deal with specific medical conditions for example, but also offer referral suggestions.

The range of services and agencies has also exploded in the last twenty years and with it the opportunities for helping training of all kinds. Many agencies offer a form of counselling as part of the response they make and either prepare their own workers or expect them to have some form of training prior to their induction within the agency.

The link between counselling and therapy has also been part of these developments and this plays its part in the roles practitioners undertake. Back in the nineteen eighties counselling was in its infancy and was more often related to the application of *counselling skills* to a broad range of helping roles – voluntary organisations, pastoral situations, academic roles etc. With the urge to make the activity more specialised and in order to claim professional status, counselling became much more associated with therapeutic work and with longer-term relationships of a specialist helping kind.

To further complicate the picture, there are a great many people who offer themselves in various helping roles outside agency settings and whose work does not have a therapeutic focus – people who offer mentoring, coaching, consultancy; the names are many. Essentially they are individuals who offer their expertise outside an agency setting and outside the need for the kind of regulation that practitioners have decided to create.

The setting. Where the help is offered makes every difference to its likely value and success. It may be that you are 'buttonholed' in the car park on the way out, or you are stopped as you walk down a corridor. Such a way of approaching you for help makes it 'safe' because very little of any consequence can take place if you are on your way to somewhere else.

It may be a 'safe' way for the potential client to let you know that they need something, but it is not the place to practise. You need the right working conditions if you are going to be able to understand the real forces at work in the situation. Such requests for help can always be met with attentiveness and suggestions for the person to meet you at a suitable time and place.

---

[8] Mind is a charity concerned with helping those with mental health issues.

The boundaries. As we've already noted, the helping relationship takes place in some context, a setting that usually makes clear the nature of the help that is offered, the purpose the agency serves and what kinds of difficulties are legitimate for its staff to respond to. All practitioners operate within a given set of conditions about the time they have available, the style of the meeting they use, and what can be offered.

The clients. Help that is offered in some work-related context often means that a good deal is likely to be known about most of the people who need help. Indeed, the practitioner may well have been given some information concerning the range of commonplace requests that people bring.

However, the practitioner should avoid the danger of reducing the individual merely to one of a type and assuming that they are simply another example of… From time to time the client who has a typical 'presenting problem'[9] will need help that lies a good way outside the usual range of responses. Although agencies and the preparation they offer are designed to give a sense of what the practitioner may expect, life is full of surprises, as we know.

Their own capabilities. Any practitioner can work with some individuals and some issues better than others. Like any other activity and any other form of practice, the practitioner changes their stance and evolves their skills over time according to their experience and interests. Capability is not a static thing but develops with further education and opportunities to reflect, as we discuss in other places in this book.

The time available. Perhaps the most overlooked issue and resource is time. If there isn't sufficient time, don't start. Arrange another meeting. If you have endless time today, don't give the impression you will always be so liberal if this is not the case. Offering a given amount of time, which is appropriate to the conditions and circumstances and not just to the extent of the person's immediate need, may be more valuable to them in helping them to learn how to manage themselves than indulging them with an unlimited portion of your time now.

As will be apparent by now, the author believes that preparation for a helping role is not simply about learning techniques or theories of psychology and personal development. Neither is it about having a theoretical understanding and then attempting to fit clients into a 'type' who can therefore be dealt with in this particular way.

"…it is the loss of person as image which opens the door to collective techniques of handling persons. Persons in bins can resemble each other only in their commonality. So we would climb out into individualism by heroic acts of rugged will." J. Hillman, 1980.

---

[9] 'Presenting problem' is the term used to describe how people make themselves available for help by disclosing something that is legitimate but not necessarily as important as other concerns that they will reveal once they have become assured of your initial interest and helpfulness.

It is much more about recognising the importance of the relationship between the people involved in the enterprise. This is a much more difficult and complex process than accumulating intellectual knowledge. It involves a willingness to really meet with the other person in order to encourage that growth in freedom that has already been described. Preparation for helping needs to be wide-ranging and, for it to be effective, it needs to address all the issues mentioned in this chapter in addition to the other areas that are addressed throughout this book.

Suggested Reading

Scott Peck, M: *The Road Less Travelled*. London, Arrow, 1990.

SECTION II

THE HELPING SPECTRUM:
Advice, Guidance & Counselling

Chapter 5
A Helping Framework

We've seen that help comes in many forms and from many sources. It is performed by a wide variety of people within a great many different roles and across diverse agencies and organisations. In practice, help comes in all sorts of shapes and sizes, from the helpful word in the ear of the colleague about to make an error, to the long-term support of someone arriving in a new town in a foreign country starting a new life. It can take the form of an interview with an official who has the complex task of evaluating your case or it can be undertaken in the practitioner's home under the term 'counselling'. It may be therapeutic help that is offered under the name of 'advice' because the tone and the manner are friendly and the relief that comes is palpable. It may be described as an 'interview' and yet feel more like an interrogation.

Despite all these diverse expressions of help, how help itself operates can be examined relatively systematically. It is clear that there are certain sorts of help that are more aligned to one another than others, for example advice and taking action are more aligned than taking action and counselling. It is also clear that some forms of help are more fitting for certain settings than others. Citizens Advice work, for example, is more about helping people take action and giving advice rather than counselling which requires longer-term contact. Similarly, drug and alcohol agencies, Youth Services, counselling agencies and other agencies of these kind often have a blend of initial counselling skills, some general advice giving and recommendations about aspects of 'problem management', which leads into an on-going 'helping relationship' that may have many of the features of focused counselling relationship.

Although the growth of 'counselling' has been enormous, and is now frequently obtainable through GP referral, most forms of help that most people turn to are not exclusively counselling or therapeutically based. Most people will refer themselves to agencies with which they identify as a result of the difficulties or concerns they have. For example, a fear of sexually transmitted disease or HIV infection would take someone to an agency that would bring specialist help alongside any supportive counselling.

One of the dilemmas facing clients and agencies is based on the issues that arise from this 'matching' process — finding the most appropriate practitioner/agency for an individual's needs. A client with eating disorder 'issues' may or may not be ready for therapeutic help but may benefit from dietary advice, a genuine desire on the part of the practitioner to understand, and a place where they can be 'heard'. On the other hand, a person seeking advice from an alcohol agency about changing their levels of drinking, which developed as a result of a relationship coming to an end or losing a job, may need help less about alcohol dependency and more skilled counselling about managing change and loss.

Whilst there is an argument that says the skilled practitioner would not only be able to spot this kind of presentational issue but would also be able to make some progress with it, it is not altogether as straightforward as it seems. The example above highlights two major issues:

1. Is it legitimate, given the agency's parameters and the client's needs, to respond to a symptomatic issue?

2. Whilst the connection might be clear that the drinking has become a 'problem' as the result of the specific experience, the counsellor, by accepting to work with it, may be entering a potentially long-term relationship where other complex forms of loss, grief and, perhaps, bereavement are waiting to be unearthed.

There are no ready-made answers to these dilemmas for clients, practitioners or agencies. Yet, given the extent of human need for help, managing these difficulties effectively needs to be a consistently high priority for agencies and practitioners.

From this it becomes clear that there are certain conditions that affect the form of help that can be offered. There are restraints linked to:

1. The agency's purpose.

2. The role of the individual practitioner.

3. The style of the person in the role.

The purpose of having a framework is to simplify and thereby highlight some key elements and essential features of help in its widest sense. It is in the first two areas - the work of the agency and the role of the practitioner – that we can be most explicit about the way helping operates. Personal style, crucial though it is, is something to consider after working out what the agency is set up to do and what the agency has asked and, hopefully, prepared the practitioner to do.

Advice, Guidance & Counselling

One common broad classification of most forms of help is to regard them as examples of one of these three types of approach:

- **Advice:** where the practitioner is taking more of the initiative.
- **Guidance:** where there is more collaboration involved.
- **Counselling:** where the influence of the client is stronger.

This is not a comprehensive analysis of forms of helping; for example it doesn't directly include an important aspect of many forms of current help – advocacy. It does, however, begin to represent help across a spectrum, from a position where the practitioner has the greater influence over the process to one where clients are becoming empowered to take greater control over their own affairs.

Practitioners and Frameworks

Type of Help	Advice	Guidance	Counselling
Power/influence	Practitioner led	Joint problem solving	Client led

One of the most important elements in any attempt to create a framework or examine help hinges on who has the power and how far the client is in charge of his or her own assistance.

The framework offered here is neither original nor unique but it is general and it is comprehensive – enough to begin to think about how helping happens and how a number of strands may be formed together to create a single *helping strategy* for a particular person or set of circumstances. It summarises the principal forms of help that are offered by one person or agency to another.

It covers a wide range of applications and many of the surrounding aspects of human relations and helping work. In that sense, it applies to almost any helping occasion and is not confined to a particular type of practitioner-client situation. Most help that takes place on a day-to-day basis fits into this framework because most practitioners are not reliant upon a single type of intervention, nor are they confined to only one type of client.

Most practitioners work with a range of people who have diverse concerns. Consequently, in order to create a workable approach to the benefit of a particular client, practitioners may require a strategy made up of a number of elements of the framework outlined here.

The more alert and conscious practitioners are as to what they *can* do, what they *do* do and what *else* they *might* do, the more they are able to construct a *developmental* approach to their own progress. Over-reliance upon one particular style of response is the ever-present temptation of any practitioner. Getting too good at one strategy and then applying it to all clients is a very real risk for the over-worked practitioner.

Whilst suitable motivation and commitment are crucial in any effective helping relationship, alone they are insufficient to secure any predictable result. *Good will alone is not enough to guarantee success* and is often the refuge of the incompetent, the mischievous and the downright manipulative. Since we never see intentions and all of us can retrospectively claim to be operating from 'the best of motives', all too often any old mess is explained away as having no link to the practitioner.

A Helping Framework

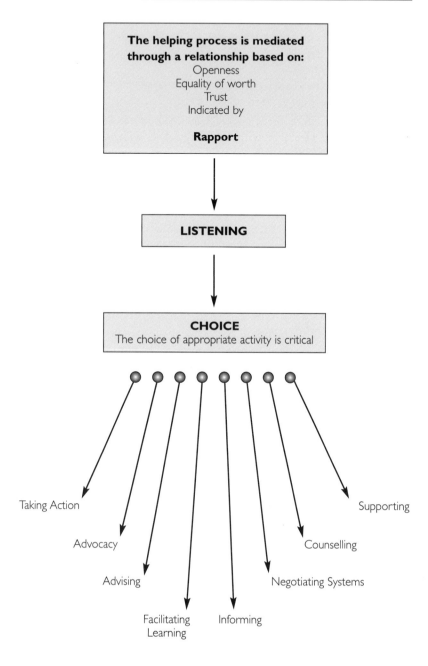

AIM OF HELPING
To promote increased self-reliance, choice and personal responsibility

The helping process is mediated
through a relationship based on:
Openness
Equality of worth
Trust
Indicated by

Rapport

LISTENING

CHOICE
The choice of appropriate activity is critical

Taking Action

Advocacy

Advising

Facilitating
Learning

Informing

Negotiating Systems

Counselling

Supporting

Tasks & Methods

Practitioners need to have available a range of methods they can draw on. Some are easier to implement than others and some take more time than others. All of us have preferences for some methods over others.

The setting, too, influences the options available and may pressurise the practitioner into relying upon *speed of response* at the expense of *accuracy of understanding*. The choice of methods – combined together to create a *plan of action* – will be strongly influenced by time, skills and so on and also, crucially, by the role of the practitioner. The role is the overt representation of the work the practitioner is providing.

Some roles rely upon one central method of help. *Advising* depends upon having effective and up-to-date responses that are given in a way that is of benefit to the range of clients coming forward for help. It is important that advising does not stray into the emotional complexities of a case or suggests that more is possible than is likely. Advising is about getting clarity of understanding and offering a clear response. This is not to suggest that it cannot be done with warmth and interest.

It is important to emphasise, though, that almost all advisory roles are clearer to recognise and perform than others in the spectrum outlined here because they require such a strong degree of clarity in the way they operate. It is one of the strengths of the advisory range of roles and tasks that clarity is paramount. Solicitors are usually very clear about what they offer by way of advice and by way of suggestion. Other advisory-based professionals are just as judicious in how they screen out the unnecessary (for their purposes) and how they make clear to the client that they will ask what they want to know. Such directive and authoritative 'performances' are often reassuring and do have the beauty that they make clear just who is in charge. Of course, they leave open the possibility of the client being too intimidated to use the opportunity to get the help that is available. But there are strengths and weaknesses in all approaches.

More broad-based forms of help and especially *guidance work of all kinds* are much less able to set clear boundaries around what there is to respond to and for how long – as we shall see. Other roles have no such obvious or single method to rely upon but will require the combination of a number of methods at different points in helping the client. Any method also gives more or less control either to the practitioner or the client. We can identify the transitions of methods from the most directive to the least directive end of a spectrum that roughly corresponds to the Advising, Guidance and Counselling illustration we introduced earlier.

Practitioner Roles

In terms of roles, the advisory end of the spectrum tends to be occupied by individuals with clear roles – and it is how they fulfil such roles that opens opportunities for their being performed in an abruptly directive fashion or in a more approachably authoritative manner. Many people who are drawn to this kind of work rightly enjoy the opportunities it gives for them to make use of their expertise and their often detailed knowledge. This can, however, lead to a lack of 'interest' in the person with the difficulty and greater interest in the problem they have leaving the individual of little account. There is no reason why someone with all the expertise in the world and all the detailed knowledge cannot show enough interest in those they serve.

In the middle area, the guidance area – not surprisingly where most helping takes place – the roles are less clear and there is scope for much fuzziness of approach and combination of methods. It also provides any number of opportunities for people to switch methods, shift roles and generally 'hop in and out' of ways of helping that can be anything but useful.

It is in this middle area of the spectrum that we have witnessed the explosion of so many roles in the helping world and the field of personal development especially. 'Coach', 'life coach', 'personal development consultant', 'mentor', and so on are only the most obvious roles in which there are elements of guidance and much more of a 'hands-on being with' the client than in advisory roles.

In new agencies such as *Connexions* and *SureStart* this is where many of the interventions that staff make with their clients occur. 'Guidance' roles such as these often require a good deal of guidance for those who are doing the guiding for two key reasons. Firstly, it is all too easy to appear far more involved with the client than more traditional roles would expect. Secondly, it is equally easy to appear far too remote to build the necessary rapport that is required to gain the trust of people who may have a long history of antipathy towards traditional forms of helping.

Method	Task/Role of Practitioner
1. Taking Action	Doing for
2. Advocacy	Representing
3. Advising	Recommending a course of action
4. Facilitating Learning	Providing opportunities to learn
5. Informing	Providing accurate information
6. Negotiating Systems	Providing understanding of systems and advice in 'living' with systems
7. Counselling	Offering time and space for concerns to surface
8. Supporting	Providing a safe haven

Practitioner Roles

Practitioners & Power

Once we think of help across a spectrum, we can immediately recognise how helping raises questions about the distribution of power. There are two important considerations here. Firstly, how far the power is maintained in the hands of the practitioner at the expense of the client and, secondly, how far it is pushed at the client prematurely, leaving them unable to manage the responsibility for the decisions they have to undertake. Many practitioners are not at ease with notions of power in something so apparently 'caring' as help. There is a great reluctance to acknowledge this dimension of power and therefore it is likely to have a way of coming into play that is not as clear as it needs to be.

For example, in the effort to be non-controlling, a practitioner may bend over backwards to help the client decide, while the client is happily delaying having to make up their mind and enjoying the struggle the practitioner clearly is having to remain non-directive. On the other hand, the practitioner, so desperate to win the approval of the client, may be quick to offer suggestions that simply do not meet the circumstances that underlie a difficulty. In the effort to bring about a result, the practitioner fails to listen accurately. We might not think of these kinds of examples as having much to do with power but they are.

Practitioners have to come to some sense of the appropriate use of their own power within the agency's ground rules and the relationship with each of their clients. If they do not, it is likely that they will be working out of their own unmet needs or expressing their unexamined assumptions about the nature of power in the helping relationship.

This is, in large part, what makes helping so fascinating an activity. If the practitioner, out of the best of intentions for their client, makes decisions on behalf of the client, the client may be appreciative at the time but utterly disempowered in the future. If, however, the practitioner steps aside and simply offers non-directive support then the client may languish in the throes of ignorance when a 'shot' of direction and problem solving may make all the difference.

'Taking Over' the Client

A further complication to this discussion comes about when thinking of the general abilities of people, especially at times when they need help. As a general rule, the more disabled and dysfunctional the person, the more the help will tend to be of the practitioner-directed kind. However, the more this is the case, the less the client is going to gain any opportunity to recover their self-direction. As we have already seen, directed help, even when offered with the best of motives, may serve to maintain the client in their dependence upon others rather than being something introduced to protect them for a time before encouraging them to resume responsibility for more and more of their lives.

In therapeutic work this is a major issue. If therapeutic practitioners see clients as 'vulnerable', 'damaged' people to the degree that they cannot take responsibility for a shared relationship; if they see their clients as 'patients' (as many do); if they require a doctor's agreement before entering into a working relationship with them (as some do), then the client is being viewed as someone barely able to function. The fact that they may have a job of some significance in the real world outside the meeting room does not qualify. To the therapist, the client is in need of protection of a fairly heavy kind.

Empowering People

If, however, you are a practitioner who views the client as someone who is functioning in society and thereby responsible for decisions about managing their money, paying their mortgage, feeding their family and the usual range of concerns that makes up the role of the citizen, then the removal of self-direction from them, however emotionally upset they may be, would amount to a termination of their rights. In such circumstances, the practitioner should be more than cautious of assuming a power role over the client. Unless a citizen is incapacitated from their role as a citizen, the therapist has no right to treat them as somehow medicalised to the point of requiring the kind of control and direction that they would receive under medical supervision.

This is a major distinction in the helping world; between those who claim the need for the strict 'policing' of the helping relationship and those who view helping as something that needs no such 'social policing' in the great majority of situations that make up the human condition.

If the client is capable of making a clear contract, then there is every indication of their capacity to act responsibly. If they do not like the treatment they receive they can act accordingly. If they are not able to make such a contract, then the chances are that any help they might gain from even regular sessions is likely to be dubious. Very often beneath these stances on the need for policing there are incompatible models of the very nature of helping.

Chapter 6
Advisory Methods
Taking Action/Advocacy/Advising

Any compilation of methods is, to a degree, arbitrary and simply serves a utilitarian purpose – to distinguish for the purposes of explanation some of the major distinctions between one method and another. However methods do frequently fall into types and many years of experience and reflection have led the author to the identification of three major forms of working with an *advisory* stance.

1. Taking action on behalf of the client: with all the attendant dangers that come from such a strong method when misused.

2. The Advocacy role: one that is increasingly required in a modern, complex society where a growing number of individuals may not be in any great distress about their lives but who are greatly annoyed by some lack of response by a system or a group.

3. Advising: the need for people to be armed with adequate and correct information to take further action.

The crucial distinguishing feature of advisory methods is that practitioners are working from a base of *expertise* rather than *relationship*. These three methods also account for the work in many occupations: medical, legal, financial and many personal services depend upon them. In addition, social problems require the mobilisation of thousands of 'rights' workers. Advisory methods take up a huge portion of the helping industry and are often the starting point for someone beginning to realise that, though they may 'have a case', it is not going to be solved as easily as they thought. Such experience may then lead to other, less directive forms of help, at a later date.

Traditional Responses
Of all the methods discussed here, those that fall within the realm of advisory methods are most weighted in favour of the practitioner. This is the case because it is up to the client to find a way to offer the information they hold in ways that unlock the expertise of the practitioner for their, the client's, benefit. It is the approach that is most dependent upon the practitioner and the one which will leave the client not much more able to negotiate their way through the complexities of similar situations in the future. The overriding concern of these methods is that the client needs help of a specialist kind they are unlikely to be able to provide for themselves and therefore needs to find a person who has the relevant expertise.

In the case of needing legal advice about the sale of a house, I can consult a solicitor. (I can also try and do it myself these days, but not unless I have a fair understanding of how to manage the kind of situations that I will have to face. When it comes to learning about the law, the sale of a house is not the best way to begin!) When faced with redundancy, for example, I might need the help of a number of specialists to discover my rights to entitlements, help with my housing circumstances, and where to look if I intend to take up some other form of employment. Negotiating a way through the domain of experts can be time-consuming, complex and not always satisfactory.

There is often a stage for people exploring the labyrinthine passages of 'the system' (whatever system they happen to be in) when they realise that if they had known then what they know now, they would have been able to make much better use of the help they were offered previously! There is something inevitable about this state of affairs for many of us. Unfamiliar with the way experts and systems work, we tend to believe our case is as we understand it, and that the expert will recognise this and act accordingly. The matter will be straightforward and unambiguous as it usually is to us and it should be 'sorted' in a matter of moments (or else it is so chronically complex that we expect no-one to really understand it). The expert will know the 'right' question to ask and avoid the 'wrong' question which it is better not to ask. I exaggerate only to make the point that most of us, when confronted with the need for experts, have a simplistic view of what they can do, the time it takes, and the results that can be obtained.

In many ways, this stance to providing assistance is the traditional mode. A problem exists; an agency or an institution is given responsibility to respond to it. Individuals are appointed to fulfil the obligations of the institution and that is the end of the matter – until further legislation or regulation requires the institution to modify its provision or its response. Those requiring the service attend on the terms and conditions governing the agency or organisation and all is well – in theory.

The underlying myth behind this stance is that once the problem has been identified, an agency created to deal with it and staff appointed to respond, then we can all relax knowing that our civic duty is taken care of. Those appointed fulfil their duty and the problem is then being 'managed' – until some major loophole appears or some catastrophic failure is unearthed[10]. A social issue is raised but there are not the resources to help everyone who might be considered to be affected.

Numbers, therefore, are reduced to an eligible and manageable proportion by various strategies, such as means testing, and a solution is applied. Things improve and we all feel better! It is a heartening view of helping; one that depends upon everything going

[10] Such forms of response are, by nature, a salve to the social conscience of us all; a way of excluding the unpleasant and unwanted side effects of our social system to the margins where others can take care of the consequences until the glare of media publicity shines through. Different social groups get marginalised and then demonised in this way. In recent years we have had paedophilia, asylum seekers as well as the continuing problems of race relations. The psychology of exploiting 'the stranger' and their differences from the rest of us (who are every bit as different if we bothered to consider it) is part of the way in which social groups create a way of bonding: in-groups need out-groups. Out-groups have an unpleasant fate. No one wants to be a member of an out-group so there is some incentive to make those groups remain the ones they are so that others, who might be made into marginal groups, remain within the mainstream. Social stratification is maintained by such distinctions and social cohesion maintained by agencies that attempt to manage the consequences of marginalising and ostracising minority groups.

according to plan and one that depends upon the problem that is being addressed having little or no emotional or psychological component otherwise it becomes much more complicated.

In times past, the white-coated expert was not expected or required to understand the dilemmas that went along with the difficulties people had and, anyway, personal difficulties had no place in the 'fair' and objective assessment of who was entitled to what level of treatment or benefit. Impartiality of the service provider was considered an important virtue in such forms of help. The 'means-tested' benefit is perhaps the most socially controversial form of this kind of help.

Considerations in Applying Advisory Methods

There are two major considerations to bear in mind with advisory methods. The first is that the advisor may well overlook the individual in favour of viewing them merely as a 'case' to be treated. The second is that treating all people equally is inevitably unjust and unfair to some – especially to those whose case is particular and unique – and is therefore socially divisive in the way it apportions its fairness. On the other hand, universal entitlements that give everyone the right to enjoy a benefit or service are controversial for the way in which they encourage people who do not need the service to indulge themselves or to exploit the benefits wastefully.

Since resources are scarce there has usually been a need for some form of regulation about access to services. The advisory figure plays this role of providing and enforcing strict criteria before anyone benefits from the service being sought. They have an enforcement role and a gate-keeping role as well as a providing role. These three elements are not straightforward to implement and inevitably individuals favour one aspect of these three responses over others. The role of enforcement favours those who like to apply clear-cut rules and conditions. The gatekeeper role gives those who wish to offer some latitude and interpretation a chance to respond beyond the strictest of interpretations. Those who desire to bring help to people in need will emphasise the provider role wherever they can.

In other professions that are strongly advisory – the law and medicine, for example – the expert stands in danger of showing more interest in the case or the condition than the person who carries it. Experts are notorious perhaps more in the reputation they have been given rather than in the numbers who are actually so remote and impersonal in their dealings with the public. However, it is a continuing issue for any organisation wishing to portray itself as more 'customer focused' or 'person-centred' to ensure that the experts providing the service have changed their stance to the way they treat people.

It is quite a change for people who have gained their prestige and authority by the acquisition of knowledge, at the expense of relating to people, to now need to become interested in those they serve. This shift of emphasis lies at the heart of the revolution in the way helping has changed over the last thirty years or so and is echoed throughout this book.

Where once the expert had the undisputed power and the client was deferential and thankful for any interest shown in them, the tables are now turned. We live in a consumer age in which the individual consumer expects choices; 'patient choice' is the mantra of those attempting to find new ways to reform the beleaguered NHS. The whole concept of 'choice' for clients, for patients, for consumers in general, is crucial in how the relationship between the expert and the client will develop.

1. Taking Action

The practitioner executes the agreed course of action on behalf of the client.

Taking action is most closely linked to crisis and emergency work. The more critical the situation, the more likely it is that some form of immediate action will be appropriate and essential.

In some circumstances, it is also the case that unless action is taken to remedy the immediate situation, longer-term help of a more developmental kind cannot even begin. Someone made homeless, for example, is unlikely to be able to respond to a sensitive counselling relationship unless the issue of his or her homelessness is addressed. Someone who is made redundant, and who has no knowledge of the benefits system, may need someone to act on their behalf as a first step toward managing a new phase in which other forms of help will then play a crucial part.

Limitations
- The individual may not learn how and why the practitioner chooses to act in a particular way.
- If the problem recurs, the client may have few extra skills or resources and may revert automatically to seeking the expert again.

Benefits
- Action is prompt, and the identified problem is usually dealt with swiftly.
- If the expert is well chosen and can be relied upon to know the best course of action, the problem is solved.
- The practitioner recognises the limits of the time, skills etc. it would require for the client to solve the problem for themselves.

2. Advocacy

The practitioner is employed to assess the individual's circumstances and represent their case in some formal process of assessment – for benefit entitlement, asylum or at a tribunal, for example.

The growth of *advocacy* is in part a reflection of the nature of the litigious world we are entering. Litigation, as we have already seen in the first section, *The World of Helping*, is an increasingly common aspect of our culture. Liability is the driving engine of many arguments of our time and, consequently, there are more and more occasions when advocacy is needed. People have rights; those rights are enshrined in codes of various kinds. It takes a form of expertise to understand the implications of the codes; how they apply when, where and to whom. All forms of advocacy are covered by the term here, including, for example, having the skill to put together formal statements, or knowing people's rights and being able to present a case.

Even someone with a strong case may well lose it if they are not represented well or are unfamiliar with the way tribunals and other formal decision-making bodies operate. Advocacy is therefore an area where the individual has to provide the information to someone who then turns it into some form of 'case'.[11] Disputes of all kinds are increasingly put in the hands of people who specialise in providing expert-based assessments of the likelihood of success.

Many who would not have thought of making claims against institutions or other individuals when things go wrong are now willing to resort to formal challenges. On the one hand, this is an example of the march of individual rights for fair and equal treatment. On the other hand, there is something of the 'see what you can get' mentality about some such claims.

When confronted with a prospective client, the practitioner has a number of tasks to manage and perform simultaneously. They have to:

- Gather the information.
- Assess the likelihood of success.
- Give due respect to the client.
- Pay attention to the distress suffered by the client.

All this is in order to ensure that they provide the client with a realistic appraisal of their legitimate chances of success if they pursue their cause further.

There is a risk for the claimant of taking up such a course of action only to find the nuances of the hearing or the terms of the codes are so stringently maintained that it leaves them with little hope of getting satisfaction. After great effort and a period of hope, the claimant may find themselves back where they began.

Sometimes the case, which is the most important thing in the world to the claimant and upon which a lot may rest, is nevertheless only one of a caseload to the advocate and has to be put into context with other concerns. It may easily appear to the claimant that the case has got 'lost', is locked up in some endless procedural process about which they know nothing and about which they can do even less. What began as a search for someone 'to stand beside me' seems to have produced someone who

---

[11] Following one plane disaster in Britain, the families were offered a settlement of £6 million per person killed: an enormous sum until you learn that over **one third** of the final amount (which will not be the full amount when you read the small print) will be required to pay for the services of the advocates involved! Advocacy can be costly in every sense and bring little satisfaction by the time a matter is resolved. Another example is how an inquiry into the way this nation was given information to build a case to go to war – the most serious act that can be undertaken – was very rapidly reduced to a lawyers 'game' and the moral and ethical issues – those which most interest people – were in danger of being obscured by those presenting their case through legal representatives. Advocacy here becomes another form of theatre, if we aren't careful.

has taken up arms against me and is yet one more impediment to me getting on with my life! The level of disappointment from advocacy cases that are too protracted, too ambiguous or just plain awkward and difficult is not hard to imagine.

Limitations
- Time, money and patience. No advocacy solution is likely to be swift.
- Underestimating the risks of losing a strong case for lack of some decisive element is not uncommon – justice may not be served and the client may not get satisfaction either.
- Often it requires the individual to pay some or all of the resulting costs of the action.

Benefits
- An individual can call upon a wealth of expertise relevant to their case.
- It may provide a solution that is solid and binding, bringing much relief to an uncertain situation.
- Causes with elements of injustice and unfairness are often settled only by some verdict from a third party – help to get such a result is almost always essential.

3. Advising

The practitioner gives an explicit recommendation to the client of a course of action the client should follow.

Offering advice may provide critical information where a lot may be at stake if a deadline isn't kept, especially in a time-limited situation such as when a contract or an appeal is involved. (Much of what is said here applies to advocacy workers too.)

There are many people who encounter the formalities of systems only rarely in their lives and, as a result, are overly intimidated by them when they do. They frequently do not know the procedures and, if they do, are often overwhelmed by the mechanics of how things operate. For those who spend their lives in such systems, these situations are no more than routine. They can therfore provide extremely effective help in the form of a recommended course of action and up-to-date knowledge of what the consequences are likely to be of specific, considered actions, without being overwhelmed by the system itself.

There is, of course, another group of 'advisors' on hand in the form of those who have opinions to offer about almost any human situation or dilemma not based on expertise, or even experience, but based upon the desire to pass on their own views about anything and everything. Such a view of the role of advice is not the one being promoted here.

The whole issue of who should give what advice to what level needs careful consideration.

An individual may have expertise in one area and, of course, have no great knowledge in any other compartment of life. I may know what your welfare rights are, but that does not mean that I am any more qualified to give advice about whether you should have more children or not. An extreme example perhaps, but only to make the point that both the advice-giver and those advised often stray way beyond the confines of the expertise of the one and into the realms of please-take-over-my-life of the other. As someone pointed out a long time ago, there are only three reasons for seeking advice:

- Because you want someone else to tell you what to do so that when it goes wrong you can blame him or her thus evading responsibility yourself.
- To go ahead and do what you would have done anyway.
- To add more information to the equation and delay doing anything.

Limitations
- If the advice is considered and rejected, the adviser can feel rejected and may refuse further help. (An unlikely response in any seasoned advisor but a consideration for clients who may think they have to comply with the expectations of the adviser to maintain the relationship.)
- It is difficult to estimate the full consequences to someone else of any recommended course of action.
- The adviser does not have to live with the consequences of any suggestion.
- There is a danger of advice being given prematurely – it may only serve to solve the wrong problem.
- Giving advice is very easy to do badly and very difficult to do well.

Benefits
- It can cut through a lot of confusion.
- It can help the individual to see a way forward without forcing them to take the preferred suggestion.
- It can provide a perspective for considering other alternatives if the course suggested does not appeal.
- It can be particularly useful when there is professional expertise involved; specific issues such as legal and financial matters, housing etc.

Chapter 7
Guidance Methods
Facilitating Learning/Informing/Negotiating Systems

The methods we have gathered under the heading 'guidance' are perhaps the methods that are the most balanced of all forms of help. There is a mutual recognition by both parties that each has something distinctive to contribute. The willingness by both parties to collaborate in a meaningful way rather than simply paying lip service to the idea of a joint venture is the key to the effectiveness of the relationship in these methods. Collaboration and willingness to work together is the pivotal distinguishing feature between these methods and the ones that were described in the previous chapter. We are now entering the realm of two people meeting in a more genuine and mutual manner.

The learner[12] (rather than 'client') has to be willing to put in effort on their own behalf and they have to be willing to enter into the kind of relationship that is necessary for them to get to the end result they are seeking. The 'guidance agent' (the generic term we'll use here) has to be willing to make allowances for learners and their own unique position. They must not 'take over' the learner's situation, mould the learner into their own version of what they believe the 'right way' needs to be, nor recruit the learner or attempt to convert them to their own particular ideology.

At the same time, they have standards to promote, a way of operating that has gained respect and recognition and they are therefore committed to being in the relationship in an active and valued way. Part of the enjoyment and success for those involved in guidance work of all kinds is making their evident talents, skills and abilities available for the successful use of the other.

Types of Guide

A guide[13] is…? There are many different anecdotal descriptions of the role of the guide.

> There is the wise figure who knows the landscape ahead and provides a sure-footed way of crossing difficult terrain, minimising the risks of unnecessary accident and danger. This is the guide as **mountaineer**.

> There is the guide who shows a long-term interest in the development of another person – often a younger person. This is the guide as **mentor**.

---

[12] Throughout this chapter I have substituted the word learner for client. It seems to be a much more useful term and emphasises the central importance of the element of learning that is involved in guidance roles of all kinds.

[13] There are a number of excellent films that illustrate the nature of the guidance relationship. *'Lord of the Rings'* is better read for these purposes than seen. But *'Karate Kid'* is exceptional in demonstrating the interests of a wiser figure who offers a restraint and a capacity of understanding to a young fatherless boy. *Donny Brasco* is another portrait of the male-male guidance relationship. A Mafia lieutenant (a 'capo') coaches undercover cop, Donny Brasco, in the culture and practices of the New York Mafia underworld, i.e. he is a guide or mentor. The resulting betrayal is an illustration of how the relationship affects even those who are at odds with each other. *'Annabel's Line'* is a film based upon the informal guidance a woman brings to a whole community in a modest and unstated way.

There is the guide who plays an important role in an individual's progress at a particular time in their development. This is guide in the form of a community leader or the swimming instructor who doesn't simply teach the strokes but helps the individual develop a wider appreciation of responsibility and practice through the approach to the activity. This is the guide as **coach**.

There is the guide who takes the form of the more experienced individual who offers more than a helping hand to the organisational newcomer or the colleague on a 'mentoring scheme'; someone who provides a point of reflection and learning for those wanting to make progress within the workplace. This is guide as the **organisational mentor**.

There is the individual who offers to coach people through life difficulties or who has a particular approach to some aspect of personal development. This is guide as the **personal coach**.

There is the guide as the person of formidable reputation who may be *consulted* occasionally by the individual with an unusual question or a particularly awkward set of circumstances that needs something extra and something from a source outside the usual range of assistance. This is guide as **mentor** in the Gandalf sense: someone who can bring a bit of *magic* to a problem.

The Need for the Guide

A great many helping occupations require practitioners to put together a number of different elements of help as an effective response to a problem. Most of the help that is delivered through organisations is of this kind; health care, social care, youth work, careers assistance all may well require the combination of a number of different elements to help the inquirer get from where they start to where they want to get to. Individual requests, though they may be typical, usually require them to be formulated into some working arrangement for the particular individual – into some form of 'learning plan'[14].

Equally, individuals throughout life from time to time face a wide range of tasks that they cannot yet solve, given the state of their own understanding, without seeking some form of support and guidance. 'Leaning on' the wider expertise of someone who knows a good deal more than you do may occur either informally or formally, but it is a form of guidance.

We might be referring to something that is a matter of life experience, never having been for an interview for example, or facing a new life situation, such as becoming a parent for the first time. Such examples illustrate the need for outside help, especially

---

[14] There is room for any number of terms to describe the programme put together between the practitioner and the learner in such circumstances. I have adopted this term to emphasise that it is essentially a plan centring upon the learner learning something. It is a complement to the term 'learner', rather than 'client', which runs through this chapter.

in a society where many of the local networks of support and traditional forms of help are no longer so readily available. It may well be that individuals are facing relatively novel situations – given the background from which they come – and there is no obvious source of help around.

Negotiating the complexities of a modern society to obtain help, establishing benefits, ensuring one's rights are respected – these are not easy matters even for those who act as guidance agents. Rules and procedures change and eligibility criteria are revised in the light of new legislation, thus making the services of guidance workers essential to those seeking help if they are to negotiate their way through a system successfully.

Similarly, the complexities of the modern workplace have led organisations to begin to rethink how best to prepare and develop people. Training is often not the best use of time for people who are learning how to manage new or increasingly unpredictable situations. People in such roles often need opportunities to explore and reflect upon the actions they have taken, or, better still, intend to take. This is best done with someone who can offer that important balance between intervention ('do this') and listening ('what do you think would work?'). Where the aim is to unlock the potential of the learner then the support of some form of organisational coach or mentor can make an enormous difference to the progress of individuals committed to their own development and/or their role in the organisation.

This arrangement of the one-to-one personal coach or mentor has also been successfully applied to children in deprived inner-city areas. Fostering a relationship with an adult who volunteers to offer a few hours each week to support a young person can make all the difference.

Part of the success of any relationship of this kind, whether at work, in school, or in life, is the ability of the two people to create a satisfying relationship. Mentors must in no sense be condescending or patronising and learners must feel real interest coming from their guide. At the same time, mentors or coaches must make real demands on learners to stretch themselves in new ways and find more capacity than they believed they had for the work they are learning about.

A good relationship of this kind – one which lasts over time rather than one that is established to solve a short-term situation – is characterised by the depth of the challenge that both involved are willing to enter. It is not an easy matter for mentors to know when to 'push' (and by 'push' we mean here 'strong encouragement' rather than directive command) and when to 'stand back'. It is equally important for learners to be open to hearing some challenging and awkward facts about how they operate, or the way their actions are understood by those on the receiving end of them. The ability to give and receive feedback is perhaps the most important element in the success of such relationships and is something to which we shall return later. *(See Section Five: The Core of Helping.)*

The wider the gap between the understanding of the learner and the expertise of the guide, the more the implications have to be considered and the bridge across the divide needs to be thought about. If this does not happen then it becomes too tempting for the 'guide' to become the director, simply telling the inquirer what they 'need' to do rather than exploring with them what they might best do. Sensitivity to the needs of the individual may take second place. When there are too many demands on your time and the request appears routine, it becomes all too easy to repeat the formula and ignore the individual emphasis.

Background & the Use of Expertise

The personal profile of the individual guide matters a good deal when it comes to implementing a guidance role and it is more valuable if they play to their strengths creatively and effectively. It is not that it is necessarily better to have the experience you are guiding people through – though it might be – but it is important that you do not use that experience to determine what someone else needs to do. It may 'inform' your contribution but should not be the basis of it. If you have such knowledge it is important that you don't assume that what worked for you ought to work for someone else from a very different sub-culture, a different background or even from the same background for that matter.

The background of experience that the guide brings to the work will strongly affect their stance to the task at hand. For example, a man in his mid fifties will approach careers work with a different set of concerns than a woman of twenty-five. Helping someone develop new parent skills is a different matter when you have brought up four children of your own compared to a professional at the start of their career and who is living on their own. Not only is each one 'seen' differently by the learner, they will each hold a different level of credibility in the eyes of different people. Some people needing help may be reassured by an older figure; others may well be wary of being made to feel they have to take up the suggestions that come from someone else's experience. Another person may welcome 'straight talking' from someone who is a 'professional', even with little direct experience, on the grounds that they will listen and then make up their own mind. Someone else may feel less than reassured. After all 'what use is professional knowledge if you have no direct experience of what it is like to be a parent' (as in the above example).

Since guidance is about influence, it is all too easy for the guide to excuse any and all influence they exert as legitimate. Even when they have doubts about the extent of their suggestions, it is still possible to explain away any lingering uncertainties on the grounds of time or the need for action and so on. The point about having influence is that it is *exercised to the minimum* and *done awarely*. 'Minimum' because the only guidance a person needs is 'enough': enough to take the step ahead of them, not enough to find their life pattern taken over by the guidance agent. 'Awarely' because there needs to be a conscious, aware and responsible willingness to account for the strategy chosen and the intentions it is designed to fulfil.

When put to this test, a good deal of guidance would be more modest in scope and more reflective in nature. After all, a person with a problem has often taken a long time to get to the point of being ready for help and needing it and so to wait a little longer may be no bad thing if it helps them design their own solution – the aim of all effective guidance agents.

Time & Relationship

Most guidance relationships are not long-term but they are certainly not brief. This is another feature that adds to the ambiguity.

- 'How do we know when we have done enough and it is time for the work to come to an end or for me to find the next figure in my search?' This is the question that arises for any ambitious learner.
- 'How do I let someone who has a great talent move on before they have gained all they could from me but yet they need the challenge of new opportunities?' This is a question that is crucial in many guidance roles, such as the athletic coach, for example.
- In more 'straightforward' relationships, the learner may be concerned about the time available to them. 'How many meetings are we allowed before I have used up my quota of your time?'
- In an organisational mentoring relationship: 'How do I find someone else when we are not suited to one another without me causing you embarrassment or stirring up your retribution?'
- 'If I don't make enough progress will the guide end the work?' 'How will I know if I am doing all right?'

Whilst the guide has to work with ambiguities of all sorts (and we'll examine some of them), the learner has their difficulties too, ones that are likely to generate a much higher level of uncertainty and concern for them than those of the guide. What is, after all, a familiar situation for the guide is often a novel experience for the learner. Most want to do well and 'get it right', but they aren't sure what 'getting it right' involves. In their efforts to win approval and gain the security of the relationship, they may be tempted to put on an act of compliance and make heroic efforts that they cannot sustain – all to keep the relationship alive.

Being at Ease with Expertise

The guide is someone who has to manage their own unquestioned expertise without taking over and doing things for their charge or belittling them for their difficulties. They also want to make good use of their experience and expertise by bringing it to bear effectively. This is not something easily done and there are accounts throughout the world of sport, politics and industry of great guides and clumsy ones.

The guide who has the necessary expertise and the reputation for getting results might well get away with a good deal of awkwardness in their personal manner. They may be anything but pleasant to those they develop, but 'they know' and they know they know, and, what's more, those who want to learn from them put aside such personal foibles and learn. There are other, more kindly and interested, individuals who put great store in fostering a 'way of being' in relation to the activity that they love that is every bit as important as helping the learner succeed at the activity. Such 'guides' are often looked up to as more than examples of good practice, they become models of exemplary conduct.

The guidance specialist must learn to work comfortably with ambiguity and hold themselves second to the needs of the person they are helping, whilst at the same time ensuring that their own expertise is a central and valued part of the exchange. The guide has to manage releasing what they know in ways and at times that the learner can make use of rather than hector or dictate the terms of the work. The guide has to assess the rate at which the learner can absorb and use new information, when to offer helpful direction and useful observations, and also judge the time for a major rethink or take 'time out'.

In activity-based guidance, there is always more to a 'performance' than the activity itself. There are all the surrounding implications of the decisions that are made; the preparation required, the care of the equipment needed, the order of the learning itself and so on. Tackling 'this' aspect of the work 'now' may only make another aspect of the task harder later. It might make sense to the learner to do what 'they want', but the guide may well know that it will be sure to bring disappointment because of the limited understanding learners still hold.

At times it may be important to give the learner their head and even for them to 'make their own mistakes'. At other times such an action could bring into jeopardy all the work to date. The guide therefore has much to assess, balance and decide about without it appearing as part of the contribution they make. The learner may only want to 'get on with it' and find all the required preparation and consideration too fussy.

In some fields of activity, the person who becomes a guide may or may not have been a great exponent of the activity, but they do need to have learned a great deal about how the activity 'works' far beyond the performance itself and the straightforward matters to hand. Some guides have an outstanding, innate talent for this form of helping but it can also be learned. The best guides are often not those who reached the pinnacle of performance or the height of their profession, but individuals who put their time into their work, did more than a 'good' job, took a pride in what they accomplished and who wish to put something back into an activity for which they have affection and regard.

Such respected figures are not to be confused with the retired 'star'; who may still be more interested in promoting their own view of themselves and trading on their past reputation rather than showing any real interest in the needs of those they are supposed help.

Developmental Learning

Implicit in all that has been said so far is the idea of *learning*, of the guide passing on understanding or skills, of the guide steering the learner toward their chosen goal as non-directively as circumstances and roles permit. Learning in this context is not necessarily formal learning, though it may be. It is more about developing a way of approaching the work that enables the learner to appreciate the way things connect, how links are formed between elements, and helping them become aware of some of the less obvious features of the subject under study.

This aspect of the role is overt in the case of a music teacher, but is no less important in the case of an organisational mentor. In this situation, the mentor is not simply helping someone 'settle into a new role' but enabling that person to reflect upon and assess how the organisation operates, and to learn the unspoken rules that will make a great deal of difference to the contribution a new individual is able to make.

Developing an inquiring approach to the work is at the heart of the successful relationship between the guide (the developer[15]) and the would-be learner. When both bring a real interest in what they come together to explore, then the development that may unfold can be enormous and a deep pleasure to both.

There are countless ways one person can find himself or herself in a guidance type relationship with another. The role may vary and the task may differ from one type of *developmental relationship* to another, but any *developmental alliance*[16] can be distinguished in one of two ways. It either seeks to *'draw out'* what is within the individual who is being developed, or it seeks to *'put in'* something that is regarded as absent from the present performance of the individual.

Drawing Out

The guide who seeks to draw out from the learner talents, skills, attributes, understanding or performance is depending upon the quality and the depth of the relationship offered in a number of essential ways that include the following elements.

> **There is sufficient time to ensure that the relevant 'bits' of the performance can 'appear'.** It is important not to attempt to do the impossible. Often the guidance specialist will make some evaluation or assessment to ensure that what is needed can be done or… They, together, will use the assessment to pace the rate of the learning that will best help the learner gain most. Learning is more important than any final outcome. This does not mean that outcomes do not matter, only that the guide is more concerned with the unfolding of the learner than in 'driving them' to the final result.

---

[15] The assumption here is that all guidance relationships that are valuable are developmental by nature. Of course if they were considered as such by practitioners then they might approach some of them from a different stance.

[16] *Developmental alliance* is a useful term first brought to the author's attention by Julia Hay in her book *Transformational Mentoring*. It covers all those kinds of relationships that are focused upon getting somewhere, problem solving and which have a shared component – such as all guidance roles have.

Learners are able to raise the issues that most concern them. Such relationships only work when learners can manage their own concerns and feel enough trust in the relationship to be able to raise them openly. Learners have to be able to confide and disclose their concerns, and at the same time not expect to be 'looked after' by the guide. Many guides are wary of creating a dependence upon their skills and understanding. They are there to enhance those of the learner.

The relationship will stand up to the strain that may sometimes be imposed. In some guidance relationships, such as the athletic coach, the relationship may last a long or a short time. Neither party knows. 'Liking' each other or not may play little part until it comes to separating and then both parties may discover they feel a good deal more strongly about each other as people than they had ever realised. On the other hand, a 'spiky' relationship can inhibit the development of any individual. Guides who take out their own frustrations upon their charges are, of course, acting irresponsibly. Yet there are moments when a good 'straight talk' can make all the difference to the next step.

The guide will also point out the blind spots and the temptations that learners may find they are prone to. The guide has to have sufficient respect from the learner to enjoy the freedom to point out errors, flaws and things overlooked. This makes it a more dynamic and engaged two-way relationship than the more supportive relationships described in the following chapter. However, it is never equal. It is always one sided. The premise is that the guide has the knowledge or the expertise and it is worth facing their displeasure or criticism because of the learning that will arise as a result. Of course this is the ideal portrayal and some guidance relationships may fall a long way short of this. What it does emphasise is that the terms of the relationship are never equal and that it is up to the guide to manage their contribution with the limitations and the sensitivities of the learner in mind and not to indulge themselves.

Bearing these aspects in mind, a guide recognises that they are building a relationship based upon the unfolding presentation of the practice of the individual and, though the pace at which this happens can be encouraged or even hastened, it cannot be dictated. The learner is in charge of their own learning – since that is the essence of the relationship.

Everything a guide offers is based on what learners suggest for exploration. Of course, this does not stop the guide raising some issues, offering some suggestions and even providing some direct and firm guidance when appropriate. However, it is all offered from within a stance that takes as the essential and overarching perspective that of *drawing out* from the learner those things that make sense to the learner, given where they are and what they regard as important.

The danger is that such trust in the learner can be misplaced and things that the learner does not want to examine may be kept hidden or not even noticed. If the guide and the learner have favourite topics or areas of interest these can be focused upon endlessly at the expense of some of the more essential and mundane aspects of the work.

Whilst drawing out what is present within the learner is appealing in theory (just as is *person centred counselling*), it can generate many ambiguities and dilemmas for both parties in practice. They must have clear understandings and a very fierce contract to ensure that they keep the work openly reviewed and regularly reflected upon.

This kind of alliance puts both parties in the work together. Each brings something, essential and different from the other, but they make of it what they do by sharing the work together. It requires patience and a willingness on the part of guides to put aside their own priorities and interests and, sometimes, their own hopes for the learner. It requires a deal of ruthlessness on the part of the learner to bring up issues that they know will not be raised unless they take the initiative to do so, even though the guide may have spotted them.

To summarise, this approach takes as its underlying principles:

- Puts the person before the task.
- Looks at development from what is 'given'.
- The learner is more important than the practice. (This does not mean the practice is not important.)
- Working out the themes together.
- The model being adopted is less important than learners developing their own model.
- It is likely to be an unfolding relationship – important to both.

Putting In

This approach starts from a very different place. Here the guide has adopted a method, an approach. In some way and at some time they have embraced a specific way of tackling the work. Along with it, they have acquired a set of understandings and are keen to transmit it to others who wish to adopt it. The emphasis here is in there being:

A way this can be done. The guide is not open to negotiation about how we proceed. They have worked it out in advance and the system works – even for you. The implication here is that you are not so important as you thought you were and if you are to succeed it will not be by your efforts alone.

A willing learner who wishes to adopt the approach. For this method to work (and the more extreme the stance, the more this has to be the case), the learner must be willing and committed at the outset. The guide ensures that only those who are serious in their interest get adopted. This has the beauty of ensuring that only those who have a real possibility of success come forward.

Standards that are being aimed at that go with the approach. The guide offers a set of objective standards and measures that the learner has in front of them to aim at. It is improvements in meeting these standards that provides an external verification of success and acts as a reward for the strenuous efforts required.

Clarity of power and authority. The enterprise is based upon the well-regulated and disciplined obedience of the learner to the suggestions of the guide. It is a tightly bounded relationship that provides a strong sense of security to the individual who needs a strong framework to hold their impulsiveness. On the other hand, it may provide the very structure against which they one day rebel.

In this approach, we have someone who is not so reliant upon the abilities of the learner deciding for themselves what to focus upon. It is, rather, based upon the willingness of the learner to adopt an approach that is the particular committed way of working that the guide has devised or, at the very least, made their own. In such a relationship, the guide will feel a greater degree of freedom to intrude and may become quite invasive in offering remarks and observations that would be in marked contrast to the 'drawing out' relationship described above.

Often such a guide uses their depth of understanding of the method to get new standards and improved practice from the learner. Both parties are interested in the externalisation of the understanding via performance in the way that the 'drawing-out' guide may not be. The emphases of this approach, therefore, can be summarised as:

- The *task* nature of the meeting is emphasised.
- There is 'a way to do this' and I can show it to you. Exploration of other methods is not part of the learning. There is a given prescribed way.
- You will know what you are doing at the end and will be able to demonstrate it. You will achieve a level of practice otherwise unobtainable.
- 'Failure' is likely to mean the end of the work together. There is little room for slippage and 'mistakes'.
- You will find your place in the hierarchy of great performances. The guide has no interest in deluding the learner as to their overall capability.

Drawing Out versus Putting In
In the case of the first, developing the talent of an Olympic athlete is a joy and a privilege, but enabling anyone to move beyond their present limitations is the essence. For the second, given the approach and the person, the question is, 'How near to the highest standard can we get?' The emphasis thus becomes more practice-focused and the development of the person arises out of their commitment and struggle to attain the highest levels, or how they deal with the setbacks that limit them.

There are difficulties to be faced with either style since there are some learners who favour being allowed to take things at their own pace and will never stretch themselves voluntarily, and there are those who will perform as long as they are 'bullied' into it. In this latter case, however, they do not necessarily become sensitive learners of anything they are 'taught'.

The dilemma for any guide lies in knowing which of these two approaches most represents their own style and how far they are able to move around coherently within it. It is not necessary, for instance, if you are someone who favours drawing things out never to attempt to put something in. Nor is it always the case for the person committed to a method to have to teach everything to the learner. It is in finding the balance of what is required from within the style the guide favours in relationship to the tasks and the stage of learners that makes for the ambiguities and richness of practice.

Having established all these aspects of the guidance role, we present three distinct methods: *facilitating learning, informing and negotiating systems*. Each needs to be considered from within the background of all that has gone before in this chapter.

4. Facilitating Learning

Together, the guide and the learner create a joint problem solving approach, enabling the learner to take increasing responsibility for themselves in the future.

Facilitating learning, as we have seen, is the essence of the guide's role — whatever particular form of guide we have in mind. Facilitating learning is not meant to conjure up classrooms and formal lessons, but to suggest something much more informal and shared. Facilitating learning can take many forms but essentially arises out of some relationship where the guide is willing to step alongside and show the learner how to...

It is important that the guide sees the value in promoting learning rather than telling, showing or doing it for the learner (adopting a more advisory role) and yet there may be elements of the whole relationship where even these responses play a part. For the majority of the time, however, and certainly during the central part of the work, the guide is assisting the learner to develop a better grasp of circumstances, conditions, choices, options, decisions and so on. The over-riding aim is to enable learners to become more equipped to act on their own behalf in similar circumstances in the future and not simply come back the next time they get stuck because they took too little notice in the first place.

This means part of the guide's role lies in motivating learners or at least ensuring they are *motivated enough* before they begin. This creates difficulties in many statutory or institutional settings. It immediately sets up a competition between the well-meaning guide and the rebellious or reluctant learner, as many institutions know only too well.

At one level this is an issue of 'contracting'. If the learner has no control over how they have come to be in the position they are in within a system, then the only means of opposition open to them is recalcitrance. Disaffection about their overall situation is then 'acted out' wherever it has an opportunity, and someone who is supposed to help offers an opportunity too good to be missed. The guide is then faced with the impossible task of helping someone who has no wish to be helped and prefers to remain in their own difficulties as a demonstration of at least their right to refuse any suggestion for improvement.

In such circumstances guidance may become little less than bullying, as those in the role of guide have to get people through the system to meet their 'targets'. It is not a helpful remedy, however predictable. No one gains and the real work of the guide is only demeaned.

However, many guidance agents are caught between institutional demands and expectations, and the reality of the opposition of those they work with on the ground. Support for managing such opposition, and opportunities to ensure that the organisation's leaders are aware that there is a gap between the problem and the solution, are an essential requirement if guidance services caught in such dilemmas are to retain credibility with their constituency as well as the institution. All too often these issues are relegated to the margins – so often the place where their clients find themselves too. There is also all too often a classic resources versus demands issue in many situations in which the guide finds themselves.

Where it works effectively, the guide helps select, plan and manage a learning experience, or structures a situation in order that the learner can improve their knowledge, acquire new skills, or develop insights further. This is undertaken on the grounds that the next time a similar situation is met, the learner will have a process to follow and a series of steps that are at least rehearsed, rather than them being confronted with a situation and no clue as to how to manage it.

Some guides are very adept at this form of help. Almost by second nature, they adopt the role of 'show and tell', of getting learners involved in their own difficulties and are able easily (so it seems) to indicate those small steps that can be taken for people to help themselves.

They are also usually skilled in not allowing themselves to be defeated when things don't turn out the way both sides had hoped. They can return, non-judgementally, to the point just before the plan started to go awry and consider what needs to be done next time. Such dedicated and patient help is perhaps the most critical type needed at a time when there are too few resources for long-term intensive personal help (of the counselling kind) and a need for guidance agents not simply to run round and take over other people's lives, however efficiently they could do it (the taking action style).

Limitations
- Real 'learning needs' take time to establish.
- Being managed through the choices of the system can be experienced as oppressive to the learner.

- Experts may wish to retain their own sense of separateness and keep their knowledge to themselves or only release it on their own terms.
- Learning skills and transferring them to a new situation is not easy, and it is often made to look easier than it is in practice.

Benefits
- It recognises the need to plan for a solution and does not expect it to appear by chance.
- Once a skill has been acquired or information gained, it can be used repeatedly.
- Individuals can be helped to plan their own learning programmes – encouraging self-direction.
- It takes a developmental view of difficulties rather than a crisis or remedial approach.

5. Informing

The guide offers up-to-date information relevant to the learner's present need.

Informing appears on the surface to be the most neutral and the most accessible way of offering help of just about any kind. However, the information given depends greatly on the perception of the guide and the intentions they wish to fulfil. This makes the giving of information far from a straightforward and neutral activity. Systems are relatively easy to establish and maintain but there is a good deal more to an effective information service than racks of leaflets. Information services rely on guides providing up-to-date data based on evidence, accurate accounts of facts and figures from reliable sources, without recommending any one as having more or less value than another.

At first sight, informing and advising may seem to be closely allied and yet they are quite widely separated here. Informing is about presenting the information that is available at the time, either from me or from others, and offering you the opportunity to consider that information in the light of the situation with which you are dealing. It may even involve exploring some of the potential consequences, in an immediate way, to check that you have a grasp of the implications that may be involved and which are contained in the information, and then *leaving you to decide*.

This may take the form, for example, of going over some information about contraception, but leaving the decision about what action to take firmly with the person concerned. It may be outlining the steps for enrolment to a course, or how to apply to another institution for training, but it is leaving you to decide which course you follow.

Indeed, part of the difficulty in information giving is to leave the choice in the hands of the person who will have to live with the consequences.

Many of us, when seeking information, actually want more than facts. We want some *perspective* through which to view the facts. We want, in fact, some guidance, but we don't want to be 'told'. We want information that we can evaluate, but we don't have the sophistication to know how to evaluate what we've got or what else we might need. We are at a distinct disadvantage. But having got the information we don't want then to set off on a hunt to find someone else to talk it over with. We want some response now!

Whether we are in the tourist office looking for bed and breakfast accommodation, or wondering whether to have a medical procedure, the provider of the information is usually related to the agency supplying the response. Information is provided at key places and through key channels because it is linked to some service or organisation. Understandably, as we approach an office for information, we expect to get some guidance to go with it. But it is one thing to give some informal 'advice' about local accommodation and quite another for an untrained practitioner at the desk to promote a particular form of medical intervention. Yet the two situations may look alike to the inquirer who may (superficially) wish to be treated alike in both circumstances!

Most information workers and those offering informal guidance in information-based services develop a comprehensive understanding of what the service can provide, to whom, on what grounds and so on. They become conversant with the operation they represent and are expected to make this knowledge available as part of the information role they fulfil. But it is then a difficult matter to decide quite where this kind of knowledge ends and where preferences and personal agendas enter into the picture.

Is it acceptable to point out that if you met these terms and conditions the likelihood of you being considered, as a person acceptable to the company for credit for example, would increase? Is it just as acceptable to point out how you might change your circumstances slightly in order to qualify for your child getting into a nearby school rather than the one she is presently attending? How far is such 'help' legitimate, and who decides?

Setting these kinds of extreme examples aside, people who work in such services necessarily develop a set of preferences and priorities over the choices they are presenting to people day in day out. Many information workers also develop a kind of collusive agreement between themselves about which choices they regard as the 'OK' ones and which they regard as second rate, and can even sift out applicants for the choice they have decided.

Additionally, many of those in information roles also develop a set of preferences about those who they wish to see benefit from the services that go along with the information they provide. They will often go out of their way to help those they favour by pointing out ways round the system or the allocation of resources (as the examples above illustrated). Since the main rationale for information-based services is their low cost, it often means that those staffing such services acquire a tremendous amount of knowledge but have little training about how their own preferences (not to say prejudices) influence the way they present information and the way they respond to people.

Understandable though this might be, it is clearly something to resist. Knowing how far to offer choice and when to keep silent is an important aspect of information giving that needs to be considered in supervision or reflection time.

Information is power in a society that depends upon gatekeepers for access to all manner of services and provision. Information workers often fail to realise just how much their observations and indirect comments influence those they are assisting and what an impact they can have on the choices people make. There is a case to be made for carefully preparing anyone placed in such a position in order to ensure that they are aware of the degree of influence they hold both by their acts of commission (such as those above) and by omission. There are many people who do not get the help they might from information providers because they do not know how to present themselves in a way that gets the best out of the staff member they have to deal with.

Information workers often acquire crucial information about the way systems manage their learners, customers, or those with whom they work, yet systems managers rarely seek it. This is taken up in the following section.

Limitations
- Not much information can be presented without suggestions being made as to how it should be used, in which case it soon becomes advice.
- It requires good inter-agency contacts to make the most of information services.
- The relationship with the learner is usually of a short span. It is not always possible to diagnose real needs, as opposed to those the learner admits to having, in such a short time.
- It can mean individuals have to seek help at another agency and tell their story all over again.

Benefits
- It leaves the learner to decide.
- It is relatively value free.
- Information services can be relatively cheap to run and can cope with large numbers of enquiries.
- It can make the most of the learner who has no great amount of training.

6. Negotiating Systems
The guide has expertise in understanding the system they and the learner are in and how to manage the consequences of the impact of systems upon the progress of the learner.

The guide often has to negotiate with an organisation or system to get a more flexible response, to make allowances or to begin to reconsider the conditions that apply in order to make sure individuals gain the experience they need, rather than the experience the system is designed to offer.

This is an important, though often underplayed, aspect of the guidance agent's role. Whether a guidance agent within the statutory sector or a guide as in a sports coach, both require an experience of the 'context' and how it operates both on a large scale and in the details of negotiating day-by-day requirements.

Any form of guidance role is limited if individuals lack knowledge and understanding of the subtleties of the context because it is often in the application that problems arise. It is not that the individual cannot perform the task at all, but at these times… It is not that the learner cannot implement their skills under good conditions but they have difficulty under particular ones. So what do we know about these times?

Helping someone improve their performance in a context (and all performance has a context) means having some inkling of the influences that operate in that context in order to separate the influences that are 'context-dependent' and those which are individually generated. So, for instance, I may be a much better runner in good weather than in the rain. Is this because I need contact lenses rather than glasses? This seems a really simple matter but big problems for learners are sometimes that easy to spot when guides bring their accumulated wisdom and practice experience to bear on the issue.

It may be that a particular staff member showed little interest in someone when they joined the class. An approach by the guide can clarify whether this was a refusal by the learner or whether it was the result of an off-putting and unhelpful comment by the teacher. Time and again the guide has the role of reassurance, offering an opportunity for checking things out and for encouraging the defeated learner to 'try it this way or that way'.

There is of course the risk that the guide simply gets the learner to run around in circles solving a problem that is all too real rather than helping them find a way through a difficulty that can be overcome. The 'real' problem can be experienced as too big and therefore impossible. It is important to guide the learner into working towards realistic targets rather than setting themselves up to fail. The remedy here lies in the guide spending time reflecting upon their own stance to these things, with others, away from the session with the learner. It may be called supervision. Whatever it is called, since so many guidance agents have a role to play in the systems that employ them or in which they are based, there is a need to assess how much the system is willing to assist the individual and how much the system demands unnecessary conformity from the individuals it is supposed to serve.

Guidance agents stand at an uncomfortable point in the organisation's flow of work. They are often seen as marginal to the 'real work' of the organisation (see above) and they are often asking those who do the 'real work' to change the way they do it to make it easier for … Guidance agents, because of frustration in trying to assist those with whom they are working, will often see themselves as change agents[17] rather than

---

[17] 'Change agent' is the term to describe anyone who has as part of his or her role the modification of a system or work situation. Many people think such work relatively straightforward: diagnose the difficulty, prescribe the remedy and visit every once in a while. However, it is far from easy. Learning how individuals respond to change, how groups respond to change and how organisations respond to change is only the beginning of learning about the work of the change agent. Oasis provides development opportunities for those seeking to understand more of this role.

working for their clients in a direct way. Influencing the organisation then becomes as important, if not more important, yet they do not have a legitimated role to take this on. Changing organisations is more difficult than people think. It is not getting people to consider change that is the problem; the difficulties lie in getting people to try solutions and learn from the results.

Standing between the learner and the organisation, holding a gatekeeper role, many of those with a guidance role find it difficult to maintain an independence of stance to these issues. Some find the organisation too unresponsive to meet the developing needs of those entering into the system, others become less interested in the difficulties of some of their learners. (See *The Upstream Helper* in *Section Three: The Helping Context*.)

Limitations
- Being viewed as marginal is a poor place from which to exercise influence upon a system.
- Systems are not easy to challenge or negotiate with.
- Negative information is rarely heard constructively by organisations.
- It is easy to be seen as being more interested in the role of change agent than 'doing your job'. The change agent role requires considerable skills, access to sources of influence and, ultimately, of power.
- Individuals who seek to change systems risk having their career blocked.
- Systems-changers are often regarded as disrupters and a nuisance to stability.

Benefits
- Learning how the system works is an important part of functioning in a contemporary society.
- The guide who can recommend ways to manage a system effectively is worth listening to.
- Improved organisational effectiveness is likely to improve morale for everyone.
- Responsiveness by the system to improve the way it meets people's needs is likely to increase their commitment.
- Change has positive outcomes for all – if handled constructively.

Chapter 8
Counselling & Support Methods
Counselling/Supporting

In the case of the earlier two types of methods – advisory and guidance methods – there are a number of provisos that mean both the practitioner and the client come to the meeting with a clearer recognition of their separate roles. In both, the practitioner has the potential for influencing the way the relationship develops and the actions the client might well undertake. This is very different in the third group of methods that cover the spectrum of helping activities – counselling and support. In this group, there is a marked shift from any suggestion of prescription. The power is now very much in the hands of the client.

Responding to Needs

The client has a need[18]; the role of the guide is to help shape a way for that need to be met within the range of experience and expertise they offer. Life coaches, mentors and guides of all kinds therefore have to know the limits of their competence. The guide who is well-regarded must ensure that the clients they assist are similarly effective in framing their needs in a way that enables the guide to respond effectively.

It is no help to either side to be working with little clarity about matters that are of no concern to or which do not interest the guide. Similarly, it is of no help for the guide to pretend to a range of competence that they do not possess. Sooner or later they will find guesswork and inventive suggestions increasingly lead to results that both parties regret. Trust about the limits to guidance is a key issue and is explored later (see *Section Five: The Core of Helping*) in relation to all helping activities.

The more advisory the relationship, the more the client seeks to follow the course of advice outlined by the 'expert' in the hope that the expert has understood the case accurately, considered the weight of evidence available and suggested a strategy that will ensure success. In guidance relationships, the learner is consulting someone who has a base of knowledge and a role that proclaims the guide's areas of interest or expertise. There is some expected reliance, not upon the guide deciding on behalf of the client (as is somewhat more the case in an advisory relationship), but in helping give shape to the chosen option and some order and progression to any course of action that may emerge.

In each case there is an understood requirement for the client or the learner to be open to the influence of the practitioner. In each case the practitioner is working with the client or learner on the agenda they have brought but which they acknowledge

---

[18] In practice, clients may be uncertain of the real extent of the need or quite who will be of best help but they approach an agency with a sense of the help they are seeking. It is this sense of knowing in advance that there are levels of potential direction involved that distinguishes a guidance role per se from that of a counselling response. A counselling response makes no preconditions about what **the** problem is.

they are unable to fulfil satisfactorily without some expert assistance. The client or learner therefore has to surrender something of their own autonomy, at least for a time, and accept the value of the practitioner's expertise.

Counselling Distinctions

In each case there is something to be done and finding out how best to go about it is the focus of the work. When it comes to *counselling* and its sister activity *supporting* this is not necessarily the case. It is not so much that there is nothing to do: it is that what needs to be done is problematic or unknown. With counselling and supporting we are in a much more provisional land of uncertainty and indecision. Whereas advisory services and guidance agents work with the problem as described by the person approaching them, in a counselling relationship the starting point is to explore what is the source of concern. Nothing is taken for granted. The territory is more to be explored, to be revealed and charted.

As we know, any guide or advisory representative would be foolish not to ask questions that uncover some of the background and history to the situation that they are being asked to help with. But the questions are asked primarily to create a richer understanding to aid the work in hand.

A counselling relationship does not assume what the work in hand is. Indeed the strength of counselling is that it is left to the client to decide what to disclose, how much to disclose, and when to disclose. Counselling therefore represents a form of help that leaves the client very much in charge of what unfolds and how far it unfolds. In consequence, counselling is a relationship that is more likely to focus upon unresolved dilemmas, unaccountable reactions, perplexing issues, preoccupations about the way events have occurred, or difficulties about aspects of decisions that need to be taken – matters that the client believes are taking up more of their 'internal space' than they are due.

A counselling relationship is thus one where nothing much may change in the world but a great deal may change in the person's understanding of it. As a result of that change, they may be able to act differently; but a successful counselling relationship does not have to lead to action in the world. Insight, understanding and developing a new view of things are all important results from effective counselling sessions.

As a result, it is also a much more open-ended form of help. It is not easy to decide how many sessions any person may require or how much time it should take to deal with some supposedly 'common' difficulty. After all, no difficulty is 'common' to the person who has it and routine prescriptions are not a usual aspect of a good counselling relationship. But if there are no guidelines as to how long or what it may take, how do we decide when we have done enough and who will pay for such an open-ended contract?

The Growth of Counselling

Twenty years ago, there were few counsellors or rather there were a great many but they were not necessarily people who simply held the title 'counsellor'. There were student counsellors, pastoral workers, people who had another role and offered 'counselling' as part of or in addition to the other work they performed. Such people were sought out by those who wanted time and space to work out where they stood about some matter that was troubling them in their own lives.

Someone with a background in counselling was the kind of person who would offer just such time and space, bring the discipline of listening attentively and keeping their own views of it all to a minimum. Counselling was thus not a separate activity for the most part, but something that was a part of what other kinds of practitioners could offer when needed.

Many people who 'trained in counselling' also recognised that they would be more effective in their other work (guidance work of all kinds, especially) if they had some understanding not only of the dynamics of people's emotional response, but also how to be present when people displayed distress or concern in a way that was not typical of 'English restraint'.

Learning how to maintain compassionate and aware attention when someone is deeply distressed rather than rushing in to console them or discouraging them from further 'outbursts' by 'shutting them down' were important skills to have. This was especially so if you worked with people who, whatever help they might know they needed, also needed a good listening to and an appreciation of their struggle to manage the emotional component of their difficulties.

As a separate occupation and a singular role, counselling had not yet really arrived. But by the late eighties and into the nineties the whole 'therapy movement'[19] took off in the UK. Counselling and therapy began to become specialised preserves for the practice of the many different kinds of therapies that were invented.

Almost overnight there was a move to establish counselling as a separate and distinct profession. But without a clear body of knowledge or a convincing theoretical base, it is difficult for something as diverse and contentious a field as 'counselling' to establish itself in the same way as 'dentistry', for example, can claim to have an area of special expertise.

After all, it is still difficult even after decades of research to be sure what it is that helps people through counselling. Many people point out that it is the feeling of being listened to, but many of us have friends who can do that. That is not what is meant by such a comment, yet it is difficult to identify what makes the difference. It is not the theoretical persuasion of the counsellor that makes the difference since there are an enormous number of theories available and they can't all be right since many of them hold contradictory accounts of what it means to be human. The problem about any

---

[19] The growth of the therapy movement has created a new industry that has appeared during the last twenty years. As a result of the increasing interest, something that was a relatively minor interest and was happily developing with the minimum of regulatory conditions has suddenly become a form of highly regulated provision.

explanation of what it is to be human is that it is not simply going to be influenced by the observation you make but by the value you give to your observations, what ultimate purpose you think human life has, and how significant you think human beings are as life forms on the planet. In addition, there is growing speculation about what forms of intervention work for what and there are deep divisions between different schools of practitioners about what approach should be taken to many 'issues' and how best to respond to such issues.

Creating a base of solid evidence for the effectiveness of counselling to stand comparison with other forms of help like the example of dentistry given above, or health care assistance and so on, is not only illusive but is likely to prove illusory. Even hard professions like dentistry have areas of professional controversy about what works when for whom. It is the case in all applied activities.

Counselling, however, is *the applied activity of the conversation*. In the end, the only things that we can be sure of about counselling is that it is two people engaged with one another, largely through the exchange of words and the nonverbal accompaniments to those words, on a one-to-one basis in the privacy of a space they share together. A process which itself is always evolving.

Whilst it surely matters what you think of people and how you view the difficulties they experience, what is really significant is how you respond to this person before you now, rather than what you believe you ought to do with the kind of person that this person is supposed to represent. When you are working with people, you soon learn that it is important to put aside the theory and respond to the person. But that makes the body of the work very shaky and not at all convincing in the way that knowledge about dentistry is convincing.

It is this underlying lack of a firm base that, in the author's view, has played its part in the hasty rush to professionalise counselling. It is an attempt to make it stand comparison as a quasi-form of medical intervention. As a result, counselling is now almost totally identified with therapeutic interventions and medical settings.

The gain for the counsellors is clear – at the moment. They have created a profession that has helped them find a place amongst the range of health care professionals who are involved in emotional and mental distress.

It has also meant that those other practitioners of the art of the *helping conversation*[20] – mentors and guides of all kinds – have distanced themselves from such an exclusive stance. They remain in the middle ground drawing upon a wide range of influences and knowledge to provide their services: services that are distinct. Such services are distinct being neither therapeutically based nor are they to be confused with counselling any longer.

---

[20] The term 'helping conversation' is not the author's, but the one I have adopted as a simple and elegant description of what is involved in helping work of this kind that depends upon deep, rich listening and working with the emotional and other subtle levels of the person. The concept is explored in depth in *Section Four: The Helping Conversation*.

The work of so many of the people in the roles described above depends more on their ability to know how 'to be with' other people in a way that creates an invitation to the person to feel increasingly able to disclose their concern. Such ability to promote self-disclosure is not easy to measure and is something that is likely to differ from one kind of person to another and from persons with one kind of concern to another.

This makes establishing what makes the difference in *conversational helping* very problematical indeed. Whilst there is every reason to applaud those who attempt to pull back the mystery and reveal the forces and influences behind what works, there are also elements that lie outside the most comprehensive of descriptions and theories put forward to explain the success of one method over another.

Individuals have differential capacities to grow and change at different points in their life and according to a myriad of factors that lie outside the actual skills of the particular practitioner – influences that compound the huge difficulty in attempting to measure the value of one kind of helping technique over another.

Like it or not, it does seem that it is the qualities of the individual practitioner that lies strongly at the heart of the success of the enterprise. The other major factor in successful helping relationships is that if the client believes that their practitioner believes that they (the client) will improve, they do. If the client believes they are a hopeless case, imagine how that will be compounded if they believe that their practitioner also sees them in that way. Eric Berne expressed these necessary qualities for 'therapists' (his terminology) but they are equally applicable to any kind of practitioner who wants to empower those they serve. The practitioner needs to convey three things to the client:

Permission: that they offer the space and the freedom for the client to do what they have to do and get where they need to get.

Protection: that they convey the sense that the boundaries of the relationship are secure enough for the client to 'fall into' themselves and the other will still be there – no matter what.

Potency: that they have the vitality, the 'juice', call it what you will, that inspires the client to the belief that you and they will get there.

Learning a great deal about the human condition is incalculably important for anyone involved in helping work, but without these kinds of attributes any help is likely to be superficial and less than effective. These attributes are not provided by training programmes but can be enhanced by them or, in some cases, be diminished by them by over concentration on expertise and skills practice, and theoretical understanding at the expense of the qualities described above.

If, as the above highlights, it is difficult to establish just what does make the difference in effective helping, then the case for a professional claim is hard to make. Yet the levels of distress in modern societies are increasing and people are in great need. Counselling quickly began establishing a domain and a terrain for itself that set itself apart from other helping methods. As we have seen, many guidance agents used a large element of counselling in their work in the past and the term was often synonymous with the application of 'counselling skills', but it has now become a form of specialist help. The word 'counselling' is increasingly identified with an exclusive focus upon the therapeutic concerns of the client and the differentiation between counselling and psychotherapy is not at all easy to establish – though it is a matter of rich controversy within the ranks of those who practise these activities.

7. Counselling

"The art of counselling is an interchange of energy with another person, a way of elucidating the realities of the client's total life situation and individual way of being." S. Arroyo, 1975.

Counselling is amongst the least directive forms of help offered here – supporting is something else again (see below). Counselling implies a process of encouraging individuals to confront their dilemmas and difficulties in a supportive framework of trust, safety and acceptance. No assumptions hold in a counselling relationship. The client chooses the relationship, chooses how much and how far to disclose about what, and maintains a strong capacity to shape how the relationship unfolds and develops – well, in theory they do.

As counselling has become more and more *the* helping word of the era, so the ways it is performed, the places it is offered, the conditions under which it is performed and the activities that pass under its name have also changed. Much information-giving and advising is more like informal counselling and relies on the application of counselling skills. Much counselling, at the other end of the spectrum, is indistinguishable from psychotherapy.

From the time this book was first written in 1986, the author has always maintained that the definition which appears here (the source of which he cannot find) is the most useful one to follow. "The helper offers a relationship to the client for the purpose of enabling the client to change." It says it all. It is primarily based upon the *quality* of the relationship, rather than the skills and techniques of the practitioner. Such a relationship is placed at the service of the client for the purpose of the changes *they* wish to make. It also recognises that the client may wish to take a long time working out whether to change and, if so, at what rate. The very form of help itself often lies in the process of change.

Many people simply have never previously experienced being offered the opportunity, attention and sense of importance that *their* choice is sufficiently important to be given the time to appear. Whilst techniques and strategies, skills and sequences of intervention are more or less facilitative and often crucial to the development of both the client and the relationship, the underlying value of counselling as an activity is its emphasis upon the value of two human beings engaged together for the one to help the other.

The sense of mutuality, equality and inter-changeability of the two roles – that today 'It is me here helping you, but tomorrow it could be you listening to me work something out' – was a vital aspect of the counselling movement's impulse until relatively recently. The drive to professionalise what for most people will always be one aspect of their wider role (a teacher who offers pastoral support, for example), has meant an increasing emphasis upon the expertise and the specialised training that primarily serves to differentiate the counsellor or therapist from the humble and inadequate client. Since no one knows all that goes on between two people, opportunities to review a session are an integral part of monitoring performance and deepening both the skills and the insights of the counsellor.

The view here is that counselling is a human activity. It is not a qualification in counselling, human behaviour, or human relationships that, in the end, makes a person an effective agency for change for others but the degree of relatedness that those involved find with one another – something that makes the training of counsellors at best problematic and at worst positively unhelpful.

Limitations
- It is often a lengthy process.
- It is very easy to do badly.
- The predicament has to be one appropriate for counselling.
- Counsellors can be asked 'to save others from themselves' and they can also be asked to save colleagues (or difficult students, customers, staff).

Benefits
- It enables people to 'own' their inner difficulties and overcome them.
- Growth and change are inherently challenging – counselling can provide support to assist such growth and change.
- Some of the difficulties people experience require a strong, stable and supportive relationship if they are to be resolved.
- It encourages accurate communication at both a content and feelings level.

8. Supporting
The practitioner is available to the client on an unconditional basis for the client to seek reassurance, support or refuge.

Supporting is an immensely important aspect of any helping relationship or any alliance for learning. If individuals do not feel cared about, they will not be inclined to risk exposing themselves to ridicule or worse. However, the term 'support' has a wide range of meanings. I can be 'supportive' of your position and not of your attitude. I can support your cause but not your conduct in relation to it.

When organisations offer 'support' to their clients or residents they often have a definition in mind that is anything but unconditional. It is support limited to particular occasions or aspects of the services provided to those eligible for the time specified. It is, in short, conditional support. This is all well and good so long as the individual receiving it understands that the support is not all-encompassing and indefinite.

It is often misunderstandings of just what constitutes the limits of support that get support workers into some of the difficulties that are inherent in their work. What does it mean, for example, to support asylum seekers? How far does such support extend? How does the 'support worker' define the limits of their contract to those they serve in useful ways given the limitless needs many asylum seekers have and the few forms of help available to them? The danger in such circumstances, and there are many employees in circumstances like this, is that support workers become the catch-all of the client groups' dilemmas and difficulties because they know only too well that there is no one else for the client to turn to. The client may well feel supported, but only at the expense of the practitioner who is on the road to burn-out (see below).

Such 'support' is rarely a feasible strategy for professional practitioners since they are paid to make a difference and bring about change. This is in contrast to personal life where support is valued precisely because there are no expectations to live up to.

Supporting is the least directive form of help offered by one person to another. It is more often associated with the informal interest of friends and neighbours than viewed as a deliberate strategy of a paid practitioner or the volunteer from a helping agency. Non-judgemental support, the knowledge that there is someone there who will first of all listen and only listen, can be a vital resource for someone moving towards accepting the reality of a difficult situation. Offering such support, however, is something of a mixed blessing, since to the person receiving it the question will be, 'How much and for how long?' and for the person offering it the question will be the same, 'How much and for how long?'

The practitioners would therefore be wise to ask themselves if they can really deliver the goods if they offer to support someone. The implication is that it is 'OK to be where you are, for as long as you want to be there'. You, as a practitioner may feel that way towards the client, but your agency may well have expectations of results. The resulting *role conflict* can put great strain on the practitioner and the practitioner-client relationship. Qualified support, however, is in almost every case worse, since you never know how far it extends, or for how long it will last. Better to work out a realistic arrangement of what you can offer one another than pretend time is limitless if it is not.

Unconditional support is better coming from within the network of the person's life rather than from an individual with a particular role. That said, we live in an increasingly fragmented social order in which there are many people who have no such network to speak of and certainly no individuals around them who either care enough, or have time enough, or have the skill and awareness, to provide the support they need. This is perhaps one of the greatest social issues of the day. But it is not eased by well-meaning practitioners implying they can give more than they have to offer, or be more involved than they know they will be allowed to be, either by the weight of their case-load or the limitations placed upon them by their agency.

It is, therefore, essential to work out in the early stages of a relationship the kind of support that is appropriate and the length of time that it will be available. Whilst this is not an easy task to manage, nevertheless it needs to be faced, otherwise the client is likely to develop expectations that have to be redefined – something that is illustrated really well by the 'granny' story in *Section Six: Practitioner Resources*.

Limitations
- Supporting can be very demanding if limits and boundaries are not discussed.
- Supporting can amount to little more than collusion; helping the client stay where they are.
- Supporting can generate a mutual dependency between practitioner and client.

Benefits
- Supporting leaves the client in control.
- Supporting enables a client to have a haven of security where they are not being asked to answer for themselves.
- Supporting can be a very powerful form of reassurance.

Summary

This section of the book has attempted to cover the broad spectrum of helping methods, offering some common dilemmas and issues that relate to each of them. Most practitioners would recognise that rarely is their own helping in practice so 'pure' as to rely upon one or even two methods. Those involved in organisational roles almost always have to combine a number of methods into an overall approach for the particular circumstances of individual clients.

Most practitioners also recognise that they favour some approaches over others. Some of us are more problem-focused, others more people-based and the resulting preferences influence where we gravitate to, both in the terms of the roles we seek and the methods we use. It is useful for practitioners to review their profile of methods and approaches from time to time and to consider how far they are developing or consolidating their approach. It is also worth remembering that as individuals change their profile over time, they may find themselves out of 'sync' with the organisation that they have long been serving. Practitioners, like clients, may need to be reminded that it is time to move on.

Suggested Reading

Brammer, L M: *Helping Relationships*. Allyn & Bacon, 1988.
Carkhuff, R R: *The Development of Human Resources*. New York. Holt Rinehart, 1971.
Dass, R & Gorman, P: *How Can I Help?* Rider, 1985.
Kopp, S: *If you Meet the Buddha on the Road. Kill Him!* London, Sheldon Press, 1974.

SECTION III

THE HELPING CONTEXT:
Careers and Conditions

Chapter 9
The Upstream Helper

Gerry Egan is responsible for the title of this chapter and it is based on a story he tells that seems to me to be important for all helpers to bear in mind.

> A farmer is ploughing his field, which ends at the riverbank. As he reaches the river bank he sees a figure floating down stream in distress and calling for help. The farmer stops his tractor, gets out of his cabin, runs to the waterside and throws himself in. He rescues the drowning stranger who is deeply grateful. The farmer ensures his charge is recovered enough, gets on his tractor and resumes his work. Not long after, he is once again approaching the riverbank and about to turn his tractor round when the same situation occurs. Another stranger is drifting down stream calling for help. The farmer repeats his actions and rescues yet another victim.

When Gerry Egan tells the story it lasts a long time and the farmer has to stop a number of times but the point of the tale comes when the farmer, on reaching the riverbank to find yet one more victim drifting down the river, gets off his tractor and begins walking upstream to the increasing alarm and distress of the stranded victim. Asked where he is going, the farmer replies, 'I'm off upstream to find out who is throwing the bodies in in the first place and do something to stop them'.

The point of the story is that practitioners are at the end of the chain of difficulty. By the time someone needs help from an agency or seeks help from someone styling themselves as a 'therapist', the chances are that they will have endured a lot of unhappiness and have had to cope with a lot of disappointment – from whatever source.

Gerry Egan was at pains to make practitioners aware that they have some responsibility for considering how people get to be in need in the first place and not simply to exempt themselves from the effort. Why? Because many practitioners work with issues that are created by the way systems injure people and work with clients distressed by the impact of systems or people who are unable to deal effectively with organisational politics.

Readers will know by now that helping of any kind is never so straightforward or conceptually neat in practice as it can look in a diagram. It is usually a good deal messier if not sometimes murkier! It is one thing to be conceptually clear and another to put it into practice!

How the need for help arises and how it appears in the forms it does, who requires it and for how long, are all questions that bring with them uncomfortable home truths to many practitioners of all kinds. They do so because they force us to recognise our complicity in the very systems that bring about distress. How we might like the world to be but how it actually is can produce discomfort; just as there can be an uncomfortable sense of recognition when facing many of those seeking help of 'there but for the grace of God'.

If helping is a means of avoiding dealing with our own social responsibilities then we stand in danger of exploiting our clients because we endorse the system that turns them into people who carry such a label. Far from feeling good about ourselves for the work we do, we need to examine how far we are privileged to be in the situation we are because there are those who need us. If we were a little more active in our examination of social conditions we might well support actions that would alleviate some of the circumstances that create the clients who need us. Unless you are prepared to respond to these social conditions you will always do what you always did and you will always get what you always got! By that I mean if we avoid the effort of making an analysis of how people become distressed enough to need help, we are likely to see suffering in purely personal terms and to respond to it only in the narrowest of ways. Sometimes we need to go 'upstream' and talk to those creating the difficulties – at least metaphorically. We are all citizens before we are helpers.

Problems and Conditions

There are five main areas that give rise to difficulties for practitioners.

- Difficulties in helping conditions.
- Difficulties generated by practitioners.
- Difficulties intrinsic to helping itself.
- Difficulties arising from those who help practitioners.
- Difficulties as a result of the world in which we live.

Difficulties in helping conditions. Many practitioners are all too well aware that the actual resources set aside to help those in difficulty are woefully inadequate and this raises questions of just what is possible and just what should be attempted. Working out these questions, so that the practitioner remains sufficiently positive of their contribution, is important.

Difficulties generated by practitioners. Many agencies struggle to survive, funding is far from easy and often a single campaigning individual has put in some over-whelming dedication to get a service off the ground. In such circumstances support for volunteer practitioners and, especially, paid staff is a major breakthrough in their work. Practitioners, however, are all too easily critical of the conditions, the circumstances, and the lack of this or that requirement. They can then become more difficult for the agency to manage than the clients.

Many agencies rely upon volunteers who have some connection to the issue and such practitioners (or some of them at least) may well be vulnerable to over-identifying with the client or their difficulties. Good preparation and reflection help to reduce the likelihood of this happening.

Difficulties intrinsic to helping itself. Effectiveness in helping is sometimes all too apparent and the result is gratifying for all concerned. More often it is problematic, unclear and may even be doubtful. To offer help is to meet with failure in others, in the world, and, especially, in oneself in the sense that we have to adjust our understanding to match the shortcomings of the world and those around us, including ourselves. It is almost inescapable that any substantial time spent in the helping world brings people face to face with their own illusions, idealisations, avoidances and escapism. Work of this kind, can, for some, be part of learning what it means to be a more complete human being. For others, it is a further step in their disillusionment of there being somewhere 'good enough' for them to find a home – or at least a haven.

Difficulties arising from those who help practitioners. Managers are not all perfect and managing committees are usually anything but, yet both are necessary to create the environment for the practitioner to practise: they have to be worked with rather than antagonised or opposed. Similarly, the practitioner needs space and time for reflection and review. Inadequate arrangements for practitioners to gain the support they need to learn from the work they do only ensures the agency remains limited in its capacity to be useful. Supervision, or whatever other term is used for the reflection upon caseload issues, the dynamics of practice and so on, is often inadequate for the needs of those involved and often poorly understood by agencies and their funders.

Difficulties as a result of the world in which we live. Our world is shifting at an unprecedented rate. From the last vestiges of the cold war twenty years or so ago, we are once more living in a deadly and threatening world. The fear of atomic war may have receded but the potential for large-scale destruction is still with us – this time perpetrated by those who are termed 'terrorists'. Our world is as divided and fragmented as ever and the gap between those who have and those who have not is continuing to expand.

These circumstances create the conditions that ensure there are millions of people seeking and in need of major help of even the most basic and fundamental kind. Shelter, food and relief from torture are not guaranteed to millions who share the earth with us. Fleeing from oppression in the hope of seeking safety elsewhere is becoming more and more a questionable solution. Economic migration, once the route for the most enterprising to escape the limitations of their immediate world, is being challenged by wealthy western states who wish to limit the numbers of people entering into their society. Closer to home, there is a greater and greater questioning of all forms of authority and less willingness to accept expert opinions. Systems are often overloaded and the frequency of breakdown or error unsurprising. All these go to make up a complex world in which the practitioner offers their services.

There are further problems for practitioners arising out of the situations in which they work and the growing awareness and understanding that can only be gained through experience. These include:

- Recognising that not all clients will make it this time around.
- Helping is a lot untidier than it is made to sound.
- There is a loneliness in practice not discovered and rarely discussed in training.
- The revolution in personal fulfilment rarely happens.
- Realising you actually cannot help *everyone* is painful.
- The impatience in wanting to get it right and give the client what you think they need means the person gets mistaken for the *mission*.
- The sheer variation in people's problems is bewildering.
- Clients do not always play by the rules even when you have taught them what they are.
- It is not easy to specify the value of what *you* did or to identify what effect it has. The School of Life might change people anyway.
- Over-ambitious expectations: most people want to be psychotherapists not counsellors, consultants not trainers.
- Lack of prestige in helping as an activity.
- Being convinced that *your* approach should work — applying the theory irrespective of the person.

Chapter 10
Helping as a 'Profession'

The Professionalisation of Helping

The professionalisation and politicisation of helping has had a crucial and distorting influence upon the education and training of practitioners. It has been the major cause for the rush to impose accreditation and registration upon practitioners. It is, therefore, with no apology that we revisit this topic with specific reference to how this influences the conditions the practitioner will bring to their helping situations.

For those of us who view the vast majority of helping situations that any of us are ever likely to encounter as exchanges between equals, transactions between citizens, then the professionalisation of helping is about appropriating skills and understandings that are the right of all and nothing less than attempts to capture them as the exclusive right of the qualified. The effect of all this is to create a profession out of what is essentially a human exchange. It is also an attempt to license only those who are deemed suitable by their qualifications as having the right to offer themselves in a role that is essentially for all free citizens to offer to each other.

For many of us, who saw in the burgeoning field of helping a reassessment of how social change might be brought about by citizens acting more fruitfully and collaboratively rather than by state intervention (which of course has withered away), the professionalisation of helping over the last twenty years has been one of the most depressing features of social life. So many of the skills of helping do not require any great length of time to practise, nor do they require being dressed up in the jargon of science and presented as mysterious and 'dangerous' procedures if they were to fall into the 'wrong hands'.

There are thousands of supervisors, managers, teachers, nurses, pastoral workers, housing staff, doctors and others who have benefited from training in counselling skills and who are able to make a difference as a result. But as time has passed, the kind of programmes where such skills could be learned about, applied and understood (often not taking too long about it) have become hedged around with all manner of 'professional' restrictions. Training in counselling is now a much more academic affair with the essence of the exercise – practice – only one part of it and not even the most essential element at that! It seems absurd that such a practice-based activity like counselling is 'academicised' and made into a subject that is assessed like literature, history or physics and that these qualifications are then used for accrediting those who are deemed 'fit' to practise.

If the major influence in successful relationships is creating and sustaining such relationships, it is odd, at the very least, that this is of so little significance in the preparation of contemporary counsellors. Indeed, most of them are no longer expected to have any significant exposure to the experience of disclosure and self-challenge in their training that they require from their clients. Such a lack of what many of us regard as essential – the experience of what it is like to disclose aspects of ourselves and experience having to face and meet oneself in the confines of a small room with a relative stranger – is a further way in which counsellors separate themselves from the experience of clients and further encourages a view of counsellors as 'experts'.

This fundamental division in the world of helping comes about as a result of how people view the world and others in it. If you believe others have a right to tell you what to do and that you, similarly, have a right to tell others what to do, and if you believe that there are people who are 'experts' to be obeyed because they hold authority and that people's difficulties are only another species of 'problems' amenable to the expertise of those who study and learn about such problems, then it is not a difficult matter to learn how to become one of those experts yourself and give to yourself the right of helping people 'get better' or improve their mental and emotional health. There is nothing to stop you doing this courteously, with regard for the fears and concerns of your clients and with a real talent for making them feel at ease, but it is all offered from an expert-base and with the belief that helping needs to be in the hands of the qualified who have been appropriately approved and vetted.

On the other side of this division are those who regard the establishment and professionalisation of helping as a deformation of the human impulse to be of service. They view it as a means of infantilising individuals who are quite capable of looking after themselves by voting with their feet if they don't like the help they are receiving. They also see people who come for help as functioning individuals in the day-to-day world who have temporarily got into something of a mess rather than as mental health casualties.

It is not some deficiency in their 'wiring' or their emotional make up that makes people need help in our complex times, so much as faulty and inadequate social learning in the first place. This is not to say that there are not extreme cases when individuals need all the expert help they can get, and of a highly specialist kind at that, but to establish a new profession on the basis that a minute minority of people who, it is claimed, need protecting from themselves and we from them is nothing but alarmist. This is especially so when those calling for all this licensing and policing of help are not themselves adequate to the task of assisting those most at risk in our societies under the terms of the work most of them do. This is apparent in that those who are genuinely in need of protection and need the most help are medicalised and in the care of statutory bodies. Clients of counsellors are almost always people holding down jobs, involved in a set of social relationships and managing the usual obligations of the citizen. The description of 'vulnerable' is therefore misleading and misrepresents the situation of most people in most helping situations but it does inspire a view that the practitioner is making a saintly sacrifice in risking their professional identity dealing with such uncertain and unpredictable people.

The Politics of Helping

One reason this fault line is so important is that it runs through everything that follows. Would-be practitioners can soon get the gist of the thing. There is a range of strategies; some give more power to practitioners than others. These need to be put together in some kind of meaningful sequence to assist clients. Clients need to be heard in order for the practitioner to be able to respond to the issue that is most important or most in need of some remedy and so on. All this is uncontroversial enough, but once we reach the matter of what conditions we are to provide and look at why we are providing those particular ones, we come to the politics of helping in a big way. It is political because we come up against questions concerning the amount and kind of preparation practitioners actually need to operate in the settings in which they are working.

Is help therapeutic or developmental? Is it remedial or crisis focused? Is it about generating new modes of response or putting right what doesn't work? How you answer these questions will deeply influence the stance you take to the 'work' and those with whom you do the 'work'.

As we have already seen in *Section One: The World of Helping*, the more remedial and therapeutic views you take of help, the more you will recognise that clients are dependent and in need of… The more you take the view that most people's difficulties are best thought of as deficiencies in learning, inadequate social experience and so on, and have a developmental view of their potential, then the more likely you are to think of working in a collaborative way. If clients, however, are not capable of self-direction or understanding the nature of what is needed (or if I believe they are not), then I am more likely to adopt the role of expert and start prescribing what should be done.

If I see help as a means of encouraging us all to become more self-directing, capable of greater and greater autonomy and able to collaborate together over more and more of our shared life – ideals to be sure – then my stance to the work and my stance to clients will reflect an essentially fraternal view. I will not need to bolster my own position by seeking to be held in the esteem of an expert and I will not seek to make out that the work I do is more than it is. Neither will I attempt to surround how it is conducted with the barbed wire and machine gun posts of a licensing and accreditation system that inhibits all but a small handful of individuals who have the time, money and, above all, academic skills to gain it.

Helping then becomes less something to do than something that happens as a part of how we are. This is *'healing through meeting'* (see *Section Four: The Helping Conversation*) and whilst it is possible to get misty eyed and vague about it, many people have evidence of having been met in their difficulties with such a degree of unsentimental compassion and such a deep level of understanding that that in itself was an experience that brought about change.

The conditions we require to bring about useful aid to another vary from person to person and from concern to concern, but it is important for us to remember that they reflect more than anything else something about how we view the world, other people, the role of expertise and the need for us to maintain our own ego.

An important aspect of the rush to embrace the world of the white-coated expert is that of making clear an important distinction to the world that 'I am not the same as those I help'. Of course there are rational reasons for white coats – hygiene being the most obvious – but, as many studies demonstrate, once practitioners get to a certain level of experience and position they are at pains to distinguish themselves from those they help. They do so because those they help are seen as having 'spoiled identities', to use Erving Goffman's phrase, and practitioners do not wish to be associated with such attributes.

The fact that most practitioners were once little more able than their clients and often became involved in the helping game as a disguised attempt to get help themselves, only strengthens this observation. Many of us do not want to betray our origins once we cross from the 'wrong side of the tracks'. Respectability is a potent force amongst those who have had little or no influence and suddenly acquire it. These are important features in the pathology of helping as an activity and are best not skimmed over or ignored by any intending practitioner. If they are, the result is that the client is likely to find themselves having been recruited to a cause they may not believe in or having to take sides in a battle they are not sure they support.

Third Sector Agencies

Helping remains overwhelmingly a non-professional activity. For most people, most of the time, their first port of call when they need help is someone they know. Only when a personal network breaks down and/or the situation deteriorates are they likely to look beyond for any assistance. When they do, most help comes initially in the form of a voluntary, or charitable, or informal, i.e. what is increasingly termed a Third Sector, response.

The Third Sector comprises of a staggering number of different kinds of agencies that vary enormously in the style, the depth and the calibre of their response. It ranges from charitably funded, high-quality counselling services all the way to organisations whose primary role is to inform those meeting difficulties as to how they might best respond. There has been an extraordinary explosion in the last thirty years of these kinds of helping agencies (another example of the Thatcher revolution).

With the exception of those people who enter professional training i.e. doctors, nurses, teachers etc., the vast majority of people explore the possibilities of offering help and their suitability in the role of helping practitioner via a Third Sector agency, in either a paid or unpaid role. There are also a large number of helper roles that are what we might call 'transitional roles'. Many people train as community workers or teachers, for example, but are then unable to find employment of their choice so, as a way of gaining experience and an, albeit limited, income, they may well take up employment in a Third Sector agency for a time.

For the purposes of this discussion, it may be helpful to illustrate the range of the agencies; there are nationally recognised charitable organisations, e.g. the Samaritans, Age Concern and Childline, all the way to the other extreme of locally based initiatives built by solo pioneers. In the middle between these two extremes, we find many small, autonomous organisations in almost every town in the country, which are operating under different names but responding to similar issues. So, for example, most towns have organisations responding to domestic violence; many towns have contact centres for parents, usually fathers, to meet their children. Mental health organisations would be found in almost every town just as there are charities looking after people with serious physical disabilities (some might be represented nationally but not always). There are drug and alcohol agencies operating under different arrangements and there are agencies to promote the rights of, for example, asylum-seekers. This is just a sample of agencies to illustrate the plethora of the provision facing the intending practitioner. Given this context, it is Third Sector organisations that provide a huge amount of 'counselling style' responses and where most practitioners begin their journey. This makes the Third sector a vital proving ground for people who are aspiring to the work.

The Changing Picture of the Third Sector

Beginning in the late 1980s, and increasingly as the 1990s progressed, the dilemmas of Third Sector agencies increased. Most volunteer-based agencies cannot hope to fund paid staff to do the amount of work they aspire to respond to. If they take the route of employing paid staff they usually discover that it does not necessarily lead to any sizeable increase in the provision of service. On the other hand, if they continue to operate out of their volunteer base they are under increasing threat of being regarded as an 'outlaw' organisation. This makes the combination of students and paid staff as a way out of its situation particularly tempting. It solves the shortage of person-power at a stroke, but only by simultaneously undermining the organisation's very existence because it changes the character of the organisation completely..

What gives Third Sector agencies their unique character is – I suggest – that they are not aligned to mainstream services, have no aspirations to be and therefore cannot be expected to perform according to the parameters that apply to such organisations. This does not mean that they can afford to care little about how they do operate, only that the kind of standards expected and required for any statutory or quasi-statutory organisation cannot apply to an organisation that is funded on such a slight basis as most Third Sector agencies.

The key issue here is that it is what you offer that is important; less important is what you call it. So long as the agency knows the level of the service it is providing, describes it clearly, monitors it appropriately and manages it accountably, the Third Sector agency has nothing to be concerned about from other bodies.

The Third Sector, in order to improve the quality of its helping, became interested in the development of counselling skills as the baseline standard for those wishing to work with their clients. The first nationally recognised counselling skills qualification (RSA) took place over approximately 120 hours, was emphatically skills-based in its nature and was designed to provide a broad-base to educate practitioners so they could make a useful contribution in almost any context. The combination of this kind of training, supported by the agency itself offering continuing development opportunities related to the specific issues and circumstances of its work, was an enormous advance for volunteers, clients and agencies.

However, this raises its own dilemma for both the agency and the practitioner. The volunteer helper is usually encouraged to gain qualifications in counselling. Indeed, in the current rush to professionalise helping, it is almost mandatory for anyone to have formal qualifications, or be on the way to gaining them, before an agency lets them loose on their clients. However, having gained the relevant and necessary qualifications, most practitioners are then likely to want to look for employment which recognises their new status and this usually means some form of paid employment – the very thing that Third Sector organisations can rarely offer.

The Third Sector & Trainee Practitioners

It is the case that many students on counselling diplomas, i.e. trainee practitioners, have their placements provided by Third Sector agencies and this appears to be an excellent way of addressing two issues:

- The need for Third Sector organisations to provide counselling for their clients at reasonable costs.
- The opportunity for new practitioners or those still in training to gain experience.

However, the extent to which any service becomes dependent upon those travelling through (however committed and loyal at the time) has consequences of a very different kind than those affecting an agency that is dependent upon the committed actions of those who have a long-term relationship to the issues and the clients that they serve. If this relationship is to be effective for all parties i.e. the agency, the student and the clients, three key issues need to be considered.

1. Students come at different stages of development and with different models of practice. How does the agency manage this?

2. What guidelines are given to students about the nature, the extent and the style of practice expected? How far would the institutions from which the students come be agreeable to such direction? If this issue is not raised with the training institution then they *de facto* define the agency's practice – something no agency should allow since the agency is ultimately responsible for what goes on under its name.

3. The more students are required in order to deliver the service, the more the agency is then pressured into finding acceptable ways of meeting demands from the training institution.

If the agency becomes student dependent, it becomes, by implication, a clearing-house for student practitioners to gain their student hours. Once the service is dependent upon this group for its delivery then *their* needs have to become central to any discussion about future developments: an issue that is compounded as the number of students increases.

It is one thing to enhance your provision with extra help in the form of students (or paid staff), it is quite another to create the service around people who may well not have (and there is no expectation that they should have) any long-term commitment to the issue or the work of your agency. The organisation cannot then develop. It can only react to the needs of those upon whom it has become dependent. It is not an exaggeration to say that under these conditions clients become less and less central to the work of the agency.

Questions that come with Paid Staff

The acquisition of paid staff and how they are to be employed needs thought. Since they are a scarce resource, it is important to ensure their contribution gives the organisation the maximum benefit for the costs and changes involved in providing practitioners with the kind of conditions that come with their appointment. Are paid practitioners to be used to clear a backlog of clients? In other words, are they a 'mopping up' service? If they are, how is that planned? An individual practitioner cannot see double the clients in half the time just because they are paid. There is something potentially misleading in thinking paid staff might significantly reduce any backlog or significantly increase the amount of work – especially if their arrival reduces the commitment of some of the volunteers. The idea of paid staff working alongside the student or volunteer helper raises many questions:

- Are paid practitioners an elite group?
- Is their role to take on the most challenging clients?
- Are they to give specialist support?
- Are they to be on hand to support existing staff at key times or at key stages of the client's journey?
- Are they to offer a screening service?
- Is it a better use of their skills to ask all new clients to see a paid member of staff to make some kind of assessment about the response the agency can offer (given the number of clients, waiting times and so on – all of which have then to be worked out), on the grounds that paid staff will have these matters to hand because it is their paid work to know these things?

The critical issue is:

- If they have skills over and above most people in the agency, how do you best use their talents?

The Cumulative Effects of Professionalisation

By the late 1980s, counselling had its sights set firmly on claiming a legitimate role in the spectrum of mainstream services. Many of us involved in the work at this time strenuously opposed this move. We believed that counselling was not a role but a way of being in the world and that there were plenty of legitimated, regulated and accredited helping roles already and counselling did not need to become another. However, the move succeeded and thus ensured that counselling would not long remain a central Third Sector activity, except as a place for those in training to gain experience. This shift is less to do with clients and their needs and everything to do with practitioners and theirs. Most clients aren't like most trained professional practitioners. First time clients often need less professionalism and more a sense of safety to disclose their concerns to themselves for the first time.

However, the counselling elite saw an opportunity to create a profession, which, once accomplished, would then impose further conditions upon succeeding individuals wishing to gain membership of an increasingly exclusive group. This is the traditional way any monopoly gains its position – by creating 'barriers to entry' that make it more difficult for later entrants to join easily. In all this, the British Association for Counselling and Psychotherapy (BACP) has been busily creating a role for itself as the professional voice of what is required – in their view. There is no longer an alternative umbrella federation to represent the interests of volunteering or informal counselling in the way BACP once was.

Just as there is no link between client satisfaction and length of training, the professionalisation of counselling has strongly favoured the interests of the training providers. The people who have lost out in this process, by and large, are the clients and the students who are being trained for a role that is unlikely to be available, certainly as a paid one. The current training arrangements for students on courses are based on something of a deception. Students are recruited onto diploma courses in FE/HE institutions when those institutions have no obligation or commitment to the cohorts of students once they have completed the courses. Staffing is often varied and many institutions regard the provision of counselling training as little, or no, different from any other form of provision. In addition, the individual has to find their own placement to gain their practice hours.

There is no link between a counselling qualification and employment other than you can't get employment as a practitioner without a qualification; but there are literally thousands of people who have armfuls of qualifications and who can't get paid work because not enough people will or can afford to pay for counselling. The current situation generates expectations of a livelihood that are largely unrealistic. An example might serve to underline this impact.

> Recently, a woman was appointed as a member of a team giving up to ninety hours of student support. She was employed solely as a student support person whereas the other members of the team were also academics and had teaching commitments too. A very short time after she was appointed, the counselling/support service was arbitrarily cut by half and most of the team were made redundant. What is significant is that it was the academics who were made redundant and not the most recent person to be appointed, i.e.

the support worker. The academically trained members of the team were, naturally, paid considerably more than the support worker and also had different conditions of employment. She is now working more hours and seeing up to six clients per day.

This is an illustration of the insecurity of counselling provision and the kind of occurrence that is happening more frequently. Elements within the insecurity include:

- In the event of cutbacks, counselling/support provision is often the first thing to go.
- The lack of political influence counselling provision has on its own future in institutions.
- The work migrates to the employees who are the least expensive.

A further consequence, unintended but a consequence nevertheless, is that those people (clients) who are already marginalised are increasingly regarded as 'fodder' (not a pleasant term but probably one that is nearer the reality than more pleasant descriptions might be) for practitioners in training to acquire their practice hours before (they hope) they go on to more secure paid work elsewhere.

It is a paradox that in the name of developing higher standards to provide better services to clients, the consequences of this drive for professionalism has been to make agencies and the way they work appeal less and less to the people who need them most! This is a dilemma a number of counselling-based agencies have had to face.

Chapter 11
Being a Professional Practitioner[21]

"I'm not sure I want to wake up in the morning saying to myself, I wonder how many more child abuse cases will fall on my desk today?" (Unqualified social worker at the prospect of entering professional training.)

Practitioners stand in danger of over-dosing on other people's suffering to the point of anaesthetising themselves to it. In part this is a result of living in a world in which information travels quickly, drama is highly valued and trouble is a guarantee of attention. Hence the ever-more heart-rending appeals that seek our attention, the ever-more strident demands that we should care enough to cough-up and then we can once more go about our business. There is nothing new or unusual in all this, it just seems to have become an acutely present feature of contemporary life. It is a symptom, no doubt, of a combination of elements including:

- The withdrawal of state intervention.
- A general lack of belief in the 'institutional solution' being capable of alleviating the social misery generated as a by-product of the 'each against all' social atmosphere that forms the background to our lives.

It is not an easy time to become a professional practitioner. Whether we think of ourselves as professionals, citizens or consumers, we are all disappointed, disenchanted and disaffected in one way or another at the social ills that beset us. Against such a background, it is a brave, or more usually a naïve, person who decides they want to be a practitioner in the first place. Not surprising then that they can quickly reach the level of disillusionment of the young man quoted in the passage above.

It is not that social ills are necessarily occurring on a greater scale (though some argue that they are), it is more that our modern media increase our awareness of such issues whilst, at the same time, our response is to exile them from real debate and consideration. As a result, we know more about more things and are involved less and less in what is to be done about them as the next issue rolls across the screen. In such a context, what is to be done? If those are the realities, what happens to practitioners and what can be done to help them help themselves?

Helping Ourselves

Helping ourselves is something most practitioners find difficult to do and are somewhat uneasy about claiming a right to. That is part of the problem. Perhaps helping has never been an easy profession to take up, but the situation facing many practitioners today has grown appreciably more acute over the last decade.

---

[21] This section of the book is particularly for practitioners as they start their careers. Since this is usually in an agency of some kind, there is an emphasis on the practitioner within an organisation/agency and how this might affect them.

Against such a background, we have to appraise the circumstances, weigh their effects and establish a strength of realism about the limitations it imposes upon how our practice is to be delivered. The costs for failing to do so are particularly high in human service professions. Helping is the kind of work that makes those who do it particularly vulnerable to the deadening effects of working in a context which many practitioners feel is working against them.

This leads to the *frustration of idealism* (often converted to its opposite – *cynicism*). Where, initially, everything might be attempted, we soon reach the stage where nothing is worth doing. It then becomes more important for practitioners to justify 'Why not' and 'Why I can't' than to become involved in the effort of doing anything wholeheartedly.

Untenable priorities are raised in competition with one another and choices between unacceptable alternatives are forced upon us. *Service delivery becomes increasingly compromised.* People say things like, 'We wouldn't have had to consider doing this five years ago'. The point of contact between the service and the client becomes more questionable or ambiguous for all parties involved, (practitioners, managers, and policy makers). When under pressure, there is the tendency for things to be redefined in a way that compromises the overall performance of the service. Guidelines quickly become inflexible or are interpreted inflexibly thus putting further pressure on the system as a whole.

Such consequences have high costs in terms of professional satisfaction, self-esteem and quality of service. The disillusioned idealism and disappointed ambition of long-serving professionals can have a deadly effect upon the initial high aspirations and enthusiasm of a new practitioner and the new entrant can quickly become socialised into cynicism.

Agencies & Systems

Most practitioners meet most clients in some system. The system may be more or less formal, more or less restrictive but it will be there somewhere lurking around, even if it is disguised, as it is for those involved in detached or outreach work.

At one level, the system, in an all important sense, is the two people involved and they will become focused upon their relationship until the wider system intrudes and prohibits an action of the practitioner or rules out of court a request of the client. The more this wider system is invisible, the more likely it is to bring disillusionment to both parties when it appears. The more the relationship is conducted as though the system is not there and not influential, the more scope there is for a *folie à deux* – the danger of any helping relationship when the two parties are so engrossed in what they are about that they forget there is a contract elsewhere with someone about the conditions governing what is to be done.

The starting point is the agency: it provides the cloak that surrounds the practitioner. Ideally, the agency provides protection from the storms that every practitioner encounters from time to time rather than being a cumbersome garment that gets in the way of moving anywhere useful. The agency:

- Gives credence to the work.
- Defines what the work shall be.
- Allocates who does it and to what level.
- Acts as a responsible agent in the allocation of the provision offered.

This means that the longer an agency is alive and well, the more complex its own life-support systems will be. From rudimentary statements of intent, the agency will need to develop its own statement of practice, codes of conduct, establish training programmes and induction courses, review its literature and its service agreements, and provide staff support to those who are delivering the service. Agencies may be charged with a direct statutory duty to perform some task, public health officials for example, or they may be not-for-profit organisations that have successfully bid to provide services in a local area against other potential providers, a sheltered housing organisation for example.

Many agencies, however, lack any number of features, from carpets to staff, from funds to premises. Any practitioner knows that helping is under-resourced and the aim here is not to bleat at how badly off helping is but to recognise that given the usually meagre resources to hand there are some more pressing anxieties than others.

Lack of confidence in long-term direction. Lack of secure funding, or the level of funding and its consequent knock-on effects, hampers the freedom of action and working climate of many helping agencies. The work of many practitioners, especially in the voluntary sector, is often undertaken against a perpetual crisis of funding; 'Will my job be there next year?' Sometimes as much energy is spent generating funds as ever gets offered to clients. Such uncertainties create problems of morale and commitment. 'Just how important do they (does anyone) think this work really is?'

Insufficient organisational support. The implications of establishing a new team, project group etc. are rarely foreseen. When they appear, the policy group responsible for the initiative often fails to acknowledge their responsibility for the team's establishment.

Stereotyping of positions, roles and styles of operating. We will, for a long time, remain in a working culture that has been influenced by the cultural assumptions of men as the predominant decision-makers. Clearly, even though the situation is changing, it is not changing at any great speed. Gender-laden ways of operating that are assumed to be 'normal' are tiring to challenge and are often met with looks of sheer amazement, if not outright hostility, that anyone could still have a concern for such outmoded ideas.

Inefficient use of resources. The failure to define clearly what can be offered, who to, for how long and with what expected results (no easy task) creates a vacuum for the inefficient consumption of resources by default.

Pay-offs & Rewards

Many practitioners work in a system with an unsatisfactory *reward structure*. The levels of pay for the level of education, skill and responsibility that are required and expected in helping are considerably less than those in the commercial world. Helping is a Cinderella profession in terms of both status and influence, and is one of the main reasons for the rush into respectability via qualifications. Rewards, whether considered in terms of financial incentives or career structure, are poor compared to industry and commerce.

The argument often advanced, (most notably from people outside the helping professions), is that practitioners are 'dedicated' or that they get a lot of human satisfaction. In other words, helping, as a way of earning a living, carries sufficient privileges to compensate for low pay. Poor unfortunate industrialists and people in commerce, on the other hand, have to be rewarded for the lack of such human involvement by huge levels of financial reward! Such attitudes betray a lack of social awareness of how routine, unpleasant and difficult many helping activities actually are. Whilst little of this may matter to the new teacher, social worker or health visitor, after six or ten years of practice, vocational dedication begins to wear thin. To find that contemporaries in other comparable walks of life are both financially better off and more secure only exaggerates the sense of feeling exploited.

The Meaning of 'Success'

What new entrants begin to realise is that hardened and experienced practitioners often have great difficulty in deciding what constitutes 'success' in the work they do. No longer being naïve, their experience brings greater understanding of the ambiguities of the helping role and a realisation that part of this role is about living with doubt and uncertainty without giving in to cynicism and despair.

Without *agreeing criteria for success* the way lies open for long arguments about just how well or badly individuals or agencies are performing. However, agreeing useful measures is proving a challenge to many organisations and groups of practitioners. Helping is a sophisticated activity in many arenas; what constitutes success and whose criteria of success are most important are contentious issues. Is it, for example, criteria set by the practitioner, the agency, the client, the funding body or some integration of all these? What criteria would they employ anyway? If you, the practitioner, apply your own is it:

- By deciding how well this person has done, given where you think they *should* go?
- By comparing how well you did against the range of previous practitioners the client has worked with?
- By looking for noticeable improvements in the situation? (Though that begs all too many questions too.)
- The number of clients that are 'processed' each week?

It is exceedingly difficult to know how to decide whether you are doing a good job and how far anyone is actually benefiting from what you offer. This is particularly so in many service organisations where the work is continually being re-defined thus making it very difficult to work out what is 'typical' and therefore hard to know what a consistent standard might be. There are many different and often conflicting views about 'a good job'.

> "The gap between initial expectations and actual accomplishments in human service professions would be large and painful enough for almost anyone, without having the additional frustration of being unable to define just what constitutes accomplishment." Edelwich & Brodsky, 1980.[22]

Starting Out

The new practitioner's belief that they 'only want to help' is actually not that simple. Motivation for helping anybody, as we have seen, is complex and often has elements of grandiosity: 'Why *I* should be the one' and 'why they should need *me*'. In coming to terms with what it is actually possible to accomplish as a practitioner, would-be practitioners again and again meet their own illusions, delusions and collusions. All of us, until we learn from experience, tend to think the job easier than it is, that we can do more than we can and that we are more talented than we turn out to be. For aware practitioners, helping is a fierce path of self-knowledge because you cannot work for long before being brought face to face yet again with your own shortcomings.

So the above elements are not resolved by self-effacing statements such as, 'Well somebody has to do it'. These only evade and cover the deeper questions of, 'What pushes you to be *the one* doing it?' and 'What in your personal history has given you the impulse to place yourself in such a situation where it is either a compulsive requirement for you or an impossible task you have adopted as your personal road to Calvary?' (As someone recently observed, practitioners are often carrying their own crucifix with them and are simply seeking someone with a hammer and nails!)

Learning to gain a realistic sense of the contribution one can make is a crucial phase in the career of any successful and effective practitioner. It requires good examples; role models of experienced professionals who have successfully made that journey and who remain sympathetic to the idealism of the newcomer. The desire to make a financial success of life, to become a great banker or a very successful entrepreneur is very often tempered in our culture in a way that the claims to want to help other people rarely are. It seems that the more we want to 'do good' on the grand scale, the greater the social approval it generates. Altruistic purity is rarely examined, let alone challenged, in order to ensure we avoid confronting potential crusaders with their 'mixed' motives.

By and large, we are willing to accept all manner of claims that practitioners want to make, and excuse all manner of mistakes on the grounds that if practitioners 'did their best', it somehow makes it alright. 'Doing their best' is meant to excuse any catastrophe but there needs to be a serious challenge to practitioners early on in their career so that they begin to recognise that:

---

[22] This chapter is inspired by ideas outlined in their book, *Burn Out: Stages of Disillusionment in the Helping Professions.*

- The practitioner too has needs of their own.
- Helping is a way of trying to meet those needs and the way the practitioner does it will have its fair share of compulsion, manipulation and distortion.
- The practitioner has no right to help anybody just because they need it.
- Clients have a right to stay in the mess they are in, even against the practitioner's better judgement.

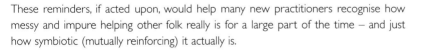

These reminders, if acted upon, would help many new practitioners recognise how messy and impure helping other folk really is for a large part of the time – and just how symbiotic (mutually reinforcing) it actually is.

Characteristics of the Stages of a Helping Career

When new entrants have settled into the role, sometimes taking only weeks to get into the culture of the organisation and how it approaches its task, it is not long before they are looked upon, in presence if not in status, as experienced members of the organisation.

It is one thing to feel you have been somewhere for years, know it all too well and have second thoughts about whether this really is the career for you, and quite another to have colleagues who now regard you as being capable of undertaking the same kind of tasks they do. Sometimes this may be no more than thoughtlessness under pressure; sometimes it amounts almost to an initiation for the new entrant. It seems that in some agencies, until new practitioners are as burdened and battle-weary as the rest, they are not really accepted. Sometimes the sheer pressure the work team or project group is under forces the new entrant to undertake duties and responsibilities that are well beyond their real capabilities or experience.

Helping has its particular dangers, as we have pointed out throughout this book. It can be assumed with dignity, care and self-respect and managed with great compassion and concern without any of the following stages being a necessary step on the way through the helper's career. However, the more out of touch the helper is with their own internal motivations, their own 'unfinished business' and their own 'drivers', the more they are likely – at some point – to find themselves visiting one of these career side-tracks. Watching for early signs of loss of freshness for the work, noticing the reducing interest in the rest of life will keep some of the more dire stages at bay. (This is something that many helpers find beginning to happen to them. As the work becomes more tiring, there is less and less interest to do those very things that raise one's energy and keep one's spirits buoyant. Soon there is work and only work – a sure recipe for trouble.)

    1. The naïve enthusiast. The early stages of the helper's career are often marked with a great determination to make a difference, a crusading zeal to not be put off by the kind of stories the old hands may well tell. This stage is, of course, one of great influence for the long-term. How far the new helper is idealistic in the naïve and unrealistic sense will often be matched by the rapid disillusionment that can soon set in as its complement. On the other hand, the tempered enthusiasm of the young or the new practitioner can be an invigorating addition to any agency.

- The eager entrant.
- High on idealism.
- Lack of experience.
- Likely to identify with the job or the clients, or fluctuate between both of them.
- A lack of understanding of the implications of the job, the agency and its role within the wider context.
- Impatience with the 'old hands'.

2. Signs of stagnation. It may take some while before the career realties begin to filter through to the practitioner. The low pay, long hours, lack of recognition – often – and the sheer difficulty of knowing if you did any good, all contribute to the sense of stagnation that can befall any helping practitioner. Add to that the increasingly driven nature of the helping culture with its targets and statistical calculation and it becomes more and more difficult for the helper to focus upon the relationship with the client. Learning that some systems work with people who are not committed to the kinds of effort that would bring about change, or that the system actually prevents the best work from happening, all begin to make helping lose some of its lustre.

- The crusading spirit fades in the face of the sheer volume of the work.
- Awakening to the fact that work is not a substitute for life.
- The growing impact of relatively limited financial rewards – free time is eroded.
- An increasing sense of limitless responsibilities.
- Personal needs re-emerge and have to be buried, suppressed, acknowledged or accepted.
- Increasing self-doubt about the role and its activities.

3. Career dead end. The practitioner may have set out with commitment and a determination not to succumb to the defeatist attitudes and stalling actions of some of those that have been in the 'helping game' a long time. However, given the lack of recognition and the difficulties of funding that besets many agencies, the realisation that there are few opportunities to extend or expand the range of the work begins to take its toll. Those who move into management rarely find that this is the answer. If it is done for a career change rather than career development, it is often no more satisfying than where they were. It can work when the practitioner is suited to management but it is not an easy move for most practitioners to undertake.

- Facing up to the way it is.
- Low pay, long hours.
- Feeling the victim.
- Career move as escape.
- Seeing the same old faces.
- The feeling of going round in circles.
- Trailing around the interview circuit.

4. Frustration. Long-term helping with too little personal support, opportunities to reflect and periods of rejuvenation, can easily lead to the creeping signs of professional 'burn-out'. The signs accumulate slowly and over time so that the unwitting practitioner doesn't recognise their overall state. They will often put down the increasing signs of weariness or the susceptibility to small inconvenient illnesses as 'just something to get over' and something that is happening 'only now'. The long-term effects of self-neglect, to which all too many helpers are prone, may lead to chronic issues of an emotional, psychological or physical kind.

- A deepening sense of increasing problems.
- Effectiveness and what it means is increasingly questioned.
- 'People' do not respond. The same old faces come back again and again.

5. Apathy. Reducing interest, lessening commitment, faltering practice, all combine to create the stage where the practitioner is simply 'getting by', 'putting in an appearance', or sometimes not, all excused as part of the 'pressure' and the lack of recognition for the difficulties that practitioners face. A long period of helping without the proper mechanisms of support and management can lead to individuals staying 'out of the way' and learning the art of how to look busy. They usually feel pretty worthless and dispirited inside whatever 'clever' observations they might make as a way of displacing their concerns away from the real cause of difficulties – their need for career reinvigoration or even change.

- Apathy as a defence against frustration.
- The task is limitless, 'What can I hope to do?'
- 'My own "survival" is now paramount.'
- 'I may need the job but don't have to let it get to me.'
- Legitimated malingering i.e. justified 'skiving'.
- Reduction in commitment and in the time given.
- 'I may have to be here, but I do not have to let it matter.'

A crucial part of on-going practitioner reflection and development is to hold the above stages in mind and ask the following questions:

- What qualities signify each stage to me?
- The dangers of each one are...

This continued awareness can identify any tendency to fall into the slide towards frustration and apathy – the death knell for an effective practitioner.

Chapter 12
The Altruistic Practitioner?

Motives within Helping

There are many, many reasons and motives for choosing to enter the helping professions. Some are open and acknowledged; others are perhaps unconscious and hidden. 'Avowed' and 'unavowed' motives for practitioners include:

- A need for other people to need them.
- A desire to have an impact.
- Self-exploration is legitimised.
- Following a powerful role model.
- 'Someone did it for me: I would like to do it for others.' Yet it does not follow that if someone was a success as a client they will be a successful practitioner.
- Job security. (Fantasy though this is likely to be.)
- The need for client contact (do not want to confront organisational problems).
- To be valued for providing a worthwhile service.
- To increase the chances of the disadvantaged.
- To bring about social and political change.
- The compulsion to share oneself.
- To enact a religious conviction.
- To compensate for having been insufficiently helped at an earlier time in life.

A crucial question when considering motives behind the desire to help is to ask what the help is for.

> Is to make the practitioner feel better? In part it is that of course, but if that provides the major motivation, clients had better look out since they are merely an audience that is expected to offer deference and gratitude.

> If the aim of help is to 'change the world', then beware the unsuspecting clients who thought they were simply souls in trouble but who find they have become a recruit for the cause the practitioner is doing battle with.

> If the help is to ensure that some deadly scourge is removed from blighting social life then beware clients who may find themselves being helped, but only at the expense of being lectured at for having fallen victim to some fallibility they should now forswear.

> If the practitioner is attempting to 'rack up' a long list of successful cases in order to gain approbation, recognition or promotion, beware the clients who may well be treated to a very successful technique that means they will be left in no doubt as to whose fault it was if the technique doesn't work for them.

No self-respecting practitioner would admit to any of these motives contaminating their blameless concern for the client, would they? Well, strangely enough, unless practitioners can begin to admit that some of, or even bits of all, these motivations play their part at times or can influence their decisions on occasion, practitioners are likely to be operating out of some cherished belief in their own spotless character.

The Compromised & Compensatory Practitioner

Such a need for the illusion of being beyond the reach of self-examination and a little soul searching is an ever-present indicator of the *compromised* practitioner and *compensatory* practitioner. Compensatory practitioners are those who, feeling less than whole themselves but desperately unwilling to acknowledge or face it, seek out others who are more in need than they are and then set about healing and helping them as a means of evading their own journey of self-repair.

Many of us practitioners begin the work this way, with motives that are far from clear and these 'unowned' aspects of ourselves are then 'projected' away from us and onto others. When there are attributes and characteristics, responses and reactions that I am not yet prepared to acknowledge as belonging to me, they have to be dealt with somehow. They can be 'projected away' from myself and onto others. So what I recognise and disapprove of most when I see it in others is what I cannot admit to in myself. Thus the 'unowned' finds a home — elsewhere — until we are mature enough to 'take back the projections' and until we recognise that we also have our share of human distress to sort out. It makes some of our helping unaccountably strange and odd, and we then have to excuse it with self-serving explanations about what we claim was 'really going on'[23].

All practitioners have to be prepared to go on a journey of self-understanding if they are to be free from contaminating their work with their own compulsions and distortions, their own distress related reactions and value judgements. This is nowhere better exemplified than in the internal struggle over getting clearer understanding of our motivation. Most of us have to find a way of learning about how some of our limiting self-beliefs (see *Personal Myths* below) reduce our effectiveness or bring other concerns into the room that are strictly speaking notthing to do with the client and their concerns. Three of the most prevalent are highlighted here.

> **1. Is it OK not to be perfect?** Many practitioners are only too aware that they are far from whole themselves — or they are desperately pretending that they are already well on the way to the summit of professional excellence. How far we can admit something of the real nature of our talents, abilities, skills and attributes is far from easy. If the work has never been done in the preparation of the helping work, then the practitioner arrives with their own shaky self-assessment running the show and a self-image to maintain that will have all kinds of shadowy, murky bits about it.

---

[23] The phrase,'what was going on with…' is counsellor speak and is an attempt to recognise that there is a surface explanation of things and a deeper level of understanding about that surface level – that is 'what is really going on'. Since what is really going on is only available to those in the actual experience, by the time it comes to be discussed in some form of 'supervision', say, it is long past and the practitioner is able to explain it away with whatever pet theory they have adopted to help shore up their faltering self image.

2. Could I be good enough given how unworthy I am? In the effort to compensate for my own limitations I may well end up running around living the client's life for them.

3. Perhaps if I hide it nobody will catch me out. This speaks for itself!

Personal Myths

Most of us walk round with our own internalised sabotage kit of statements, beliefs and attitudes that others have applied to us as we grew up. These beliefs, our *personal myths*, ensure the world 'out there' continues to remain the world we know. They also help us remain who we know ourselves to be and keep others how they are supposed to be. These myths usually operate outside our direct awareness and appear so self-evidently true that it seems pointless to question or challenge them. Personal myths restrict us from making the fullest use of our potential and the opportunities we encounter in our day-to-day life. Some of the most common are:

- People who matter to me must always love and approve of all that I do (and if they don't I will feel miserable and worthless and make sure they know it).
- I must always, under all circumstances, appear to be in complete control of everything (never letting anyone in on the secret that I am as unsure as they are about what is going on).
- I must always have my own way, and things must always work out for me (and when they don't, I will find something or someone else to blame, because it must never appear to be my fault, even when it is).
- I must never be wrong (and when I am, I won't admit it at the time but wait until much later, and then I will acknowledge I might have been 'a little bit mistaken' – never wrong, you understand).
- No one must ever do anything that might hurt me (and so when someone says something thoughtless and insensitive I can feel as misunderstood and helpless as I like but never say so).
- I must never appear to have any problems (and when I have, I must never admit them openly, but show how bravely I am coping with all the demands that have been so unfairly placed upon me).
- I must always appear to be strong, no matter what the emotional cost (and when I need to express how sad, hurt or upset I feel, I will instead complain at how weak other people are who always play for sympathy, never realising I do that myself).
- Whenever anything goes wrong in my life, I am a victim (and therefore all responsibility belongs to someone else for causing me to have to put up with all this unbearable suffering, which I shoulder bravely and with a smile).
- I must always try hard (and although I may never succeed I will always put in every effort to do the impossible expecting you to notice – which you never do).
- Because I am so immensely sensitive, I should not be expected to cope with anything (and if you make me, you will be responsible for all the suffering and hardship you may inflict on me).

- I must always appear perfect in all things (and if for any reason I am not, I must remind you that you have not understood me, and will therefore put you right – just so you know).
- The reason why I can or cannot do anything lies a long way back in my past (and as everyone knows you cannot change your past, so do not expect so much of me).
- Everyone knows things always change and so I must never be expected to decide anything about myself or my life (and if you try and make me, that just shows how mean and inflexible you are).
- I must always do everything for everybody all the time, especially now (and the fact that I cannot, means you should appreciate me all the more for all I do, and not complain about how badly I do it).
- I must always remember to put everybody else before little old me (and though I resent the fact that nobody ever puts me first, and wait for the day when they will, I will never actually tell anybody what my needs are, or that I have any).

Practitioner Myths

There are also many common myths that influence practitioners and reduce their effectiveness. Ignorance of the existence of these myths can lead to practitioners falling into the trap of holding them and being unaware that they are doing so. In reading them through, it may become apparent that we, too, are prone to some of them or that we may move in and out of different ones at different times and under different circumstances.

- I must always cope.
- I should never bother anyone with my troubles.
- I always do my best so I can never be wrong.
- To really help, it's important to identify with other people.
- If the other person gets upset, it must have something to do with what I've done.
- Burnout is a reflection of the agency, not my practice.
- When I overdo it, there's always a good reason.
- No one's really interested in my work.
- Clients are never grateful enough.
- And the organisation's never grateful at all.
- It's my job to solve it all.
- After all I do, I'm still not winning.
- If only I had more resources, I'd do a better job.
- It's the system that's the problem.
- Clients must always come first.
- It's essential that I am available to anyone who needs me – at any time they decide.
- I think it's important to feel what the client feels.
- No gain without pain.
- It's always left to me in the end.

Further myths that are particularly strong in the helping professions at the present time include the ideas that[24]:

[24] Taken from *Burn Out: Stages of Disillusionment in the Helping Professions* by Jerry Edlewich and Archie Brodsky.

- It is a dire necessity for a helping professional to be loved or appreciated by every client.
- One must always enjoy the favour of one's supervisor.
- One must be thoroughly competent and successful in doing one's job if one is to consider one's-self worthwhile.
- Anyone who disagrees with one's own ideas and methods is 'bad' and becomes an opponent to be scorned or rejected.
- One should become very upset over clients' problems and failings.
- It is awful and catastrophic when clients and the institution do not behave as one would like them to.
- One's unhappiness is caused by clients or the institution.
- One has little or no ability to control one's emotional reactions.
- Until clients and the institution straighten themselves out and do what is right, one has no responsibility to do what is right either.
- There is invariably a right, precise and perfect solution to human problems and it is catastrophic if that solution is not found.

These kinds of statements may carry more or less power and investment, but under stress there can develop a culture of heroic struggle that is ultimately undermining. Realistic descriptions of the work as well as of the effects it has upon those involved are important. Contradicting these kinds of responses can be useful.

Chapter 13
Practitioner Survival and Support

Survival Strategies

Dead practitioners are no good to anyone; dying practitioners simply add to the problem; 'burned-out' practitioners are a danger to themselves and others, so mere survival is not the aim. *It is healthy, functioning, able practitioners* that are needed. But in order to function in a healthy way, survival strategies that protect the individual from overdoing it, from taking on an overdose of guilt and that enable them keep a manageable sense of proportion, are all-important.

The difficulty with such strategies, like so many other useful things in life, is that when you don't need them they seem so obvious and when you do, how on earth do you find a way to free yourself to benefit from what you know would be useful? The risk then is of simply adding more guilt and incompetence to the overloaded and poor self-image you carry. Here are some obvious strategies that are worth keeping pinned up on the notice board, positioned on the desk, or kept to hand in the organiser that you carry. No one can be reminded of these things too often.

1. **Accept the givens.** It is important to accept the actualities of the situation as they are and not what you want to believe or hope they are. Having a steady realism of what is possible, given all things considered, is a key element in practitioner survival.

2. **Establish realistic and agreed targets.** Working out what these are is as much an individual exercise as anything else. You know your energy levels, health, capacity for work and your own rhythms. If you let external agents dictate the targets without recognition of you in there somewhere, the chances are they will not be realistic and you will be on the way down the spiral. What is realistic for you, given what you know of yourself and what is going on in your life?

3. **Focus on successes – even small ones.** Stop and consider who gets what from what you do and remember how much difference you do make. It is all too easy to see a client leave a session and know nothing much will be the result of it but there are times when there is a magic about what happens. There are also many, many times when something marginally useful worked. Don't only count the great successes; include the 'good job'.

4. **Focus on where you can do the most good** and have the courage to choose it. When there are too many places to be and too many people to see, working out who will make the most effective use of your time and skills, whilst apparently cold and clinical, is nevertheless a wise strategy. It is important to learn to make the most of the time and skill that is available. Too many practitioners put in time with those people who they like working with (and

who would, by and large, make progress anyway) or spend time with those who are unlikely to make much progress at all (those who are more in need of support and management rather than direct, active help). Those who could make useful progress, given sufficient resources, are often left to manage with too little and the progress that could be theirs does not materialise.

5. Focus on the process and not the results. You cannot always guarantee to bring about real and lasting change with every client but you can ensure that they get you as an attentive, resourceful and capable individual. Monitoring how attentively you approach the work and how sensitive you are to cues and nuances are all important ways of heightening your own performance and maintaining the control where it lies – with yourself.

6. Develop a longer-term perspective. Go from weeks to months; short- to medium-term. Many inexperienced practitioners believe that results happen fast and, when they don't, go on to believe it is their fault. Many experienced practitioners, whilst knowing things won't happen fast, still feel downhearted. Having a realistic time-scale and modest goals are important for maintaining a sense of proportion about the work.

7. Create slack in the system. Make sure you have enough space for yourself to revive, relax, reconsider and reflect. Make sure you have a life!

8. Do not interpret results self-referentially. Many practitioners believe it is their entire fault when things go wrong and too little to do with themselves when things go right. It is unlikely that you were the person who made the client the way they are and it is also unlikely that you will be the one to solve the difficulties that they have had for years. What you can do is make a modest contribution to their journey towards wholeness. It is important to remember that you may not know how much good you did – ever – so do not rely on client approval for your self-esteem.

9. Reframe success as... a modest improvement in another person's well-being or circumstances. Maybe it won't change the world overnight, *but it will change the world in the end* if more and more help manages to reach that standard. Most practitioners would also be functioning with more available space in themselves if they held this as a criterion for success.

10. Develop your own reward system. What useful and appropriate ways do you have of giving yourself some appreciation and support? Check that it is in keeping with the setting you operate within.

11. Identify your sources of strength and support. Complete the exercise on your support networks (see below) and review it from time to time – especially at points of transition, major change, or development – and see that the support system has enough of the range of things that you need to support you through what is coming as well as what is appearing now. And make sure that you use them.

Most of these suggestions are deliberately framed so as to remain under the control of the individual practitioner. They do not require the agency to do much, managers to be other than they are, or clients to suddenly develop angelic qualities. They are within the reach of most of us. The more practitioners are in control of themselves, the more likely these things will be done and it is certain that they can be. If that is what works for those you help, it is good enough for you too.

Support Systems

The exercise described here can be reviewed periodically. It is a way of making explicit the kind of network that supports you in the work you do and where the conflicts and tensions within it might lie.

It is rare for someone to look at their support system and find everyone and every aspect of it in alignment with their human relations role. Most of us have 'helpful critics' who point out how overworked we are getting: friends who tell us we are neglecting them, or children who moan all too strongly that we are not available when we said we would be.

Looking at how much conflict and tension exists in the system itself may help some practitioners realise their effectiveness is reduced markedly. This may be despite the total amount of time committed to helping itself because much of that time is taken from other commitments (like family) that generate guilt and irritability for having been neglected.

The more openly this exercise is completed, the more useful the information will be. (Fill in using either yes/no responses or with individual names).

The People Around Me

Have you someone:	In my work setting	Away from work
To share new ideas and projects?		
To share concerns with in confidence?		
To depend on in a crisis?		
To help you feel warm/wanted?		
Who respects your competence?		
To enjoy things with?		
Who gives accurate feedback on your performance?		
To challenge you?		
To have a good time with?		

Others Around Me

Have you someone:	In my work setting	Away from work
Who are they?		
What role do they play?		
Who/what is missing?		

Overall

- Have you a place to go and lick your wounds?

Have you access to:

- Resources?
- Information?
- Getting things done?
- Is there a good enough atmosphere? (Most of the time)
- Is what you've got strong enough to face the future?

When you have completed the exercise find a like-minded practitioner or someone whose support and challenge you appreciate and sit down and talk your way through how this picture looks.

- Is it adequate?
- Where are the strengths?
- Where are the limitations?
- In what ways might you be vulnerable?
- Do you rely upon the same source for too many aspects of support?
- Is this a long-term picture of stability or is it changing?
- Where will the next moves in the system come from? From you or from someone on the map?
- Given your plans for yourself, how useful will this map be over, say, the next three years?
- Is there any form of assistance you could usefully add to this picture?
- If so, when and how might you do something about getting it?
- Who is most important to you now?
- Who was most important, say, three years ago and who do you think will be most important to you in the next three years?
- What changes, if any, do you think would be useful to make?
- Is the frequency of contact adequate, too much, too little?

Suggested Reading

Edelwich, J & Brodsky, A: *Burn Out: Stages of Disillusionment in the Helping Professions.* Human Sciences Press, 1980.
Hillman, J & Ventura, M: *We've had a Hundred Years of Psychotherapy: and the world's getting worse.* HarperSanFrancisco, 1993.
Bauman, Z: *Postmodern Ethics.* Blackwell, 1993.

SECTION IV

THE HELPING CONVERSATION

Chapter 14
The Helping Conversation

Relating & 'Training'

We are always relating. We do not suddenly become 'good enough' to relate in some special way to others for the purposes of 'counselling' them. The process is much more like: 'I become conscious that my way of relating in 'this' context with this 'person' is somehow inadequate either for me, the other, or the results that seem to occur.' In other words, I recognise that I am not acting and relating as well as I might. This gives me the impetus to explore how I can relate in different ways. I seek out ways and places to try things out.

The experience may take the form of a relationship with a counsellor, it may be in a group or it may be on a course to prepare myself to become a counsellor. Many of those attending training courses in activities such as counselling start out with a more or less conscious acknowledgement that they have something to sort out whilst they are learning how to help others. Training as covert therapy is a strong feature of just about all human relations work.

Depending upon what the trainers believe and what they tell me, I might emerge from this process having greatly improved how I relate and having acquired a belief system about why, where and when to do this. I will become 'socialised' into the norms of the activity as part of the learning I do. I may or may not have a critique about this process of socialisation but I will pass through it.

What I am introduced to, how it is offered, what emphasis it is given and what requirements there are for me to demonstrate my learning, are all ways of inculcating the would-be practitioner in the underlying values and the ideology of their new occupation (or profession, as many would like to have it). Much of what goes on in relationship training may, however, have little to do with me learning about how I relate to others, especially my peers and my 'facilitators', and much more about absorbing the mystique that serves a profession in pursuit of its own identity and the acquisition of its own territory.

Human Relations

'Human relations' covers a wide spectrum of encounters, meetings, purposes and activities. Wherever people are engaged upon a task together then they must have some form of relating in order for their work to take place. However, it is the two-person relationship (the dyad) where human relations is most readily recognised and most commonly experienced in the helping world and in our day-to-day lives.

What are the forms and condition of our human relations that we want to govern us, to influence us, to promote or to practise? If all collective human endeavour requires those involved to establish a relationship of some kind in order to succeed, then what are the most suitable, the most creative or the most productive of relationships to pursue?

Once we ask ourselves such questions we are, of course, in the land of *values* and *purposes* and on the continent of *means and ends*. We must then consider how we offer ourselves to others in order to achieve our ends, how they offer themselves in order to achieve their ends and what claims we can realistically or ideally make upon one another and ourselves in order to conduct our efforts.

Relationship is a potent force for change that can bring about an inexplicable quality of healing to a situation, just as it can remain determinedly absent from a helping relationship if either party is trying too hard. These are just two simple illustrations of the complexity of relationship.

At one time it seemed that counselling was a place to experience and explore such dimensions of human relating, a 'laboratory' in which to study and a 'field' in which to play every bit as much as it offered a 'role' to adopt. In recent years, however, the ever-growing preoccupation with licensing and registering practitioners has made counselling a specialist field. Counselling is in danger of being eclipsed as a term to describe a diverse range of practitioners predominantly employing counselling skills. We now have experts who can be consulted in order to explain the nature of our relationships and their difficulties to us.

However, the work of Rogers (1961) and Egan (1975) remain good indicators of how a counselling approach can respond to a wider set of concerns rather than it becoming appropriated to a specialist function that only the 'qualified' people with 'credentials' are licensed to perform.

'Professionalising' help removes the importance of the citizen as someone who is able to make a particular form of active contribution to civic affairs and the well-being of his or her fellows. There are two major elements contained within this process:

- Qualifications to practise.
- Expertise.

Qualifications give practitioners the respectability to practise; however, they do not necessarily give an indication of ability and effectiveness. This is not helpful to clients who mistakenly believe that qualifications and credentials equal expertise and competence. However, such credentials are more and more based in the needs and demands of an academic institution, and what it needs in order to preserve its status, than anything that might meet the client's needs. They also act as protectors of the members' vested interests and usually go hand in hand with protectionism and the reluctance to allow paraprofessionals to undertake duties. They also tend very quickly to align themselves with the status quo – something that professionalisation is centrally about after all – and become part of the establishment rather than a force for questioning the current orthodoxy.

In addition, the idea that a 'foreign' body should take it upon itself to claim the authority to approve another individual as 'fit to practise' with a third party in order to promote the third party's capacity to act independently is not only somewhat bizarre, it is decidedly contradictory. It also detracts from the importance of the citizen as an agent for social improvement. If everything is left to experts, then the role of the individual, unless they possess the requisite white coat of respectability, stands in danger of being neither required nor welcome. The common weal stands, then, in danger of collapse.

Once 'counselling' becomes specialised and the preserve of only a few specially qualified and trained folk, who 'know' how to do it and, moreover, have particular ways of doing it, then *the 'mystery' of relationship soon flees elsewhere and we have to go elsewhere to find it.*

A Matter of Education or Professional Training?

There are only so many suffering people out there willing to pay for the help that is available and most 'therapists' and 'counsellors' cannot realistically expect that they will earn a living by counselling or by calling themselves a 'therapist'. Those who are already in practice see the legions of trainees pouring from institutes and training centres, individuals who are ambitious and idealistic enough to think they are about to enter into the role of therapist or of counsellor, only to find that the requirements get tighter, the training gets longer and the qualifications become more complex.

Most of those who began practising in the late eighties when the explosion first began usually had little more than the rudimentary training that was available. They developed the skills that have stood them in 'good enough' stead to be 'accredited' – if they could be bothered with such a pretentious idea in an activity that was essentially about promoting individual choice and self-direction – by having supervision and developing themselves as they went along. To a great many who developed an interest in practising counselling in the eighties, it was essentially an adult-to-adult activity.

Counselling during this period was viewed as an alternative to other forms of professionalised help. It was deliberately developed and promoted as an alternative for those who sought out the confines of a relationship where they had the opportunity to be listened to by an adult and regarded as capable of making decisions about their concerns like an adult. It had none of the current pathological overtones that have so influenced the need for professionalising the activity.

Clients are no longer assumed to be adults capable of making sound decisions but are now regarded as being infantilised by their 'problems' and 'issues' to the degree that they cannot possibility be expected to decide whether the help they obtain is of the kind they need or not. Instead, they have to be 'protected' by august bodies that are made up of individuals who have exempted themselves from the requirements they now insist are necessary for all subsequent practitioners.

The ad hoc, leaving-it-to-the-individual to develop the profile of training and development that fits their style of their practice is far too anarchic for the new entrants to this work, or so it seems – a matter forcefully expressed by those who managed to thrive on this very system and who now want it changed for everyone else! The inconsistency in all this is something that rises high on the swelling tide of activity connected to regulating human relationships.

If training, practice and supervision are crucial to the would-be practitioner, it equally requires much self-examination and willingness to scrutinise all aspects of practice. There is a way this can be imposed punitively on oneself just as much as by others. The would-be practitioner might do better to take a more generous view and realise that folk who are really interested in helping know that they have to:

- Look into themselves.
- Enquire into what makes up the activity of helping.
- Enquire into the many complex moral and ethical issues that arise when one person sets out to help another.

From such a view there is, then, much less need to insist upon externally imposed conditions. It is something any individual with aspirations to become self-directing would choose, without being told to undertake it and monitored to discover if they have, and whether they have done it sufficiently with this and that approved individual. Such a regulatory prison-house removes discernment, discretion and the practice of choice from the very people who set out to promote these same qualities in others!

More and more, I have come to think of counselling, at least as I have practised it and as I model it, as no more than *being in relationship*. It is not even about being in relationship in a 'special' way or for a special purpose. However, that being so, it is easy to get to the place that seems to imply:

> If all counselling is about is 'relationship' then there doesn't need to be much time spent on either boundaries or core conditions but only on this thing called 'relationship'. If counselling is only a relationship then there is no useful way of making a distinction between counselling and other forms of human relating.

Well, I am not there and this is not my argument. I present it in order to dismiss it and begin the more challenging exploration of what it might mean if relationship is the heart of real help and certainly of counselling.

The Implicit View

In much of the literature about the counselling relationship, there is an implied view that the intending practitioner trains in how to relate in some 'special' way ('special' according to the theoretical school of the institution where the training takes place) in one arena. Then, at some suitable, agreed and decided upon moment, they become capable of offering a 'counselling relationship' to another because they have now mastered the art – or at least they can do it sufficiently to be neither a danger to themselves nor those they practise upon. Indeed, training alone is insufficient to become 'accredited'; many, many hours of supervised practice are a requirement as further proof that the practitioner is capable of being 'accredited'.

I know, too, that this is only a caricature; merely a way of highlighting and exaggerating the situation but it does approach a description of what lies behind much of what happens in the training of practitioners. They may have 'clients' from an early stage and they may practise upon each other, but the fact of the matter is that until they have finished their training, they are not regarded as being adequate enough to work as 'counsellors', unless of course they are that already and are simply training to acquire the right pieces of paper to make them feel secure in their work.

Relating First

There is much written in counselling on the importance of boundaries and the core conditions. Boundaries, it is usually argued, are what keep the enterprise safely in place in order for the work to develop. The core conditions are what the practitioner brings, adopts or models as a way of enabling the client to enter more fully into the work or the relationship.

The argument about boundaries seems to me to have potential conflicts with the nature of the core conditions[25] and what they essentially promote. It is not that I believe that boundaries are not crucial; I believe they are. It is not that I view the core conditions as other than central, because I think they are. It is more that the two topics are inseparable in the activity that is counselling because the two topics are embodied in the way the practitioner offers themselves. I think of them as being aspects of the same topic and that topic is relationship.

It is important to recognise that relating comes first and no amount of clarity about boundaries or understanding and modelling of the core conditions can displace that priority. The way 'I relate' is not something that is 'special' to counselling or in some ways unique to helping. My way of relating is in large part connected to:

How I am in the world with others – wherever I am and whoever the others are.

It is, in part, a 'given,' something that I bring that is unchanging and, in part, something that is indeed capable of modification, development and growth as a result of my experience of relationships themselves. In some ways, this is the whole rationale for counselling itself: that *'it offers a relationship to another for the purposes of change'.* However, when that was first written, it is unlikely that the author had themselves in mind as well as the client! That is part of what makes the difference in my view; that the change under review is not exclusively that of the client.

'Helping the client' may be the focus, it may be the intention and it may be the purpose of the enterprise, but there is no relationship which doesn't have the potential for and the actuality of *changing me* if I am willing to be engaged with the person. The 'person' here means neither some helpless, hapless individual who is looking to me for guidance or direction nor some clinical 'case' or 'patient', but it does mean any human being that I am willing to enter into relationship with – helping merely providing one pretext and one set of concerns.

---

[25] There is a comprehensive discussion of the core conditions of helping in *The Core of Helping* and of boundaries in *Practitioner Resources*.

Counselling as a Task or a Role

Part of the dilemma is that, for many, counselling is a task, a job, and the title 'counsellor' indicative of a role i.e. an identity that goes along with a set of preciously won skills and competencies that are essential and which are applied to the 'problems' that clients present.

In short, it is a profession and, like all professional identities, it is something that can be assumed and taken off by choice and at will. The concerns of those who practise this profession clearly indicate these features. There is less and less interest in the wider questions of what it means to be one person with another and there is more and more concentration on establishing the rules and the conditions about just who should be allowed to do what, with whom and with whose say so.

The idea that we are all incompetent at human relationships is removed from the agenda and hidden away in further training requirements and supervision, whereas the starting place needs to be that we are all able to benefit from further development in our human relationships.

Such a description may draw howls of protest from many practitioners and trainers, claiming that this is 'not the way it is' or 'this is not the way they were trained'. But, like it or not, most counsellor training has had to get into this terrain and most practitioners have willingly adopted the-preparation-for-a-job way of approaching their work. This is because they are unwilling to face the alternative – that counselling is not a job, is not a profession and that it doesn't require 'mysterious' skills or endless practice to perform it competently. Nor do those who have the necessary competencies in great measure, numerous amounts of qualifications and all the paraphernalia of credentials by the truck load, necessarily inspire their clients toward health, improvement or change.

When counselling is defined in this way and when the centrality of relationship is removed or reduced in its significance, then the way is open for endless concentration upon technique, method and the search for the 'right way'. There is then a retreat from facing, 'How am I in relationship with you, now, here and how far can I meet you where you are with a steady awareness of where I am in myself'? It enables counselling to become a technical activity so that much counselling is no more than helping others adjust more satisfactorily to the same kind of situations that the practitioner has not managed to resolve either!

Preparation

It is the task of training to equip the practitioner with a series of skills and strategies that enables them to offer themselves as a *valuable resource* to the client. This requires a balance of personal awareness of motivation, values and beliefs, in order to know *what not to do* and a range of strategies and skills to promote effective development that stems from within the client. Since personal change is an experiential process, the training method needs to model the process itself and should be experiential wherever possible.

Good preparation ensures that the intending practitioner knows that their own development and their own needs will be just as active in the work they do with clients as it was in their search for the programme they attended. Many people who undertake programmes do not always intend to become practitioners but they recognise that this way of learning and this type of exploration is hard to find in any other forum. Therefore counselling training is, for some, a programme of life development that is an attempt to make up for what they were unable to experience elsewhere in their lives.

All helping activities that take place within the privacy of the relationship formed by practitioner and client are open to collusion, illusion and delusion. In preparation, therefore, it is important to draw attention to the potential distortions of the helping process and to encourage openness to self and others in the safety of a learning group. Since human relations is also an activity which promotes client self-direction and self-evaluation, the process of preparation should encourage the development of these tools and provide substantial opportunities to practise ways to assess and evaluate progress. The learning group is therefore an essential element in such a programme and *the use of self and peer assessment methods central to the style of such preparation.*

Since the client and practitioner come together from separate contexts and create yet another in which to operate, an understanding of the influence of personal networks and support systems is a vital part of assisting someone to change and in evaluating the potential for resistance they may encounter. The overall social context in which client and practitioner pursue their lives is also marked by rapid change, so some understanding of the major forces at work within our society is important in the effective preparation of an intending practitioner.

Many will bring questions concerning accreditation, qualifications and the whole issue of licensing practice. All these anxieties reflect the world in which helping takes place: the uncertainties of practitioners in knowing quite how far to claim an expertise for all they do as well as issues about the legitimacy of claiming a professional identity. Such concerns tend to make the philosophic inquiry into the nature of the enterprise subsidiary to managing the occupational anxieties of a role the person is a long way from yet performing. That said, that inquiry is none the less vital.

When a practitioner has developed a sense of relationship with their own higher self, the more easily can they step inside the client's own world, experience and nature and they need then to project fewer and fewer of their own unconscious assumptions upon the client and what the client ought to do.

How far an individual understands that the relationship itself is central to the enterprise will influence how far they are challenged to meet themselves in their own awareness of what is driving them. 'Investment in self' at some level or another is likely to be a strong element in bringing anyone into a helping role and certainly into training.

The 'Helping Conversation'

"I define 'helping' as supporting and enabling the well being of another person. There is clearly something odd about turning human helping into a profession with training, accreditation, status, case conferences and institutional politics. Does the wise flow of love from person to person require all this apparatus of paternalism?" J. Heron, 2001.

Why find another term when 'counselling' is perfectly adequate? Because counselling now so confused a term, so 'contested' an activity, that it is almost certain to be taken to mean anything but what a 'helpful conversation' implies – *two adults, coming together as peers*, to establish a relationship, however long or short, for the benefit of one of them.

'Helping' is an overarching term that encompasses many forms of offering assistance to another. The term, 'helping conversation', implies a mutuality and an equality that is increasingly questioned in the world of counselling, where clients are frequently seen as 'vulnerable' and counsellors referred to as mighty figures of wisdom and power who have 'the interests of the clients' at heart – but only if they are vigilantly policed.

The concern of those involved in the helping conversation is not how it might go wrong and how to stop it, but how it happens all the time amongst all kinds of folk and how it might be done better.

A helping conversation may be brief or long, it may be focused or discursive, it may take place in a work setting, or it may be arranged independently. It may arise out of the role relationships individuals have to one another, staff member to participant, for example, or it may be an explicit search by the client for someone who will give particular kind of attention and understanding to their deeper concerns. The helping conversation isn't an exclusive term and will encompass most counselling sessions coaching and mentoring relationships, consulting, most supervision, most therapeutic approaches and most informal helping. This is one reason why those who are status conscious prefer specialist labels – it separates them from those less 'trained' than themselves.

Adults & Peers

Such a kind of conversation is an adult activity capable of being decided about by both parties. Although it is one person putting themselves at the service of another, it is not one person putting themselves at the *mercy* of the other. It is important that we respect the client's freedom of action, choice and decision. It is also important that we do the same for ourselves, for where is the client to gain a sense of these things if not with us? It is crucial therefore to recognise the importance of the context of help in shaping:

- What can be attempted.
- How it can be conducted.
- The kind of focus of interest.

And in remembering:

- Counselling is only one form of helping conversation out of a range of ways of helping another.
- Other people may be doing as much, or more than, I am in 'helping the client'.

Perhaps as nowhere else in the helping relationship, the brief counsellor is tempted to overlook the relationship and 'get on with the job': to 'fix the client' and send them on their way. Or, alternatively, they can become so bemused and transfixed by all the potential strategies that they could adopt, they actually do little that has any real effect. To remind ourselves that the aim is to work with and through the relationship, and that the most effective help arises out of the quality of the relationship, is always a useful starting place before launching into the acquisition of techniques and skills.

Philosophy & Method

Help is neither neutral nor private. It requires choices to be made about where, when and how much (resources) it takes up and has implications beyond those directly involved (social impact). The more attention is directed at the dynamics of those involved or the dynamics of the individual receiving the help, the less these other concerns are likely to be made explicit or brought to awareness with any real strength.

In our time, we have seen the retreat of the civic and the social, the appeal to the psychological as a primary means of explaining difficulties, and the 'subjectivising' of most impediments as the 'description of choice' by society's legislators. The promoting of explanations of individual difficulties and dilemmas as examples of personal shortcomings that have nothing to do with wider social arrangements has been one of the great confidence tricks of the age. Together with the attendant condemnation of the individual as the agent of their own circumstances, they have made great inroads into our communal understanding and our sense of the way many individual dilemmas are structurally linked, politically implicated and socially determined.

Not all clients are capable of making the changes they know they would like to make, given the life chances they have had. Much help is so focused upon the psyche of the client that little time is left for the radical appraisal of our social obligations to one another and how far their decline provokes the increase in suffering that finds its way into the practitioner's room. Little time is spent exploring the way in which the counselling profession is largely composed of those in retreat from social and organisational pressures that contributes to making so many of their clients' lives difficult. Help itself is never straightforward and has many implications in all areas of life, including the following:

- Personal   - Social   - Emotional
- Political   - Spiritual   - Economic

However, it seems to be the case that practitioners, who claim they simply want to 'help people', rarely examine these facets of helping or how they inter-relate.

The Role of the Practitioner

As we have seen, the world of helping and counselling is changing rapidly. There are now a prodigious number of folk who are 'trained' as 'counsellors'. There are legion of therapists and cohorts of psychotherapists roaming the world claiming territorial rights to the client's psyche. The emotional world is under siege from an army of competing factions all determined they know best what the other needs.

'Who and what are we dealing with?' are primary concerns in any helping domain. Techniques, methods and approaches proliferate, all claiming cure – instantly. It was not always this way. A time was when growth, development, change and taking oneself seriously enough to work at the 'work' was an expected commitment for any lasting change to take hold.

Most helping and counselling work and certainly preparation, focuses upon the method, approach, technique, or framework that the practitioner uses. Most approaches are concerned to ensure that the practitioner gets it 'right' within the paradigm of the approach or within the framework of the method.

The relationship may be a matter of importance but it is less and less the central concern. The client is seen more and more as a person with 'difficulties', or 'in difficulties' and it is 'the difficulties' that we are there to help with. This quickly leads to the client being little more than the 'site of operations' for the skilled practitioner to do their work; the relationship no more important than that required of the dentist, the doctor or the travel agent. This is hardly an exaggeration.

The role of the practitioner may take many forms: conscious and chosen, spontaneous and 'natural', without thought or with a careful sense of priorities. Much effective planned help consists of the practitioner refraining from doing things that impede the individual being helped from making clear their own needs and offering their own best efforts to move toward some improvement. Consequently, the preparation for a humans relations practitioner needs to pay attention to the fact that even the practitioner is not simply a practitioner but an active social agent who may well occupy other helping roles and certainly will have contact at other times with individuals where they may be a practitioner, whether a parent, friend, neighbour and so on.

Human relationship is increasingly fragmented, difficult to sustain and under constant revision in our turbulent world. It is hard for practitioners to offer relationship to clients when their own are under so much strain and collapse. It is easier and less painful to work with specifics, complaints, difficulties, the ubiquitous '*problem*' rather than reach into the client's world and be there with them for a time: that is arduous and soul-searching work. Much preparation leaves this out and much counselling leaves it out too. Putting the relationship at the heart of the work, the willingness to be there, to engage, to work out with the client how and what to work with, is not to ignore method or technique, it is to give them their *due place and their proper role*.

In an important respect, the practitioner is the instrument through which their help is offered. Personal insight and development are important for both practitioner and client. An understanding and considerable experience of the process of personal development and growth is central to the formation of any effective practitioner. The core conditions of *empathy, respect* and *genuineness* find expression through the behaviour of the practitioner towards the client. The practitioner not only has to develop and extend the range of their capacity to enter the client's frame of reference through the development of effective rapport, but also has to be able to offer appropriate techniques and strategies that will facilitate the client's progress towards a more effective resolution to their dilemmas.

Arriving with an Apparatus

The danger is that of bringing to the meeting a set of boundaries and conditions from elsewhere, from previous experience, from what I have been told or led to believe *should* be the case or from the theoretical model that I hold. We know that practitioners guard against their own preferences coming through, but we know, too, they are there and we know they are influential – whatever we would like to believe and however much we guard against them intruding too noticeably.

As a practitioner, I may, indeed, respond from whatever emotional or psychological reservoir I have available to enable me *not* to have to be there in the moment with you, relying upon my experience as my guide in how to be with you in your experience. Instead, the practitioner models a way to respond, through the adoption of the core conditions, that seriously reduces the capacity of the practitioner to make themselves fully available to meet the client – who may well know nothing of boundaries and core conditions, but a good deal about their own torment and pain.

The practitioner who takes a limited view of human potential, who sees individuals as capable by and large of making only incremental shifts or changes, will not be looking for ways to bring about major shifts or great leaps of progress. When this does happen, they are likely to dismiss them or remain suspicious of their capability of being sustainable. Similarly, the practitioner who views the client as simply another like themselves, struggling and making the best of it, will perhaps create the kind of relationship in which the client feels deeply understood but is not much challenged to re-investigate their basic assumptions about themselves or their world. If the practitioner views most difficulties through the lens of gender politics, for example, then the client is likely to discover that their difficulties are in some way related to gender issues.

Indeed, many practitioners, when looking for help for themselves, choose someone – a colleague – with a strength of conviction and experience about a particular issue or range of problems. This is usually seen as someone's 'speciality' – something all to the good but not something that should be offered to the naïve client who might be easily persuaded by the practitioner's preferences! Yet the very methods that the practitioner adopts also influence the whole enterprise. It is as though with the naive client we should all aim to be benignly neutral (or is it indifferent?) whilst with one another our expertise is really valued.

When I am tempted to meet the other as 'a person in difficulty', what takes place may well be a useful and helpful meeting, but both parties may leave it believing that what they experienced was not all that they could have experienced together. They never realise they met in such a way that a whole dimension of meeting was not free to show itself.

When I approach the meeting with a trust that the boundaries we need will indicate themselves and bring more of myself to the meeting, then the more likely it is that the client will do the same. As far as we are able to enter into 'this coming together', the deeper the potential meeting can become. Such a meeting will create the space and the presence for those healing forces that are, in the end, mysterious, but which nevertheless can be sensed, to enter and help facilitate our time together.

'Self as Helper'

Human relations practitioners, those working with developmental relationships and counsellors, bring with them to any meeting their own beliefs, attitudes and values regarding themselves, others, the practice and the world at large. They also bring with them a legitimate degree of human 'woundedness'.

In the beginning, practitioners need to attend to the issues that arise for the client – they need, in other words, to be able to make a useful contribution in *helping the client manage the problem*. With greater experience, the practitioner begins to *locate the problem within the person*, which, in turn, leads to a firmer recognition that it is the process of the client that is the common feature of all helping relationships and that the challenge is in finding the way to work with the client's process.

Only by exploring these same aspects of the practitioner's own make-up does it become possible to work effectively and sensitively with others. In some ways, if counselling is about enabling another to live out the life that is 'theirs', then it is in some measure dependent upon the practitioner having a notion of what it is to live out the life that is 'theirs' too.

It is therefore important for prospective practitioners to explore their own 'image of the person' and clarify, as far as possible, the influences at work upon how they learn to respond to those they help. The individual practitioner needs to begin to identify areas of particular interest or concern and become more thoroughly acquainted with approaches and suitable theory to enable them to work more effectively.

It takes time, experience, reflection and considerable commitment to one's own development to gain that deeper understanding of one's own way of life which becomes formulated into a working philosophy, i.e. a working theory. Such a working approach is therefore not something fixed and determined for all time, but evolving as one's own living sense of meaning in relation to one's own life and circumstances deepens. Such deepening of learning, such 'knowing', enables the practitioner to accomplish a number of things:

- It helps foster a centeredness from which we can meet the client in the face of all their turmoil.
- It promotes a deeper level of patience.
- It helps us gain a steadier view of the human condition where we hold ourselves in relation to the other with a degree of equanimity. Concern for the other is then deepened.
- At the same time, we grow in insight and acceptance of ourselves as we are. No longer are we so interested in how the client views us, how we 'come across', or whether we are doing it 'right'. We have confidence that we have taken enough care to do it well.
- It helps relate the individual moment or issue to a wider sense of periodicity, cycles and rhythms.

As a result we are no longer isolated in our difficulties and our pain; we are living through events that mirror universal processes.

Helping in general, and a developmental relationship in particular, is a means of offering assistance via relationship, yet counselling often takes place in a context and between people who have unequal power and influence. Exploring the dynamics of the helping relationship is therefore an essential dimension in adopting an aware and conscious use of the *self as helper*.

In part, this is no more than a skilled performance. In part, it is also a decision based upon expressing in action the underlying view of the person, the nature of their difficulties and the purpose of the help that is being offered. A skilled practitioner not only knows what they do and can discuss it, they also have some competent description that explains why they are choosing to do what they are doing in the way they are doing it at the time and given the circumstances. A humanistic perspective in human relations work requires an acknowledgment of three important dimensions:

- A recognition that we are all creators, actors and participants in the world in which we live. (This is not the same thing as saying we are all free to do as we like.)
- An emphasis upon the positive potential for growth and change, which is seen to lie within the individual
- A whole-person perspective, which regards the conventional mind/body split as largely artificial.

Consequently, such an approach is primarily interested in enhancing the individual's capacity to take increasing personal responsibility for their own and others well-being.

In such a view there is less emphasis upon 'illness' and the search for cures for the dis-ease that attends much of modern life. Individual growth and development are regarded as life-long processes and the distinction between education and therapy is superseded by an emphasis upon 'affective' as well as cognitive competence, a view well expressed almost thirty years ago by the radical humanistic educator and transpersonal thinker John Heron, who wrote:

"I see the facilitator as an educationalist, not as a therapist – whatever the setting. The concept of education is thus extended to include such notions as personal development, interpersonal skills, working with feelings both expressively here and now and cathartically through regression work, transpersonal development, social action skills.

The concept of therapy maintains an arbitrary excessive and unreal distinction between the mental state of the helpee and that of the helper. I see human beings, by virtue of certain general features of the human condition, as vulnerable beings who are differentially distressed: some have manageable amounts of distress that coincide with the prevailing behavioural norms in the culture – but all require a mutually supportive education for living which shares skills in relating to feelings and other features of intrapsychic life, in relating to persons and social structures and situations, as well as skills in relating to data and information of all kinds, in relating to objects, things and the natural order. The heavily distressed and disoriented may require specialist remedial education, but to call this education rather than therapy provides a more honest, authentic and promising climate for change." J. Heron, 1977.

Meeting

I am at pains to indicate here that helping, whilst it is different and in some sense 'special' – like rounders is special amongst the species of activities played by groups with bats and balls – it is special amongst the species of activities that make up human relationships. In such a framework, helping is, of course, 'special', but just as a game of rounders can be enjoyed and played with dedication by all who have a mind to do so, so helping too can be offered by one to another.

This is clearly at odds with many of those involved in helping in its many forms and from its many theoretical positions. This is especially so for those who enthusiastically claim how different or special the way they do it is and how necessary it is, therefore, to spend a great deal of time and money learning how to do it 'the right way' – i.e. their way. I dispute such a view because I think it leads to a view of helping that removes the centrality of relationship and substitutes technique, method or theory over two people being there together and 'working it out' – 'it' being what they have contracted to attempt together.

"Whenever a counsellor begins to formulate a theory it seems increasingly to me that whatever the theory actually is, whatever the framework consists of in the end, counsellors like any other individuals who penetrate beyond knowledge into wisdom find some universal laws that can both help an individual and help the counsellor. Among these laws is a certain sense of order, a sense of compensation and balance, an understanding of cause and effect or KARMA, that life has an essential vibration about it, that there are rhythms or cycles, and there are polarities. What we think, we are; like begets like; that we all get the clients that we deserve and clients get the problems that they need and our job is not to 'help them' but to be there for them.

Such wisdom enables both the counsellor and the client in time to realise that the personal, subjective and immediate sets into a wider and more important plan. It is a reflection or a fragment of the whole. It can help too to not get hung up or lost in a particular experience, frustration or blockage. We can see it as being out of a particular place in a cycle.

Developing such an understanding of the phases of developmental cycles can create a sense of faith in something greater and more developed than ego consciousness and help begin to get a sense of the 'real' or 'higher self' at work."
J. Hillman, 1980.

I take the enterprise of being human as centrally involving relationships and the more I know and learn about relationships, the more effective a human being I will become. The more effective a human being I become, the more 'helpful' I will inevitably be since a by-product of being effective, in my scheme of things, means having a capability of responding to an ever widening range of other people with an ever increasing sense of one's individual awareness. There is much to say about the notion of an 'effective human being' and here is not the place, except to say that it is not a mechanical measure of utilitarian worth but much more about the unfolding of the individual in all their potentiality and richness.

In the end, helping is about how much more freedom the client has gained: not necessarily the freedom to say or do things differently, not necessarily the freedom to be more assertive and challenging of other people – though these are important freedoms to acquire if you haven't already got them – but the freedom to experience more of themselves.

This is an existential quality that arises out of relationship. Depth of meeting and quality of relationship are neither predictable nor 'prescribable'. They emerge out of the distinctive creation of relationship that is formed by the separate presences of client and practitioner 'merging' together to create something unique and transcendent of their individual contributions. There is always *me, you and a context* and who knows which is the more important and influential upon our endeavours? Often it is what we do not yet know that is influencing what is happening.

It is this relationship, more than skills, techniques and knowledge, that is the crucible for healing to arise. As a result of the practitioner's willingness to meet me, I then begin to discover my own willingness to meet myself. In that way I begin to grow and change, not only in the world of action but in the world of being; in the-being-for-myself rather than in the doing for and with others. The client is also enabled to take up their place within the relationship that will enable them to bring about changes both agree they are working toward. This has sometimes been described as *healing through meeting*:

"... to embark seriously upon healing through meeting is to leave the safe shores of the intra-psychic as the touch stone of reality and to venture on to the high seas in which healing is no longer seen as something taking place in a patient.

Although one hopes that the client becomes wholer in the process, and although the therapist has a special role as initiator, facilitator, confidant, brother or big sister, and representative of the dialogical claim of the world, the healing itself takes place in that sphere Buber calls the 'between'. This healing cannot be limited to the client alone, or even to the relationship between therapist and client. To be real healing, it eventually must burst the bounds of psychotherapy and enter in all seriousness into the inter-human, the family, the group, the community, and even the relations between communities and nations...

Buber calls for a more 'musical', floating relationship of therapist to patient, for the deciding reality is the therapist and not the methods. Although no therapist can do without a typology, at a certain moment the therapist throws away as much of his typology as he can and accepts the unforseeable happening in which the unique person of the patient stands before the unique person of the therapist." M. Friedman, 1992.

However, if my practitioner does not hold this perspective then, however much I am helped, I will not necessarily experience or learn much about this kind of freedom. I may well leave the relationship entirely satisfied and deeply appreciative because I am now more successfully 'adjusted' to the world that I already knew, accepting that 'it is as it is'. The practitioner has enabled me to manage it better and to understand more of how to manoeuvre myself through it. These are not inconsiderable gains.

What my practitioner may well not do is challenge me to meet myself in such a way that the questions I arrived with begin to stand out against a more and more developing sense of questioning how it all comes to be this way. This is not just about an individual questioning their own world view, *but questioning the very structure of the world in which we are together.* This is part of the political nature inherent in the 'helping conversation'. The more the practitioner is invested in techniques that 'work', in solving the client's 'problem', the less 'political' they are likely to be and the less likely to encourage their clients to enquire into the nature of the way things are.

Presence & Openness

The practitioner takes responsibility in entering into the meeting to be of service to the other, whilst recognising that they are there as themselves and for themselves. This creates tensions between the need to 'be there for the client' and the need to 'be real in the encounter' which both bring about together. Human relations *is a shared enterprise, a collaborative endeavour,* in which both parties need to take up a clear understanding of the limits and conditions which are to frame the way they decide to work together. Together they have to form a working alliance within a set of more or less clearly understood boundaries. The work has to be undertaken and some evaluation of its consequences and value has to be made. The Seven Stage Model of Human Relations (Section Seven), which includes counselling and helping relationships, is an applied model that has been tested in a wide variety of fields and fits with this view of the helping conversation i.e. as part of a human relations approach to service and helping.

If a working alliance is not created, whatever help may be given and however valuable the time spent, it is not based upon the mutuality of relationship. Fundamental to a working alliance is the recognition that the client is a potentially self-directing individual in their own right. The practitioner is making themselves available to facilitate the growth of the client's experience towards development and change. The relationship must establish the minimum conditions for the time spent to be at least instrumentally rewarding and it may flourish into the possibility of an '*I-Thou*'[26] encounter. The practitioner must ensure they remain open to the client sufficiently for the client to unfold their difficulties and be present enough to be engaged in the relationship.

There are two aspects to the activity: *presence and openness.* The client must experience a sufficient degree of presence from the practitioner to be inclined to enter into the relationship in order to meet themselves. The practitioner must also enter into the relationship with a willingness to be open to the possibilities which lie waiting to be discovered. In this lies the vulnerability of the practitioner to be touched and to offer their '*realness*' in the exchanges that take place. The practitioner continually monitors their presence so as not to intrude upon the client's experience, boundaries or subjective reality. They enter only by invitation and it is always conditional upon the choice of the client.

The openness of the practitioner offers an example to the client that it is possible to be in relationship, to meet and to be unafraid of change and development within the human relationship. Relationship then becomes a creative force for both contributors, whilst it does not equalise the encounter into a sharing of similar concerns, or of a healing of the same wounds. Techniques do not become unnecessary, conditions irrelevant and modelling unimportant, but they do take on a much less prominent role and develop from within the space of the meeting and they arise out of the created need of those involved.

Authenticitiy

As we noted earlier, empathy, respect, and genuineness are the essential requirements for any effective helping relationship. They were first promoted by Rogers, reaffirmed by many other practitioners and supported by the available research. Within the core conditions there has to be a sensitive, and not easily achievable, balance between several forces if the client is to find the necessary safety to begin to unfold themselves and undertake the painstaking task of self-disclosure.

The struggle to engage with the issue of *authenticity*, what it is, what place it holds and how it is offered, puts much of the rest of what we learn into a less crucial context. In the end, authenticity is about the degree of 'in-touch-ness' I have with my experience of myself in the moment, as the moment develops and the relationship unfolds. It illustrates a good deal about how far I have come to learn to trust myself, the other, the work itself and how far I am still trying to 'get somewhere', 'do' things for the client, or rely on a technique to make it 'alright' or 'better'.

---

[26] Whatever terms or conditions are present when the meeting begins there is the willingness to encounter the other in all their fullness and, likewise, to be seen in the same way leading to real depth of communication and meeting. *I and Thou* is the title of a book by Martin Baber, see the bibliography for details.

Experience is the most reliable and direct guide in relationship; this requires trust. In many ways, trust is no more than living out of the authentic experience of the encounter with the other. Authentic relationships, in this respect, are more important and influential than are 'correct' relationships. I won't get to be authentic by doing what someone else says. And I won't get to be me either. Similarly, if an important aspect of any helping or counselling relationship is fostering encouragement in the client for them to become more of themselves, then there has to be room somewhere in the process for the practitioner to be themselves within the relationship that they create together.

This is not always so simple as it seems and to some people it would immediately be apparent that this is a most unreliable indicator of what needs to happen within the relationship. There is a major dividing line over the issues of authenticity and openness as the guide for what to do next within the relationship. How people practice the art of helping, how they view the nature of the relationship within which help occurs and the nature of the image of the person that guides them in the work they attempt, are all influencing factors in how people respond to the issue of authentic presence and how willing they are to be open.

For those who hold a contained view of human potential, or who see the capacity for individuals to misuse their position, to exploit their role and to take advantage of the client, albeit unconsciously, then authenticity as a testimony to the development of the relationship will simply not do. It is far too uncertain a guide and far too open to misunderstanding and exploitation.

People can, in their claim to act authentically, damage and hurt one another and later realise that there was little that was authentic about it. However, authenticity is a more demanding challenge than simply the right to label all that I 'wish' to do as an indication of the authentic expression of myself. It has much more to do with sensitivity to self, other and relationship, and requires great commitment in order to remain engaged in exploring its implications.

Authenticity is also the point of return in attempts to establish where I am with myself and with the other. It is by becoming more and more alert to the moves and shifts inside my own experience that I begin to develop a reliable guide for working out what is happening, both in myself and in my relationships. The challenge of authentic relationship within the helping session is an important and essential element. If part of the impulse in becoming involved as a practitioner is to offer a relationship as a way to enable another to become:

- More self-directing,
- More self-initiating,
- More in charge of their own choices and actions,

then all this has, in some measure, to be reflected within the helping relationship itself. Depth of presence and the quality of openness foster the strength of relationship in which the *growth of the person becomes possible, rather than the increase of individuality.*

Co-operative Inquiry

A humanistic and a developmental approach can look upon the endeavour we are describing here as sharing the features of a *co-operative inquiry* into aspects of personal experience and the human condition. A strong element of such work, at all levels, is the promotion of self-reflection. It takes a developmental perspective in relation to individual progress and the unfolding potential for growth and change within the person, group, or organisation. It also recognises the importance of values and belief structures in shaping the individual's responsiveness to change. The role of such beliefs in the creation of meaning, including the transpersonal dimension, is an important strand in this way of working with relationship at the heart of the enterprise.

It helps us have a sense of perspective, a 'world view', that is held not as a set of fundamental tenets but as a living expression of our regard for ourselves, others and the planet. Such a 'way of being' about the work enables us, whether in the individual session or in a group, to recognise the symbolic struggles, the wider resonances and the universal themes that bring a wider significance not only to the client's personal life but equally in their wider life as another individual on a human journey.

Having worked hard to wrest some nuggets of understanding out of the experiences of life, a practitioner can tune into another with their own inner power of thought, will, and creative vitality by offering a model paying attention to the client in a deeply rich and satisfying way.

Suggested Reading

Egan, G: *The Skilled Helper: A Model for Systematic Helping and Interpersonal Relating.* Wandsworth, 1975.
Rogers, C R: *On Becoming a Person.* Boston, Houghton Mifflin, 1961.
Daloz, L A: *Effective Teaching and Mentoring.* Jossey Bass, 1986.

SECTION V

THE CORE OF HELPING:
Listening & Responding

Chapter 15
Listening

There's not a lot of point in helping someone to solve the wrong problem
because you didn't listen properly in the first place.

Introduction

An understandable reaction might be to regard 'listening' as being simply confined to
what happens between our ears, and responding is what is said or done in 'response'
to that. However, the whole process of listening and responding in any effective helping
relationship is much more complex than this suggests. In order to explore further the
complexities inherent in listening and responding, the process has been separated here
in the next three chapters into three different elements:

- Listening.
- Between listening and responding.
- Responding.

Although this separation is arbitrary, it does highlight the process; firstly, the ability to
listen and attend, secondly an awareness of the effect this has upon the listener's[27]
internal response before, finally, they respond outwardly. The aware and reflective
practitioner will learn how to separate out these three elements in their practice.

Listening[28] as the Foundation

Helping of almost any kind is based upon listening; listening accurately to the concerns
and dilemmas of the person in their difficulty. We may listen to:

- How the other speaks: the various dimensions of the use of voice.
- The content: what the other person is actually saying.
- The linguistic structure of the speech: the choice of words, use of
  grammatical and other linguistic structures.

When we listen, however, we bring much more than hearing – which is complex
enough in itself – into play. There is the impact of *facial expression*. There is the impact
of the *relative position* the people occupy in relation to one another, both in respect to
their physical position, seated, standing and so on, and in their social position, head
teacher and teacher, for example. There is the *use of the voice* itself to convey the range
of affective elements to the accompanying description. There is the use of *eye contact*

---

[27] Listening is an integral part of life and occurs in every context where there are people, so in this section 'listener' is an
overarching description used for anyone who finds themselves in a listening role. They might be practitioners, helpers or simply
citizens fulfilling their normal, day-to-day activities.

[28] Much of this section is similar to the chapter found in the book *Forging the Future Together* (Bryce Taylor, Oasis Press, 2003).
Since the heart of listening is the base of any form of human relations it was outlined there. The author has modified it to reflect
the exclusive concern with the one-to-one relationship that is the focus of this book.

and how far that is relaxed and open, contrived or avoided. There is the role the other senses may play in our ability to enter into the meeting and in giving our full attention to listening and responding. *Smell, taste, touch,* may not be things that occur in relation to the client but they may well play a part in establishing or limiting our degree of ease in relation to the meeting.

What We Hear

How someone expresses his or her concerns and difficulties may be clear and concise, or long-winded and elaborate. The difficulties themselves may be simple and straightforward, or complex and in need of unravelling. *How we talk and what we say* may need separating. Some people are very capable of describing nightmarish experiences they have had but find it much more difficult to give voice to the accompanying feelings that are part of the story. Others are hardly able to give a coherent account of a situation that on the face of it seems unproblematic and yet… It may be that their difficulties lie in their unfamiliarity with talking at all, or the challenge of finding a way to explain themselves even to themselves. The practitioner has an incalculably important role to play in encouraging the client to bring forth what they want to say and they do that primarily through the art of listening.

By listening we mean something much more complex and rich than simply hearing what is said and evaluating it. Listening here suggests a willingness to take part in the world of the client and become engaged with the nuances and subtleties of their exploration in order to encourage them to give voice to their preoccupations.

Learning to listen is not as straightforward as many of us suppose. In fact, it requires a strenuous effort to remain open to hearing what someone else is saying, and the more challenging the content, the more difficult it is to stay that way. Add to that the pressure on many practitioners to come up with some 'useful' response and the way is open for the listener to decide early on what the speaker 'must mean'. The listener then responds from that base rather than truly paying attention to the real meaning that the speaker is attempting to grapple with.

There is some evidence to suggest that there are differences in the listening skills of men and women, differences that are in line with the role-stereotypes for each of the sexes. How far this is innately true and how far a matter of cultural conditioning is not clear. Women are regarded as having a more finely developed 'intuitive grasp' of things, whilst men are said to be more rational, logical and so on. Perhaps the most important thing to be gained from such studies is a reminder that we are all inadequate as practitioners and all have skills that are in need of development.

We also need to bear in mind that though the capacity to listen varies from one person to another it also varies markedly in the same person from one day to another – a good reason to continue to deepen our capacity to listen.

Social Trust

But underlying the issue of learning to listen is the need for trust in the relationship in the first place[29]. Social life is based on a degree of trust that you will act in a way that is consistent with the way you appear[30] to be and that you will follow the expected conventions of our meeting. As we grow up into the society around us, so we become socialised to the norms and expectations of being a participant in the network of relations in which we operate. Social trust is hard to overestimate: it is the glue that holds our social world together.

We depend upon it and make use of it without giving it a thought – until some exchange takes place that reveals just how fragile our meetings and exchanges really are. Social trust is based on people being relatively congruent and relatively consistent in their behaviour and their agreements. It is precisely this, of course, that confidence tricksters employ to take advantage of others. Painful though it may be, the value of the confidence trickster is to remind us of the importance of holding our social trust in high standing; not taking advantage of others, not exploiting their good will and not manipulating them for our own ends.

We are living through a time of massive change and social upheaval. Social relationships are under revision; their expectations are being recast and our expectations that other people will act as they appear can no longer be taken for granted. All this together gives rise to a declining degree of social trust. The instability that ensues is one of the causes of the kind of distress and insecurity that bring many people into helping relationships of all kinds. Where formerly they might have depended upon their family network or their social friendships to sustain them through a crisis, many people find they have no such resource to fall back upon and are left feeling adrift, alone and isolated, coping with whatever crisis has provoked their sense of need for help.

There are many issues that individuals face in modern urban societies about identity, sexual preference, employment, life-style choice, questions of entering into relationships with others who bring children with them, problems of ethnicity and allegiance, faith and social expectation. These kinds of problems or dilemmas of the human condition in the 21st century are a relatively new phenomenon on the scale in which we now see and experience them. Old certainties that, however restrictive, once gave those who were brought up within them clear expectations and understandings are fast disappearing bringing doubt, uncertainty and a desperate search for some sort of answers.

Those answers may be found in fundamentalist movements and appeals to simplified ways of thinking of all kinds. Under pressure, many of us opt for the simplicities of an easy answer rather than struggle with our own dilemma until we find some resolution that meets our own sense of things. Some may attempt to fall back upon the appeal of traditional roles and identities without much success and some may seek a form of helping conversation to explore their own reactions and responses.

---

[29] The Reith lectures for 2002 were based on the changes taking place in relation to the question of social trust at a time of great social and economic change. (See the bibliography for references.)

[30] 'Appear' is a general term which relates to not only one's physical appearance but also the way people express themselves and their body language in, for example, the way they stand or sit or move.

This fracturing of social trust makes it particularly important that the practitioner recognises the influential role they play in creating the kind of spacious interest for someone else to discover their own views and develop their own sense of direction.

The kind of trust the practitioner has to form together with those they help is one that recognises the worth and value of the other in their own unique identity and the value of them as a person working out their own solution to their own quandary – whatever that is. Whilst these ideas are taken up further in the discussion about the 'core conditions of effective helping', it is worth emphasising that this is not a stance to adopt in order to help someone, but a deep regard for the diversity of human experience and the richness of human flourishing. This is an easy sentiment to write, however it can be extremely difficult to maintain that deep sense of acceptance and regard in the face of some of the more primitive and damaging expressions of personal freedom that some people bring to the practitioner.

Effective Listening

'If I do not listen well, then I can do none of the rest that I am supposed to be doing well.'

We have to learn to listen just as much as we have to learn to speak, perhaps more so, since we have to speak to get our needs expressed. Many people seem well able to do that but not at all able to know how to assess accurately what someone else's needs are. Listening is so invisible a process that there is nothing much noticeable by way of action. It is all too easy, therefore, to assume it is going on when, as any parent knows, it is anything but!

In our day-to-day life we may 'drift off', hear the intonation of a word and be called away to a whole set of associations from another time and place. We can hear a person give an account of something, believe we've got the 'gist' of it and be satisfied, but know full well we would be hard pressed to give any kind of précis of what we heard – yet we still believe we know what was said.

Because we are listening all the time, we tend to believe we can do it. But listening to someone else enter into their experience of confusion and uncertainty; listening to someone wrestle with the dilemmas of what they should do about…; listening to someone identify and manage themselves through the difficulties of facing some deeply unpleasant experience from their past, is listening of a very different order.

All of us can recite experiences and the consequences to us of how it feels not to be listened to. We can also quite genuinely believe no one would make the same observation about ourselves but we are as guilty as anyone else of failing to listen intently at times. This is something that cannot be allowed to enter into the helping relationship.

Listening, in any kind of effective helping role, is the base upon which all else depends. If trust is the quality required to bring the meeting into form, then listening is the agency by which something useful may begin to appear. Listening in this way is an active and demanding activity. Indeed, it is sometimes termed active listening to distinguish it from other forms of listening, like listening to the radio, listening to someone comment upon an incident in the office and so on, i.e. listening that does not require us to get inside the meaning of the person who is doing the speaking.

Research into interpersonal communication reveals that listening is a complex matter and itself involves many skills – skills that can be identified and improved. How well a person can listen and how well in fact they do listen are not the same thing. There are numerous factors that influence the quality of any communication between individuals or members of a group. Some of these relate to external factors and some relate to the rapport[31] that develops between those involved. External factors include:

- The situation itself.
- How it is organised.
- Who organised it.
- The stated purpose of the occasion.
- The intended outcome of the meeting.

The more we can separate the occasion from our own agenda, the more we can recognise a difference between an occasion being 'successful' and whether or not we fulfilled our personal agenda.

Listening is also connected with the individual's ability to select and structure what is being presented and to remember it. Perhaps the single most important skill in listening is the capacity to summarise accurately, to restate, very largely in the client's own words, what they have been saying as a way of indicating that you:

- Are indeed listening.
- Have understood.
- Have kept track of what the client is relating.
- Have been bothered to hear it as they said it.
- Haven't re-interpreted the content into your own perspective.
- Can remember the salient points in the sequence they appeared.
- Are with the client in their story.

This capacity to enter into the story of another will be influenced by such things as intelligence, motivation, familiarity with the subject and so on. The *willingness* to listen is probably as important as the *capacity* to listen. It is possible to have the ability to put aside one's own life for a moment and truly hear what the other is saying, i.e. have the capacity for listening, but not have the willingness to make that active commitment to the other. An ability to listen that is never put to use is no good to anyone. Some people seem never to listen; others seem to distort whatever they hear. Poor listening habits cause many of us to listen much less well than we could.

[31] Rapport is discussed later in this section and is also explored much more deeply in the companion book *Forging the Future Together*.

Listening 'With'

The most engaged form of listening is not simply listening to but listening *with* another person in an active and involved way. This means that we are no longer observers, but become active 'experiencers' of what we are being told.

As we have already seen, the foundation of all responses and courses of action is based upon an assessment of what is known, what you have been told. Accurately hearing what is being described, hearing 'the music behind the words', is an active process, which involves overcoming many of our habitual ways of acting when others are talking.

The major barrier to better mutual inter-personal communication is the natural tendency to judge or criticise, to approve or disapprove of what the other person is saying. In this way, a good deal of communication begins to resemble a game between those involved. The speaker assumes they are being listened to and the listener conveys the impression that they are listening and reacting, even though, for the most part, they may have 'tuned-out'. Such listening has no place in an effective relationship.

Although we like to think of ourselves as offering other people our undivided attention, in fact we are often busy doing our 'own thing' whilst they are talking. Most people use the time during which others are talking to prepare what they are going to say. Although we like to believe that talking and listening goes something like:

YOU SPEAK   I LISTEN
I SPEAK   YOU LISTEN

In truth it is much more like:
YOU SPEAK: I LISTEN – EVALUATE – LISTEN – PLAN – LISTEN – REHEARSE – SPEAK (at the first opportunity I find to stop you).

As you are talking, I am already deciding what you mean and what I think about it, as well as what I am going to say to you about it.

There is not much time in all those processes for listening with deep concentration, and with a search for the nuance, the subtlety and the richness of meaning, to what the other person is actually saying that may be all-important. Even the good listener is guilty of evaluating critically what is being said before attempting to understand what specific meaning the speaker is trying to convey. The result is that they often jump to premature conclusions about what the speaker is driving at. This, rather than assisting, only disturbs the flow of communication. The speaker has to try to explain what he means a second time – or give up, as happens more frequently than we might think.

In an important sense, individuals learn the art of 'not listening' from an early age. We become adept at 'screening out' what we don't wish to attend to, ignoring those requests that get in our way and being selective when hearing those sounds that register as calls for our attention that we would rather not respond to. 'Not listening' is one of the ways human beings cope with an overload of demands. We learn not to listen to those echoes from our past that remind us, all too strongly, of associations we would rather not recall. We make decisions not to listen without being consciously aware that we are doing so. We can see the difference between making a response based on having listened and making one that indicates that we have simply 'heard' by looking at a few examples.

Example one: Over-talking

Speaker: I had an accident yesterday; fortunately no one else was hurt and I'm OK now.

Respondent: I was busy yesterday so I wouldn't have been around if you had phoned me then.

Here the respondent offers a response that is unrelated to the issue of the speaker. The expectation is that conversation will continue moving back and forth with no agreed subject and even a serious topic may well be missed.

Example two: Indirect talk-over

Speaker: I had an accident yesterday; fortunately no one else was hurt and I'm OK now.

Respondent: Have you got your mobile phone handy? Oh there's Ian, I'll ask him.

The respondent uses the pause in the topic to introduce their own agenda and to get their own needs met. In other words, the respondent hijacks the topic.

Example three: Direct substitution

Speaker: I had an accident yesterday; fortunately no one else was hurt and I'm OK now.

Respondent: Driving is such a problem these days isn't it? I can't be bothered most of the time any longer.

The respondent assumes they know the cause of the accident and offers their particular take on the topic. The experience of the subject is merely an opportunity for the respondent to 'sound off'. This is an interesting interruption when it turns out that the accident was a domestic one and that the washing machine flooded the kitchen!

Example four: Action not feeling

Speaker: I had an accident yesterday; fortunately no one else was hurt and I'm OK now.

Respondent: Have you checked if you're covered on the insurance – do you want me to do it for you?

Here the respondent is out to demonstrate their recognition of the event and even to get involved but only at a task level and in an inappropriate way. The purpose here is to stay away from the domain of feeling and any distress resulting from the accident.

Example five: Amateur psychologist

Speaker: I had an accident yesterday; fortunately no one else was hurt and I'm OK now.

Respondent: I wonder how you managed to engineer that? Do you often create accidents for yourself?

Here the respondent offers the benefit of their half-baked New Age understanding or their current pet psychological theory that we all create the events that happen to us. Whether this is true or not is beside the point at this stage. The person needs more empathic recognition.

Example six: Computing response

Speaker: I had an accident yesterday; fortunately no one else was hurt and I'm OK now.

Respondent: Do you know that people of your age are more prone than other types of driver to have an accident by a factor of 3?

Again, the respondent ignores any distress accompanying the event in favour of using their acknowledgement to illustrate a pet theory, provide an opportunity to offer a point of information or avoid what might be difficult emotional territory for them.

We might all be guilty of responses like this from time to time in our day-to-day life – though we may well be horrified to see them written on the page like this. But they do go on and day-to-day life does not fall apart. We are insensitive or realise long after the event that we could have been more empathic and interested than we actually were. We may learn to change our stance in future as a result.

It may be that we meet a friend who has suffered an experience that is all too reminiscent of some unfinished situation of our own, or too much like a past experience that is full of distressing memories and we wish to push it aside. As a result, we may well respond either truculently or with minimal interest. Sometimes we simply withdraw and stay away out of a sense of not knowing how to respond at all. Such a reaction may come, not out of a past experience of our own, but out of the fear of our own state should we be suffering the experience of our friend.

Acting as though the other is enduring some form of bereavement is a way of keeping the 'contagion' away from ourselves. It is a way of maintaining the psychological barrier that suggests 'that might be happening *out there*, but it isn't going to get to me, even symbolically through the experience of my friend!' This is a form of denial well known to those who work with grief and bereavement.

Blocks to Listening

There are a number of commonly experienced blocks to effective listening. It is possible to identify certain areas that radically influence how effectively we are able to really hear the words of another.

External features: the environment is unsuitable

- An overheated room.
- Noise.
- Interruptions.

All these and many others make for an unsuccessful meeting.

Practitioner issues

Feeling out of their depth. The 'material' is too powerful for the practitioner to manage effectively. However it is worth remembering, 'You get the clients you deserve', as someone rightly pointed out and, if they have found their way to you, don't be so sure you can do nothing.

Distracted by their own internal pre-occupations. Having concerns of their own, the practitioner finds that the concentration needed to 'stay with' the client is simply not there and they are only offering an appearance of interest.

The information offered is not what the practitioner wants to hear. Unexpectedly, the practitioner realises that the client is exploring a concern or expressing a view that touches their own 'unfinished business' and they are no longer able to be equanimous and dis-interested in the disclosure but are busy now managing their own emotional reaction.

Judgements of liking or approval are not forthcoming but are being sought or expected. To the surprise of the practitioner, they find themselves not being loved, approved of or worshipped in the way they have come to expect and are disgruntled as a result.

Client issues

Judgements of liking or approval are not forthcoming but are being sought or expected. Similarly for the client, there can be the expectation that they will be something of a 'hit', and if it does not manifest in the way expected, the client may allow themselves to become distracted from the work and more preoccupied that they are not getting the attention they expected.

The content is shocking. The client has a fear of expressing the content of events, which they find shocking and is sure the listener will also. The client then begins to act as though they have been judged by the listener and withdraws.

Shared differences

If either of those involved has a **strong accent or an appearance** that is extreme in some way, the likelihood is that it will have some effect that needs to be dealt with, preferably overtly. The appearance of immediate difference and obvious distinctions of class, age, appearance and so on will have an effect, at least for a while, and can often be dissolved by surfacing them and discussing them.

If there are **significant differences in education, experience and class** background between those involved it will have an impact. This is a little like the example above but where the differences are not so visibly obvious and only begin to become revealed in the sessions. Nevertheless, the two people may have to make some fairly important internal adjustment to accommodate to one another once they realise neither is the kind of person they quite thought.

Where those involved hold **different value systems** there will be some adjustments to make. Because our values are often only revealed when they are expressed, the relationship can be some way developed before one or other of the parties begins to realise that there are significant differences in the values each holds – and they may be incompatible for effective work. If the difference in values between the practitioner and the client's view of things relates to the issue they are there to explore, the more awkward it will be to manage. Good work can be interrupted or even brought to an end[32] if a new issue arises about which client and practitioner are at odds.

Very different vocabulary is used by those involved. If the practitioner is committed to helping the client learn from what they themselves say, they will endeavour to reflect and summarise the content in the language the client uses, but the more that language and content are different from what the practitioner would usually use, the more it may begin to feel like a pretence. Sincerity of communication is perhaps more important than glibly repeating what someone else says if it is an unfamiliar language.

The aim of effective listening is to *allow the other person to explore their own experience in more depth*. Only by coming to terms with their own sense of things and the emotions that accompany events will they be able to cope with and understand new information, or formulate a policy of action.

The Importance of 'Refraining'

The problem of learning to listen well is further compounded by the fact that most practitioners – certainly at the outset of their work – suffer from an overdose of needing to prove they are keenly interested and willing to be helpful. Sitting saying nothing, they believe, does nothing to convey any of that.

---

[32] This illustrates the difficulty of applying the core conditions of helping as though they are a once gained forever held attribute.

The emerging practitioner hits a major dilemma here: How can less mean more? How is it that 'getting out of the way' enables the person to somehow become freer to say more? Naïve practitioners look upon their role as one of encouraging, enabling; in short, 'doing'. However person-centred they may be, they know that they are there for something to happen and that they therefore should be willing to do their bit to ensure it does. In large measure, it is this energetic eagerness that is a stumbling block.

The client will already have met the over-helpful friend, the over-identifying and sympathetic listener, or the individual who can offer them a solution. What they are unlikely to have met is someone sufficiently at ease with themselves to be able to settle back into the shared space, and who is able to offer a real and committed invitation to them to reveal themselves at the pace and in the way that suits them, given all they carry.

To do that means *refraining* from all kinds of habits, patterns and responses. It means:

- Not giving invitations.
- Not showing how impressed you are at a client's dedication to their struggle.
- Not affirming them in their need for approval.
- Not finding opportunities to show how much you have understood by practising all those skills that you have been busily learning.

Instead, you are able to offer the *appropriate minimum* to enable things to progress. Such a measure of inner stillness is not something that can easily be found.

There is a paradox in all this. Those who can do it, can. Those who can't often don't know what is meant. And if it is more than the skills or if it is unrelated to the skills, why learn the skills? Like so many other practice-based arts, it is not that the skills aren't important – they are crucial at the time they are needed. But above and beyond 'the doing' there is 'the being'; a way of simply offering the client the space and the opportunity to unfold their concerns in the way that makes sense for them. 'But how can you be sure that will happen?' 'How can you do it all in an hour?' 'What happens if...?' As the practitioner's anxieties intrude into the shared experience, they begin to create the expectations. The client then obediently attempts to fulfil them, if we are not careful.

There is another dimension of trust involved here: trust that the client will find the sincere invitation one worth entering into; trust that you will be able to hear what is being felt – not just what is being told to you – and that together you will be able to work out a set of steps to move towards progress. Hurrying won't get you there any faster and may well ensure you don't get there at all.

Learning the art of *refraining from*, being alert to all those distractions and evasions which prevent you from offering your full presence, is a continuous part of the work of leaning how to be more effective in any helping role.

The Use (or misuse) of Information

A considerable risk for those practitioners in small communities, either of friends, networks of associates or in a workplace, is that information gained in one setting or on one occasion can be used inappropriately elsewhere in another context for quite other purposes. Sometimes this may be deliberate, in order for one person to 'use' the information in order to disadvantage the other. Often it is a result of a lack of thought or consideration of the boundaries that need to limit what information is held where and what information is available to be used elsewhere.

If much of social life is distinguished by a variety of what Eric Berne termed 'games'[33], the practitioner must be careful not to make use of the information they have gained in their helping work in any 'games' they may play. The kind of information that is disclosed in helping situations is often potentially damaging to the person who discloses it, or to those about whom the client is disclosing. The practitioner must not make use of such information to settle their own scores or even to act on behalf of the mistreated client. Their role is to be there to assist the client to come to their decision about what action might or might not be needed.

Non-verbal Cues

'Messages' are the overall statement given by someone. They can be divided into two principal categories:

1. Content: providing us with the meaning.

2. An emotional, or affective, component: telling us something of how the speaker feels about what they are saying.

How an individual feels about what they are saying is often more important in establishing what they really mean than what they actually say (content). This second element, the affective component, is conveyed through the use of such things as tone of voice, facial expression, gestures, posture, stance and so on. It is often said that over 90% of a message is conveyed by the non-verbal features and less than 10% by the actual content of the message. Whether the figures are strictly accurate is not so important as to note that the proportion is very much weighted towards the non-verbal elements.

John Heron, in *The Complete Facilitator's Handbook*[34], describes five basic kinds of important cues in the 'facial expression and body language' and how to work with them. Although he is primarily relating these to working with groups, the underlying principles are equally important for one-to-one relationships. The following examples are taken from *The Complete Facilitator's Handbook*.

---

[33] 'Games' is part of TA (Transactional Analysis) terminology. See *Section Six: Practitioner Resources* for further details.

[34] This book is an excellent resource for anyone interested in working with other people, either individually or in groups and is recommended for further study.

Picking up on pensive cues. You ask the open question 'What are you thinking?' of someone who has that typical brief reflective facial expression indicative of an inner reaction to what has already been said. The person may not verbalise the thoughts unless asked. 'What are you thinking?' is an open question rather than a closed one. There is no single right answer. The pensive person's presenting thought is usually at the leading edge of a whole cluster of related thoughts.

Picking up on wanting-to-speak cues. You put an open question such as 'What is your view?' to someone whose facial and other movements show that they want to say something. Or eye contact and bringing in the person with a hand gesture might be sufficient.

Picking up on emotional cues. These cues may combine with pensive cues, or wanting-to-speak cues, or may be evident on their own. They show shock, surprise, delight, loving care, irritation, impatience, anxiety, and so on. You can use 'empathic divining'[35], 'It looks as though you...'; or open questioning, 'How are you feeling?' Again, the presenting emotion may well have other sometimes quite different facets.

Picking up on cathartic cues. This is a special case of the previous kind. The eyes, facial expression, other bodily cues, show that distress emotion is coming up, moving toward discharge. The fists are clenched (anger); the lips and jaw are trembling (fear); the eyes are filling with tears (grief); laughter is about to break out (embarrassment). Empathic divining may bring the distress a little nearer identification, ownership, acceptance and release. So for filling eyes you may say 'It looks as though you're holding on to so much hurt and pain'. For sustained discharge, of course, you will move over into full-blown cathartic interventions.

Picking up on alienation cues. The facial expression and perhaps the posture show that a group member is alienated, has mentally and emotionally cut out of the group, and is sunk in their own internal process. You can use empathic divining and say 'It looks as though you...' Or you can gently ask an open question: 'What is going on for you right now?'

Recognising and using such non-verbal cues has received a good deal of attention in recent years and NLP[36] has highlighted many of these features of communication. The whole non-verbal approach of the listener can, therefore, exert a significant influence upon how the exchange develops, especially if they remember to:

---

[35] Empathic divining' is a term used by John Heron to describe that ability to identify an unstated content/feeling and put it back to the person.

[36] Neuro-Linguistic Programming (NLP), is one of the most influential approaches in the study of personal communication and subjective experience to emerge in the last thirty years. Devised by Bandler and Grinder and their associates, NLP has now spread widely and programmes in NLP are available almost everywhere. Quality of what is offered, however, does vary widely. Anyone interested might consult the Association for NLP (ANLP) and visit their website.

- Sit in an open expectant, but non-threatening way.
- Hold an open gaze rather than a stare.
- Invite the other person to choose where to begin.
- Mirror the other person's body posture and movements.
- Match the other person's language and use their preferred channels of communication (see below).
- Pace the other person's world-view in an attempt to understand their *frame of reference* rather than challenge their ideas and beliefs too early.

'Pacing', in this situation, refers to the ability to anticipate the implications of the person's belief system. The ability of the practitioner to learn how the other person understands the world is more important than getting into arguments whether their beliefs and views are 'right' or 'wrong'. Getting into such an argument immediately loses rapport.

At a simple level, pacing someone is literally working at the pace and in the way that enables them to be most at ease. More sophisticated ways of pacing enable the practitioner to ask questions about the implications of what is being said. The risk here is that the client feels they are being caught out or having their mind read. The value of such sensitivity by the listener, however, lies in having a fuller grasp of the internal world of the client. In this way, pacing moves into 'leading'.

The phrase, 'preferred channels of communication', refers to the fact that most of us describe events in preferred ways that can be listened for and responded to – thereby making communication more easily accepted and fostering rapport between those involved. In 'matching' the preferred channel of communication, the listener will encourage the client to enter into their experience more fully. Many people, for example, describe their experience using visual metaphors, omitting some of the sound elements and the feelings that are attached to the pictures. Being able to respond with questions that invite visual information enables the speaker to continue to respond in their preferred, in this case, visual channel. Examples of such questions might be:

- What else did you see?
- When did you see things change?
- What did you observe when…?

This enables the flow of their narrative to unfold more easily than if they have to translate questions asked in another channel, such as:

- How does it feel?
- What do you think about that?

Either response could be offered as a form of encouragement to the client to say more, however, the impact is to 'shift' them from their preferred channel into one from which it is less easy for them to respond.

Barriers to Effective Listening

The key points of which the listener needs to be aware include:

- We tend to listen least well to the middle of a statement.
- Previous knowledge and expectations tend to mean we hear only what we expect to hear.
- Because of previous knowledge and existing attitudes, we frequently reduce a message to conform to our expected meaning by eliminating detail. In other words, we listen selectively.
- Before the speaker has finished delivering their message, we are almost always formulating an answer. This means we do not listen to the end of the message, and may even finish off the sentence for them.

The listener inevitably brings their own world-view with them to any meeting. There are two key factors for the listener that will make the difference between effective and ineffective listening. The first factor is vital in being able to achieve the second.

1. The level of their self-awareness and their ability to put their own world-view to one side.

2. Their ability to reach that place of stillness in themselves so they are able to be fully present to the person with them.

There are many elements that affect the level of effectiveness and some of the most common are described below.

Anxieties and uncertainties. People who do not know each other well, or who have some reason to be wary or apprehensive of one another, are more likely to find it difficult to hear clearly what is being said to them. Anxiety in the practitioner increases *defensiveness* and the propensity to misinterpret statements and the tendency to find unintended threats and challenges increases.

Supportive encouragement from the practitioner, on the other hand, with the use of gestures and expressions of encouragement, can help reduce anxiety and lead the way to a more open form of conversation. Such encouragement indicates to the speaker that they are being listened to and that what they say is being valued. The more space they are given to talk, in an encouraging way, the more they are likely to take up the invitation to explore what they think and feel.

Mismanagement. All relationships are open to mismanagement through neglect, oversight or deliberate exploitation of one party by the other – another aspect of the issue of trust. The client may use the time to circle around the issue or deliberately obfuscate matters. The practitioner may seek the opportunity to convey their own views to the client. They may seek to impress the client with their own display of skills rather than help the client get where they need to be.

Defensiveness. Most communications and interactions that go on in the world are used to influence an individual or an outcome. In such cases, it is highly likely that those involved will become defensive. This may make it difficult for individuals to hear accurately what is being said. Deliberate attempts to coerce, exploit or manipulate the other are likely to be counter-productive in the long run and usually lead to deterioration in the quality of the relationship, whatever its purpose. Even with goodwill on both sides, successful communication cannot be guaranteed.

Assumptions and prejudices. It is also worth reminding ourselves that we all experience the world differently and our concepts of things rarely match exactly those of anyone else. This leads to some of the most common difficulties when listening because we assume that the speaker's meanings match the ones we have. Almost certainly this will not be so: their own personal experience of events (the major influence upon the development of their frame of reference[37]) will almost certainly have given them a different shade of meaning from that which we possess.

How we feel about and look upon what we are being told affect profoundly how we respond to it. What we decide is important and what we choose to screen out and overlook influence the way we feel about what happens to us. Being aware of our own *prejudices* can help us to listen better, but strongly held attitudes have a pervasive effect upon how we respond.

Attitudes and expectations. These effect the judgements we are prepared to make about others, often on the basis of relatively little information. The attitudes and expectations that accompany us as we meet new experiences derive from our past. We attempt to integrate new events into our existing outlook. When we discover that we cannot accommodate some event or experience into our familiar world-view it generates conflict and internal stress (the term often used is 'cognitive dissonance'). The resulting tension means we either have to modify our existing assumptions because the evidence is overwhelming, or deny the evidence and discount its value. (We minimise the information: 'Smoking kills people, but not me, or not yet', or 'I will quit one day'.)

We make our judgements based partly on socio-cultural influences and partly on personal experiences. So, for example, in European societies it is disrespectful for children not to look into the eyes of their elders when being chastised but it is the exact reverse in some cultures.

The attitudes we hold operate largely out of conscious awareness throughout our daily life and any attempts to question our basic assumptions tend to be met with rejection and even hostility. Fox-hunters, as we have seen recently, are not likely to be persuaded by the arguments of their opponents, nor are those in favour of banning fox hunting much open to discussion either.

---

[37] This term means the composite of ideas, beliefs, feelings and impressions that give the person their own unique internal world.

Attitudes and expectations are not frozen, however. They are, as we've observed, influenced and modified by the day-to-day experiences that invite us to review, amend and revise what we understand. We meet individuals, have encounters with new situations and come into contact with other groups. All these influences help us to reconsider how we believe things to be and how we believe things *need* to be.

When it comes to being influenced, it is important how we assess the person to whom we pay attention. The degree of respect or liking is likely to determine just how far we are prepared to consider adopting their views and how far we are willing to accept new views and integrate them with our existing assumptions.

Evaluation and interpretation. All of us tend to evaluate what we hear far too soon and, once we have made our evaluation, it takes us a long time to give it up. We are all too often listening with a view to, 'What is this worth?' 'What does this mean?' 'So what, but how does…?' We are working on the information we are being given rather than attempting simply to receive it and sense its impact. We need to sense, first of all, its impact for the person sending the information and the meaning it has for them, before sensing its meaning for ourselves.

It is very difficult not to evaluate what we hear because we listen for some reason and that provides a screen. However, the motive we think we have for listening and the way we actually listen are often far apart. If we really do want to help someone, then listening for longer and deeper might well get us nearer the heart of the matter, rather than continually asking questions and raising issues that we believe might have something to do with the essence of things.

Aspects of Disclosure
All language is selective – a reduction of particulars of experience into a representation that is then further diluted by being put into words. It is not possible to convey the experience itself, only a part of it, and the principal ways in which language operates in and of itself create many of the difficulties we find in miscommunication.

In order to tell you about what I did last night I will inevitably leave out some details (*deletion*). I will emphasise some aspects of the experience over others (*distortion*) and I will give you some portion of what took place as a summary in terms of what it meant to me (*generalisation*). As a result, you may believe you have an idea of what I did but it may be a long way from what actually took place. These three processes are critical for affecting how people think about their experience and how they talk about it.

Deletion. Aspects of experience are omitted from the representation offered. It is both necessary (to limit the information being offered) and impoverishing (because we leave out vital cues without realising it). It saves us being overwhelmed with data but only at the expense of losing key elements.

Distortion. We exaggerate, often without intending to, the way things occur. We note features as significant to ourselves but which may not be 'read' the same way by anyone else present and which may be relatively insignificant to the purpose for the narration. We can distort the sense of time or the value of aspects of what took place and even what we do to make it 'fit' our perspective. In addition, we can make deliberate shifts in our experience by inventing elements that are not there or were never there.

Generalisation. We come to allow one element in our model of the world to represent an entire category of which it is merely one example. We all have an enormous number of 'operating assumptions' that enable us to function in the world without having always to think about what we are doing. We drive based on generalisations about what other road users will do and the 'rules of the road'. In the same way, we have our own personal rules about where things 'should' be placed, what kinds of actions should follow others, and so on.

Without realising it, we live in a very well-defined map that we only recognise when something deeply at odds with our expectations begins to happen and highlights the assumptions we have about how things 'ought' to be. Generalisations allow us to operate more efficiently across contexts. They allow us to distinguish the *'deep structure'* from the *'surface structure'*. This is similar, for example, to how we open a door but sometimes fool ourselves – when it opens the 'wrong way' and we look foolish.

A key element of effective communication lies in developing the skills to recover what is missing, what is exaggerated (one way or another) and what actually took place, rather than being satisfied with a phrase like 'it was a very satisfying meal'. (Satisfying because of the food, the wine, the place, the people, or all of them?) Recovery of the specific content of what took place often lies at the centre of effective agreements about what needs to happen.

Chapter 16
Between Listening & Responding

Just as there is a great deal more to listening than simply hearing what is said, so too there is a great deal more to communicating than speaking. As we will see, responses that may fit the day-to-day conversation in ordinary life are not suitable as the considered response to someone in search of assistance in any context.[38] It is one thing to over-talk as someone is speaking, change the subject, offer an opinion or simply direct the conversation away from the speaker's topic in the office, over a drink, or sitting in the relaxed atmosphere of the living room, but it is clearly not helpful when offered as a reply to someone in difficulty and seeking some response that connects to their concerns.

The Space Between

There is, then, a space between simply hearing what is said and knowing what to do about it. That space, as we began to describe in the previous chapter, is the *space of refraining from,* of suspending our usual ways of conducting ourselves in favour of … what?

If we are busy 'not doing', how does that help? If we are not intervening then what use are we going to be? These are often the kinds of concerns that begin to surface once practitioners face not being able to do what they usually do or what they think the role requires of them. But, as someone famously said (I don't know who), 'well-meaning good intentions don't get you very far in helping without some effective skills'. Just about all practitioners are well-meaning and well-intentioned – in theory. On the day, given the wrong kind of client, we can all lose our impressive tolerance for humanity, excuse ourselves and 'blame the client' for promoting a reaction that actually has no useful place in the array of helpful responses.

This is also something we have already touched on throughout this book. There is a gap between the 'avowed' motives of the practitioner and the 'unavowed' motives that accompany the performance. Our conscious and deliberate reasons for being in practice have to be balanced by those other influences that affect how successfully we are able to work on the client's behalf for whatever reason.

If we are busy 'not doing' then what is the client experiencing about us? The absence of action is often linked to inactivity, stasis, non-involvement. However, when we are not behaving outwardly, it does not mean we are not actively engaged. But how will the client know?

If, as a practitioner, I identify how effective I am by the degree to which I demonstrate how helpful I am, then by 'just' sitting listening I well may feel like I am 'doing nothing'. It isn't though. When a parent sees their child performing their first Christmas play, they

---

[38] This is something organisations are increasingly learning to give attention to, as indicated by the training offered to staff in customer care (not always very successfully).

aren't doing a lot but they certainly show a lot by their expression! When friends meet after a period apart they may not demonstrate their affection audibly, but it will be apparent on their faces. When someone fails their driving test, for example, they may say little but their appearance will speak volumes. In other words, when two people are engaged in important communication, it shows.

In these signs and indications lies part of the key to 'not doing'. When someone is not busy with their own performance, concentrating on what they should be doing or finding an opportunity to demonstrate how well they have listened, it leaves a great deal more time simply to enter into the space of the other person's story. That space will lead to a greater *appreciation* of the other person's circumstances and conflicts. It will also ensure there is more space for a much deeper understanding of how it feels for them to be in the difficulties they are describing than is possible when listening at the surface level of description.

The Space Within

We hear with our ears but there is much more to listening than hearing, as we have already explored. Before we respond with any kind of skilled intervention we need to open up that other space inside us, which, however linked to the ears, is actually more to do with the heart. 'Openness to the other', 'willingness to enter into their experience' and phrases of this kind, all attempt to convey the experience of feeling secure enough in one's own reality to be able to journey from it temporarily and learn how it is in someone else's. Such phrases suggest and convey that quality of willing suspension of one's own concerns to be available to sense and resonate with the concerns of someone else. We may talk of it as a certain 'fellow-feeling' or 'emotional resonance'. It means that we are 'attuned' to more than the simple meaning – the content of what we are being told – and are willing to enter in to the complexities of the internal experience of the other.

Writers as diverse as John Heron and Zygmunt Bauman note that the essential basis of the human community is, in the end, this important over-riding connection of feeling (not emotion); the ability we have to have an all-encompassing openness of sensing the situation of the other that is above and beyond language.

For Heron, feeling is the "participatory form" of our being in the world. It is that which "interrelates us with the network of beings". Like sentience, it is a universal aspect of the human condition and one that extends beyond the human. This sense of feeling is different from emotion. Feeling is what enables the mother to grasp the fact that the child is in distress in the other room without hearing a sound. Feeling is what makes the mother cow bellow in grief for the lost calf. Feeling is what ensures the geese fly in 'V' formation and have their own forms of caring patrols when one of their number falls behind. Emotion, on the other hand, is the individual expression, the distinctive manifestation of the "feeling sense". It may be theatrical, limited, controlled, inappropriate. We assess emotions and adjudicate how appropriate the emotion is to the situation (the felt sense of event) rather than the personal significance we are expressing in our distress or elation.

Feeling, then, is not the same thing as emotion but it is very much linked to it. It is important in developing our connection with others that we don't simply attempt to feel the emotions they are feeling but 'feel' the 'weight of the experience' they are describing or expressing. All this is very difficult to describe and just as hard to do because we are divesting ourselves of the luxury of the emotional content of our own situation, letting go of any consideration of 'how we would respond in the speaker's situation', and even of how the speaker is responding to their situation. Yet we are acknowledging that we are strenuously attempting to sense where the other is in their feeling about the events that the emotions express.

We might be helped by thinking that emoting links to an individual's needs and the assessment of the likelihood of those needs being met; they relate to fulfilment, inhibition, threat or frustration.

The Core Conditions of Effective Helping

The less self-preoccupied the listener is, the more *genuine* their presence. The less they need the client to recognise them or to validate their status, the more 'real' their presence will be. In counselling these attributes are termed the *core conditions* of effective helping. They are not skills. They aren't separate responses: they are a way of 'holding oneself' that gives a steady and open regard to the unfolding story the client offers. Developing these attributes is something all practitioners can do to a degree but how far they develop these attributes is, in large measure, dependent upon their commitment to deepen their willingness to engage with the world of the other.

There is an abundance of research evidence, which goes back a long way, that most of us want these three major ingredients to be present in the practitioner's stance to us. In simple and direct terms Truax and Carkhuff (1967) described these core conditions as:

Respect (Acceptance). Respect for individuals in their own right as they struggle with their dilemmas and difficulties. This is often termed 'unconditional positive regard'. This represents the practitioner's communication of their willingness to accept and respect the client.

Genuineness (Authenticity). Genuineness represents the practitioner's willingness to meet the client halfway and the successful avoidance of posturing with the client, playing a role, or erecting a facade or barrier between themselves and their client.

Empathy (Warmth). Empathy represents the practitioner's successful attempts to comprehend their client's thoughts and feelings in the way in which the client comprehends them – and to communicate that comprehension.

It is not sufficient for the practitioner to possess these qualities; they have to be able to communicate them and communicate them effectively to the client. These conditions are expressed through the skills and behaviours *demonstrated* by the practitioner.

This aspect of the helping relationship is often called *rapport*. It includes a readiness on the part of the practitioner to work at the client's pace, to start from the client's position and to attempt to understand the circumstances as experienced by the client. Rapport is about understanding and not about liking. People do not have to like one another to be in rapport, nor do they have to agree: they have to be in a *working alliance* aiming for a commonly understood goal.

It's nigh on superfluous to repeat once more, following all that has been said, that the more the practitioner appears to offer these conditions but is insincere, the more likely the client is to play games too. On the other hand, of course, the more the practitioner offers those qualities, the more likely it is that the client will find themselves willing to trust the relationship as being safe enough for…

The importance of the core conditions, or essential elements, of any helping relationship cannot be overestimated. No amount of skill, for example, can make up for a lack of interest in the client. No one, however competent, can engage in a real meeting if they are simply too exhausted, or find that they cannot release a willingness to enter into the client's reality. The more the practitioner reflects upon and learns about their own relationship to the core conditions, the deeper their response is likely to become. Development opportunities and skills practice are vital components of the preparation of all helping practitioners, but there comes a point when a deeper exploration and investigation into the complexities of our individual relationship to these essential conditions are needed and not simply more practice.

The process of such an exploration raises certain questions:

- How are we developing our human openness to the other?
- How far are we seeking to find the places of movement and change within ourselves?
- How far are we willing to investigate the reality of our own experience in the way we explore that of the client?

Almost any helping relationship one can think of will be more effective the more the individual offering the help is able to establish a sound relationship, based on a sufficient level of *trust*, with the person they are helping. The issue of trust is paramount in all but the most superficial of helping relationships. It is not sufficient for the practitioner to know what they are doing; they have to communicate they know how to manage the concerns, the anxieties and the fears that arise for the person being helped, in a way that is more than simply being courteous and which goes beyond a purely professional manner.

The more help remains at the advisory end of the spectrum – the repair man, the person being hired to decorate, the solicitor being consulted and so on – the more the matter of trust is based on competence to produce the result required, in the time agreed, for the price negotiated. The more personal the matter and the more it concerns personal disclosure, the greater the level of trust required.

If I need to tell you things about what has happened in the past for you to help me at all, then, of course, I won't do that until I have confidence that you will not judge me, or laugh at me, or make light of my difficulties, for example.

The gaining of trust may be the most significant aspect of the helping relationship itself – especially for someone who has learned through bitter experience that other people can take advantage of their vulnerability. Asylum seekers, for example, may be amongst such people. Not knowing who to trust or what the implications may be of any disclosure they offer, they may prefer no help to risking exploitation of the kind many of them have already experienced.

Respect (Acceptance)

In order for anyone to enter fully into their dilemma or their difficulty, to share their problem or outline their concerns, they have to come to feel that they themselves are not going to be judged as failures. To admit failings is one thing but many of us believe we are a failure if … happens. As a result, many people 'project' onto the practitioner the belief that they aren't going to be accepted by the person in whom they are about to confide.

Respect is the term used to convey the quality of non-judgemental acceptance offered by the practitioner to the other person. It is the quality of expressing a genuine regard for others and a warm dispassionate interest in what they are attempting to disclose and understand. It is a non-threatening, non-evaluating acknowledgement of the reality and integrity of *the client as a person*. It needs to be carefully distinguished from a dependent wish to be nice to people or to make excuses for people. It is a realistic, not a sentimental, posture. Rogers (1961) uses the term 'unconditional positive regard' to convey his understanding of this essential component of the helping relationship. It means holding to the belief that the client has the potential to move beyond their current difficulties in a positive and life enhancing way. Rogers explains:

> "It means there are no conditions of acceptance, no feelings of, I like you only if you are thus and so."

It is all very well not holding the person in judgement for who they are and keeping that separate from what they have done, but all practitioners quickly realise that some of the acts people perform do actually express who they are in a fairly decisive way and that withholding a judgement is a far from easy matter. Additionally, some of the things people do 'press our buttons' i.e. inflame our own emotional responses because we have unacknowledged or unworked-out 'material'[39] relating to the action, the topic, or some aspect of the situation.

Our judgements are part of what holds our world together and our security, such as it is, intact. It takes mature individuals to allow other, very divergent views to be

---

[39] Material is a common term to indicate that we all have psychological and emotional garbage that erupts or appears from time to time and needs attention. Material is a handy term to mean anything of this kind.

expressed and to view with equanimity the right of another to act in potentially hostile and damaging ways to the values we ourselves hold, whilst still listening attentively and with respect! The nearer the perceived threats are to my security, the easier it will be for me to lose my detachment and get carried away in struggling not to judge.

For the practitioner, it may be difficult to suspend judgement enough to allow the client to be in their difficulties and the more tainted by judgement the practitioner's response, the more controlled will be the response of the client. In the end, I may be using so much energy refraining from letting my disapproval or fear show that I cannot really be with you at all. Such a situation is more likely when I have done little to develop my understanding of how my judgements and beliefs influence me before you come along and 'press my buttons'.

This is an important reason for practitioners having a place to work on the issues that reduce their capacity to offer free, undivided attention to others. In the end, most judgements are self-protective. Reflection and self-disclosure with others (with peers or in supervision) help dissolve judgements with insight and greater understanding. Learning what my judgements are and where they come from doesn't somehow abolish them, but it does give me some inkling of the way in which they can undermine the clarity of my helping – of my being able to be there with you.

This is not to suggest that I will have no discernment but that I will be more able to separate judgement, which is condemnatory, from distinction, which is discriminatory. Many would-be practitioners somehow assume it is important to erase all trace of value judgements from their work – not that it is possible – and then adopt some anodyne version of the current politically correct code. 'Realness' is important in helping. And realness here means recognising that the person who has sought your help does not provide you with a free opportunity to run your own ideology over them. Discovering that you find something the client says is not to your taste simply indicates you have some remedial work to do on how come it gets in your way.

There are times when it is clear that the client wants some indication of where you stand on a matter they have been disclosing. It is often in the asides, the small comments at the close of a session, or as the client leaves, where I might let them know how I really stand on issues that I have been attending to with detachment through the session. Sometimes it may be important to indicate to the client openly, 'I have a position on this and you may need to know so that it doesn't get in our way'. If a practitioner offers their view or stance at the request of the client, the client is then free to set it aside or adopt it, knowing where it has come from.

More insidious are the judgements that we collude in together, that we both understand we actually share and hold by being in this same space together but never openly identify or confront. These may be judgements to do with the practitioner being 'on the client's side', feeling empathic towards the client's distress, or accepting the current myths of the day for our social group, gender, class or race. These kinds of judgements are there because the dividing line between discrimination – essential in any development of awareness – and judgement is itself a difficult 'judgement' to make.

The distinction between discernment and judgement is that discernment is about having a relatively uninvested way of assessing a situation or a set of circumstances, whereas a judgement is an invested part of a person's world-view. A problem for the practitioner is in the effort they make to be open, tolerant and free of any judgement. The danger here is of reaching a place where the belief is: *if all things are equally important then nothing is*. It is not that all things are equally unimportant; it is that the practitioner needs to be able to hear how the client understands their own actions/beliefs and so on, rather than to feel obliged to analyse, interpret, excuse or condemn the client.

Enabling the client to find meaning and value between experiences and within them is an exercise in helping someone to make informed judgements. Most of us are subject to being influenced by the uncritical adoption of attitudes from our background, or the counter-dependent rebelliousness that comes from the same source. The practitioner cannot enable their clients to find their meaning unless the practitioner has some inkling of the process themselves.

Egan (1975) also stresses the importance of regarding each client as unique – another element in the quality of *respect* – and says that although the practitioner is committed to helping the client change, this does not mean that they are determined to make the client over in their own image and likeness. This may mean that a client ultimately will choose a course different from the one the practitioner would choose for them. Or a client may choose one that the practitioner thinks is less than the most effective available to the client. But the practitioner, if free, will unequivocally respect such choices. Respect for others forms part of the underlying core of beliefs that the effective practitioner holds. In this sense, it is not something simply acquired once and for all, but something to be striven for and developed both as a belief and as a communicated act toward those with whom the practitioner works.

Essentially, respect means recognising the separation between the client and yourself, between the client's world and your world, and having the equanimity for your own world to be unthreatened by what someone may say in time spent exploring concerns that are theirs.

Genuineness (Authenticity)

"It indicates an openness in dealing with others and behaviour that is truly reflective of the core of the being." Pietrofesa, 1978.

This is a complex aspect of relationships. In each exchange there is what we believe, what others see, and the gap between them that needs to be explored. Genuineness is about *risking being real*. Genuineness itself is not necessarily beneficial or therapeutic but without it the therapeutic process is unlikely to get very far. Genuineness is an easier term than *authenticity*. Some examples might help to distinguish these elements.

I have met a number of people who are *genuine and inauthentic*. They were genuinely inauthentic and they exploited that ambiguity very well. Confidence tricksters depend upon it: that we will be taken in by their pose and that we will believe that they are what they sincerely are not! They know they are being inauthentic in that they have very strong ulterior motives for wanting us to believe them. They are taking responsibility for their deception of others.

Then there is being non-genuine but *authentic and real*. This would be someone who is so compulsively conventional that their only response is to do what is expected and not to have genuineness about a personal response. This is the person who is unaware of how out of touch they are with their own inner reality. They are sincere but from a place of absence of self-knowledge.

People can be *genuine and authentic but unreal*. In this case, people are not pretending to others and not pretending to themselves. These are people who are in touch with themselves but who avoid disclosure. They restrict how much they reveal of themselves to others. It is the resulting lack of depth that makes them seem unreal.

Much counterfeit genuineness can be found in helping relationships where the practitioner and the client sometimes begin to form a way of acting together that is genuinely intended but patently unreal and insincere. The effort to be real in the encounter does not seem to me to be anything like so hard as the effort required to 'be there'.

It is not hard to be real when I am attending to someone else's story, or witnessing their hurt, or their delight, but to be fully there – that is always in doubt, a project always requiring more. To be real in how the practitioner meets the client cannot happen unless the practitioner is real to themselves. However, it is possible to be real and not be present to yourself. For example, when I show anger, I may become lost in my anger. In such a case, the reaction is real but I am not very present since the emotion is so strong. There are no simple formulas. It is about integrity, presence, realness, authenticity and sincerity, and not getting hooked by any one of them.

If the client thinks you are hiding behind a role, what encouragement does that provide for them to take risks? Genuineness is therefore about being at ease and at one with oneself in the helping relationship, and not employing facades or deploying pretences. Other terms often used in this respect are *congruence, transparency or internal consistency*. Congruence lies in the balance between the practitioner's usual sense of self and how they appear to be to the client: in allowing themselves to be known as real and authentic people.

People are not internally consistent in real life, not even skilled and experienced practitioners; life brings difficulties and dilemmas, choices and conflicts, which create internal tension. What is indicated here is not that the practitioner is beyond such human struggles of their own but that, in relationship to their helping, they are not at odds with what they are doing, in conflict with the organisation they work for, or finding the client so difficult to work with that they can't wait for the session to end and are somehow trying to 'see it through'.

Genuineness is also linked to the capacity for *appropriate self-disclosure*. The willingness of the practitioner to display and take responsibility for their own life, for their personal values, ideals, feelings and experiences, and their own integrity as a practitioner, is related to their ability to be both *spontaneous and self-controlled at the same time*. Spontaneity here means behaving freely, without constraint, rather than acting impulsively. When offered appropriately, such behaviour has the effect of offering a model of disclosure to the client that indicates that risks can be taken without exploitation, loss of self-acceptance or dismissal being the result.

These qualities require a certain level of maturity and genuine non-defensiveness in the timing of their expression, or they may be in danger of being seen as little more than the outpourings of the practitioner's own unresolved difficulties. Such revelations, however well meant, would give no therapeutic encouragement and would be likely to close down the client from talking usefully. Jourard (1968) writes:

> "If the counsellor spontaneously and honestly conveys his thoughts and reactions, I believe they are not only communicating his concern but they are in effect both eliciting and reinforcing kindred uncontrived behaviour."

It is clear, too, that the practitioner may need to talk about their own feelings, after all, isn't this exactly what they are encouraging their clients to do!

> "Certainly the aim is not for the therapist to express or talk about his own feelings, but primarily that he should not be deceiving the client as to himself. At times he may need to talk about some of his own feelings (either to the client, or to a colleague or superior) if they are standing in the way." Rogers, 1961.

Combs (1969) writes about this element of the helping role:

> "We suggest the major problem of poor practitioners is the fact that their methods are inauthentic, that they tend to be put on, contrived."

Paraphrasing what Combs goes on to say; the methods can only be utilised so long as the practitioner keeps their mind on them. That, of course, is likely to be disastrous on two counts. In the first place, it separates them from the client and the message conveyed is likely to be that they are not with it, are not really interested and are phoney. Second, it is almost never possible to maintain attention on the right method for very long. As a consequence, the poor practitioner relapses frequently into what they believe their previous experience has taught them. So the method they are trying to use fails, because of the tenuous, interrupted character of their use of it.

This is the dilemma of all preparation. You cannot learn without going through the stage of thinking about doing something that would be better done if only you had internalised it — but you haven't yet. The time of preparation for a helping role is an important place for sharing these issues and thus developing flair and style rather than a wooden professional persona.

To be fully there, to be engaged and to 'be with' the client is a huge undertaking, or so it seems to me. Without the determination to make the effort to be there, much that I would otherwise bring to the relationship is unnecessary or conditional. The desire to be there as fully as I might be, if it is to figure in my work at all, will take precedence, because if I am doing anything less, or anything other, then I am not committed to offering my authentic presence. Developing a professional persona is a sure way to make the struggle to work out the contribution of authenticity in the relationships with which I am involved less and less central to the enterprise. A professional persona offers a way of holding to the importance of boundaries, yet the core conditions are only useful if the practitioner does not adopt a professional persona as soon as they enter the room. In many ways, Rogers' impulse has been betrayed; his core conditions were for anywhere, not simply when entering a room and stepping into a 'role'.

Inauthenticity is unhealthy and removes people from experiencing themselves truly. Inauthentic behaviour makes it very difficult to know what's going on in situations for two reasons. Firstly, it is likely to be assumed that everyone else is as inauthentic as you are, therefore making any accurate interpretation impossible. Secondly, it is difficult to make even tentative assessments of atmosphere and dynamics if you are out of touch with the instrument you rely upon, i.e. yourself.

Authentic behaviour encourages others to take risks and offers a model of how it might be done. In summary, there are five key elements that relate to genuineness and authenticity:

1. Self-concealing takes time and energy away from the opportunity of full relationship with others.

2. Techniques are almost always less important than the ability to experience and convey genuineness to the client.

3. Authentic behaviour encourages others and models how it might be attempted.

4. Genuineness indicates being at home with oneself, an important quality for anyone helping others move towards the same sense of unity with themselves.

5. Spontaneity and self-disclosure are indicators of genuineness.

Empathy (Warmth)
Fielder's work (1950), supported by other research since, indicated that it was the quality of empathy communicated to and experienced by the client which had most influence in promoting positive change for the client, irrespective of the particular

theoretical orientation offered by the practitioner. It is not only important that the practitioner makes every effort to understand what the client is saying, but also that the practitioner communicates that understanding effectively, so *that the client feels understood*. This is the area of helping covered by the word empathy.

Empathy is perhaps the easiest of the three core conditions for the practitioner to embrace. It may not be easy to do well, especially when the practitioner comes to know more and more about the nuances and the subtleties of the other's experience that are overlooked, ignored or misinterpreted by every reflection and paraphrase. However, the simultaneous commitment to 'get out of the way' and to 'be there', and also to let the client find out for themselves is something most practitioners take to with little philosophical difficulty once it has been grasped experientially. Helping the client to live their own life rather demands it.

Empathy is the ability to listen and understand other people's experiences in a way that is as close as possible to how they themselves experience it. Clearly you cannot experience what the client experiences, since they are talking about something which has already happened. You can, however, begin to build a sense of their experience and what it is like for them to have experienced what they describe, rather than wonder what you might have felt if the same thing had happened to you. In the latter event we are only finding a response that *identifies with* the client and what they have to say, and is very different from attempting to *construct* a sense of the client's frame of reference. Being able to communicate that you are making the effort to do this encourages the client to begin to feel understood and therefore contributes to the likelihood of their sharing more of what concerns them.

> "What man needs more than anything else to be healthy is a sense of meaning. Meaningfulness is defined as passing through a number of phases which, related one to the other, become the frame of reference for whatever happens in your life." Rudhyar, in Arroyo, 1975.

Empathy ranges from simply understanding the content of what someone says through to a deep 'I-Thou' communication. A *working alliance*, however, must be formed for anything productive to be possible. An elementary level of empathy is the capacity to reflect back the essence of the content of what the client has described. *But the more the practitioner can reflect the emotional complexities and the hidden 'music' behind what is described, the deeper the level of empathy achieved.*

Everyone experiences the world differently and builds up an individual frame of reference. By suspending their own frame of reference and attempting to get inside the client's frame of reference, the practitioner can begin to gain a sense of the way each client's world is organised and how different facets of experience link together to make up an individual's *world-view*. In order to build an *empathic response*, the practitioner needs to attend carefully to the variety of cues the client offers, especially the non-verbal ones. To devote such detailed attention to the other person, the practitioner must be free from internal preoccupations and concerns of their own, external distractions, or any defensiveness or over-protectiveness towards the client.

It does seem from studies, even as long ago as Carkhuff (1971), that people from similar backgrounds are more likely to be empathic to one another than people from widely different backgrounds. Carkhuff found that those from similar ethnic backgrounds had more empathy than those from different ethnic backgrounds and so on. This might be especially the case on occasions when the practitioner is using their own experience of what a situation is like to guide them toward understanding the effect it has upon the client. The danger of such use of self is that it can be wide of the mark! Another quasi-empathic response is to offer a normative response, i.e. to offer a reaction that would be typical of most people in that situation. The danger in this situation lies in generalising that what most people might feel, this person actually does feel.

Such quasi-empathic responses are often offered because they are the nearest the practitioner can get to the experiences of the client. They are offered as better than nothing but they are far from experiencing the world through the client's frame of reference. And sometimes it is useful to share just that, 'I have no reference for what that might be like, but I am doing what I can to sense what that might be like for you.'

This theory is also used to claim, for example, that only women should counsel women or that only those that have been abused know enough to help others in a similar position. Whilst there is some evidence to support this, it also seems that it is only true for some clients. There are people who deliberately look for practitioners who are quite different from themselves, because they want someone who is in no danger of using their own experience as a guide for determining what they, as clients, are actually feeling about *their own* situation.

> A pregnant woman deliberately chose a male practitioner to help her work out the birth plan she wanted for her baby: a man, at that, who had little expertise in the world of childbirth and midwifery. It was deliberate on her part. She wanted to ensure that there was no chance of him using his own experience of what had happened to him to contaminate his ability simply to be there and let her work out what she herself wanted. This was a skilled client, but not an experienced one: *someone who had thought of who would be most useful for her to work out the questions that were important to her at that stage.*

A real empathic response, therefore, is one in which the practitioner attempts to help explore the client's understanding rather than the practitioner offering suggestions and advice. *It is usually part of the clarifying stage of the helping relationship but it must be available throughout.* The practitioner is not therefore 'taking on' or 'taking over' the client's problems in order to solve them. The practitioner is outside the dilemmas that the client experiences, and knows it, *but they are inside the understandings.* The practitioner attempts to stay with the pace and to resonate with the emotional tone of the client. In this way they encourage what is available to emerge but don't attempt to drag it forth. It is clear that any suggestion of judgement or evaluation by the practitioner at this stage will undermine the level of empathy achieved.

Empathic responses place a value on the person and give recognition that the individual in difficulty is worthy of care and attention. They help the individual to experience themselves more deeply and therefore more completely. To give this kind of *permission* can have a swift and liberating effect. To encourage, for example, a bereaved relative to find, experience and express the accompanying anger at the loss of a loved one, as well as the sadness and longing, can provide an important realisation that such feelings are part of the total process of grieving, though a part that is often overlooked. The following are indicators of empathy:

- Being attentive, physically and mentally, to what is happening.
- Listening carefully and noting the key words.
- Responding encouragingly to these core messages and being willing to move in new ways if indicated.
- Being flexible. If what you are doing is not working, try something else.
- Giving permission for the emotional tone to find expression as well as the content.
- Looking carefully for cues that you are on target: be aware of signs that you are not and be prepared to change. It is not the client that is resistant[40], but the practitioner who is not effective in finding the right strategy.

Empathic Divining

"Empathic divining is when someone says something that 'has an implicit feeling, or intention, which is lurking between the lines and which is expressed', you divine this unstated content and put it back." J. Heron, 1977.

Heron goes on to describe ways in which this can be implemented. If someone says, in a certain context and with a certain tone and inflection, 'I can't say any more', then the listener may say, 'You sound as though you are quite frightened'. You are divining the speaker's attitude of mind that is just below the surface of what is being said and that is affecting how it is being said. It may be a belief or an intention, or some mixture of these. This will be picked up mainly – within a given context – from the form of words, the tone of voice, aided perhaps by facial and other bodily cues. The listener must express it always as a statement, never as a question, with an opening such as, 'It sounds/seems as though you...'

"This intervention often needs a little practice before people get it right. It is a very precise test of empathy. The key to success is only to reflect what is actually emerging between the lines. Sometimes you put back something that goes way down below any lurking and this throws the speaker in too deep too soon. Sometimes listeners actually divine their own projected agenda." J. Heron, *ibid.*

Empathic divining can also be used with confronting intent and effect; to raise consciousness in people about some emerging attitude they are defensively trying not to acknowledge. It may also be used with cathartic effect; bringing the distress further up toward the surface or even into discharge.

---

[40] There are stages in the work when the client becomes irritated with themselves, disappointed at progress, or any number of reactions that make them appear resistant. This needs to be distinguished from the client who really does not want to be helped. Of course, on the surface in the early stages, it might be difficult to tell the difference. Good contracting skills help enormously.

Chapter 17
The Importance of Rapport

Rapport is a pervasive requirement in the development of any helping relationship — long or short-term. Only if the practitioner is willing to demonstrate their interest in the client is the client likely to gain any sense that they matter enough to warrant the attention they need. No matter how interested the practitioner is, if they fail to communicate that interest or are too reticent in their response, the client will not experience the strength of presence they need if they are to bring forth the kind of issues that they may well seek to voice.

Rapport runs throughout the whole of the helping relationship and is separated here to emphasise that so many of the key elements are crucial at the beginning of a relationship, yet they are equally important throughout it. If it is true that you can't get far without it, you certainly can't get started without it. So whilst the emphasis upon rapport is placed at the outset and in the formative stages of the relationship, it is not to be left there, as something needed only for a time.

Rapport comes out of the awareness of the need for and the provision of the core conditions by the practitioner. Some people can recognise the importance of the core conditions yet they are unable to communicate them to their clients. Communicating the warmth of interest is essential — it is important that the client is aware of the practitioner making the effort to develop understanding, offering respect, empathy and genuineness.

Real interest ensures that people lean towards one another rather than sit at a distance. Real interest is indicated by mirroring of key body postures and gestures, and is noticeable by the alignment of vocabulary and linguistic expressions that individuals use. However, the more preoccupied I am with my own performance and whether I am really listening, the less I can truly attend to you. This is one good reason for practising the skills of rapport in training rather than on real clients, who may find you so busy trying to be 'there' for them that you are practically the star performer of the show.

Rapport truly is the key to any effective relationship; if you haven't got rapport you haven't anything worth having. You may be talking and the other person may be responding but without real rapport it will only pass the time. Rapport is the surrounding atmosphere in which the task is attempted, or the 'emotional glue' that keeps the two parties in communication together. At its best, rapport is illustrating your capacity to be with the client: it is putting empathy into practice. At its worst, it is a cynical experience of a set of skills that are designed to convince both the practitioner and the client that they are really engaged in something real. When this occurs, such unreal rapport can be collusive, deluded and illusory.

Practitioner Role

Successful rapport relies on two important considerations with regard to the willingness on the part of the practitioner to:

- Begin their conversation at a suitable place that is near to the major purpose of their meeting i.e. somewhere close to the topic at hand.
- Move at a pace that does not upset or put the client off, thereby making it more difficult for them to respond well.

The practitioner has a crucial role in setting the tone and in creating the context for the client to respond. Any helping activity has to begin somewhere but, if you do not know the client well, there is a danger of starting too close to the subject matter and increasing the client's anxieties. However, if you begin too far away from the topic there is every danger of never getting to it at all, or only when the time available is running out.

There are five major elements relating to how the practitioner presents themselves to the client that will enhance the development of rapport. They are:

1. **Willingness:** a genuine interest in accomplishing a result.

2. **Freedom from distractions:** the ability to give your full attention to the task at hand.

3. **Joining and leading the subject:** the ability to match the client's language, mirror the client's behaviour and pace their belief systems, before moving anywhere else.

4. **Remembering what you are doing:** being flexible enough to respond to the client rather than expecting the client to adapt to you.

5. **Acuity:** having sufficient awareness to both detect and understand the signals the client gives and the responses that they make.

Rapport & Skills

Rapport is all too apparent when it is absent in others, as observing a restaurant full of people will quickly illustrate. Those who are at ease immediately show it; just as those who are having a difficult time illustrate it very clearly too. It is also the case that noting when rapport is absent in others is much easier to detect than being attentive to its disappearance in relationships of our own. And for many people, rapport is so 'intuitive' a thing that the very idea of developing it, or of practising the skills that improve a person's capacities at demonstrating it, is regarded as far too contrived and artificial. Yet the skills we have now were acquired somewhere and somehow. The fact that they were randomly acquired by our travelling through a process called 'life' does not mean they are somehow more valuable than those consciously acquired skills in learning to relate more effectively to others. All skills are artificial until they have been integrated and become second nature, as anyone who has learned to drive knows. The skills used to promote rapport are no different.

Once you are aware that certain ways of using your non-verbal behaviour support what you are hoping to accomplish, then you have a degree of influence over yourself that adds to your likely effectiveness. This may seem manipulative, and of course it is, but it is consciously manipulative in order to be a more effective practitioner.

The ethics of this issue run throughout all forms of interpersonal skills training. If I learn to do something different will it really be sincere? Of course not, if you don't have a commitment to it. But, if your primary intention is to improve the range of skills you can offer to another in order for them to bring about changes in their life, then how can you not take time to consider how you use the skills you already have and assess how effective they are in comparison to others? And, as we all need to remember, the skills we already possess may be far more manipulative than any we are likely to learn consciously. It is how we use what we learn that is the test, not the skills themselves. Finally, these skills are being learned by a lot of people who may not have the same golden intentions as you and, if you are not aware of how they work, you are open to manipulation yourself.

Rapport, the art of creating a working atmosphere that is appropriate to the task and degree of relatedness required, can also be thought of as one of the social graces. So when confused and unhappy individuals need help, meeting someone who can help them settle into themselves effortlessly and begin to talk about what has happened without apparently doing much of anything to ensure it happens is a godsend. Such a person is far more responsive and sensitive than the individual who pours false reassurance over the client, or who becomes fazed at not knowing what to do. The more difficult the situation, the more unfamiliar the client, the more remote the experience being described. the greater the challenge to our capacity to stay in relation with the other person in a way that facilitates their process.

Practice in learning how to read and understand other people's cues and signals is crucial, as is knowing that individuals represent their experience internally in specific ways that may be very different from your own. Assuming that because you visualise events this is the way everyone remembers things can be a costly error to make. As we have already briefly noted, some people remember much more by the auditory dialogue and commentary that accompanies a particular experience, whilst pictures are much less important. This is the realm of NLP – the structure of subjective experience.

More than most approaches, NLP has emphasised the crucial significance of attending to how the other person 'sorts their experience' into categories and elements, and then goes on to create significance and meaning. The practitioner who meets a broad cross-section of clients, or clients in stressful situations, can improve their abilities immeasurably by training in 'acuity drills' (detecting emotional states from clues given off by the person) and by other NLP practices. Because rapport runs throughout any relationship and is especially important in helping relationships, the more confident the individual becomes in their skills at putting the client at ease and managing the transitions of the relationship with elegance and timeliness, the more the client is free to disclose the experience that they need to bring forth. In practice, there is a tension between two elements – putting at ease and getting on with the job.

Shared Understanding & Reality

The central purpose of establishing rapport is to promote a climate of shared understanding, whilst you are able to gather information central to the task that you are there to accomplish. And, of course, you cannot understand the client until you have spent some time listening to them and learning how they come to experience the world in the singular and unique way that they do. The more there is genuine interest in the client's story, the less the practitioner has to worry about the technical aspects of rapport. When the relationship is underway and the practitioner begins to relax, it can soon lead to the realisation that they are no longer on the same wavelength and tracking where they lost it may simply be too intrusive. Rapport requires a continuity of attentiveness.

Learning the art of understanding someone else's world also can mean you can become so good at joining their experience in order to understand them that, if you are not careful, you will become like them for a time. This is not always a good idea, especially if they are depressed or deeply unhappy. Building up a sense of how the other person's world works and what it might feel like to be them in it (always a tentative idea since you are not them and therefore can't 'know' for sure) is an essential aspect of rapport and there are those who forget that the purpose is to learn and end up turning their own state into one like that of the client. You then have two people in the same state and neither is much able to be of help to anyone. It may, however, mean that the client momentarily sees someone in as much distress as they are and start rescuing the poor practitioner who lost the plot! This is an exaggeration to make the point. Rapport does not mean ending up where the client is or being *how* the *client* is but understanding where the client is and 'how it is' from where they are.

In this sense, the whole idea of 'reality' is only a convenient hallucination — it just happens to be the one most of us agree to pretend is how it is and the one that everyone has to go along with. It is wise not be deceived into believing it is *true*. The client has their 'take' on reality and a whole way of experiencing the world that ensures it remains real in the way they know. It is better not to be taken in by it in the way they are or you will end up there too.

Because our 'take' on reality is so pervasive and provides us with a coherent sense of ourselves, others, the world and how things work, we are very committed to maintaining it — even when the rewards it produces are painful and self-defeating. It is literally a self-fulfilling prophecy because it is all we know. This makes it difficult for people to help themselves with some of life's crises because the loops they use to understand the world are the very loops that cause them the problems they are in. In addition, the loops they have are not going to get them out of the problems those very loops create. It needs another process from outside to start to unravel how things are 'wired' together to produce the results they obtain so repetitively and, in that sense, so successfully. As Richard Bandler once observed, "You could think of a client's problems as a major achievement". It is a form of learning that has been very strongly established and runs repetitively.

This accounts for the fact that, when confronted with 'incongruity', people have to distort their experience in order to make it congruent. They exclude a part from consciousness and then it simply is 'not there', or they risk having to amend their world-view and their sense of how 'reality' works. This is another reason why working with serious incongruities (which we all have) is best left for the time when the relationship has got some time and substance behind it. The impact of facing a major incongruity and the revision to my belief system, and self-concept that is likely to result, is something best done in a trusted relationship and not with someone I have just met.

Rapport & the Use of Questions

Often, recovering experience and memories, prompting the client to recall how things fit together or how a sequence of actions took place, is part of relationship work. It is worth remembering that with good rapport skills — matching, pacing and leading — when you have a fragment of someone's experience you can find the rest if you know how to help them build and overlap from the elements that they do possess. Asking questions like, 'Can you recall the last time she said that to you?' when asked in a well paced fashion will invite the client to stop and actually recreate the occasion and the experience by remembering it.

So long as you are open in your interest and gaze, allow the client to 'sort' through their memories and only ask minimal questions when they have 'accessed' the memory, you will find yourself obtaining much richer descriptions of what people are basing their ideas and views upon. When someone 'travels' back to a memory and accesses it strongly, they usually indicate that they are no longer in the 'here and now' in the way they usually are. They defocus their eyes and look a little 'spacey', all indicators that they are sorting their memories and finding the occasion requested.

If, however, such questions are asked hastily and followed by another in quick succession, you get not so much the memory but the stock 'response' about when it must have been. Thinking 'back to a time' (as trying it for yourself will immediately demonstrate) takes a few moments and you can't both be here and there at the same time. Attention shifts and, by knowing how to ask useful questions once the client has accessed a particular experience, you can enable them to learn more about what happened than they ever experienced in the moments when it took place.

People will always attempt to make a communication *mean* something. That is not to say they will make of it what you intend but you can rely on them making something of it. The question about communication is not, '*Is this true?*, but, '*Is this useful?* If the responses you get are not what you want, you could take that as an indication that what you are doing is not working. You then have to be able to alter your behaviour until you get the response you want, i.e. demonstrate behavioural flexibility. You will always get answers to your questions in as much as you have the sensory *acuity* to notice the response. The verbal response is rarely the most important.

Asking someone, for example, how they get up in the morning may or may not get you the 'truth'. It may get you the description of how they did it that morning or the answer that they 'sleep standing up'. But the question elicits a response. So long as the response it gains is one you can work with, you can keep going. This is helpful not only with shy and reluctant individuals who need to be shown a lot of interest before they start to respond more easily, but especially when you are attempting to learn more about how someone understands their world.

If 'getting up in the morning' is a way of asking, 'What is the sequence of events from the moment you achieve consciousness to leaving the house or flat in which you live?', then you need to be much more specific in the questions you ask. 'Getting up in the morning' to many people means 'what is your basic routine' and, since they are not as wide awake as they might be, they are a little hazy on the details. If it is the details you want (and in problem solving it usually is) you need the most accurate account of the steps taken you can get, not the ones people think they employ!

When it comes to getting help, many clients want to do the best they can and they often believe they know the 'real' question you are asking as opposed to the words you are using. Sadly, they are sometimes right. If the client you are trying to help has first to translate what you mean before they can get any help at all, it indicates that the questions you ask leave a lot to be desired! Additionally, they try to give you the kind of answers they think you want rather than the answers that the question invites. So between these two slippage points there is a lot of scope for ambiguity and loss of meaning. Learning the art of asking for the kind of information you really want, rather than what the words bring about, means you have more of a chance of getting it sooner. But, whatever answer your questions bring, it is important to be able to build upon it and move the topic further toward a more useful direction. Rapport, in this sense, is the major responsibility of the practitioner.

Levels of Rapport

Rapport can be considered as having four levels. The third and fourth levels are much more complex and difficult. However, if you can confidently create rapport in depth, the work that you can do with the client will have consequent benefits. Accurately identifying the emotional component of the client's experience requires considerable skill and practice. Not only do you have to assess it accurately, but also you need to offer it in a way that does not leave the client feeling that you have *interpreted* their experience rather than understood it. Most of us want to be understood – desperately – but *few of us want to feel analysed and interpreted.*

The four levels, in order of increasing complexity, are:

1. **Content. Can you tell the client what they have told you?** Can you repeat back what has been said? The practitioner relays back what the client has said in such a way that the client feels understood.

2. **Feeling. Can you reflect the underlying feeling behind the content of what has been said?** Can you assess the feeling 'tone'? The practitioner can convey to the client a sense of understanding of what it is that they feel about what they are saying.

3. Advanced empathy. Can you tell the client what they are hinting at? Can you infer what the client means? Can you offer a suggestion in such a way that indicates to the client that the way is open for them to tell you more of what they might want to say? Can you highlight what might need to be approached? This means taking what the client has said and drawing attention to what has not been described but which is also meant. It is akin to filling in the spaces between the words. If done sensitively, the client not only feels understood but feels understood in a way that they themselves are groping to discover.

4. Projective empathy. Can you take what the client has offered and enter inside it, offering it back in such a way that it indicates to the client what else is related to what has been said? For example, 'you said that the situation was already difficult before you had to face redundancy and that you were feeling pretty bruised by it all. I wonder if, when that happened, there was a sense of being really let down?'

Here the client is not only understood but the practitioner can so closely identify the frame of reference the client is using that they can give other examples of similar situations or of other situations which are congruent to the world-view of the client. The effect is to help the client realise that someone else can begin to understand even what they themselves are not yet able to express confidently and can help them clarify the implications.

When working with a client, it is important for the practitioner to have flexibility, to observe how the empathic level is developing and to maintain the rapport between them. If there are difficulties, it is the practitioner who needs to change.

Chapter 18
Responding

In the last chapter we observed the difference between 'being responsive' and 'responding' i.e. having the ability to be engaged without necessarily making overt demonstrations. When someone stands before a magnificent picture in an art gallery they may be highly responsive but not usually externally. Of course they are, strictly speaking, 'responding' but they are not demonstrating it much.

Similarly, when someone sits down to listen to a favourite piece of music they may or may not respond to it a great deal externally but they will be responsive. The internal capacity to experience wonder, pleasure, mystery, fear, dread, pain and suffering as part of our proximity to events and other people is part of the human condition.

It is hard for us not to be responsive and the argument here is that such responsiveness – being in touch with the instrument that is you, sensing its movements and shifts – is a vital part of being effective in the helping relationship over and above the particular combination of skills the practitioner may have available.

This is an aspect of relating professionally and practically that is often neglected or passed over in the preparation of practitioners and discussions of the helping relationship. In part, this is because it is something so hard to get at and to unearth except through inference and suggestion and, in part, it is also because alone it will not necessarily bring about any change. To share in someone else's situation by imaginative participation may make them feel less alone and even more understood but it will not necessarily suggest a way forward.

Sooner or later the work must begin. And here is the shift. Helping is work; it is paid employment for many and unpaid work for thousands of others, and where work is concerned we need results, measures and improvements; targets have to be met and improvements made. This is no bad thing but it does indicate the way in which 'the work' gets made into 'work'.

What people express, what is demonstrated, is much easier to focus upon and soon it becomes all too easy to assume it is all that is of concern. In passing, we might comment upon this aspect of connection and 'fellow feeling' but, in practice, it is more likely to be the skills and interventions that offer a much more overt and direct aspect of the helping effort – they are certainly much more easily identified. The skills and interventions are often given far greater importance and recognition than such elements as the power of the relationship and the practitioner's understanding of the human condition.

However, beyond a certain point of practice and experience, most practitioners begin to realise it is not more sophistication in the timing or the range of their interventions that has the impact upon helping the client. The impact is much more in their depth of understanding of the situations people experience and in their capacity to know much more of how human beings operate in relation to their issues and concerns that enables 'less to mean more'. In other words, to accomplish that level of practice where an inquiring look or an invitation to say more is enough for a great deal more information to come forth than was ever produced by impressive interventions in the past.

When it comes to interventions, it is, of course, more useful if the interventions are positive and encouraging than simply a contribution to fill up the space vacated by the client who does not know what to say next. And it is far better that the intervention promotes the work rather than stalls or inhibits it altogether. First we look at interventions that are likely to do the latter.

Unhelpful Interventions

There are a number of interventions which do not encourage the client to disclose with any great ease and in fact often bring about the very opposite – put them into retreat. Nevertheless, many practitioners find themselves falling into the trap of using them if they are not vigilant and attentive. Among the most common are:

> **Inappropriately probing.** *Example: 'Why exactly do you feel this way?'* 'Why' questions rarely bring about useful information because they drive the person into justification and rationalisation. It is more useful to ask how something occurs or when or, better still, *what* is the result of it occurring. When someone feels that they are being probed, they usually feel they have something to hide (though they may not know what it is). It raises the spectre of interrogation and being put on the spot rather than being helped.

> It is possible to ask the most challenging of questions with a degree of lightness of touch and the freedom for the client to reject the need to answer. 'You might not want to answer this, but I am wondering just how far you think you did put the knife into your colleague at the meeting.' I am being deliberately absurd here to make the point that the lead in to the question is a lot softer than many probes are.

> **Offering excessive reassurance.** *Example: 'Everything is going to be OK. I'm sure it won't turn out to be as bad as you expect and you'll probably feel better in the morning after a good night's sleep.'* There are numerous objections to such interventions. One is that you cannot possibly know whether any of your predictions are going to come about. Another is that you may not know the full extent of what is causing the upset. More importantly, such interventions almost certainly arise either out of your own unacknowledged distress at seeing someone in difficulty and having to recognise that you have no magic wand with which to help. Or it may well be that you have similar distress about similar issues and this is an all too painful reminder. In such a case, you are serving your own needs whilst pretending that you are being helpful to the other.

Evasion. *Example: 'Please don't be upset.'* At least this has the merit of being more direct than the response above and does recognise that the practitioner wants the client to stop what they are doing because it is too much for them. Our culture is not at ease with the ups and downs of emotional life. We are somehow supposed to rally after every setback, never appear distressed and certainly never express how upset we are. Such attitudes are changing but we have a long way to go before people can express their discomfort in a mature fashion, leave it behind them and get on. Suppressed distress (and repressed distress) is present in most groups and workplaces, ensuring that it is difficult for anyone to get a straight, direct and supportive response to their difficulties.

Minimising. *Example: 'You feel upset, but just think how your wife feels.'* Most of us have been on the end of this kind of well-meaning *minimisation* of our pain by asking us to compare it with that of someone else. It is a demeaning and damaging intervention because it suggests that only certain degrees of distress are worthy and yours isn't. It suggests that you are somehow exaggerating the importance of what has happened to you and that other people have more right to be upset than you have. Minimisation can be of:

- The extent of the situation and problem: 'it wasn't that bad, or it wasn't so difficult'.
- The extent of your reaction: 'I'm sure you are exaggerating when you say you are feeling…'
- The extent of your view: 'I don't think you really mean that when you say you think he doesn't like you'.
- Of you per se: 'You're just being dramatic – again!'

Expressing judgements. *Example: 'Your behaviour is stupid and foolish.'* Such judgements have no place in a helping context. Indeed, much of the work of the practitioner lies in observing those judgements arising in themselves as and when they appear.

Such judgements indicate that we have unresolved material of our own, *unfinished business* as some call it, that the client's experience has ignited. It provides us with the reminder that we have more work to do to leave such judgements behind. And, whilst we need to manage such reactions, we also need to continue to 'see' into what is happening for the client and not let our own 'material' take over the session.

As someone observed, and the author found to his cost, 'you come to live your judgements'. In other words, every judgement you make one day comes back and you realise you are living the very thing you condemned so freely at an earlier time. It is a very sobering experience and teaches that whenever a strong judgement appears (in life, in a session, anywhere where you find yourself with an overheated reaction of disapproval), it is better to seek some help to unlock it rather than wait for it to appear in your own life.

Expressing hostility. *Example:* '*Are you really suggesting that you would do that?*' (Tone is all here and it is one of disguised disapproval, of the client letting you down for the very thought that they might go ahead and do something which you don't like.) Displays of hostility and lack of patience at the client's very real concerns have no place in any useful helping conversation. When coupled with the judgement that often accompanies it, it can have a lasting impact upon the recipient.

Relationship & Skills

If you are in relationship with someone, really in relationship, the skills needed to offer a helpful role are likely to arise out of the *understandings* that also begin to emerge as the trust and mutual collaboration grow. This is not to be taken as a message that skills don't matter, so much as to emphasise the value of the relationship.

The more time is spent in preparing new practitioners through skills-based practice, the more there is the risk of creating the impression that help is a technical matter of application at the expense of the relationship. It cannot be emphasised too strongly that it is the relationship that is essential in order for the practitioner's skills to truly serve the purpose of aiding the client.

The skills outlined here have been set out in a relatively progressive way. Thus we meet the role of questions first since that is usually how most relationships begin; with inquirers asking the person they are meeting, 'What brings you to this meeting?'

Whilst some skills are much more in evidence and more likely to be in greater use at some stages of the work than others, they are not confined only to those stages. The skilled practitioner:

- Uses what is needed.
- Can say how come they have chosen what they are doing and what effect their intervention is likely to have.

Such *reflexive* practice is the most reliable guard against the relentless application of technique and something that needs to be fostered throughout practitioner development. It is not so much, 'Can you do this?' or even 'Can you do it appropriately?' as, 'Can you express how it arises in you to offer yourself in this way?' This is an altogether more challenging invitation, in my experience, because it includes motivational issues as well as technical considerations.

Empathic Building

Empathic building is another term that describes an overall activity rather than a specific skill or set of skills. As we will see, an important aspect of the work at the clarifying stage[41] refers to the *facilitation and elaboration of meaning*, which enables both people

---

[41] Clarifying is one of the key stages in the Seven Stage Model, see Section Seven.

involved to investigate the possible implications of suggestions, nuances, unexpressed thoughts and so on. Such elaborations are offered non-possessively and are made to aid the client, not to suggest the practitioner has great depth of insight. All this work comes under the rubric of building empathy.

As already noted, the practitioner's use of appropriate self-disclosure, sharing a feeling, an experience or an observation from within their own life, can bring about a helpful release or further work in the same area by the other person. To know that someone else has experienced similar events in similar ways can be a great relief and can help someone in difficulty to begin to accept what is happening in themselves.

Using Questions

Most practitioners are convinced, or at least act as if they are, that their main role is to ask questions. If questions are removed from their range of possible responses, many practitioners feel that all their responses have been removed – a sinking feeling often follows! It is not that questions do not have their use, it is that there are often more effective interventions.

'Client-centred' questions are questions that enable the client to explore their own experience and understanding of their external or internal world. In that sense, almost all questions at the early stage of a relationship and throughout any kind of helping relationship need to be focused upon enabling the other person. The questions need to be tuned into their reality rather than satisfying the curiosity of the practitioner or the practitioner's determination to be proved right.

There are some points to consider whenever you find yourself asking questions:

- How come you are asking questions at all?
- How come you are asking those questions out of the range available to you?
- Which types of questions do you usually use?
- Have you considered alternatives to questions: simply pausing, making a non-verbal sound such as 'mmmm', showing your interest and being prepared to wait for more disclosure?
- Will the next question you are about to ask further or inhibit the flow of the process?
- Are you assisting the exploration of the other person's world or satisfying your own curiosity?
- Will another question get you what you want and, more importantly, will it help the client get closer to what they want to say?
- What question is the person asking of themselves, whether outright or not?
- What is the next question they need to be asking themselves?

Open & Closed Questions

"…any question, however open, leads off in a certain direction." J. Heron, 1977.

Most of us are conversant with the idea of 'open' and 'closed' questions. The value of open questions is that they allow the person a generosity of interpretation and response. The open question does not have one right answer and therefore gives plenty of space for the person to come up with several possible answers. In general, open questions tend to be more eliciting than closed questions simply because they give more scope for self-directed exploration and discovery. But there is no hard and fast rule: it depends on the context and the timing.

Closed questions, on the other hand, often seek specific information and are more likely to be used in the problem solving part of the Seven Stage Model rather than in establishing a relationship. Closed questions are also often experienced as either too challenging or as leading to all-too-specific responses (sometimes very important too but often misused when a more open question would allow the client to respond with their own starting point and travel in their own direction). 'Do you always travel that way?' invites a yes or no. 'How do you make the journey?' is much more open and yet remains fairly specific. The question, 'What do you do?' is too wide a starting point to indicate it is the journey that is the topic. However, as John Heron points out:

> "The distinction between open and closed is not an absolute one. Some questions are ambiguous, e.g., 'Do you believe in school?' may be heard as open or closed. And there are degrees of openness (or closure), e.g., 'What do you remember about your first school?' is more open than 'What do you remember about the head-mistress of your first school?'" J. Heron, *ibid.*

The skilled practitioner can ask both open and closed questions as and when appropriate and can control the degree of openness of open questions. Highly anxious or compulsive practitioners often have difficulty mastering open questions since their anxiety contracts their questioning into the closed form.

How, when, where, with whom, what else, where else? are all **open questions.** (Why? questions, as we noted earlier, often move the person into rationalisation and justifications.) Open questions serve a number of purposes. They:

- Allow the client to develop their response in their own direction.
- Invite the client to widen their perceptual field.
- Solicit views, opinions, thoughts and feelings.
- Open the door to good rapport.

'Did anything happen?' 'Do you feel depressed?' 'Why did you do that?' These are all **closed questions** and they have a number of limitations. They:

- Narrow the focus of response of the client.
- Reduce the perceptual field of the other person.
- Usually demand cold facts only.

Framing questions at the level that is best for the client rather than what you believe will get you what you think you need is the art here. For those in an expert or advisory role, asking specific questions is part of their need to diagnose a situation effectively and strip it of the opinions and feelings of those involved. This is important, for example, in accident investigation and crime scene interviews as well as in GP consultations about specific medical conditions. The art of using such closed questions lies in the practitioner balancing the need for specific information with the ability of the client to be in a state of consciousness where they can supply the information effectively.

So, for example, if the patient is clearly distressed, asking information only about the type of injury, when it was sustained and so on, is not going to gain the information needed. It is important to settle the patient down and offer some minimal reassurance that help is now at hand. Nevertheless, once this is done, the specific events leading up to the injury, actions taken following it, and why it has taken three weeks to arrive at the surgery may all be critical.

One of the things that helps here is that situations are 'framed' by the expectations that accompany them and this leads people to expect to be managed in a certain way. So a visit to the doctor is an occasion where we expect to get asked very detailed questions about our condition, for example.

A helping interview, especially for someone in any of the guidance-based roles, may require some of each kind of questioning; questioning that enables the client to outline how come they are there at all and what has happened up to date, as well as detailed information about the specific circumstances and actions already taken. Moving between the two modes is an indication of the successful practitioner who can enable the client to feel at ease as they go about their work.

Forms of Questions

A number of forms of questions can be identified. They include:

   1. **Open invitation:** 'How are you?' indicates acceptance; allows any response to be acceptable.

   2. **Seeking information:** 'When did you last visit the centre?' identifies an area to develop and focuses the person's response.

   3. **Seeking feelings:** 'And how do you feel about that?' invites an emotional response; deepens the perspective.

   4. **Seeking opinions:** 'Do you regard that policy as useful?' identifies values and beliefs.

   5. **Requesting comment:** 'Can you say more about that?' gains further elaboration and/or clarifies a particular aspect.

   6. **Clarify Understanding:** 'Am I right in thinking...?' is an invitation to check both parties share a common understanding; gives a tentative suggestion of meaning.

There are other forms of questions – ones that are best avoided. They include:

- **Multiple questions:** supplying too many possibilities.
- **Leading questions:** suggesting what the answers ought to be.
- **Rhetorical questions:** to which you already have an answer.

Clarifying Skills

Many of the skills used during the exploratory stage of a session help someone clarify or enlarge their ideas, thoughts or feelings further. *They are designed to elicit self-direction.* These types of intervention aim to broaden the shared information between the two people involved in order to:

- Help clarify the issue under review.
- Explore an aspect further.
- Examine the implications of the way things are.
- Consider alternative strategies.
- Increase choice, understanding and self-direction.

In addition to open questions the main clarifying skills are:

Prompting. Repeating the last few words or last word when someone hesitates or appears stuck, almost as a question. Or, when there is a hesitation, adding a prompting word such as 'but…' or 'and...' In both cases the client is encouraged to continue and take themselves further.

Key word repetition. Restating just one key word, or a phrase, which holds a charge of feeling or which invites the client to consider the weight of the meaning. This can be an important way of moving beyond prompts and into the further range of clarifying skills.

Example: Client, 'I don't like doing that first thing on Monday morning.'
          Practitioner, 'First thing?'

The art of key word repetition is to recognise that some words are like 'neon lights' in the overall total of the remarks being made. When they are spotted and just held in front of the speaker, they lead directly to something much more illuminating. 'First thing' may lead to the client exploring that getting started at the beginning of a day is a problem every day but especially so on Monday morning. The response then is not, 'Me too. It's a pain, isn't it?' but to move into what significance that *pattern* holds for the client in relation to what they are talking about.

Restating. Asking the client to repeat a statement, phrase or word exactly in the manner they have just expressed it.
Example: 'I wind myself up before every exam – do I really do it to myself? I'd never thought of it that way.'

Such interventions have the effect of re-emphasising the weight the client is giving to particular ideas or expressions. On hearing them repeat the phrase once more, it reminds them of how far they 'own' the sentiment or not. Sometimes asking to repeat the phrase with an opposite intonation is also very effective.

Reflecting. Playing back a complete statement or key words in order to enable the client to hear what they have said and to measure its effect.

Example: Client, 'I really don't like my boss'.
      Practitioner, 'You really don't like your boss?'

Selective echoing. This is related to reflecting above, and is described by John Heron in the following way:

> "You are listening very fully and with fine-tuning to everything a person is saying. You then reflect or echo back something not at the end but from the middle of the speech, some word or phrase that carries an emotional charge or stands out as significant in its context." J. Heron, 1977.

As Heron goes on to say, again there is no interrogative inflection or any other kind of inflection in the echo. This gives space for people, if they wish (they may not), to explore more fully and in any chosen direction the hidden implications of the reflected word or phrase. Selective echoing is usually used to follow the speaker deeper into territory already entered, but it can be used to echo something that leads into new territory.

Paraphrasing. Taking part of a statement from within a longer speech and *selectively reflecting* the phrase or image back, either with a similar tone and intonation or with the tone and intonation deliberately exaggerated. The impact in either case is to provide the client with the means of sensing how far they 'own' (stand by) their sentiment now they are hearing it from outside themselves.

Testing understanding. Deliberate attempts to summarise and test out the practitioner's growing understanding of the whole matter and to check if they have got the essence of the story or scene. Frequently, the client discovers what they mean as they talk. Such tests for understanding are therefore useful to both parties.

Checking for understanding. This is used when the client is struggling for words or they say things that are clearly confused or contradictory. It is very similar to *testing understanding* above and the difference lies in where the main focus is. *Checking understanding* is to enable the client to understand what they (the client) is saying/feeling; *testing understanding* is when the practitioner is testing their (the practitioner's) understanding of where their client is. Heron describes this as:

"You try to divine what they want to say, tidy up their statement to express this clearly, and put it back to them with the preface, 'Let me see, are you saying that...?' Then they can either agree or disagree, clarify what they meant, and get back on a more coherent course." J. Heron, 1977.

Summarising. The practitioner summarises the main points from within a series of statements and provides the client with an opportunity to confirm, deny or change the suggested version.

"You organise the explicit content of a whole chapter of the discussion, summarise it, maybe interrelate parts of it, maybe indicate directions in which it seems to be leading, and put all this back succinctly." J. Heron, 1977.

This intervention can be used at any point, not simply when the client is indicating confusion or contradictions (as in checking understanding). John Heron describes this as 'logical marshalling' and views it as a complementary intervention to empathic divining. Empathic divining, as we have already seen, is sensing between the lines of what the client says whilst logical marshalling focuses on what the client has actually been saying. For example, the practitioner might say, 'Let me see if I've heard what you're saying...'

Challenging Skills

Challenging skills move all the way along a spectrum from mild requests to major confrontations. It may be a simple request to reconsider the weight of a statement and its appropriateness to the context, such as, 'Can you describe what you mean when you say you feel angry?' It may take the form of a much more challenging intervention that confronts the individual with aspects of thinking, or attitude, or behaviour which are severely limiting their action. 'You appear pleased with that statement. I see you smile and even laugh a little. What is so funny about saying you think that there's nothing left to do now but give up the ghost?' Such challenges are often a strong way of bringing to the client's attention the way in which they are colluding with their own mistakes, misassessments of situations or themselves. This approach helps open the way to deeper exploration of how far they have brought themselves into the situation they have, up to now, felt was 'accidental' or not their 'fault'.

Confrontational interventions often fall in the realm of feedback, where the practitioner is in the position of external monitor to the client, able to make helpful comments and suggestions as a result of what they hear and see, especially when there is a mismatch between what is said and how things appear.

Many people have little clear idea about how their behaviour is seen by others and, therefore, have little accurate information about its effects. The deliberate request for feedback can seem little more than an invitation for others to become negative and judgemental. However, once we know how others who have offered the information supportively interpret our behaviour, we might then decide to change it.

The main challenging skills are:

Focusing. Focusing means bringing attention to select those strands that possess most charge or significance.

Example: 'Which of the last few remarks seem most important to the topic we have been talking about?'

It is usually experienced as a mildly challenging intervention. By use of such interventions, the practitioner exercises responsibility for maintaining some focus of interest or pursuing some theme.

Defining. To move from a general description of the problem or the issue at hand into a specific and detailed definition of what it is, where and how it happens is not straightforward. If pushed too hard, it can back the other person into a corner. If left unclear, it can make the following effort all too vague and uncertain.

A consideration of the internal responses that are linked to the external steps also needs to be included. By this we mean that it may appear to you that, given all that the client has said, now is the time to move into a more problem solving stage. However, if you introduce the topic of 'planning the next phase of the work' without realising the client is still nervous and apprehensive about their overall progress, you may have only an obedient individual in front of you: someone going through the motions who has an underlying issue that has been passed over once again. Refined work on defining is crucial and one of the most under-developed skills in most practitioners.

It seems most practitioners, even those who specialise in helping people in counselling sessions, stop at this stage and prefer to work with the meaning of the person's problem rather than help them change the basis of their experience itself so that they no longer have the problem. This shift requires detailed and careful questioning of a very different kind than that of clarifying, which is what most practitioners are comfortable doing.

Pointing out 'mixed messages'. People can be alerted to discrepancies between what they say and what they do.

Example: Practitioner, 'You say you feel happy about it, but you don't seem to be happy – your face is all drawn and tight...'

Example: Practitioner, 'A few minutes ago you were telling me how good this relationship was, now you seem to be saying that it's "too painful".'

Pointing out a mixed message is not intended to trap someone. If a trap is suggested the other person will immediately become defensive.

Immediacy. Immediacy, or using the 'here and now', occurs by encouraging the client to draw upon their reactions and responses to the immediate situation they are sharing together.

Example: If a woman says it is difficult for her to talk to a man, in a male/female meeting the male could ask: 'You say it is difficult talking to a man, how do you feel talking to me?'

Example: Practitioner, 'You said you aren't at ease talking about personal issues when you are at work. I wonder how that affects you here?'

Direct questions. Supportively asking a direct question aimed at the core of the issue — an area the person may be avoiding, concealing or hesitating in sharing — can be a useful challenge.

Example: Practitioner, 'So what is most hard to acknowledge in this situation?'

Challenges to personal restrictions. When someone celebrates their inability to do something or when they are yet again recycling familiar stories of failure, interruptions and mimicking their script can be sufficient for them to recognise it for what it is. Putting one's self down before others do it is not something to practise! The practitioner can discourage it and ask the client to do the opposite. Ask them to find some aspect of the session or the work for which they can validate themselves.

Being specific. Asking for a specific or actual example can be useful.

Example: Practitioner, 'Can you tell me the last time you felt you were performing well?'

Ideally, all challenging interventions come out of a desire to assist the other person and not to serve the practitioner's needs. Therefore there should be no great investment in any of them. If the observation does not fit for the person, you don't have to pursue it until it does.

Feedback

Feedback is a way of giving and getting help. It is included here because it is an area of interpersonal skills that, if better understood and practised, might well go a long way to reducing the kind of interpersonal distress in the workplace that leads to people seeking outside help.

Feedback skills are integral to any functioning relationship. It gives individuals important sources of information to assist them in learning how well their behaviour matches their intentions. It increases the chances of accuracy, success and confidence in interpersonal behaviour and helps to promote a healthy and open atmosphere of mutual regard. The free flow of constructive feedback is a powerful tool for the promotion of mutual learning.

Feedback requires an atmosphere of sensitivity and support because most people find the deliberate request for information about themselves threatening. If I am to learn from what you tell me, if I am really to appreciate your experience of me, then I need clear and direct remarks that are not vague and abstract, i.e. wrapped in cotton wool with all the energy drained out of them. If the feedback is coming with the best of intentions, it will be better if it arrives at me straight and uncluttered, not packaged for my protection. Effective feedback needs to be:

Related to specific behaviour. There is little point in telling someone they dominate the gathering. They need specific occasions that illustrate what is being meant. For example: 'Just now, I felt that you were not really listening to what I was saying, and that you were just wanting to tell me what you think.'

Identified as a subjective impression. Feedback is often given as though it is a judgement from on high, delivered with all manner of claims to authority. *Feedback can only be a subjective impression.* For example, I cannot know that you are angry, though I may believe you are. To own the impression as a subjective one is both more honest and more productive. To say, 'I think you look angry, are you?' is to offer a personal impression which does not label the other person, and leaves them free to accept or reject the suggestion.

Directed toward behaviour that can be changed. To offer feedback on aspects of life that the other person is powerless to change is both threatening and frustrating. For example, if someone who is self-conscious about their height is told, 'You look like a dwarf!' it is not likely to help them listen to feedback next time.

Descriptive not evaluative. It is more effective to say, 'When you point your finger like that, it makes me feel as though you are treating me like a child', rather than, 'Don't point your finger at me, you berk'. The first describes what happened; the second makes a judgement of the person.

Well-timed. Almost always, feedback is better for being given sooner rather than later – providing the receiver is ready to hear it and there is support available.

Requested. It is most useful when the receiver has actually invited the feedback. For example, 'Do you find the way I behaved just now threatening?' implies an openness of response to the feedback the individual may receive.

Checked for understanding. Check to see if what has been heard is what has been said and meant, and work at it until it is.

Cathartic Skills

The expression of strong feeling in our culture tends to be reserved for special occasions when few witnesses are present. There are strong social inhibitions about 'letting go' of anger, grief, sadness and so on, and this can strongly restrict the choices individuals make. For example, individuals may ask for time, care and support to talk about the loss of their parent without realising that 'talking about' it is only part of the process of grieving: *feeling* is also part of that process.

The inhibition about experiencing such feelings fully and openly in the presence of another can give such sessions an unsatisfactory quality. There are times when people living through post-traumatic periods are still processing events. At such times people dip in and out of feelings. It can often be the case that the person is unwilling or unable to choose either to express the feelings or put them on one side. Ultimately, it must be they who decide, but a willing practitioner who has some experience in working with feelings of anger and distress will play a very great part in the decision. In emotional terms, it seems very unlikely you can ever take anyone to places you haven't at least visited yourself.

The following elements are all part of work with strong feelings and enabling the client to fully experience their feelings.

Physical support. Physical contact is another area of social taboo. Who can touch who, where and in what circumstances is an issue full of uncertainties. In the workplace it is all but absent. However, what is being acknowledged here is the human need for 'contact' at times of acute crisis. The holding of a hand, or an arm on a shoulder, can simply tell those suffering that they are not alone.

Validation. To share strong feeling is a considerable risk; appreciation and respect for having taken the risk, and gentle encouragement and support as it happens are ways to validate the person.

Critical scene descriptions. Reliving a traumatic scene by retelling the events from within the present tense evokes the unfinished and incomplete elements of the original experience. Psychodrama is one way of doing this. Returning to an occasion of distress that has resurfaced and saying all the things not said at the time, as though the person or group were present now, can begin the process of 'closure' and start bringing an incident to an end.

Associations. When people begin to speak of emotionally laden events, their attention may switch, signs of feeling may become apparent on their face, breathing may become more rapid, shallower, and so on. Inviting them to share the thoughts, images or words they might be experiencing internally can enable them to experience the emotion more fully.

Contradictions. Asking the person to repeat the opposite of a negative statement can have a powerful effect and will often bring emotional 'material' to the surface to work with. For example, if a person says, 'Work is just a waste of time', the contradiction, 'Work is wonderful!' is much more likely to bring to their awareness what the original statement actually hides.

Summary

This is a summary of the key ideas addressed in this section. They are perhaps the ten most important dimensions of human relations effectiveness in just about any setting.

- **Empathy:** the ability to perceive accurately what another person is experiencing and to communicate that perception.
- **Respect:** appreciation of the dignity and worth of another human being and of that person's right to make their own choices in their own time.
- **Genuineness:** the ability of an individual to be freely and deeply themselves.
- **Concreteness or directness:** specificity of expression concerning the client's feelings and experiences.
- **Confrontation:** the capacity to challenge the client on discrepancies in their statements, feelings and actions.
- **Self-disclosure:** the revealing of personal feelings, attitudes, opinions and experiences on the part of the practitioner for the benefit of the client.
- **Immediacy:** the ability to deal with the feeling between the client and the practitioner in the here and now.
- **Warmth:** the expression of verbal and non-verbal concern and affection.
- **Potency:** the dynamic force and magnetic quality of the helper – convincing the client that you and they together can get there.
- **Self-actualisation:** the capacity to live and meet life directly; to be effective at living.

Seen as personal traits none of these can be taught. Seen as helping skills all of them can be taught. That is, one cannot be trained to be empathic, but one can be trained to give empathic responses. One cannot be trained to be warm or to be 'concrete'; one can be trained to manifest warmth or 'concreteness'. (Drawn from the work of Sidney Wolf quoted in Edelwich & Brodsky, 1980.)

Suggested Reading

Avila, D L, Combs, A W & Purkey, W L: *The Helping Relationship Source Book, Volumes I & II.* Allyn & Bacon, 1977.

Bandler, R: *Using your Brain for a Change.* Real People Press, Utah, 1992.

Rowan, J: *The Reality Game.* London, Routledge Kegan Paul, 1983.

Grinder, J & Bandler, R: *The Structure of Magic, Volume II.* Palo Alto, Science and Behaviour Books, 1976.

Heron, J: *Helping the Client.* Sage Publications, London, 2001.

SECTION VI

PRACTITIONER RESOURCES

Chapter 19
The Transition from
'Helper' into Practitioner[42]

The previous chapters highlighted and explored the principles and basic skills that are fundamental to any effective helping relationship. These principles and skills are crucial for anyone who finds themselves in a helping role, whether teachers, social workers, friends, neighbours, colleagues… or, indeed, 'professional' helping practitioners. This chapter, however, begins the process of looking at the helping relationship and the work of people whose overt role it is to 'help' to greater depth, including people employed as specialist counsellors. Hence the title of this chapter. It is indicative of the transition from helping of the kind we are called upon to offer as members of the human race to helping that is a more formal, explicit part of someone's work and which may involve working with strong, deep issues and emotions.

As the new entrant to the world of helping is quick to realise, the desire to help is no guarantee of success. People are more complex than we ever thought and the techniques that promise so much when demonstrated by those with great experience don't seem to fit or apply when we use them. The sheer effort of 'staying with' the client can be exhausting and the fatigue of listening to several people over the course of a day can be an enervating process.

There are dilemmas to practice that need help and time to reflect upon with those who have an interest in, and an understanding of, the kinds of concerns that the practitioner is meeting. The best help for such a stage of practice is someone who knows much more than you do about what you do rather than the best person in the world at the work, or even the most advanced practitioner you can find.

A good practitioner does not always make a good mentor or supervisor. Someone who is brilliant at doing the work may not have the time or real interest to work with the issues of practitioners and be much more interested in teaching the new practitioner all they themselves have learned. It's fine to develop new ideas based on someone else's style and experience, but it is best done when you have some sense of your own style and stance to the work. In the early stages, whilst you are finding your feet, it is best to work with those who have considerable experience and a real wish to help others gain their own stability in the work than with the most dazzling of performers at it.

---

[42] We have used the term 'practitioner' to describe any kind of helper because we believe that helping is an applied activity. However, there comes a point when the helper either settles for a certain level of work and is satisfied with that or becomes increasingly absorbed in the complexities of the human dilemmas people present when they are looking for help. This section forwards is addressing the issues that this deeper exploration of helping raises and it is equally applicable to an experienced volunteer as someone who has a paid named role as a helping practitioner.

Practitioner Naïvety

It is often a considerable dent to the self-esteem of the newly prepared practitioner to realise that their efforts will not reduce the sum total of human misery by any measurable proportion overnight. It is even more disheartening to realise that the very agency within which they work actually generates some of the kinds of problems that people come seeking help with!

The levels of naïvety in helping are often enormous. People have high expectations of the agencies that offer help, their own capacities to help and the effectiveness of strategies that will work to bring about changes to people's lives. Learning how to face one's illusions and not become cynical was discussed in *Section Three: The Helping Context*, but here it is important to point out that the practitioner has to recognise the reality of the difficulties that go with work of this kind. The problems or challenges come from a number of sources and some practitioners are more prone to being undermined by those from one source rather than another.

For example, some people never lose heart with their clients but do despair over the agencies they work in. Others find themselves able to work within an agency setting but are bemused at the reluctance of clients to make progress. And there are those who think it all should be easier than it is and can't decide where the fault lies, but it is all a lot more complicated than they believe it 'should' be.

Meeting Helplessness

We can't help but meet dilemmas in the work we do, whether it is at the advisory end of the spectrum or offering remedial and therapeutic responses. We can't help confronting ourselves either.

We often find on reflection that something we were all too pleased with at the time was not quite the best intervention and was used more as a chance for us to practise a skill we believed important. We may find that we completely missed the cues the client offered because we were too busy listening for the 'story' we had decided was the one we were expecting. We sometimes come away from a session with a real unease that we just didn't have the resources needed and the resulting sense of powerlessness and helplessness undermines our self-confidence about our fitness for the work at all.

All these and more are part of the repertoire of learning that the new practitioner has to meet over the course of their first stages of working with people. Of all, it is perhaps the sense of helplessness and powerlessness that most upsets the practitioner and is often hardest to recognise too. For many of us, the determination not to give up on the client is the 'driver' to keep us making suggestion after suggestion long after the client has given up any engagement with the idea of doing anything at all. A client's underlying belief that nothing can be done is almost a taboo in the helping relationship and one so hard to face for many of us that we would rather not believe it. Consequently, we continue to avoid hearing the message that is running underneath every 'yes, but…' answer a client gives that demonstrates their reluctance to move into effecting any committed response.

In such cases, the new practitioner is likely to persist with ever more imaginative or desperate suggestions in the hope that one takes hold, all because a willingness to recognise the fatalism of the client would put the practitioner's own uncertainties on the rack of self-doubt. Practitioner powerlessness undermines the very enterprise and is not something easily recognised or admitted, hence the importance of good support in those early phases of the helping career.

To recognise that it is acceptably human and altogether predictable that you will feel the utter pointlessness that comes with that similar sense of hopelessness in the client is a painful part of learning that helping is just being able to do what you can. There will be occasions when the problem goes further back or needs more than you can bring to bear to it. Helping is not the power to make things different, only the power to enable others to make things different.

Remembering that at some level the client is already doing the best they can is another of those hard lessons that brings more compassion to the plight they are in and less frustration at the lack of motivation for taking up the suggestions you make. Working to understand how come they are where they are and how come it makes sense to respond in the way they do, repays the effort far more than coming up with yet another solution (many of which they will have already heard before and found good reasons why they don't work).

Working with Clients

The importance of early experience in the development of the person cannot be over-estimated. Such experience lays the foundations for the ways in which people interact in their wider world as they move through life. There is insufficient space here to discuss this at any length, except to note its bearing upon the relationship that is to develop between the practitioner and the client. Though therapy is not being suggested here, it is important to realise that clients in difficulty arrive with wide differences in the personal resources they can call upon to meet the challenges of their inner lives. How successfully or otherwise someone has coped with life changes in the past will affect how far and how freely they can respond to the one they are experiencing at the time they come for help.

The client is always individual and their dilemmas are always unique. Nevertheless, three broad categories of client are worth noting. For convenience I am terming them:

- The temporary client.
- The problematic client.
- The serious client.

The temporary client. There are times in almost everyone's life when a crisis or problem emerges beyond our resources to deal with it effectively. Such an individual who comes for help will usually have a personal history that has enabled them to establish effective and valuable relationships. They will have a measure of *internal personal security* (however much it may be off-balance at the moment) and a sense of personal *responsibility* for bringing about the changes they are seeking. They will not have excessive illusions about the value of the practitioner or seek to foster an unrealistic dependence upon them.

They will come to resolve a specific dilemma, will appreciate the help they get, and will leave the relationship once they have made the gains they are seeking. Often their difficulties will be focused upon inter-personal issues – specific crises to do with jobs, study and so on – or with enquiries into a particular dilemma they confront. Such clients are often those who offer the practitioner relatively early signs of change and development. The relationship is more nearly that of peers in which one party is temporarily drawing upon the resources of the other.

The problematic client. This second group of clients often enter into counselling for reasons similar to those above. Some current dilemma, an important relationship or a life crisis stimulates the search for help and assistance: a need to talk it through with someone outside the situation. But such a client differs from the temporary client described in the previous section in that they have much less in the way of personal resources to enable them to overcome the current concern. Their essential wholeness cannot be taken for granted. There may be past experiences, not consciously recalled, which have significant influence upon how the individual relates to themselves and others. There may be long-standing and underlying problems of moodiness and depression, for example, or a long history of repeatedly unhappy experiences in certain areas of life.

Involvement in a helping relationship thus only begins to indicate a more serious state of affairs and a past history of incomplete or unhappy experience. Sometimes the very relationship that counselling offers – the exclusive time and attention of another – is itself something that may complicate matters. Such care and attention can come to be seen as an expression of 'friendship' in its widest sense, leading to an expectation that the practitioner will somehow become involved in the life of the client and be someone available to the client as and when the need might arise. Initially, such appreciation may be gratifying and, inadvertently, the practitioner can come to reinforce such false assumptions, taking a readier role in the life of the client than is either desirable or useful. Such 'boundary' problems then become a matter of concern, and lead to circular arguments about how the practitioner is failing the client, which have sufficient validity in them for the practitioner to feel unable to put them aside. The scene is set for poor helping of any kind.

Not all such clients end up attempting to engage the practitioner in this way. They are more likely to present the practitioner with a sense of almost hopeless expectation that nothing they attempt together will really change anything significantly. Being prepared to work with commitment when the client displays signs of passivity, reluctance or even hostility is a demanding role for any practitioner and the temptation to make comments or challenges that come from frustration and anger, rather than concern, is not always easy to avoid. It is just because these issues only emerge as contact increases that makes working with such clients so difficult. Often referral only gets thought of when the situation is practically uncontainable – a time long past when it can be most effective. Guilt, frustration and the sheer sense of impotence are not uncommon outcomes for the practitioner dealing with such a difficult client.

The serious client. The serious client is the client most in need of help, for whom counselling will often change little in their lives, and who are often easiest to identify.

These are people who, for all manner of reasons, are psychologically damaged, who have aspects of their lives that are seriously impaired, or who function in certain situations with tortuous inadequacy. They will often come to counselling as part of an organisational response to attempt to enable them to integrate more successfully within the culture of the group to which they belong. Such clients have more serious difficulties than most practitioners can expect to cope with. What the practitioner can do, however, is something that is far more constructive than inadequate psychic explorations. They can become a reliable source of safety and support – an anchor point for the individual to seek out at times of acute stress or challenge.

Such long-term support can make all the difference to such an individual. It can help them to make progress with dignity and success through a placement or work experience that otherwise might simply collapse from the unsympathetic and unskilled efforts of others who are unused to providing such a role. It is not always the case that an individual with serious difficulties must be moved on elsewhere by being referred to another agency. Often they can be very positively helped with the appropriate support and caring attention of specialist practitioners on-site who are themselves in touch with appropriate referral agencies.

Using Limitations to aid Development

All practitioners at some point lose clarity. We can lose sight of what we can bring to the helping relationship, lose clarity about the purposes of our interventions, and we can get distracted – by clients or by ourselves. When we reflect, we can recognise that there are any number of ways we have yet to learn in order to improve our helping. For many, however, surfacing these 'issues', facing their 'failings', acknowledging these kinds of 'limitations' is something to be avoided. Development, therefore, is not possible. Challenging though it is, surfacing the times, places and people that stimulate us to offer distorted help and then working through the issues that all this raises is not only a powerful activity but it also enhances our emotional and spiritual wholeness.

After a period of practice, reviewing the experience against some of the considerations outlined here will perhaps assist the practitioner to renew their understanding of where they have more to learn and what aspects of their style of helping would repay further investigation and reflection. There are a number of blocks to effective helping and some of them are related to lack of skill, confidence or awareness on the part of the practitioner.

'Degenerate' Helping

There are four important ways in which help can become *degenerate* rather than productive as a result of the practitioner's behaviour.

1. Unsolicited help. Here the practitioner begins to intervene without first clarifying whether help is being sought and whether they can supply it adequately. This can be a subtle form of interference and can take important areas of personal decision-making away from the client. It is often very difficult for the client to challenge such help out of fear of appearing ungrateful or being accused of being arrogant. Fear of rejection can also play its part in someone going along with this process. Unsolicited help can encourage passivity and dependence, and leave the problem little improved.

2. Compulsive help. Help that is narrowly restricted to the same set of suggestions or formulae that have been well tried already would suggest compulsive help. Similarly, repeatedly fishing over areas of the client's life that may have abiding interest to the practitioner but no crucial relevance to the problem is another example of the same process.

3. Manipulative help. Help that is motivated primarily out of the self-interest of the practitioner is manipulative. In its extreme, it is the clear, conscious and deliberate making use of others to fulfil our own needs or personal ends. An example might be where the client is invited to disclose information of a personal relationship for prurient reasons.

4. Perverted intentions. Such forms of help are not necessarily the result of deliberate intent, so much as anxiety, over-concern and inexperience. However they can, of course, be deliberate attempts to exploit the client and when they are, they are *perverted*. To continue the example given above, when the help is perverted the information gained would then be used inappropriately. The level of exploitation determines what you call it, with perverted help being more damaging than manipulative help.

The kinds of anxieties and compulsions that are highlighted above can lead to some distorted forms of practice. The balance between aware use of self and the degree of distress-ridden need of the practitioner gives shape to the practitioner's profile. It also influences the kind of help we prefer to offer. In addition to the above examples, there are other stereotypical distorted forms of help that occur and some of them, hard though it may be to believe, are nevertheless demonstrated by ourselves on the 'right' day and under the 'right' conditions with the 'right' client.

'Jim'll fix it'. The over-zealous practitioner is determined to answer the need no matter what the cost and to do it 'now'. 'What's the problem? Well, here's the solution.' 'No problem, let's move on to the next one.' 'Can't be done that way, well, let's try another.' 'You can't do it, well then why don't I?' 'I can't do it, but I have a friend who can.' Suddenly, and without warning, what were the client's problems have now become the site of the practitioner's performance to the degree that the client often feels their whole life has been invaded. The work of the client then becomes not that of seeking help for the problem they had, but of keeping the practitioner at bay and preventing the practitioner from running all aspects of their life. It takes very little of this approach before becoming highly intrusive and removing all real initiative from the client, who knows that you will do it anyway, no matter what they themselves want.

'Have you thought of a paper bag or a bicycle?' What is this you may wonder? However, in the early stages of helping preparation, briefing the practitioner who is to work with their colleagues in practice sessions to enter the situation armed with only these two solutions, and to work as hard as they can to 'sell them' generates no small measure of amazement and disbelief – until they try it. It is quite astonishing how many people will (apparently) show a willingness to learn to ride a bike to cure their moodiness or imagine their irritations fitting into a paper bag that they can put in the waste bin.

Having only a limited number of solutions is fine as long as the problem fits. When it doesn't, the chances are that the client's problems will be made to fit the solution to hand. And the amazing thing is that many clients oblige. This exercise is a sharp reminder of how pliable and compliant most of us are at the early stage of a relationship when we need help.

Subtle take-over. Some practitioners are highly adept at empathically indicating to the client that they well understand the nature of the difficulty in all its lurid detail because they themselves have only recently, or once a long time ago, suffered the same fate! Here we have what starts out as an eagerness to indicate a sense of empathy being confused with a recounting of the practitioner's own experiences. All we need to add to the mixture is the full rich details of what a disaster it became and how much worse it will get, and we have a client with a much bigger problem than the one they arrived with! And we also have a practitioner who will not allow their client to experience their own response to the situation.

Distracted practitioners. Being very interested in the client's story whilst fiddling, overtly checking the time or flicking through the latest edition of a favourite magazine, all provide vivid examples of the way in which the slightest distraction on the part of the practitioner can serve to shut down the client from really entering fully into all they need to say.

In the face of these possible reactions, it can be a very difficult and painful admission[43] to recognise you can no longer manage and that you need the assistance of someone else. It can be made worse if you feel you really 'ought to pull yourself together and get on with it'. Other difficulties that many of us experience include being told that we somehow ought not to have the problems we have now admitted to having.

---

[43] It can be equally difficult for the practitioner as well as the client to acknowledge a need for help and perhaps especially so for the practitioner if they are seen to be 'failing' in their work.

Dilemmas in Helping

There are three major influences acting upon the practitioner in sessions and only rarely do they act harmoniously together. Most of the time we are helping there is at least some degree of dissonance or tension between the conflicting demands placed upon the person in the practitioner role. These three sources of pressure are:

- The setting.
- The role.
- The level of skill a practitioner possesses.

Frequently, practitioners confront dilemmas about the legitimacy of their involvement, which may then begin to raise one of a number of questions. Sooner rather than later, most practitioners have to ask and work out their current understanding to such matters as:

- How far should I get involved?
- Have I the skills required?
- How far do I surface deeper issues in a task-based meeting?
- How far do I encourage people to relate their concerns in one setting with those that appear elsewhere as well?
- How far do I go in working at depth?
- How do I manage when the contract needs to change?
- Is it permissible to stop and for what reasons?
- How far should I go in offering 'support'?
- How far should I challenge clients to take some measure of responsibility for what is happening to them?
- How do I offer support in such a way that it can be rejected if it is not the right time for the client – all without appearing casual in my concern?
- How do I approach issues when there might well be a catalogue of painful experiences behind them?
- How do I cope with the fact that some clients are dealing with lives that are far more emotionally distressing than anything I have ever experienced myself?

There are no easy answers to such questions and issues. Establishing appropriate limits which will lead to a satisfactory involvement for all concerned – client, practitioner and setting – is not easy.

Help versus 'Rescuing'

In part, the answers to the above questions lie in the level of skill possessed by the practitioner, but skills are only the starting-point. Assuming the role of practitioner immediately places an individual in a position in which difficult choices still need to be made about the role appropriate to those skills and to the setting. A designated practitioner often feels a tremendous obligation to be 'doing something' because they believe it is expected of them.

Equally, the feeling that it is their task to solve all problems places an unrealistic burden of responsibility and later of guilt when problems do not get solved as neatly or as easily as the practitioner would like. Burnout amongst practitioners is high for these reasons. It is useful for the practitioner, therefore, to distinguish between *rescuing*[44], or inappropriate attempts to help, and helping which is a legitimate response to another person in difficulty.

'Rescuing' is a game in Transactional Analysis (TA) terminology. Games are distorted ways of getting involved in relationships by either or both parties. Such 'games' may involve mild anxiety, serious forms of humiliation or even downright violence and aggression. It is important to recognise 'games' – both those you play and those that other people play with you. Psychological games can easily degenerate into the *Drama Triangle*, which is exactly what many people spend a good deal of their time doing in social situations. *Rescuer, Victim* and *Persecutor* are never very far away from each other. It is a very useful description of the ways in which well-intentioned exchanges quickly degenerate into fiercely destructive patterns.

For those employed in a caring or helping role, the *Rescuer* position comes all too easily as a response to feeling pressured to be seen to be doing something at the first sign of someone in difficulty. Over time, it can become a patterned response that may well not meet the needs of the situation. Rescuing of this kind has a compulsive quality about it. The client comes to be seen as a *Victim*, and may well identify themselves as such. They are also inadvertently encouraged to become dependent on their *Rescuer*, who gets the things done for them that they cannot do themselves. Far from encouraging self-reliance, such 'rescuing' perpetuates dependence and exploits the difficulties of the client in order to enable the practitioner to meet their own needs. The important question is to find out if your help is appropriate in the first place. Four questions can help to clarify this:

- Is this person able to do without my help?
- Will what I am doing contribute towards their independence?
- Did this person ask for help or accept my offer of help?
- Is there a clear understanding between us about the nature of my help?

Once the client senses that they are being rescued the way lies open for deception, manipulation and exploitation of the practitioner. Deception can take the form of the client pretending the problem is solved to get out of the stifling clutches of someone who may take over their life. Manipulation can take the form of praising the practitioner for being so wonderful that, 'Here's an even bigger problem for you now!' Exploitation can take the form of generating new crises to maintain the practitioner's involvement in the client's life whenever the practitioner suggests it is time to consider terminating the relationship.

[44] See the Bibliography for references to TA titles. The originator of the Drama Triangle was Stephen Karpman and it is sometimes known as the Karpman triangle.

Between the 'helpless' client and the 'all-wise' practitioner, the competition is set up to find out who is going to get to the place of frustration with the other quickest and turn from their present role (either of being *Victim* or *Rescuer*) into that of *Persecutor*. Will it be the client who first becomes the *Persecutor* taking out his or her accumulated revenge and frustration at the demonstrable failure of the practitioner to deliver all they had promised? The practitioner then joins the line of incompetent professionals who 'do nothing' in the eyes of the disaffected client. Or will it be the practitioner who subtly treats the client to morally uplifting homilies about how they really aren't trying and how they really should do better?

In whatever form it appears the *Persecutor* is a sure sign that neither the practitioner nor the client are getting enough healthy value out of their time together.

The Effects of Pressures

As we have already seen, the accuracy of assessing the scope and implications of any problem or situation is determined by the ability of the practitioner to listen and to ask useful questions. Pressure of time may greatly reduce the quality of questions and therefore of the information obtained from them. Since the basis for any intervention derives from this information, the wrong strategy to assist the wrong problem is more and more likely as pressures on the practitioner increase. Pressures may be generated externally, in such things as the need to provide results, or internally by an unrealistic wish to 'make things better for the client'.

When someone sets out with a sense that what they are attempting is actually not possible, they create a certainty of failure for themselves. Many relationships start out just this way, because the person holding the relationship does not have any clear sense of what may be possible in the time available and considering the two people involved. In such circumstances, the practitioner is likely to become more and more internally controlled, more and more influenced by their own concerns, and less and less attentive to the information and the responses that the other party is providing by way of verbal and non-verbal behaviour. They go into an 'internal loop', stop paying attention to what is happening and start responding out of their own internal 'material'. They become more and more controlled by their own internal anxieties and less and less by the needs of the situation and the requirements of the client.

This point leads into the question of *contracting* – establishing the terms and conditions under which the two people attempt their work together.

Contracting

The word *contracting* can sound very cold, clinical and formal. It is. Yet the contracting process need not be carried out in that way. *How* it is carried out, how far and at what point it is carried out are all important. The contracting process is not about setting a 'contract'; it is not about a finished product or creating a fixed form. The real aim of contracting is to help both parties to learn how to negotiate and ensure that assumptions about such issues as who does what and for how long are questioned. The value of the contracting process, therefore, does not lie in the end result, but in learning how to review where we are and what we are doing as we go along. Adaptability to changing circumstances and responding to what arises are also important areas to consider. When the practitioner insists on sticking rigidly to contracts, they are often unawarely punishing the client.

Contracting is also about setting out the understanding people have about their respective contributions to the enterprise they are to begin. If, out of fear of putting off the client, the practitioner refrains from discussing the times they will meet, how long for and how they might spend their time together, then the client may well end up believing they have found a friend. If, on the other hand, the practitioner is so insistent upon dealing with the client in a brusque, businesslike fashion, the client may never get round to talking about what is troubling them and how much help they may need. Raising the question of the conditions and the boundaries of the work is a skilful task, and must be judged according to the development of the relationship, the depth of rapport and the potential for drama in the situation.

For some people seeking help, the more the boundaries are spelt out – and the sooner the better – the more they feel secure. For others, the very discussion seems an intrusion and they want to get on with sorting themselves out. Only later may they realise the value of talking through how the help could be offered and in what way because it puts a stop to the person developing unrealistic expectations. The longer the discussion is postponed, the more likely it is that unrealistic expectations will develop. It is much easier to do more than you have agreed if you only agreed to do a little, than it is to do less once you have offered the world[45]. Indeed, offering an unrealistic contribution is a form of 'rescuing' clients from themselves by making it appear you have some limitless resource on call. When the practitioner then realises they have made a mistake they have to get themselves out of it by some nifty 're-contracting'. Clarity of what can be offered is the foundation of effective helping of any kind.

There may be a clear *explicit* contract surrounding any meeting between practitioner and client, or it may be *implicit*, left unspoken but nevertheless understood. The less explicit the contract is about what is offered and what is being attempted, the more likely the help is to be unfocused, open to challenge and questions of purpose at a later stage, and this may detract from the real needs of both parties. In situations of open access, such as drop-in centres, *there may be no clear contract* and the practitioner can then be left feeling at the direction and mercy of the client, only able to respond on terms the client sets. *Contracting is a particularly crucial skill for effective helping* in brief, short-term or crisis work since it enables the practitioner and the client to prioritise their time effectively.

Setting clear and agreed boundaries may be an intrusion in the actual sorting out of the problem, but without it the problems may end up multiplied by the confusion that surrounds the relationship. For someone entering into a complex helping relationship for the first time, being enabled to understand how it works can be very useful, otherwise they only have their experience of other (non-help related) relationships with which to make comparisons.

---

[45] See below the story of the old lady travelling to Australia.

In much of the literature on the helping relationship, secure boundaries are described as 'holding the client'. They provide not only a holding of the boundaries of the time and the meeting, but they indicate also an 'emotional holding' of the client – they send a message that the practitioner is there for the client in clear ways and to a clear degree. Offering what is appropriate, given who you both are, needs to be worked out. The question of whether you are the person to be offering the help in the first place, is also something that always needs to be borne in mind.

Helping, as all practitioners quickly realise, is an easy thing to get into and something very much more difficult to get out of. Thinking ahead with these kinds of questions can help:

1. What is this person asking for? How clear are you and they at this point of what you are letting yourself in for?

2. What do they need? How far does their need for help extend? Is it a need easily satisfied or one that has far-reaching implications and is better managed than unsuccessfully sorted?

3. Are they asking for help? Is the individual at the point where they have recognised the need for help consciously enough to benefit from it, or are you reading into what they are saying the fact that they need you?

4. Are they asking me for help? Am I the only, or even the best, person to help and is now the time to offer it?

5. Am I the person to help? Do I have the requisite balance of skills, time, expertise and commitment?

6. What do I have to offer? What do I bring to the meeting by way of baggage and limitations at this time with this issue?

7. Is this realistic given you, the roles, the task, the time, and me? After all this, am I still the person to do the work?

It may be that the contracting phase takes place over a series of meetings rather than all at once, but having enough security at each stage of the relationship for the client to at least express their concerns is important. A really good cautionary tale of the importance of clear contracting is the story of the little old lady travelling to Australia for the first time.

She is delayed on her way to the airport and arrives just as the Qantas jet is leaving the runway. Undeterred, she approaches the passenger desk and meets a trainee staff member. Pointing out of the airport window she says, 'Get me on that plane, young man!' to which he says in reply, 'I'll see what I can do.' He hurries off and returns only a few moments later to attempt to apologise, but it is already too late. The old lady's handbag is already travelling towards his ear!

What she heard was, 'I will solve your problem', and she was not prepared to hear that he couldn't. At an early stage in a difficult situation few of us hear clearly or understand fully. The practitioner may have spelt out the conditions, but the client may not have heard them.

The Issue of Confidentiality

The more ambiguous the context of the meeting or the roles of the practitioner and the other party, the more important it is to consider aspects of confidentiality rather than to assume that 'confidentiality' is understood in the same way by each of those involved. For a manager or member of staff acting in the role of support, or for someone acting as a practitioner to a colleague, for example, there needs to be some clear understanding of the limits of the potential information that is being shared. Where the possibility exists for the practitioner to be able to make use of the information gained in a counselling session, for example, in other roles or in other settings, both must make clear how this is to be managed. It is not that such ambiguity should bring the enterprise to a halt, only that the trust that is required for the relationship to develop successfully needs to be supported by clear contracting.

It sometimes happens that the sheer weight of a problem pushes an individual into confiding in another who, in other circumstances, they would think twice about. This may cause unavoidable problems to both parties later. When this happens, it is better confronted sooner rather than later. Where there is time for the practitioner to discuss with the person they are meeting their relationship and its boundaries, the question of what information may go where and why, should be an essential aspect of the *contracting process*.

The limits of confidentiality are one of the essential elements to establish at the outset of any working relationship but especially helping ones.

In informal arrangements, the issue of confidentiality could well be overlooked until someone finds information that they thought was to be held within the relationship has found its way into the social pool, and they then, understandably, feel cheated. At other times, those with a management responsibility may feel themselves handicapped by having offered a guarantee of confidentiality to staff members who then reveal information relating to their work performance that needs to be challenged.

As we have already noted, there are many organisations that take for granted the role of managers as supervisors[46] for the work of their own staff. Agencies and organisations may also have policies of their own about the limits of confidentiality and the appropriateness of who should offer a helping relationship to whom. Clearly, the line manager is a most unsuitable and inappropriate figure from whom to receive clinical supervision or confidential counselling.

In an increasingly impersonal society, individuals are rightly concerned whenever they speak to anyone in an official role about what might happen to the information they give. Individuals working in medical settings, for example, need to be extremely clear about the range of information they seek and what they intend to do with it.

---

[46] There is a difference between 'managerial' supervision, i.e. supervision of one's overall performance at work, and 'clinical' supervision, i.e. the exploration of the dynamics of a practitioner's caseload.

The Issue of 'Control'

The more the client is in control, the more the practitioner *works with* the client as in teaching, informing, mentoring or guidance work of almost any kind, and the more the solutions are likely to be *developmental*. The less the client is in control, the more likely it is that they will be *remedial*.

Many practitioners are control freaks; people who want things to be better, otherwise why would they get involved in helping in the first place? Most practitioners are also under pressure to do more in less time for more people. Put these two conditions together and you have an inevitable push towards working at *the taking action and advice-giving end of the spectrum*. Number-crunching clients through a system is far more the trend of the times rather than offering sensitive responses to individual distress. There is the fear that there is too much distress around for the practitioner to do much about. Managing control in such a context is no easy matter. Holding to personal boundaries and managing oneself become crucial: looking after oneself indispensable.

Many practitioners are introduced to the helping role at some stage in their childhood. They often acquire it unconsciously and as a way of compensating for or dealing with some situation in which they find themselves. It may be a way of gaining approval or belonging, of finding a place within a family or a peer group. It will have elements that are less than wholesome about it. No practitioner arrives to the scene with an unsullied history of purity and transparency and there is nothing wrong with this.

All of us bear a degree of *woundedness* from the rigours and stresses of life and all of us have a degree of wholeness, of functioning at an aware and reflexive level that enables us to manage, or keep under direction, our less wholesome characteristics. Good preparation (rather than training) in helping needs to concentrate on raising these elements to the surface and enabling the practitioner to recognise their patterns – the rigidities and compulsions in their helping approaches – thereby reducing their appearance in an out-of-conscious way and promoting the 'reflexive use of self'.

Control is usually one of the major issues most practitioners have to come to terms with. The desire to see the client get better, however plausibly worthy, can be a rigid and fierce imposition on both the practitioner and the client to work harder, to do more, and generally to adopt a regime that is simply oppressive and of no real help at all. Similarly, the desire to 'get it right' for the client, to make a difference and to be the one who brings about a change that has eluded previous practitioners, whilst understandable enough, can be a tyrannical force upon the practitioner and can create a compliant client who will pretend to be improving simply to please their present practitioner. Watching for the compulsive behaviours and learning to recognise them at an early stage can go a long way to ensure that they do not take over and run the show.

Appropriate Disclosure

Most help involves various degrees of disclosure either of personal circumstances or of personal feelings and understandings. For many people, it is hard to even admit they need any help at all because of ... (some event or decision) 'that has caused difficulties

I believe make me look foolish and there is the risk of being told yet again that I am.' On the other hand, 'it may be even worse if you sympathise with me – that might only serve to make me feel patronised!' The practitioner stands in danger of not doing right for doing wrong in such circumstances, which is why all but the most routine of situations requires thought, consideration and some personal understanding of just what is involved in personal disclosure.

This is just one of the reasons – and an important one – for practising disclosure and sharing individual dilemmas as part of the preparation of any would-be practitioner. *Personal* exploration of the link between awareness and disclosure[47] is crucial for anyone preparing to be a practitioner. It simply is insufficient to believe that you will be compassionate and understanding of the concerns of another because you 'believe yourself to be'. Try to share some of the less well thought-out decisions you have made, the way you got into some of the situations you've found yourself having to deal with, or how you are subject to anxieties even some simple decisions have caused you, and you soon realise that the whole matter of trust is central to what is possible.

Unless, as part of their preparation, the practitioner-to-be experiences deeply and subjectively just what it means to enter into an exploration of their own experiences and find the difficulties it arouses in sharing what's there with another who may or may not be empathic, they handicap themselves from ever being able to understand a huge part of what the client necessarily has to experience. In the view of the author, a practitioner disqualifies themselves from taking others through that process of disclosure if they have not experienced it themselves. Many practitioners ignore the difficulties the client experiences in making disclosures and discovering the levels of distress and hurt through which they have had to live.

Developing the Relationship

There is a major fault line surrounding the whole issue of trust in the helping world. It is the point at which the helping world breaks down into factions and divisions. 'How much trust is enough?' And if the client is to decide, then the client may or may not trust you. 'You don't surely have to prove you are trustworthy to every client in order to get on with the job, do you?' 'Who will define what we mean by enough trust?' And, 'What about actually being able to do something, does that not count?' Most help does require the practitioner to do something. How much of it, for example, when and to what degree are matters of fine distinction according to all kinds of influences. But without a satisfactory level of relationship first, no amount of skill can get an airing. That's why the issue of trust is so important.

But it is a complex issue. Levels of trust vary from occasion to occasion and from one individual to another, and even vary within the same individual according to their own sense of the level of risk about what they are disclosing and what possible consequences might follow. Many practitioners know that trust is important but they are more interested in reassuring clients by regaling them with their qualifications than spending the time necessary to establish a sufficient relationship.

---

[47] See *Forging the Future Together*, Bryce Taylor 2003, for an in-depth exploration of this issue.

Individual practitioners will go about creating their helping relationship in very different ways and, so long as it is satisfactory[48], it will be successful. However, there is a deeper matter about the nature of relationship itself contained in this whole issue of trust – the question of means and ends.

If human beings are an end in themselves and not a means to anyone's ends, then when they seek help it is on their terms that the work should take place. If, however, I am a fully paid up, well-qualified professional of whatever stamp of approval, I am likely to take some of that for granted and assume that the client is going to co-operate with me, if not on my terms, then at least on the terms I outline. Before long, the helping practitioner stands in danger of adopting the stance of many professional counsellors, whose commitment to a particular approach or theory leads to the position that expects every client to co-operate on the terms they set and to comply with the procedures they themselves determine.

In dentistry, for example, this may work well. Even so, I took a long time finding the dentist I go to because I wanted someone who I could trust and who would tell me what he was going to do in my mouth, in terms I understood, before he started! So, even here, technical expertise alone is not sufficient for *this* patient to feel able to trust enough. In matters of personal concern this is even more vital.

My fear of flying may be a phobia and a matter of a few sessions of relaxation and 'cognitive restructuring' to put right in your expert eyes, but it represents both a major limitation to my self belief as a competent individual able to manage in the world and my judgement about my own lack of ability to be able to 'put this on one side and get on with life'. My 'practitioner' may well be developing a relationship based only on the 'presenting' issue and not able to create the safer relationship that comes with deeper questioning that would reveal my fear of flying is related to some of the concerns I have about heights and being in confined spaces – all as a result of having both legs broken when a lift collapsed nine floors up![49]

Examples like this bring us all up short and remind us that we need to be open to hearing what people say! But once the practitioner feels 'competent', and especially if they have been 'approved' as competent, they are in danger of operating on these kinds of assumptions based on the surface description rather than finding the deeper structure.

Those who take greater care in establishing the relationship in more depth, however, do not avoid all difficulties either. It is just as easy to look upon every potential client, no matter what the presenting problem, as someone in need of long-term therapeutic help of a very elaborate kind. Since most of us have a past that is littered with 'material' that we *could* sort out, the 'would-be therapist' can easily convince the naïve client of the need to go back and tidy everything up rather than work with the issues for which the client has sought assistance.

---

[48] 'Satisfactory' here refers to all parties who have a legitimate interest. It may be client and practitioner, or it may be client, practitioner and agency.
[49] This is a composite example and not related to the author's own personal experience.

Chapter 20
Working with a Plan
Steps & Sequences

Choice of Approach

It is one thing to build relationships and another to develop them in useful directions. Creating safety through building sufficient rapport[50] is vital but being able to make some useful interventions is just as important. 'What works works', is the thing to remember.

Many practitioners attempt to apply sincerely what they have learned in the form of conceptual understanding, i.e. their theoretical view, no matter how the client behaves. The value of theories is that they simplify, and the purpose of practice is to abandon the theory in favour of *meeting the person*. Whenever there is a conflict, it is usually better to abandon the theory and be open to learning something new rather than make the client over into the description within which the theory says they should fit.

A theoretical approach that requires a particular way of working will be very useful for those things the theory was meant to account for and those conditions it was designed to deal with. It will, like any other theory, be limited by all kinds of factors, not least of which is that many people do not behave according to the theory, even when they suffer from a given condition. Theories are always incomplete explanations.

In most helping and even counselling situations, it is likely that a number of approaches and strategies will be combined to add up to a working stance to the difficulty in question. It may involve some research, some learning, some rehearsal and practice, some development of insight about how things occur, as well as some expression of feelings about the distress caused. But it is not likely to be a simple matter of any *one* of them. And if it is, you can be sure the next person needing help will not be so straightforward!

Therefore, having a range of skills and strategies to put together to enable the client to increase their capacity for choice is a critical aspect of the work of an effective practitioner. The practitioner must find the best fit or blend of helping approaches to meet the client's needs and the situation in which they meet. This is rather easier said than done. It takes time to stand back from the situation and:

- Evaluate the factors involved.
- Assess the range of responses possible.
- Select those that make most sense of the situation now and where it is likely to move to.

This process usually needs someone else as a sounding board. The author is all too well aware that this is far too idealistic for many practitioners, and yet without being willing

---

[50] See *Chapter 17: The Importance of Rapport.*

to articulate *why they are doing what they are doing and what they think doing this will achieve,* the practitioner can all too easily develop a self-referential approach that is unquestioned. Much helping then becomes routinised and far from being as effective as it might be.

Most helping situations for most practitioners are, as we have seen, far from straightforward and most practitioners work within agencies that give some guidance and direction about the stance the practitioner is expected to take toward the client and their difficulties. These influences shape the range of strategies and choices that are available to the practitioner.

A further factor influencing the practitioner's choice of approach is their own preferred style. There are, for example, practitioners who have little interest in exploring the nuances and ambiguities of an issue, but who are highly effective in mobilising resources and getting things done. The practitioner needs to recognise their preferred style and to understand something of its strengths and limitations before they find themselves repeatedly and unthinkingly applying a single strategy, which may be inappropriate to some situations.

They also need to consider their style and profile in relation to the work their agency takes up. As a practitioner gains experience, they develop interest and attention for new issues or variations on the work they have been doing. If the agency is also undergoing change it can sometimes be the case that the disgruntled practitioner is unaware of the drift between their own interests and skills, and those the agency now requires. Working for an agency with an approach at odds with one's own is a sure way to be a dispirited and ineffective practitioner.

With the exception of counselling, the remaining strategies that we outlined in the helping framework (see Section Two) assume that an individual's needs are clearly known and have advanced to a stage where a specific intervention is both necessary and appropriate. In practice, this may not always prove to be the case: a fact which underlines the importance of taking time to review the situation in order to understand accurately the nature of the real problem, particularly before any of the above strategies are undertaken. This is an important and over-riding helping skill.

A particular problem may well require elements drawn from a number of activities in order for it to be resolved. For example, in order to leave college earlier than expected, students may require counselling to discover if this is the best decision. They may also need information about alternative options, jobs, voluntary work and so on, and may feel the need to be taught new skills to enable them to cope with new situations.

Referral

Referral is not separately distinguished within the range of helping strategies illustrated in the spectrum. Rather than being seen as one particular skill, referral is better regarded as an over-arching resource that needs to be available irrespective of any particular strategy. For first-in-line practitioners, knowing the extent of their involvement with those in difficulty is only part of the information required to work within their boundaries effectively. They also need to learn about the appropriate referral agencies and the contact persons within these agencies. Identifying local agencies alone is rarely enough to make referral an effective step in helping someone.

Referral usually takes place when a client is presenting difficulties or experiencing dilemmas that are beyond the ability of the agency or its practitioners. There are, therefore, high levels of insecurity around for everyone. The client is likely to experience further insecurity at the thought of having to retell their story all over again to someone else and the thought of being so odd that they need yet another type of help may discourage them from going elsewhere.

Such circumstances are not the best in which the staff of one agency have to attempt to make contact with those of another for the first time. This is a separate task that needs to be undertaken in preparation for such a crisis and not during one. It is very often the informal, personal links between staff from different agencies that make all the difference in effecting the smooth transition of the client from one agency to another. Opportunities for individuals from different agencies to meet their respective contacts generally receive too little encouragement by the host agencies, and yet the pay-offs can be immense in the improved effectiveness of the help offered and in the efficient use of time and skills of the people involved.

As the helping world is increasingly specialised and agencies become more focused on specific aspects of helping, referral becomes both more important and more problematic. Is a homeless alcohol user a client of a housing organisation or the alcohol agency, or both? And if both, how do they liaise and how much does the client get told of the work going on behind the scenes in order to help him or her? Referral is one of those concepts that is fine in theory but in practice many practitioners find that other agencies are already overloaded, may even know the client, have done all they believe they can and wish you to continue anyway. Before talking through with the client what referral may involve and what course it will take, it may be wiser to make a few general enquiries first.

Many practitioners find that though the clients they have are more suited to another agency, the fact is they are *with them* and the other agency is unlikely to make a better job of it – even if it can help. This is not to encourage agencies to begin 'rustling' prospective clients or 'rounding up' suitable lost souls and herding them into their own corrals, but to remind the practitioner – who has high hopes of solving their problem and easing the client's difficulties by sending them elsewhere – that they may often be disappointed. That said, there are some issues where only some specialised agency or practitioner can offer the up-to-date and knowledgeable information that the client needs.

A Model of Counselling

Every practitioner has to start somewhere, the work must end sometime and something must go on in between. With no more than this, we already have a model of the helping relationship that has three stages:

- A beginning.
- A middle.
- An end.

The more sophisticated models of helping divide the work up in many different ways. This section is more about the larger stages that over-arch the specific sequences of a helping relationship, so the steps below outline the major tasks of any helping relationship. These steps are the basics from which a more detailed view is developed in the Seven Stage Model (see Section Seven), the principal model around which this book is based.

All the forms of help that have been examined so far have a place in the overall aim of helping another to achieve constructive change. Helping is a person-centred activity – in the most general sense of the term. The first priority is to establish accurately the type of help that is most appropriate: that is, to understand accurately the nature of the predicament. Any type of help is likely to pass through a number of steps in moving towards the solution of the difficulty.

An individual enters the counselling relationship to make sense of some dilemma or to move towards the resolution of some problem. They look to the practitioner to bring their experience and expertise to bear to facilitate that process in a way that combines specific skills and strategies.

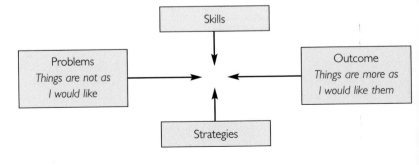

Essential Steps

1. Initiating contact: establishing a good working rapport.

2. Exploration of themes / issues.

3. Identifying options.

4. Assisting towards choice and decision.

Such a simple four-stage model of the helping process identifies the importance of establishing an effective working relationship, something that takes precedence over everything else. Once it has been established, an elaboration of the themes and issues can begin. This in turn leads towards the identification of options: a consideration, say, of the types of help available and the cost and benefits of each. Finally, the stage of choice and decision-making brings the process towards some closure. A decision to meet to review progress might form part of this stage.

Brammer's Model

An early, yet comprehensive, model of the helping process is described by Brammer in his book *Helping Relationships*. Brammer's model breaks down the four stages above into greater detail to give a more precise formulation to the sequence effective help takes. The model is reproduced below, in relation to the four stages discussed here.

1. The meeting phase
- Initiating satisfactory contact.
- Clarifying: exploring the apparent cause of coming together.
- Constructing: devising a suitable structure to work in.
- Contracting: agreeing the boundaries of working together.
- Relating: developing the helping relationship.

2. Exploring themes and issues
- Exploring: outlining the range of the problems.
- Identifying related issues.
- Clarifying implications.
- Consolidating: focusing on areas to work on together.
- Developing a theme.
- Challenging: confronting the incongruities.
- Challenging restrictions and self-imposed limitations.

3. Identifying options
- Reviewing: understanding the ground covered.
- Reviewing progress.
- Identifying learning and implications for change.

4. Assisting towards choice and decision
- Decision-making: outlining options, considering alternatives.
- Devising strategies.
- Agreeing and implementing action plans.
- Concluding: drawing the session and ultimately the...
- Relationship brought to an appropriate close.

Outcomes or Results

Effective help produces change; how much, how valuable and how pervasive are important questions, but they are other questions. The outcome of effective help has to be in relation to what has been attempted. If the practitioner never states what that is to the client and it is *done* to the client, the client may have participated in a wonderful mystery that has been deeply successful but the practitioner takes on the role of magician. However, if the two parties have worked together on the steps and the progress they are each working toward and each knows something of the role of the other (especially where the exchange or use of skills is involved) then the process is likely to be less mysterious. The client will then be more realistically appreciative and more empowered to attempt more for themselves in the future.

There is a very strong *educational element* in helping. The incidental learning that takes place as a result of *how* the help is offered is one of the most neglected domains of the whole helping process. An individual is not only learning about a *what* and a *why*, they are learning a *how*. The way the practitioner offers themselves will model a great deal that is undiscussed but which nevertheless will be having a deep effect. Knowing more about one's own style of relating and preferences is therefore critical for any would-be practitioner.

The more developmental or therapeutic the help, the more the outcome will fit those of the broad counselling frameworks reproduced here in both Brammer's model and the Seven Stage Model. There is a spectrum of possibilities that needs to be considered when looking at the outcomes of help. The different levels of outcome are useful for practitioners as a way of asking themselves at what depth they expect the work to go:

- Getting something done.
- Deciding to get something done.
- Deciding something needs to be done.
- Considering that something needs to be done.
- Recognising that something needs to be done, but not yet.
- Realising that there is nothing to be done yet.
- Accepting that things are as they are however unpleasant or distressing.
- Appreciating how come things have reached the position they have.
- Becoming aware of how things are.
- Discovering that there is more to a situation than first appeared.
- Exploring an idea, feeling or decision.
- Understanding things more.
- Discovering options
- Deciding on a course of action.
- Working out how the desired outcome might be implemented.

These different levels can be summarised under four principal outcomes (Lowry 1974).

1. An increase in understanding. For some difficulties, the most useful result of a helping session is the opportunity to work things out and understand more fully how come things are the way they are and, maybe, even how they got to be that way. Changing them at this stage may be too unrealistic, however much it may be desired. Until I know where I am, it is very difficult for me to know where I might go, let alone how I might get there – though it leaves me wide open for others to take me over and decide for me.

Issues like the break-up of relationships, sudden or recent losses, redundancy, and the kind of issues which involve a need to come to terms with the events, or to learn more about the part the person has played in what has happened, are typical of this need.

2. An increase in the tolerance of ambiguity. Similarly, but with more depth and challenge attached to the first outcome, increasing a tolerance to ambiguity may help someone facing up to the ambivalent and irreconcilable reactions they have to events that are taking place or the circumstances that are changing in their world. The person in such a stage of change does not need to understand the narrative or the sequence of events so much as to learn how to be in touch with the range of contradictory ideas and feelings that are generated.

Living through a separation or divorce, or working out the consequence of a redundancy or a disability, may well require short-term help or a brief counselling relationship. The expression and discharge of feelings may well accompany this difficult human process.

It has been suggested that in a modern society, such as our own, one of the key skills in coping is this very talent of tolerating increasing levels of ambiguity. Living in uncertainty is something we all do; it is the degree of uncertainty that individuals find difficult to manage. The more uncertainty someone is able to manage, the more flexibility they are likely to have in responding to the unpredictable. The less able individuals are to tolerate uncertainty, the more they are likely to have 'brittle' responses to sometimes even minor changes to their routine or their expected view of things.

3. Making a decision. For some, the time has long passed for working out what has happened. They need to begin the process of taking back the initiative and moving into the land of action. Making a decision is the core of the work. Identifying the options, working out the potential consequences, evaluating the level of realism and the requirements of each, before settling on any one course of action, are all important strategies here.

4. Implementing a decision. Finally, the client may have gone through working things out, dealing with their own uncertainties and ambivalence, sorting out their options and now they need help in planning and implementing the one they have decided upon. Now, they need someone akin to a guide or theatre director; someone who will not do it for them, but who will help *coach* them in the steps that they need to take so that they may take them with as much finesse and skill as possible. In this way, the client can take a step, albeit a difficult one, in their life with a sense of inner command and self-respect (which may have been all too lacking through the period of whatever events have happened to them).

No one would expect all clients to fit neatly into the stages of any model or the levels of outcomes described above, but sorting out where the work needs to be most *focused* can be a help to many. Many people can also be helped when the practitioner realises that the choice of focus that they have been using is no longer what a client needs. No one is helped by the practitioner throwing in something from here, there and everywhere at the already unsure client in the hope that something will stick and become useful. A small problem managed more effectively may be more useful than a bigger problem mauled by an overdose of badly applied technique.

Deconstructing a Situation

If you consider for a moment any recent situation in which you were even vaguely helpful, some things become immediately apparent:

- There is a situation.
- You become involved – somehow.
- Others may be involved.
- Something happens.
- Things change and are either more or less remedied, or at least alleviated, and the situation comes to a close.
- People go on their way and life resumes its normal course.

Of course life doesn't, as even this curt account makes clear. Set any real situation against this description and most people recognise immediately that life is rather more complicated than the description would suggest.

Explorations of any helping situation through this simple formula will, however, begin to make more explicit where, what and how the complexities of intervening in any situation arise. If *ordinary caring* is important, then ordinary life is a good starting point for looking at the complexities of helping. There are six key elements to the deconstruction of a helping situation that are useful to distinguish.

    1. What was the situation? All relationships take place in a context. Sometimes it is clear and unambiguous: sales person-customer, parent-child, doctor-patient, for example (though when asked, most people recognise that situations are not at all unambiguous). Sometimes it is much more uncertain: a friend asking for guidance, a volunteer in a group wanting to talk something through.

As we have already seen, the purpose and the setting in which the people meet will partly determine how effective a relationship is likely to be. Only certain kinds of relationships – particularly helping relationships – are appropriate to offer in an advice centre or from an agency offering specialist information. In any relationship, we need to be aware of the underlying assumptions that are influencing the context and any guidelines that might exist which determine what is appropriate.

Information usually exists which outlines how inquirers, clients or the people we are meeting are to be treated and, indeed, induction programmes and other training measures are essential in preparing staff to respond effectively to those they serve. But the interaction with other people, in whatever role, whether they be clients or friends is always 'live' and a working alliance has to be formed together.

The *apparent* situation is not always the situation and in clarifying its elements we begin to establish the forces at work and begin the task of isolating the influencing elements. This is part of the diagnostic phase: of assessing a situation effectively *before* committing oneself to developing the relationship. It gives some indication of just what might be required and helps us assess whether we have the time, the skill and the appropriate relationship to become involved.

2. How did you become involved? The means by which a person becomes involved in a situation often limits what can be achieved. Someone who enters other people's homes, a Health Visitor for example, has to work within constraints that are very different from someone who sees people at their office and by appointment.

The way of relating to someone who is, for example, having to confront sudden unexpected bad news, will be very different for a stranger than for a practitioner who the individual has been seeing for some time. Very different skills and understandings are required when working with people at this emotional level. People referred for help will offer different responses from those who seek help out. What anyone can accomplish in a relationship is often directly related to how they became involved.

3. Was anyone else involved? The role third parties have played, are playing or might play in relation to an individual's circumstances may have an enormous impact on what can be attempted. This involvement may support or frustrate the best efforts of anyone else becoming involved. Even professional practitioners, for example, can get into competition over who can best help the person seeking their services, just as some of the client's supportive friends can undermine progress by offering 'useful' advice. Knowing who else is involved can make all the difference. The game of playing one practitioner off against another is a common one in such situations[51].

---

[51] See the notes on 'games' earlier in this section.

4. What sequence of events occurred? An effective relationship isn't random or unplanned: nor is it neutral. There are patterns, stages and sequences of activity that come together to create a strategy. Reflecting upon what was proposed, how it was implemented (or not), what else might have been tried and so on are important aspects of reflecting upon practice. Identifying and refining strategies is an essential element in the development of the reflective practitioner.

5. What was the result? All situations have an *outcome* or a result. It may not be what you wanted or intended, but there will be one. Identifying the relationship between the results obtained and the contribution made enables the practitioner to revise their practice in relation to the result. It also enables them to begin to observe areas of the work that can be modified or developed further.

6. What was your evaluation of the experience? How the situation closes is not simply a matter of what action results, but also of how the parties *feel*. Individuals have to achieve enough rewards to retain commitment and enthusiasm for the work they do. Those responding to us have to feel sufficiently assisted to make future visits worthwhile and an agency or workplace needs to monitor, review and evaluate its work, not only by numbers but also by the level of satisfaction obtained.

Elements of Relationships

In looking more closely at any working – especially helping – relationship there are a number of things to consider. Four of the most important elements are highlighted below.

1. The moment of commitment. There is a point in any situation where the practitioner stands on the edge of becoming involved and a moment later when they have become *psychologically engaged*. This is true whether or not the meeting is official or informal. The moment of commitment is the point at which the individual is '*in it*' – for better or worse. The more you know before making your commitment, the more likely it is that the relationship will be effective.

2. Dilemmas. Frequently, even a good working relationship will generate dilemmas for those involved, creating conflicts and choices that are not easy to reconcile. These may be dilemmas about priorities, such as the need to be elsewhere versus the need to give time to the other person. There may be internal dilemmas centring upon the ambivalence in the practitioner about the subject matter at hand, a lack of experience in dealing with a particular difficulty, questions of prior knowledge or confidentiality, or an over-investment in wanting to '*get it right*'. The practitioner may discover an emotional attachment in relation to the client or their dilemmas.

3. Issues. The situation described may sometimes have a charge or significance that reduces the practitioner's ability to listen clearly and work effectively. This may well be due to the '*triggering*' *of old* 'unfinished business' from the past which interferes with their clarity of understanding and response at certain times or in particular situations.

4. Challenges. It may well be that the other person presents themselves in a particularly challenging way. They may well have unrealistic expectations, or present themselves in ways that we find difficult to respond to well. The client may cast doubt upon the usual boundaries, perhaps in terms of the style of response they expect or perhaps in terms of the way they respond to what is offered and what the agency expects.

Chapter 21
Approaching Problems

All problems occur within some context[52], as we see reflected throughout this book, and there are internal and external elements that are always influencing the events. This book focuses upon both the context generated *in*[53] the client and that generated between client and practitioner.

The context is determined by what individuals decide to pay attention to and what they screen out. What people pay attention to is determined by what they value. When people don't know what to do, they do not know what to value. When in difficulties, people, for most of the time, are responding not to what is actually 'out there' in the world, but to what they think it might mean, what it 'should' mean, or what they believe they 'ought' to do about it! They continually look for what is the same in this experience compared to the past and not for what is novel and different.

People in the helping professions often refer to the difficulties of those seeking help as 'personal' problems in a loose kind of way. They are well aware that not all the difficulties people experience are either personal, in the sense that they have their origins in decisions the clients have made for themselves, or problems in the sense that they have a clear solution.

In what sense is the loss of a parent a problem? Rather, it is a naturally occurring life-crisis that the majority of people will one day have to face. Some people will meet this and other crises with little or no need of outside support, others will not. This is not a judgement upon those who, at times of crisis, seek out a listening ear to help them shape their experience into understanding. Some people are fortunate to live in a network of support that is freely available but many people have no such network. In times of difficulty they are without close contacts to share their difficulties and must look outside for support.

It is often the case that people who are seeking help find it difficult to request it openly and initially may offer a more tangible and practical need as the reason for seeking help. In such cases, the practitioner needs to be alert to clues that might suggest that other issues or concerns are present and provide opportunities for the client to broach them. Even when people experience a dilemma, issue or concern in their lives as a 'problem', the desire to lose weight or give up smoking, for example, they may not be capable of solution in a straightforward fashion. The suggestion to 'just eat less' to someone with a weight problem immediately demonstrates this.

---

[52] Other aspects of context are explored much more fully in the companion volume, *Forging the Future Together*.
[53] The internal context – what the client thinks and feels about it – is an important, and in some cases much the most important, aspect of the way the individual functions in the external context.

Self Limiting Strategies

When people confess to 'not knowing what to do' in a particular situation, it is not that they lack the kind of information they need, despite what they might say. Most people interested in dieting, for example, know too much about diets and calories for their own good. It is simply that such information is not crucial to solving their problem. What they lack is not information, but a way of knowing how to evaluate it usefully in relation to the outcome they are seeking. They do not have a secure enough base upon which to make a selection. Also they probably have little confidence in the application that would be required to maintain a change even if they knew what change they wanted.

A *reference system* – the way a person decides something, the value that underlies the choice they make – for making decisions about whether to stay in a relationship, or whether to buy a new house, or to change your job, will not necessarily be the same. However, many people use the same strategy to make many of their decisions, or they try to. This will mean they will be good at deciding some things (things which are related to the kind of activity that the strategy was developed to help with) and not others.

They are unlikely to know why this is so, or even to realise that there is a range of activities or decisions for which the strategy serves them well, since the development of such a strategy is largely unconscious and related to underlying beliefs. Sometimes it is the very opposite: an individual has a very successful strategy in one part of their life that they simply never think of applying elsewhere to bring about enjoyable results there too. An example helps highlight the point:

> A man who was good at making decisions in his business and was well regarded by his staff was singularly unsuccessful in his home life. (He had come wanting help because he was puzzled at how come he was regarded as 'successful' but didn't feel it.) His way of remaining popular with his staff was to show interest, keep them motivated and show real concern for their welfare. By doing that, the results the company gained were beyond the typical and everyone enjoyed the work. At home he did almost none of these things because he believed it wasn't his job to motivate his family – indeed he almost believed it was the reverse; they should motivate him and appreciate him like he did his staff. Now, we can argue about the wisdom of this approach; the corrosive effects of capitalism upon family life or even about how men expect to be looked after, but getting lost in the argument about how come this occurs will not change anything.
>
> What did enable a change was to get him, in this case, to realise he had a strategy that provided him with good relationships in one setting and that a bit of it, just a little of it, brought home would improve his home life no end. At first he rebelled against the thought, believing it would be too much of a sacrifice. There was any number of 'reasons' he could find why it was not a good idea. But the question was, 'Is your family life important enough to you

to do something that you know would work and make you and everyone else enjoy having you around more?' Of course, he agreed eventually.

He applied it and it worked. Here was someone who had a strategy that was about showing interest in people that extended to everyone except those most important to him.

Many of us are like this. We use the same strategy over and over again even when it doesn't work: a sure way to perpetuate failure. If it didn't work the first time, then it will not work on the fifty-third either. If at first you don't succeed – then do something else. If, for example, you use pictures from your past to determine what you do in the future, then you are likely to condemn yourself to living out the same kinds of relationships and to making the same kinds of choices you have made in the past. You may then be doing little more than repeating the past in slightly different versions. Such a strategy can be useful for solving conceptual problems and planning things, but it is not a useful way of solving people problems, especially if you don't want to end up in the same place again.

The Three Components

To solve any problem successfully, you require as much reliable information as you can get. There are three aspects to the solution of any problem. There is a *knowing* component, a *feeling* component, and an *action* component. Most of the time it is very much easier to gather the information than it is to act upon it. It is important to realise that the way a person feels about things will have great influence upon what they decide to do.

1. Knowing. To gain information quickly, it is often better to seek someone who already knows the information you require than to try to do it all by yourself. You need to make sure the source of the information you seek is reliable. It is useful for the practitioner to suggest ways the client can do 'homework' of this kind: to gather information, ask other people, find examples, collect thoughts together.

It is useful for two reasons at least. Firstly, it makes the work extend beyond the meeting and not confine it to something that happens separately from life. Secondly, it begins to help the client engage with the real world and start asking themselves (albeit unconsciously) how the world works and how they relate to it. As they get more information that builds toward an action sequence, they then find they are acting in novel ways. They realise they are not operating in a 'strange' environment after all because they have already familiarised themselves with much of what was beyond them at the outset. The client needs to take responsibility for ensuring that the information is accurate and relevant to their needs. Useful questions they might ask themselves are:

- What do I already know about the problem?
- What do I need to know?
- How could I find out?
- Who might be able to help?

2. Feeling. Having information relating to a problem does not always lead to an individual taking positive action. The evidence connecting cigarette smoking and lung cancer is not sufficient in itself to actually stop many people from smoking, though it probably makes most people think harder about giving it up or feel guilty if they continue. For some people, to admit that they have a particular problem would be to lose self-respect or self-esteem.

Denying the problem is a way of avoiding having to confront the implications and the challenge to an individual's self-image. Alcoholics often refuse to admit they have a drink problem until it is acute and therefore harder to change. Sometimes solving a problem is resisted or avoided because those concerned would then have to consider what to do instead of complaining or feeling sorry for themselves. The person with the problem could ask themselves:

- How do I feel about the problem?
- Do I feel that way at other times?
- How important is it to me to solve the problem?
- What effect would it have upon my life if I were without it?

Working with feelings is a major part of the work of those in helping roles since how people feel about their circumstances, their options or about the institutions that they are dealing with, often impedes them from making headway in their decisions. This is something taken up later in the book.

3. Acting. Knowing all that is required to solve a problem and then becoming motivated only gets someone to the starting-point. It is only by doing something about it that gets a problem solved.

It is important to identify the sequence of activities and skills required to achieve a solution, and to isolate those that are most difficult, or those that require the most support or practice before trying them out. Once those behaviours, which are most difficult or most risky, have been identified, they can be practised away from the situation until confidence has been developed and until the person feels easier in trying them out in the real situation. Talking, in this sense, is a form of practice and so is role-play. The advantage to this kind of practice is that it provides an opportunity to evaluate the results in a risk-free environment and allows the client to modify anything with which they are not satisfied.

Helping & Counselling: An Interactionist View

Contemporary discussion amongst practitioners often separates into two groups:

- Those who define symptoms in precise behavioural terms such as a specific behaviour; 'twitching', for example.
- Those who rely upon more abstract terms like 'anxiety'.

Some practitioners formulate difficulties in ways that can then be construed as 'acts' whilst others define the issues as an expression of a character disorder. All emphasise the individual and the pathology as part of the individual: the individual is thus the site of the problem and is the problem. An interactionist approach does not begin there.

It is true however, and remains true, that if there is no noticeable relief for the person then the work – by whatever chosen method – has not been successful. The effort is made in order to alleviate the suffering of the individual. Nevertheless, what is of crucial importance is the recognition that the social context, dynamic circumstances, call it what you will (and it becomes more and more important[54] what you do call it), the social dimension of the problem must be given a place on centre stage.

'But a problem exists in a person,' you might say. And indeed it does. 'And we only have the person to help,' you might add. Indeed we do. 'So what does it matter to think of the social context?' Well, it matters in all kinds of ways and it matters more the shorter the time you are to spend helping someone.

> "A problem can also be thought of as a particular type of behaviour that has been singled out (as being a problem) that occurs as part of a sequence of acts that take place between several people. It is the repetitive sequence of behaviour that is the cause of the intervention.
>
> Thinking of such symptoms as 'depression' or 'phobia' as a contract between people and therefore as adaptive to relationships, leads to a new way of thinking about helping." J. Haley, 1981.

Shifting thinking from the individual to the social context and other influential players has a number of consequences. Haley outlines them very well:

> "Not only must the therapist think in different ways about human dilemmas, but he or she must consider himself or herself as a member of the social unit that contains the problem. The therapist must be considered a part of the social dilemma of the client, and this can be a disturbing idea. Now it is becoming uncomfortably evident that a presenting problem includes the professional world in which the problem appears as well as the larger society."

He goes on:

> "When a therapeutic problem is defined as the social relationships of the client, a therapist must include himself in the issues since he helped define the problem. To label a child 'delinquent' or as suffering from 'minimal brain dysfunction', means that one is participating in the creation of a problem in such a way that changes may be made more difficult. A therapist who describes

---

[54] How things are named influences the way people respond to them and nowhere is that more important than in what we call what we are doing with our fellow human beings.

a family situation as characterised by a 'dominating mother and a passive father' or a 'symbiotic relationship between mother and daughter' has created problems even though the therapist might think he is merely identifying the problems put before him. The way one labels a human dilemma can crystallise a problem and make it chronic."

Haley explores this further with the example of a school refuser – a routine problem you might think and the task of the practitioner to get the youth to function appropriately. Yet suppose the school is in a slum and is such a bad school that the therapist can only sympathise with the young person for avoiding it as a waste of time? The problem is thus not simply a boy's truancy but also a problem school. If one includes the school, the line between therapy and social or political action becomes obscure.

A depressed wife; an excessively drinking staff member; a fraught and over-anxious manager may all be defined as 'the one with the problem' and worked with. However if the context is ignored, the social circumstances not explored and who provided the definition that 'this condition needs help' discovered, then we might actually be working with the wrong bits of a system and making someone responding reasonably (if not rationally) and doing them no favours.

> "When one accepts the idea that the problems of a client include the social milieu, including the therapist, the therapist must always consider the coalitions he is involved in when he acts. Not only must he consider whether he is acting as a social control agent of society whose job is to quieten the trouble makers but he must also think of this function in social frameworks smaller than that of society as a whole. Problem solving from this point of view is not as simple as some behaviour modifiers would suggest." J. Hayley, 1981.

Learning & Information Model

There are a variety of approaches that have been designed to help individuals solve personal problems. Many are recent in origin and derive from techniques developed in what are often called the 'new therapies'. The approach outlined here is based upon a learning and information model. The underlying assumptions are:

- People can learn to solve their own problems and, when they do, they acquire skills that are transferable to other situations.
- Many people lack sufficient information in their awareness to solve their problems. The role of practitioners is to help them to raise the information into their awareness so they can act for themselves.
- Many problems are possible to improve through the help of another.

Such an approach would not be suitable for dealing with long-standing emotional difficulties or critically serious disruptions to an individual's life, unless it were accompanied by skilled specialist help. Force-field analysis (see the end of this chapter) is an additional resource for personal problem solving and draws on the work of Kurt Lewin (1946) and Gerard Egan (1975).

Problem Solving & Behavioural Flexibility

Effective decision-making is about choice and choice is related to outcomes – knowing what you are aiming to achieve. The outcome needs to be stated accurately and specifically, because 'sloppy' language produces sloppy results. 'A better relationship with the boss' may take many forms and not all of them would be appropriate or useful. The key question is, 'What does 'better' in this context mean?' Until we know what it means, and whether it is achievable and worthwhile, we had better keep going.

Outcomes that are framed in changing the behaviour of third parties are not useful either. I may want 'my son to be more pleasant' but that gives all the power to him and he is unlikely, this side of adulthood, to change. Coping with adolescence is not easy, but I would be better served figuring out a way to influence myself, and my responses to him, rather than him directly because, in the end, I only have control over myself. I can only attempt to *influence* him. Outcomes have to be under our direct influence or we need to keep working at them.

Once you have a clear outcome, you have to have the behavioural resources to gain it. This requires *behavioural flexibility*, which is often limited by underlying beliefs and concerns that are not always consciously known. Most personal problems have some function or purpose in the total life circumstances of that individual. Somehow and at some time, it made sense to acquire whatever habit or behaviour pattern they now seek to change. However, if change were such a simple and straightforward matter, practitioners would quickly be out of business.

The fact is that problems give people certain kinds of *secondary rewards*: ways of getting particular kinds of attention that are extremely important to them and which they believe they cannot get in other ways. If, for example, I repeatedly complain of my ill-health, and it gets me noticed, I nevertheless remain heavily invested in staying the way I am, since it gets me something that I want – time, sympathy and attention.

Making technical suggestions to solve a personal problem is the least difficult aspect of helping. It is more important to establish what 'pay-off' comes with having the problem for the person concerned (since they vary from person to person and from problem to problem) and to find ways for the client to get the same reward more safely and more effectively.

Changing Behaviours

It may be unfortunate but it is true that the only behaviour you can do something about is your own, as we observed with the parent of the adolescent example a few paragraphs ago.

You cannot change other people; you can only help them to change if they want to. The problem may appear to be centred in someone else, but the only parts you can act upon immediately are the parts that influence and affect yourself. Learning and accepting that this is the case may be the greatest potential learning for many people who come seeking help believing that if only someone else would change it would all be different. How right they are, but how utterly unimportant it is to the work the two of you are capable of doing together.

You cannot work with people who aren't present in the room – only with the response of the person in the room to those who are not. That immediately limits the opportunities for endless conversations about 'how awful things are' and so on that distract from real, useful work.

Once you have taken the first step and begun to concentrate upon your own behaviour, you can begin to apply the steps below.

1. Identify the problem. Express the essence of the problem in a simple sentence that a seven year old would understand. Keep at this stage until you get it. This may mean facing that there is not one problem but several all wrapped up in a situation. Then you have to decide which 'bit' you are going to tackle first.

2. What have you done so far? Briefly get an outline of the strategies attempted and the results obtained, so far. Explore when the individual first became aware of the issue and the signals which indicated that it was an issue. What are the signals they notice now that indicates that the problem is about to appear? This is about finding out what the lead-up to the problem is.

3. What have you not done but could attempt? Explore alternative options and ask, non-judgementally, why they have not been attempted. If they have been attempted, then ask, 'What happened?' This begins the process of identifying the underlying restrictions of belief.

4. What gets in the way? What are the factors that hold the person back? What might they be saying to themselves that limits them? What other self-imposed limitations might there be that they might need to explore? At this stage, reference to the personal *myths*[55] of the individual may help.

5. What do you want? What is the outcome sought in solving this problem? Keep on going with this until you have a positive and specific description that you are clear is potentially achievable by the person concerned. It has to be capable of achievement by them and, once achieved, sustained by them.

6. Is it realistic? How does this outcome stand up to rigorous analysis in the light of potential experience? Modify the plan and do more work, rather than allow the person to go out and discover more pain and frustration.

7. Reduce it to manageable chunks. Reduce the overall aim to manageable time-related pieces. Make sure the time scale is realistic.

8. Implementation. Work out together the steps to be put into effect – by when? Ensure there is sufficient support – if needed. Consider what will happen if the unexpected appears and confounds your efforts.

[55] See *Personal and Practitioner Myths* in Chapter 12: *The Altruistic Practitioner?*

9. Evaluate. Review the actual events against your expectations. Invite feedback. Stay involved. Once you have put a plan into action, it is important to check how they went about it so that they can remember it next time or go over the areas of difficulty. Reviewing enables people to build upon their success and to identify skills they already have and use.

Future Pacing

Remember to check that agreements built together are going to be effective where they are to go and by those who will execute them. 'Future pacing' is the term used to describe the importance of paying attention to the implementation phase of any work. A good deal of useful effort fails at the last stage when not enough time and attention are given to asking, 'Will this fit where it is to go?' or 'Will those who have the task of dealing with our decisions have the capacity to manage the consequences?'

Asking the individual if they have thought of how they will manage the impact of any decision they make ensures they do! Sometimes, when a piece of work gets to the final stage, it becomes apparent that those designing the plan and those left to implement it, do not share the same overall aim. As a result, more work needs to be done – not necessarily on the design but on persuading the implementers of the need for the action.

Similarly with individuals: it seems like a good idea to learn how to speak more assertively until I consider how I am going to deal with the effect of having the skill when I meet my manager next week! What I couldn't do before and now can do may make me more aware of the implications of the skill I wanted. With any new personal skill comes a whole host of revisions to our self-image and a whole new set of implications that start with being 'seen' in a different light by others.

Summary: Facilitating Change

"The degree to which I can create relationships which facilitate the growth of others is a measure of the growth I have achieved for myself." C Rogers, 1961.

The work of the practitioner might be summarised as that of facilitating change in the client. It seems from the evidence provided by research studies that to facilitate change it is important to:

- Communicate in such a way that people feel able to trust you – enough.
- Establish contact and build rapport.
- Communicate clearly and unambiguously. Be aware that your behaviour matches your intentions.
- Know how to handle feelings.
- Have a genuinely positive attitude towards the people you work with.
- Be mature enough to allow others their separateness and respect your own, so that you do not become engulfed by their fears or overwhelmed by their griefs.
- Enter fully and sensitively into the other's world of feelings and meanings.

- Behave in a way that provides the safety for clients to grow. The freer from threat they feel, the more attention there is available to deal with any feelings of conflict in them.
- Respect people's ability to make choices – even, especially, when they differ from those you might like to suggest.

A Problem Solving Model

This is a way of thinking that is useful for both the practitioner and the client. It can be operated anywhere and for almost any problem.

P:	Pose the problem accurately.
R:	Refine the problem areas into manageable chunks.
O:	Outline the 'right' kind of questions to ask.
B:	Bring back the data: information accurate and relevant to the problem.
L:	Look for solutions.
E:	Evaluate options.
M:	Make a decision.
S:	So what next?

Force-field Analysis as a Problem Solving Method

Force-field analysis can be used when working with someone on a problem they wish to change. It provides a step-by-step approach that covers all the factors in the situation. It includes those that promote change, and are therefore helpful, and those that oppose change, and are therefore restraining.

1. Identify the problem
- Does the client own the problem? Are they willing to take responsibility for the problem?
- Is the problem solvable? Is the problem expressed in concrete terms understood by both parties?

2. Clarify the problem
- Break down the problem into sub-parts and explore their interaction.

3. Establish priorities
- Choose a 'chunk' of the problem to begin with that can be handled easily. Ensure that it is under the control of the person being helped.

4. Establish a workable goal
- State the object in a behaviourally descriptive way that ensures that you will have indicators of its achievement.
- Ensure that the client owns the goal and is committed to attaining it, and is not merely saying so to keep you quiet.
- Break the goals down into workable units.

5. Means to achieve the goals
- Look at all those forces, however incidental, that may well facilitate and encourage the client to achieve change. Include internal approval, success, external praise, environmental support etc.
- Do the same for all those factors that will undermine, inhibit or restrain the client from moving ahead easily.
- Put this into two columns as below:

Facilitating	Restraining

Once you have the information on the two 'sides', it needs to be evaluated and each element given a different force, or weighting. It is not the sheer volume in one column or the other that is important so much as the seriousness or impact of each of the aspects listed. It may now be necessary to spend some time fleshing out the scenarios; considering the implications of each one and what impact it has in influencing the effectiveness of the change process.

Suggested Reading
Jongeward & James: *Born to Win: Transactional Analysis with Gestalt Experiments.* Addison-Wesley, 1976.
Harris, T A: *I'm OK – You're OK.* Pan Books, 1969.

SECTION VII

THE SEVEN STAGE MODEL
of Human Relations

Chapter 22
The Seven Stage Model
An Overview

Stage	Purpose	Skills
1. CONTACTING	Establishing rapport Relationship building	Listening Attending Matching Questioning Mirroring
2. CONTRACTING	Creating conditions and agreeing boundaries Establishing an initial outcome Establishing mutual responsibility Identifying areas of concern Establishing time, frequency, style of meeting Gaining commitment for the work Developing a working alliance	Questioning Checking Negotiating Contracting
3. CLARIFIYING	Developing safety to allow disclosure Enabling gains in understanding of dilemmas Understanding the implications of difficulties. Identifying issues Listening for and identifying themes or patterns	Reflecting Paraphrasing Open questions Restating /Key word repetition Prompting Testing understanding Summarising
4. CHALLENGING	Identifying the impasse Working with themes or patterns Offering permission Encouraging self-confrontation Supporting through discharge Holding the challenge Developing new/latent strengths	Defining Confronting Immediacy Tough loving Cathartic skills Specificity Focusing
5. CHOOSING	Opening new perspectives Widening and considering options Generating choice Identifying resources Anticipating consequences Helping move towards change	Problem solving Re-contracting Dreaming Imagining Testing out ideas Planning
6. CHANGING	Enabling the individual to take charge, learn and manage the change process Bringing action into the world Monitoring and evaluating results Managing consequences	Goal-setting Action-planning Rehearsing Homework Implementation Revision
7. CLOSING	Bringing the work and relationship to a close Reviewing and evaluating the work Saying 'good-byes' and parting	Managing endings Disengagement Letting go

The Development of the Model

A model of how human relations evolve or develop over time is an important aspect of the preparatory equipment for the individual who aims to be effective in working with relationship. The Seven Stage Model of Human Relations arose out of a need to provide people from a wide variety of backgrounds with a simple overview of the stages of an effective interpersonal or helping relationship – of human relations. It was developed as an *applied* model to fit a variety of contexts from the outset. It is therefore comprehensive. It also has the potential for each stage to be extracted and given focus and attention according to the needs and priorities of the kind of relationship under consideration.

The model as outlined here is a description of an evolving way of practice. It has been generated by many years use and honed by reviewing it in the light of newly developing theoretical influences alongside the experience of an overwhelming group of practitioners and users. It is under continous evolution and refinement.

The principle issue at the time the model was first being developed was, 'How to get those wanting to be of service to pause long enough to think not only about what they do, but also about the implications of what they do'. (On the grounds that many human relations issues are made worse by thoughtless interference – however well-meaning the person concerned.) The common position is that many people move from the initial response to an inquiry to the *swift and direct offer of a solution* without considering the relationship or the role implications of the response offered. The model moves away from the traditional problem-answer model. The Seven Stage Model differs from many in that it offers:

- An initial *linear sequence of discrete and easily identifiable stages*, each with its own characteristic tasks and skills.
- A *narrative approach* to the evolution of the relationship.

The model has made sense of the experience of people from every conceivable background and setting. When it is linked to the deconstruction of a helping situation, as described earlier, via a series of questions, most practitioners are able to sense where in the model they work at their best and where they are in need of further development. By enabling the developing *human relations practitioner* to attend to the types of issues 'fitting' to each stage, they gain increasing confidence in their abilities for working with a wide range of issues and with more complex human dilemmas.

Effective Relationships

Effective human relations depend upon more than the particular skills a person has, the personality they live with and the interest they show in what they are doing: they are both an art and a science. There are things that can be learned and there are things which can be 'discovered' inside us – things which can only be discovered through the encouragement, interest, or challenge of an 'other'. We need some sense of what we are coming into relationship for, a sense of how and what the influences upon each of us are and a sense of trust in the potential between us to make the meeting successful – whatever its purpose. Roles, tasks, purposes all surround the meeting and the more we can disclose and acknowledge our understanding of these things, the freer we are to discover what else we might bring and what else we might learn from our meeting together.

The skills required for any effective relationship are not something that can be assembled in the wings and brought out on the stage – they are not a performance. However, it is true that there are key skills and attributes that make up effective ways of relating to other people and which can be identified, isolated, practised, learned and acquired. All of us had to go through some similar process as we were growing up to develop the repertoire we currently have. It is just that we didn't do it deliberately or thoughtfully – one of the reasons why our style of relating will work well in some places and with some people but will have limitations in others.

All relationships happen somewhere and have with them a more or less understood set of expectations. Part of the difficulty we experience in relationships that have more than a measure of goodwill is adjusting to the changes of response or behaviour which the other person shows us that fall outside what we have come to 'expect'. The context of the meeting and the expectations of those involved all shape what may be possible, no matter how skilled and effective those taking part are themselves.

The Seven Stage Model is a human relations model of *effective* relationships, not simply counselling relationships, nor even helping relationships. The model is applicable to short-term crisis work and longer-term helping relationships, including psychotherapy. It does not provide a theoretical base so much as a working model of the stages, sequences and skills that foster a progressive relationship in order to bring about effective change. Most of us in most of our relationships would benefit from knowing the stages most relevant to whatever task is at hand, and having fluency in the skills of the various stages that could enable us to respond with flexibility and finesse. The model draws on a wide range of influences for its inspiration and its stimulus, and is capable of being adapted by most practitioners as one way of reflecting upon the progress of their working relationships.

The model also recognises the importance of the social context which forms an underlying and pervasive influence upon the potentialities of the relationship itself. In crisis work, for example, it would recognise that direct action may well be the way in which the relationship is formed. There is no presupposition that the stages require two people to be meeting in a comfortable room together; the model is robust enough to travel to outside contexts and less orthodox settings. Those involved can be anywhere and in any circumstances.

Also, the relationship may concentrate upon only one key stage of the whole model because of the issues to be faced or the work that needs to be done. For example, some types of relationship are more concerned with *clarifying* the nature of the meaning of what has happened or of developing a better understanding of what is going on. There are a series of useful skills that promote this activity. Other relationships are much more concerned with managing the processes of *changing* as a result of a decision that has been taken (itself usually as a result of matters having been clarified and the application of other processes which precede effective change). *Choosing* precedes changing – exploring options before implementing decisions – and there are useful skills that can facilitate that process.

That said, however, even in short-term relationships, it is often the case that there is development from 'contacting' to 'contracting' and through many of the stages of the model to reach some fitting way to end the time together.

Levels of Involvement

Each practitioner will develop a range of skills and modes of operating that favour their personality, style and interest and the more they are aware of the range of strategies they seek to offer most productively, the more they can intervene at the most appropriate moment for all concerned. Those who are especially interested in counselling, for example, are not likely to be so interested in direct action. It is also crucial to know the boundaries of the situation before you offer anything and, if you don't know them or they haven't been outlined, it is better to impose some upon the situation rather than operate without any sense of limits at all.

For example, if the person you are meeting is given no information about your availability and the time-scale over which you will be involved, they may well be thinking and hoping that you will be around for far longer than anything your agency can afford. It is yet another loss for them to manage if the relationship ends after thirteen weeks (or when the agency pulls you out), especially if it is just beginning to be effective. In addition, for many people suffering a major crisis, it is only some weeks after the event that counselling-type help can be really beneficial. If the amount of time available is limited, then making good decisions about where to put what type of effort is crucial – these are all issues in preparation for practice. If a third party is involved, a commissioning agency for example, it is particularly important that the practitioner does not imply they can offer long-term support if there is absolutely no likelihood of gaining the agreement of the organisation to provide it.

Such a commitment can leave both parties able to maintain the relationship only as a private arrangement. This is something that needs to be discouraged because of some of the long-term difficulties such relationships create. Relationships formed in a work-related context give both parties certain kinds of formal expectations of one another. It can both protect and give safety to the work that arises. Taken outside those conventions and into the wider world it may create long-term dependency problems that the practitioner finds difficult to contain, manage or satisfactorily close. On the other hand, if both people are clear and work out an understanding together of how they wish to 'meet' following their more formal arrangements, then there is every reason to suppose it will work well. Perhaps what is most important is that both people make explicit the nature of the change of the relationship and the different kinds of freedoms that come into play.

A Collaborative Endeavour

As we have seen, relationship, to be effective, is a collaborative endeavour between both parties. Together they have to form a working alliance within a set of more or less clearly understood boundaries. The work has to be undertaken and some evaluation of its consequences and value has to be made. The Seven Stage Model is an excellent tool for fulfilling these needs. The model is summarised below:

Contacting:	Initial meeting and expectations.
Contracting:	Agreeing boundaries, conditions and contracts.
	Finding the level of commitment.
Clarifying:	Outlining and exploring the range of concerns.
Challenging:	Confronting ambiguities and inconsistencies of belief.
Choosing:	Moving towards consideration of new responses or behaviours.
Changing:	Initiating and maintaining a strategy.
Closing:	Ending the session and closing the relationship.

Not all effective relationships are required to go through all the stages at each meeting but someone skilled in developing effective relationships will know which stages are important to draw upon during a meeting or a working session. They will also know something of the specific skills that would be useful within each of the stages to enable them to display flexibility and responsiveness to situations that they would otherwise find difficult or overwhelming.

Although the model clearly is applicable in a linear form, it can also be described as a cyclical model or as a spiral. In many situations, individuals find that they need to revisit certain stages. The model is sufficiently flexible and adaptable to meet that need.

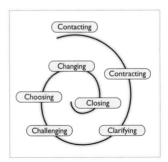

Applying the Model

Having a model is one thing, knowing when and how to apply which aspects for what purpose in the messiness of real life is quite another. In other words, gaining understanding in applying the model needs to be part of a developmental process.

> A *developmental* approach to the counselling relationship is the one which has most relevance to most people across a wide range of settings and for a wide range of purposes.

When we look at practice-based activities, people are often taught the theory disconnected from the practice and the practice has a very tenuous relationship to the theory at the time it is being offered. We all know examples of the individual who understands the theory of some practical activity but who is an incompetent performer. Most of us have encountered the dentist we would run away from, the doctor we would never see again or the receptionist who would inspire terror in Attila the Hun! The pressure of performance, of the need to be seen to 'do', often generates high levels of anxiety in the practitioner, which reduces their *awareness* (reflection in action) of their practice. The Seven Stage Model is designed to free practitioners, not limit them. It is a model and not a prescription. It is a description of what so many effective practitioners actually do, rather than a code of what practitioners *should* do.

Many people encountering the model for the first time are delighted at realising that they do all this already. They simply have not ordered it in this particular way. The model is a means to simplify the realities of practice, it reduces the disparate experience into manageable pieces and provides a guide to what the practitioner *might* do. In the following chapter, the seven stages are outlined, explaining the central tasks of each stage, the themes and issues involved, the central indications of the need for that stage and the skills that are most in demand from the practitioner.

In presenting the model, the intention is to expose the sense of narrative progression and to highlight the thematic streams that run through one stage and into another. It is more an overview of the working relationship than a dissection of the minutiae of what goes on between client and practitioner. It is not meant to suggest that these are the only skills possible to use or that one stage must follow from the preceding one. The model is an idealisation, an abstraction of what would happen if... in order to throw light upon what does happen.

Once the practitioner has grasped this they can then roam around the model and identify the parts they use most frequently, the skills most needed and the work they often find they avoid. It provides a conceptual map against which the practitioner can assess themselves but which has no prior score sheets that individuals have to achieve. In practice, this enables the individual practitioner to select stages of the model most relevant to their practice. So, for example, those who have short-term relationships to initiate and manage as part of their work, those with home visiting for maybe only an hour or two say, would find it useful to recognise that the focus of their work will be on the use of the skills of:

- Contacting
- Contracting
- Clarifying
- Closing

Those involved in crisis and grief work will need to work on some of the refinements of *contacting* and *changing* as well as understand issues of helping someone who is learning to manage closing so that they can help the client. Careers staff would be most concerned with issues of *contracting* and *clarifying*, (contacting would, of course, be important but getting down to some clarity of work in a short time is vital). The model also has the virtue of separating out into constituent skills particular tasks, such as:

- Reviewing and appraising.
- Assessing and clarifying.
- All types of counselling.
- Therapeutic work.
- Joint problem solving.

Although the model can be divided and separated out according to the key concerns of the practitioner, this does not imply that other stages of the model may not be useful. On the contrary, having a comprehensive understanding and familiarity with the other stages immeasurably increases the resources that any practitioner brings to the work they do. However, it is imperative that every practitioner is conversant with the skills that are central to their existing task

Flexibility of Context

Any model that hopes to travel usefully to a range of settings must manage contrasting trends. It must be general enough to travel. It must have applicability to where it is intended to go and it must be specific so that, when it gets there, it offers a useful map of what the land looks like. It must have relevance to the particular context. Since the Seven Stage Model is more interested in the relationship that takes place than in the specific task, it can be overlaid on any working relationship. Of course, it cannot identify the contextual issues but it emphasises the crucial influence context plays, both in a general sense and in the narrow confines of the relationship itself.

Many practitioners work within agencies or are sessional workers employed by agencies and without some common framework there is no guarantee that they will have a shared approach. It may be that we all do the same work and even talk about it in much the same way but, without a common framework to use as a template, individual practice may be more varied than is good for the individual or the agency. Developing a profile of the key stages and skills is not a mechanical exercise but a way of talking about practice that can usefully inform it. Once done, it can be repeated regularly as a way of assessing changes in practice, development in the work and individual progress.

No developmental alliance exists in a vacuum, as we have noted at various points throughout this book, and no two people meet free of all concerns and stripped of all illusions, hopes, issues and worries. We have already highlighted the external context and, as we move into exploring the practice issues of the relationship itself, we need to bear in mind that the contextual issues may have more influence on what is possible and what is attained than the ambitions of either of the two parties.

Similarly, we must also remember that each person brings their own contribution to the relationship; each will be striving to influence what takes place and each will have an internal context to manage. Surfacing some of those concerns and having ways to encourage a client to disclose them are part of the formation of the relationship. The early stages of contacting and contracting may be far from separate tasks and the contract may itself arise out of the introductions and exchanges of expectation that form the basis of many working relationships. On the other hand, the *commitment* may be established almost ahead of the contacting. The two parties may come together with a very clear understanding of what they are there to do, how and over what time, and it is this that creates the need for them to establish a working alliance. The *depth of contact* and the *strength of commitment* are highly dependent upon the overall aims and nature of the relationship that is to be developed.

Commitment, Conviction, Capability & The Seven Stage Model

The Seven Stage Model, as a description of the progression of face to face relationships, is founded on three key assumptions about people when they work collaboratively together. These are:

> 1. There has to be sufficient *commitment* from each of the parties: both to the relationship and the work. This phase would broadly link to Stages 1 & 2 of the model: contacting and contracting.

> 2. There has to be sufficient *conviction* about the value of the work and the belief in it of those involved. This phase is present from the later clarifying stage through challenging.

> 3. Those involved have to have the *capacity* to do the work. This phase is closely connected with the change process and includes elements such as developing the necessary skills to implement the desired change.

These three conditions of *commitment, conviction*, and *capability* run throughout all working relationships and are often guides as to how successful any working relationship is likely to be. In almost all instances, it is not that people are unable to do what they set out to accomplish, nor is it that they do not believe (at least consciously) that they cannot do whatever they intend, it is that they are insufficiently committed to what is required. Either they are not committed to the effort involved (when they discover that it is more complicated than they thought) or they discover that they have insufficient belief either in themselves or the work and then they withdraw or give up altogether.

The more one person is in the position of helping another, the more these things are critical. It is no good a manager being committed to helping a staff member with their development if that person has no commitment to it themselves. It is not useful to exhort someone to improve or change, take action or otherwise behave differently, if that individual has a set of self-limiting beliefs about their own performance.

When people say they 'can't do' something, it is not always a capability issue in the sense of them not having the physical equipment to do it, the mental agility to understand it and so on. It is more likely that they have beliefs that get in the way of them making a successful performance. This means that there is a great deal more work at the first phase of any working relationship (especially one that requires time and trust) than many people think. It also means that the second phase of conviction has much more influence upon the end result than the person's abilities.

The traditional model is based on an assumption that what people can do, they will do, but we now know that values and beliefs influence people's behaviour in very powerful and substantial ways. The human relations approach, therefore, acknowledges that commitment is the key to the whole enterprise and holds it at the core of the relationship.

Chapter 23
The Seven Stage Model
Stage One: Contacting

Purposes   **Skills**
Establishing rapport   Listening
Relationship building   Attending
                                Matching
                                Questioning
                                Mirroring

Creating the Working Alliance

The first stages of any effective helping relationship are strongly influenced by how the parties come together, how they meet, what expectations they may hold and what prior knowledge they have of what they are there to explore. For much of the time when people come together there is some initial period of getting into the work, creating the atmosphere. In some cases, the initial period may have more to do with working out the time available and clarifying the appropriateness of the task – both identified as part of *contracting* and *clarifying* respectively. But the underlying purpose of even such discussion lies in developing a *form of contact* or of *meeting*. This may be a delicate and lengthy process (especially if the topic is sensitive to one or both parties or the stakes are high) or it may be fairly cursory.

It is worthwhile noting here that when a relationship is not working later in its life it is often the failure to establish strong rapport or develop an effective contract in relation to what the work was to accomplish that is largely responsible. The first two stages of making contact and developing the contract therefore overlap and they can be taken together as forming the two essential halves of the process of forming a real working commitment to:

- The task.
- The relationship.
- The conditions that will operate.

Before any help can succeed the practitioner and the client have to form a working alliance. It is primarily the practitioner's job to 'model the process':

- To indicate how the relationship will work.
- To observe the boundaries that are in operation.
- To manage the balance of contributions.
- To keep to the task.
- To manage, in a generally facilitative sense, the unfolding meeting and process.

This in itself can be a major feat since some people have never had the experience of really being listened to or being given time and attention by someone else. Facing the prospect of entering such an unfamiliar space may cause embarrassment or anxiety. For others, the opportunity to explore their circumstances is an invitation that leads to a lot of unfocused talk that at some point has to be harnessed into a directed dialogue. 'Shaping' the client's responses so that they become oriented to the nature of how the meeting works is part of helping the client learn what it means to be just that, a client – something many practitioners assume the client knows when, in reality, they may not.

The practitioner can do much to put the client at ease by picking up cues from the client early and responding to them appropriately. There are two principal tasks to accomplish in promoting effective contact:

 1. Removing distractions and minimising the potential for interruptions.

 2. Promoting an atmosphere that enhances the client's safety to disclose those things they need to talk about.

However, there is no point, for example, in slavishly making someone feel at ease who patently already is at ease, or laboriously working out a contract in detail when the person concerned knows perfectly well the purpose of the meeting. It does, however, need one of you to remind the other of it – or the opportunity to revise it unilaterally later becomes possible. Artistry here is all.

This raises immediately the question of, 'Where to begin?' If the practitioner spends too long relating to the client warmly and openly, this may be a way of never getting round to the crucial material at all. Lots of good chat may happen but nothing much may change. If the practitioner begins with too abrupt a request to get to the heart of things, the client is likely to back off and freeze up.

Whilst the content of our communications is critical, the non-verbal accompaniment has the greater influence upon how what we say is received. (More on this topic is to be found in *Section Five: The Core of Helping*.) Some useful reminders though include remembering to:

- Sit in an open, expectant but non-threatening way.
- Hold an open gaze rather than a stare.
- Invite the client to choose where to begin.
- Monitor the client's overall body posture.
- Mirror the client's body posture and movements in a non-overt way.
- Match the client's language and use their preferred 'channels of communication'[56].
- Pace the client's world-view in an attempt to understand their frame of reference rather than challenge their ideas and beliefs so early.

---

[56] Identifying and matching a client's preferred channel of communication is an element of NLP.

Once the client begins to feel you are interested enough in them as a person (as opposed to them simply being someone with a problem) to want to understand how matters really stand for them and are taking the trouble to learn about their individual *model of the world*[57], they will be more willing to let you lead them into new areas of exploration and clarifying – the next stages of helping.

It is worth noting, however, that it may take a good deal of time for things to move beyond early stages of developing the relationship. This is not to suggest that there may be a lot of unnecessary conversation or that topics will be superficial or trivial, but that the client will often not know the possibilities of the relationship. Only as it develops will they begin to sense that here is a place that they might just test out one or two other things that may or may not be connected to the matter that brought them here in the first place. A useful form of self-assessment for a practitioner looking at this stage of the work is to consider their approach in relation to the following elements:

- **Balance:** between interventions and listening.
- **Pace:** the speed at which things unfold.
- **Flexibility:** the willingness on the part of the practitioner to respond to the client.
- **Management:** the practitioner's success in creating a sense of the context and purpose in which the client can respond.
- **Development:** the continuity and growth of the session.

Levels of Understanding

There are three levels of understanding, which are progressively more effective in enabling people to explore their experience. Being aware of these levels enhances an understanding of the level of engagement of the practitioner within the helping relationship.

1. Understanding *about you*. This is the level of understanding of the client and their supposed difficulties as viewed through someone else's perceptions. Practitioners are often working within this level following a referral from another practitioner or carer. This is a second-hand, or remote, form of understanding.

2. Understanding *you*. This is the level of understanding someone through the perceptions of the person in relationship with the other. It is based upon the practitioner's awareness, sensitivities, knowledge or skills. In other words, it is a form of understanding based upon *my own internal frame of reference* of what you disclose to me.

3. Understanding *with you*. This is the level of understanding that is most demanding to acquire and demonstrate and the one required for developing effective rapport. It requires us to put aside everything but our common humanity and strenuously attempt to see the world as the client sees it. In doing so, we enter into their reality without becoming lost in it.

---

[57] 'Model of the world' refers to how the client construes their experience in the particular ways that they do in order to explain how they understand what is happening in the terms they use.

Stage Two: Contracting: Conditions & Boundaries

Purposes

Creating conditions
Agreeing boundaries
Establishing initial outcomes
Establishing mutual responsibility
Identifying areas of concern
Establishing time, frequency and style of meeting
Gaining commitment for the work
Developing a working alliance

Skills

Contracting
Negotiating agreement
Checking understanding
Using appropriate questions

Levels of Commitment

"Until one is committed, there is hesitancy, the chance to draw back – always ineffectiveness. Concerning all acts of initiative and creation, there is one elementary truth – the ignorance of which kills countless ideas and endless plans: the moment one definitely commits oneself then providence moves too. All sorts of things occur to help one that would never otherwise have occurred. A whole stream of events issues from the decision, raising in one's favour all manner of unforeseen incidents and meetings and material assistance, which no man could have dreamed would come his way. Whatever you can do or dream you can, begin it. Boldness has genius, power and magic in it. Begin it now." Goethe.

People may be committed, but have no clear idea about what they are doing. They may know very well what they are doing, but they are not necessarily committed. Commitment has a number of levels:

- I can be committed to the work but not to you.
- I can trust you but not be committed to the work.
- I can trust you and be committed to the work but afraid I am somehow going to be exposed by what might be revealed so I am not committed to my part in it.
- I may not be competent to undertake what I believe will come out of our meeting so my commitment is ambiguous.

All these things make commitment anything but a straightforward matter. Living in a time when the notion of commitment itself is less and less an influence on people's behaviour, it may seem like something of a hopeless pursuit to 'gain commitment'. However, if people are enabled to understand what it is they are getting into, how it operates and what the consequences may be, one way or the other, it does help to focus the mind. It can, in some cases, be an awakening to the whole notion that commitment has a point to it and that it is not something that one party imposes upon another but is a condition that one can enter into freely.

Contracting & Commitment

Contracting is partly a way of the client testing out the determination of the practitioner to 'hold them'. It is also an opportunity for the practitioner to gauge the likely continuity of the commitment that the client is personally proclaiming. As the contracting phase unfolds both sides are testing out the resolve of the other but it is the practitioner who:

1. Must have sufficient *potency:* the 'juice' to get things done.

2. Must offer sufficient *protection:* for the client to feel safe.

3. Must provide sufficient *permission:* the freedom for the client to begin to change without judgement or interference.

All three aspects are tested out in the contracting phase. And if the contracting is not done, or done poorly, it may be that the relationship spends much of its time, either in each session or from time to time, negotiating whether the client is seriously in the relationship or not.

Contracting is about 'being in' the relationship, and is concerned with the issues relating to how deep and strong the relationship may need to be to undertake the work that is required. In *Practitioner Resources* we saw how contracting is about reaching a *mutual* understanding about the work the client and practitioner are to undertake. It is not about forcing the compliance of the client to your own particular control needs – though they will be reflected in the way you do the contracting and the kinds of contract you negotiate.

Setting Boundaries

The stages of contacting and contracting are often closely linked in time, with the practitioner building the relationship through the discussion and exploration of what the client hopes for from the practitioner and the relationship. It is important to recognise that the practitioner is responsible for making clear:

1. Time: the length and frequency of sessions.

2. Space: the location and the provision of sufficient freedom from interference and distraction.

3. Interventions: the range of ways of working with the client.

4. Structure: overall clarity so that the client cannot misconstrue the situation or the reason for the meeting.

Having set the boundaries together, which may range from a supportive comment to a more detailed addressing of the above issues, the scene is set for the client and practitioner to focus on the client's needs. The concept of establishing a mutually agreed contract with the client is based on a number of underlying philosophical assumptions about people. These include the view that people:

- Have the ability to change.
- Can take responsibility for their own destiny.
- Can work collaboratively.
- Have the ability to fulfil more of their own potential.

Berne, the founder of Transactional Analysis, made it clear that none of us are functioning fully rationally and aware the whole time or even much of the time. A contract that simply assumes people are rationally agreeing to conditions, which they will then fulfil, betrays a level of naïvety that is foolish.

People may desperately want to change now, but in three weeks time when the situation has become more manageable and coming to talk about it seems less exciting, they may find their motivation slipping. Also, even when 'I know what I want', it is not always what is realistic, or even manageable if I got it.

Deepening the Working Alliance

Motivation to help and the desire to be effective are no guarantees of success. The issue for the effective practitioner is how explicit they need to make the purpose and the nature of the way the time shall be spent together. This is not an easy matter to decide upon – especially in advance of the meeting. And yet, without holding some general parameters in mind, there is the risk of the client leading the practitioner and them both wandering unhelpfully across all sorts of interesting, but essentially tangential terrain.

If the practitioner arrives in the situation with a rigid plan, it may well only serve to distance the other person in the relationship. On the other hand, if the practitioner arrives with no plan, the resulting communication, however engaging at the time, is likely to be indecisive or inconclusive. All relationships, however brief, have some conditions attached to them. The art is to raise the conditions that are most relevant and that can have most positive influence upon the task that the meeting is setting out to accomplish.

> A *working alliance* is what needs to be aimed at in most human relations encounters; a relationship that has *sufficient commitment and involvement by both parties* to achieve what is needed.

Some (usually informal) helping meetings may well have no explicit contract, whereas more formal helping relationships are most effective when they do. The more explicit we can be about what we are here for, what we want to do and how we will know when we get there, the more openness, commitment and accountability will be promoted between those involved.

In many ways, helping relationships require a strong focus and clarity of role and purpose if later work is to be successful. In such relationships the idea of a contract is a wise step to take. The whole contracting phase helps to give focus and a plan of progress to achieve a result. Without some such plan there is no guarantee either of going anywhere or of knowing how we have ended up wherever we happen to be.

Contracting & Context

It is worth remembering that the *context defines the contract.* Therefore the practitioner needs to be aware of their own and the client's external situation, internal world, beliefs, values and how they determine and influence the area of work they are to engage in together.

Client: *Internal:* the internal world the client lives in.

     External: the world they live in, expectations, external boundaries.

Practitioner: *Internal:* their degree of openness, attentiveness, presence, centredness.

     External: the organisational boundaries, role boundaries etc.

The practitioner needs to hold some useful questions in mind for themselves when approaching the contracting stage since, once the contact is established, though it can be changed, it does have a large influence over what happens and how far it can be changed.

- Am I willing to enter your world?
- Do I have time?
- Do I have commitment?
- Am I best suited?
- Are you asking for help?
- Are you asking for *my* help?

The client has only one essential question:

- 'Can I disclose enough to get the help I need?'

It may be that the client is expecting more from you than you are able to offer. It may be that they are skilled at getting others to take on their problems and expect you to do the same. It may be that they are wholly inexperienced in contracting about the conditions and they only need some encouragement. What is perhaps most important here is that the initiator of the relationship, the person who is in the enabling role, needs to *manage the situation.* They need to ensure that:

- The required minimum conditions are made explicit.
- The boundaries are clearly established – even if they are changed in the light of new information.

Avoiding this stage of the work (often a single session to outline the broad contract which may be reviewed throughout the work at different times), on the grounds that it is too artificial or too formal, is no excuse. This leads to the insecurities and uncertainties that are generated by open-ended meetings that leave both parties unsure of what is possible, how long is available and what type of exchanges are legitimate.

n cases where the client is naïve or inexperienced, it is nothing less than simple courtesy to spell out some of the possibilities that are available for them in the time available. Once practitioners become used to dealing with contracting they raise it as a matter of course and usually have little difficulty with it. It is the newcomer to such a stage in the helping relationship who finds it odd or strange and who will often pretend to themselves that both parties already understand what they are there to do. Unless you have agreed the contract between you, you are working on assumptions. The assumptions may be right or wrong but that's all they are.

The underlying purpose of this stage of the relationship is to test out the strength of commitment that the other person has to the work that you are hoping to do together. If you are doing more than 50% of the work you had better be sure that the meeting is for your benefit if you are working that hard. In effective helping relationships, the client needs to recognise that the problem is theirs and that you can help them to solve it by putting in no more than 50% of the effort.

The importance of an *explicit contract* that practitioner and client make in assessing the potential success of what takes place cannot be overestimated. The less explicit the contract, the more each party is likely to be pursuing their own individual agenda and the less they are likely to be working conjointly. The more rigorous the contract, the more at ease the client is likely to be in the long run. That said, it is important to remember that a distressed individual is hardly likely to be able to sit down and bring their adult, aware functioning to the issue of the boundaries and conditions that are to operate in this or future sessions – they may need some indication that you care first.

But that should not mean abandoning the contracting phase of the work, simply delaying it. It is a useful reminder that, important though the contract is and that the work would be better not started until it is clear what is being attempted, it doesn't mean it has to be forced upon the naïve client or the unhappy individual as though they are signing up to some double-glazing deal.

Developing Contracts

Initially, the contract will often be loose and informal and only through further development will it become more specific and clearer to the client and practitioner the deeper focus of their work together.

The contract need not be too detailed or too rigid. It needs to offer structure for the relationship and the work to progress without scaring or overwhelming the client. Therefore the contracting stage is not a one-off event but will be re-visited in the form of review, revision, focus and evaluation throughout the helping relationship. This avoids inflexibility and irrevocable commitment to whatever the initial goals were.

It is important to have a sense throughout the work that the map drawn at the outset is not necessarily the territory and, through the stages of the helping relationship, walking the territory may well result in changes to the map. The changes are best made explicit, rather than being implicit. Often the issues individuals bring are based on their living out implicit contracts with people in their wider world (partners, colleagues, parents – others who the individual has allowed to determine what they believe they 'must' do) that would be useful if made explicit as a way of surfacing how we impose upon ourselves expectations that may well be unreal and/or unnecessary.

The whole process of contracting provides a good model for reviewing implicit contracts in the outside world.

The contracting process is more about 'modelling' for the other person (or teaching by example) so that what is happening can be planned and consciously managed rather than left simply to occur as a mysterious by-product of the time spent together. Much about helping is mysterious, but this doesn't need to be. Often, contracting enables the client, perhaps for the first time, to begin to recognise that most human relationships work according to a set of assumptions and these can be surfaced, evaluated and then modified or changed.

Types of Contracts

Some practitioners work with 'loose' contacts and others with 'tight' contracts and it is worth considering the differences and when each has a place in a helping relationship

> **'Loose' contracts.** A loose contract is more likely to reflect a broad relationship that has, as yet, no central or concrete aim. It may be enough to let the person know that if they find this meeting works for them that you would also see them regularly, for an hour each time (say), and they would be able to talk about any other concerns they have.
>
> Such an agreement is, in the sense used here, a contract. A loose contract is likely to be more useful for a client who has few boundaries and finds it difficult to work even within so few. Many people are so afraid of others controlling them that a tight contract is simply an invitation to run away because they fear what might be waiting for them further down the line of the relationship.
>
> A loose contract is also useful if someone is aiming to explore and learn rather than setting out to bring about a specific change. Where a specific change is the desired outcome, a loose contract can be no more than a pretence at working at something.
>
> **'Tight' contracts.** A tight contract is useful:
> - When planning for specific changes.
> - For projects and actions.
> - For bringing about a focus.
> - For ensuring that the work remains well gathered together.
>
> Some clients need the support of strong clear boundaries so that they always know where they are with you. Such boundaries give them the security to let go and find out what is happening to themselves. Others know that they have a tendency to be distracted too easily and feel more able to be committed if

they are reminded of the conditions that they would like to be working within. Others find that only when the terms, conditions and boundaries, even down to absence and telephone clauses, have been fully discussed can they feel ready to do the work.

Contracting Questions

Contracting questions are a way of making both parties aware of what, in reality, the commitment will require. In this way, they are similar in essence to the questions for looking at *changing behaviours (see Practitioner Resources)*. These questions also provide a check for both on the likelihood of them being able to work together effectively. So once the working conditions are established, getting down to the question of, 'What are we here to help you accomplish?' is best done slowly and thoroughly.

It was Eric Berne and his particular approach to helping, Transactional Analysis, that made strong use of contracting questions. For establishing a working alliance the following questions can hardly be bettered. Contracting certainly needs to cover each of these questions, whether done in a formulaic way or by way of a more casual set of words. In whatever way it is done, the practitioner needs to have established a confident sense of how much the commitment to change is 'lived' in the client. And any reservations and get-out clauses need to be reworked and re-explored.

1. What do you want... what do you really want? A contract goal needs to be phrased in a positive way such as, 'I want to spend more time reading'. Negative goals, such as, 'I want to stop wasting my time' rarely result in long-term change since the very process of working on negative phrases reinforces the negative state.

Much of the work in the helping relationship is related to assisting the client to find something they really want that is worth working towards. Then they have to establish if they have sufficient energy in relation to the desired change. If the motivation for change is external to the client, i.e. if someone else wants the client to change, then the outcome of the work is unlikely to result in any long-term change.

2. Is it realistic for you? This is an important reality check. Has at least one other person in the world achieved this? It may be true the client wants someone else to 'treat me better', but it is impossible to make someone else change. Such forms of third party counselling are rarely successful. 'Given your present circumstances and network, is this change possible for you?' If it is, 'Is it sustainable in the world you move around in?' If it is, 'Will you be more at ease inside yourself with having made the change you are proposing?'

All these questions simply provide checks to ensure that the client has more than a rough idea of where they want to get to and has some idea of how it might live once they are there. That said, the idea is not to encourage some ruthless interrogation of the client, only to help them explore the ramifications of a change they may only now, for the first time, be articulating with clarity and discovering the implications of as they go along.

3. How will you and I know when you have achieved the change? If the goal is too general it will be difficult to tell if the client has achieved it, and they may well be working on it for an eternity. The more the person has a *detailed* perceptual sense of how it will be when the change has occurred, the more useful it is. Positive visualisation/sensing and asking questions like those below are all useful strategies here.

- What will you be doing?
- How will you feel?
- Who will notice?
- What thoughts will you have?
- How will others see you?
- What will you sound like?

Any change needs to be specific, reportable, demonstrable or observable.

4. What will you have to give, or 'give up' to get it? All change has a price. It may be in terms of facing a fear, a sense of power or powerlessness, money, endings, time, commitment, loss or turmoil. It may be that the client decides that having explored and stated the goal, confirmed it is possible, outlined clearly how they would know they have achieved the change only to decide it is not worth the price ... yet ... or maybe ever. The helping relationship may end at this point. If it doesn't then the next question is...

5. What is the first step and by when? This aims to help the client to begin to change from the start. It checks the level of commitment to change i.e. if the client is ready to take on the challenge of change *now*. It builds the beginning of an action plan and enables the next phase either to build on the success, or to explore how come the first step was not achieved. It may be within this area that the client outlines who might support them in their change i.e. what forces around them are supporting their endeavour.

6. How might you sabotage yourself? This question focuses the client on past behaviour and how they 'get in their own way'. All of us have favoured ways of not quite succeeding in doing what we *might* intend – and often the very language in which we put the claim gives it away (as you might observe by the use of *might* in the phrasing earlier in this sentence).

Sabotages often take the form of unhelpful internal messages, re-runs of past critical observations (especially from authority figures). The client is assisted to explore their self-defeating instructions, which may have been very helpful at one time but which are now old patterns that get in the way of the grown-up situation. Bringing the potential sabotages into the open will help to reduce their influence. Specific work may be done on how to reduce these influences further.

Another part of this question relates to the practitioner: are you aiding the client to sabotage themselves by not helping them to be specific and detailed, not challenging them on what seem to be incongruities, or on the way they seem to be getting in their own way, even in the contracting phase? Letting a client leave the session with the practitioner thinking 'they'll never do it' and not voicing this is a form of sabotage and of assisting the client to re-live their old patterns.

Stage Three: Clarifying

It is useful to think of clients as needing their problems. Since they have usually taken a long time to get them, have spent a while hanging on to them before asking you for help, it is also useful to remember that it will do no great harm for them to keep their problem until they come up with their own solution.

Purposes	Skills
Developing safety to allow disclosure	Prompting
Listening for themes or patterns	Using open questions
Identifying issues, themes, patterns	Key word repetition
Understanding the implications of difficulties	Restating
Enabling individuals to gain greater	Reflecting
understanding of their dilemmas	Paraphrasing
	Testing understanding
	Summarising

The Purposes of Clarifying

The third stage of a helping relationship is to help clarify the concerns the client is attempting to express. In many ways, this is where the work begins in earnest and it is the stage of helping that is most concentrated upon and written about. Of the many practitioners using counselling skills, it is 'clarification skills' they already have and know about. They use them all the time and, just as it is easy to confuse help with counselling, it is easy to confuse clarifying with counselling.

Discovering more about the internal sequences of the client is an important aspect of gaining information throughout the clarifying stage. Clarifying has three main purposes:

1. To contextualise: to help generate a sense of the overall circumstances in which the client understands the event, experience, or problem. The client, in sharing the story, is attempting to gain a sense of how it fits within their life, *their* circumstances, or who they think they are.

Tasks: to hear the story; identify the themes and issues; listen for *generalisations, distortions and deletions*[58].

2. To retrieve meaning. As the story unfolds, and the client begins to reveal themselves to themselves, they are also likely to begin to gain a richer sense of meaning. This may relate to the events they describe and their importance, the relationships between each of the parts, or the consequences of the different parts to the totality that is beginning to appear. Helping the client gain meaning may be all they need. Through the art of reflection they may come to realise,

---

[58] These three aspects of disclosure are explored further in *Section Five: The Core of Helping*.

'This is where I am in relation to...' As a result they will gain greater understanding and learn from the accompanying uncertainty.

Tasks: listen for '*nominalisations*'; break up abstract concepts into specific experiences. For example, 'respect is really important'. What are the elements that make up this concept?

3. To construct meaning. Telling one's story, describing events, may be an unfamiliar or uncomfortable process and many clients only discover the implications of what they are saying as they tell their story. This occurs as the story moves out of the land of predictable narration and into something new and altogether more challenging. Using a relationship to explore and discover some of the implications that result from what has been happening may increase awareness of consequences and limitations. The challenge to the practitioner is to develop a frame of reference as close as possible to that of the client: that matches the client's descriptions and how they code their experiences into their personal meanings.

Tasks: listen for how the elements of the story fit together, for the values these elements illustrate and how they are important in the client's unfolding view of the world.

The Power of Story

Story is one of the elemental modes of human understanding, along with art and movement. To be human is to tell stories, to relate to pictures of events and to take part in or witness ritual and drama. We listen to a story and we are 'moved to tears'. We observe actors perform a drama or create a ritual and we are similarly transported into deep feelings of 'identification' with all that they are portraying. We look at cave paintings of early societies and we are taken back to the scenes of our ancestors and the acts they performed. Art, sound, movement are the ways we bring order to our experience, incorporate what happens to us, shape it into meaning and give expression to the result. The result is a shared world; a world in which the teller and the listener become co-creators, participants in a joint endeavour to make something of experience and find meaning in what has occurred.

Help reflects these elemental forms. We have 'narrative', or story, as at least part of 'talking cures'. We have art therapy and there are countless variations of working directly on the body. Psychodrama is one that connects all three forms: it relates events that have taken place (the story) by enacting them (through movement) and we then get to see a new picture of just what else was involved (tableaux picture forms) beyond our starting point of understanding.

One of the reasons why these methods are so powerful is that they bring forth more of the sensory elements that are part of the experience itself; they help highlight new features or reveal alternative possibilities. It is also one reason why people fight shy of exploring their experience in these ways, saying things like, 'I can't draw', 'I never know what to do in role play', 'I can only be myself'. We use these kinds of excuses, which arise from our negative social conditioning, to keep ourselves imprisoned in the narrow confines of our present form of understanding and especially to remain the person 'we know ourselves to be'.

In effect, we are really saying, 'I cannot let go of what is, after all, only a provisional sense of what is, but instead hang on to it compulsively as though it is *all there is* and all I have to make sense of things. Give that up and then where would I be?' All of us, as we reach thresholds of change, find ourselves experiencing some of this trepidation and uncertainty; encountering fear at having to let go of the comfortable understandings we have grown used to in favour of a new arrangement that we will have much less control over.

When we are listening to someone's story, we are not simply letting them catch up with themselves or gathering the necessary 'information' to get on with the 'real work'. Telling our story is a deep and important aspect of learning to be who we are and how come we are who we are: how come we got here rather than somewhere else. The stories we tell influence how we become who we are; they shape us and we, in turn, learn to tell stories in the way we do to reflect the person we think we are and the way we believe that events take place around us. Stories in this sense help create us and confine us. And many of us have never really explored our own story. We settle for the usual descriptions, find the typical meanings. We accept the long-standing interpretations that we have found available or been given and, however uneasy we may be about the results that come from them, rarely do we re-examine them and seek a different narrative.

Story as Metaphor

Stories depend upon symbols, metaphors and images as well as straightforward description. What things are and how we understand their quality is, in part, linked to what they resemble. We say, 'this story is like a fairy story', 'his descriptions remind us of a heroic adventure' or 'her account has the makings of a myth'. This is not mere 'talk', and not simply a way of making more of what has happened, but is, quite literally, a recognition that inside even the simple descriptions of things there are often major thematic resonances, overtones or echoes of grander themes and forms from earlier times in our shared history.

If earlier societies used story as one way of finding shared understanding of events and of explaining the significance of key aspects of life, then in a secular age it often falls to individuals to seek out patterns and shapes amongst the random, fragmentary experiences that can seem to make up a life. It may be that ultimately (and who knows what ultimately is in this sense) human life may only be a blip in the cosmos but if we act as if we are no more than that, we are sure to make little of our circumstances. Whereas if we recognise ourselves as part of the living fabric of the planet, linked to our ancestral past, with a role and responsibility to those who will succeed us, then the stories of our forbears are not mere entertainments but a living resource upon which we can all draw for sustenance and enrichment.

In a similar way, we can take the personal experiences that make up the day-to-day of our lives and, through the way we tell what occurs and with help to look into it a little further, we begin to give expression to patterns, themes and recurrent images. We might begin to see some of the influences that affect our sense of who we are. We might see what is worthwhile, what is important and what is significant. We might begin to get inklings of the way in which concepts and ideas like 'loyalty', 'friendship', 'commitment' and so on are living in the way we conduct our lives.

Story depends upon the accessibility of the imagination; the symbols and images that come directly to us and which somehow give expression (often without our quite knowing how) to certain elements of our overall experience. A single image can sometimes contain enough facets of understanding that it takes a long time to unravel it all. Similarly, an image can often hold in a condensed form what would otherwise take a long time to explore and explain. A symbol can provide a rich source of nourishment that may never be exhausted; there are always more nuances to be found.

Such symbolic forms hold 'information' that is both ours and not ours simultaneously. Symbols 'come to us'; we do not decide upon them. They arrive reflecting something vital or important about our current situation but they cannot be possessed by us and they cannot be reduced to just our concerns. In an essential way, a symbol is always autonomous and independent from our connection to it. Working, for example, with archetypes, it becomes apparent that key figures which might appear, such as the 'warrior' or the 'mother', carry so many meanings that they are not capable of being made into any single one, nor are they reducible to merely our personal history or concerns. They become ours and yet are only on loan for a time. They visit us in order for us to develop our understanding and then return into that great ocean of the collective unconscious from which they arose.

The whole point of such work is then to enter into relationship with the creativity and imagination of their presence in our inner landscape and explore the possible dimensions of their influence. As a result, we are able to enter into a different kind of relationship with our inner world. We no longer approach our difficulties or our concerns from the point of view of a mechanistic problem solving model, but begin to develop a more inquiring, creative and investigative aspect to the messages contained in our 'stories', images and dreams.

Just as a description of events, a chronicle if you like, has its place, so too does problem solving. However, often it is more than a simple description that is needed to bring meaning to events, so it is more than simply solving the problem, as though it exists in a vacuum, that brings useful change to people's lives.

Most of us are familiar with the imaginative realm through dreams and reveries and it is a much neglected aspect of the helping relationship. It is one few practitioners feel confident to approach, yet one which many know from their own inner lives to be a vital element to informing who they are and what they do.

As people 'tell their story' they use language that is their own. It contains images, metaphors and allusions that begin to give some sense of their inner way of shaping experience into meaning. Only by listening and inviting them to explore their images further can we begin to sense what that world *might* be like. If we ignore the metaphors and images, looking only for a report, then we will lose something quite vital to the future well-being of the client. It is in the richness, or not, of the client's description that we will get a glimpse of how to help them develop an imaginative understanding of their own situation that is far-reaching in its potential. It might be the case that a new client talks almost all the time in well-worn images, clichés of the day, but as they probe further and further into the detail of their experience, they will gradually begin to find that the ready-to-hand language is inadequate. They discover that it is only by grappling with the need to find the 'right' word', the particular comparison or the appropriate image, that they can enhance their current sense of their own living history.

This interest in the unfolding of the story, not simply at the level of narration and sequence, but in the way the telling of it proceeds, can be a major part of what makes helping work so fascinating and rich an experience for the practitioner.

Finding a new story is not the same thing as making it up or of creating a 'fiction'. (Though it is the case that all stories are fictions in the sense that they are accounts of what we understand to have happened: they can never be what happened.) Stories depend on metaphor, making one thing resemble another, in order to highlight the particular aspects of the original to which we want to draw attention. Even clichés do this. We might say 'it rained hard' but the phrase 'the rain came down like stair rods' gives us a more graphic sense of the quality of the rain. And so often in helping work it is not the event but the *quality* of the experience of the event that is so important. Simply asking the client to find the comparison can be greatly revealing. 'You found it a difficult experience, difficult like what?' immediately invites the client to find an image or comparison to bring more of the qualities of the event alive and into the room.

A picture of buffalo being chased over a cliff, for example, is a representation of the event: it is not the event itself. In just the same way, the re-enactment of a sacred act is not the actual event itself. The crucifixion of Jesus that takes place in the York Mystery plays, for example, is not Jesus himself but a man portraying Jesus (portrayal is a form of representation). It is a *representation* of what people of the medieval period believe happened. Two important things about all forms of *representation* are that they are only partial and that they stand in place of the thing itself.

Distortion, deletion and generalisation[59] are common elements that help to give shape to any account (in any representational form). So I say, 'It was a terrible night' and, given the description that has gone on before, you may or may not recognise what I mean. But the description, 'It was a terrible night' is a *generalisation* about a whole set of events and experiences occurring at the time. In each of these three ways we simplify the complexities of our experience in order to communicate them first to ourselves and then to others.

---

[59] Distortion, deletion and generalisation are discussed in greater detail in *Section Five: the Core of Helping*.

Telling my Story

If I have only a limited understanding of my life story, my *biography*, and I am asked to recall events that are similar to the difficulties that I am now facing, (something almost all forms of help get into, many sooner rather than later) I may begin to learn that the past is the place where everything 'went wrong'. It is not hard then to go on and believe that somehow the past 'ought' to have been different because that's where the cause of things lies. This view of the past is one many people have learned to take as a result of being 'helped' because the only use of the past is to find what went wrong and why.

However, the past is full of all kinds of experiences – joys, pleasures, resources, forms of creativity and expression. Our past is all that we have experienced and not simply the 'bit' that 'went wrong' (which itself is only a story and not the truth). When individuals are encouraged to take *a biographical approach* to their own story they begin to live inside the fullness of events and sense the past as a much more complex inheritance, with all manner of useful elements within it.

Of course there are events that were painful: we cannot be long on the planet without learning that there is suffering, but that is not all there is. Finding out who I am by reassessing what has happened and how I have made sense of it is a liberation for many because they have, until this point, taken on a view of themselves that is 'partial' or limited, and which ignores much about them. But in order to do that they also have to be willing to let go of the pay-offs and advantages that come with the limitations they have long accepted. When the time for that approaches, we move out of the period of 'getting the story' into the next phase of the helping relationship: challenge.

'Soothing to the Heart'

Whilst ever we are in it, however, the practitioner would do well to remember that, 'A good listening is soothing to the heart', as the Ancient Egyptians knew. Learning to let people explore their story, inviting them to examine it from other positions (points of view) with other values in mind than those they impose upon it as a matter of course, or inviting them to be open to what else might help explain how come things ended up 'that way' as opposed to some other, all help unlock the story teller from telling the story in the same way to get to the same place they always have.

When people simply narrate what took place as though it is a report, something hardly belonging to themselves, then they are talking in a way that is 'dissociated' from the experience itself and from themselves. However, helping people connect to the events and re-experience what it was like at the time, how they felt when it happened, and asking, 'What else happened'? all help bring the person and the story together in potentially new and enhanced ways of understanding. They are then free to 'inhabit' their story and connect to the feelings that live there. This is something they may have been hoping to avoid but it is essential for the healing of old wounds to occur.

Themes & Thresholds

Stories have *themes*, carry issues, illuminate dilemmas; describe repeating patterns or conflicts about values and choices. The story is an important part of who the person is and how they come to be the person they are. The themes and issues that lie inside the story do not appear accidentally. The discomfort that causes someone to seek help now is in itself a statement about the place they are in. 'How does it come to be now they choose to talk to someone?' 'What is it that makes the story need to be told in just this way or at just this time?'

We live out repeated patterns and themes until one day we get enough insight to realise, 'Hang on: I am on the hamster wheel here. And I want to get off.' Efforts to use our own ways to change the way we understand life are not going to succeed. Only by getting some insight from outside the way I usually understand things will give the *leverage necessary* to have another set of choices.

There are thresholds too in stories – not in all stories, but very often. There are experiences to be faced or decisions to be made that represent to the individual a major restatement of who they are, the kind of person they have thought of themselves as being, or the position they believe they need to maintain. Such thresholds are often to do with important aspects of our self-image and are, as a result, deeply personal to us.

It may be no problem for you to be getting older but to someone like Peter Pan it may appear as something approaching a death wish. *You* might have got your children through adolescence with all its hazards but that doesn't mean it isn't a nightmare for *this* father contemplating the prospect of what some youth is likely to get up to with *his* daughter. You may have come to terms with the fact that you are not going to run Shell Oil or even the local garage, but that doesn't make it any easier for the person who has so identified with their career, been a loyal corporate player and is now made redundant – and the fat payout is no help either.

We have to learn to listen to stories for the themes of those who tell them. What is the issue *this* person is carrying in this story they are telling? What are they attempting to reach in themselves as they outline what they believe about what has taken place?

Getting Past the 'Report'

If, however, the practitioner sees the story phase as no more than a report, a necessary preliminary to getting on and doing the 'real' work then the client's story will become just that. A rich and meaningful opportunity will then be lost for the individual to begin to rewrite themselves in a way that is much more comprehensive than the restricted view they took of themselves at the outset.

When people tell their story they are usually trying to exonerate themselves, blame themselves or someone else, but not learn – usually. They need safety and encouragement to do that. Someone who recognises that inside every report is a story, and that inside every story there are other possible ways of understanding what happened, will be helpful to the teller.

Points to consider through this stage of 'getting the story' include remembering that some stories:

- Are complex.
- Are only discovered in the telling.
- Deepen as they unfold.
- Reveal many possible directions.
- 'The story' may turn out 'not to be *the* story'.

It is also worth paying attention to the way the story arrives and how it is offered:

- Some people may show little commitment to telling the story in the beginning – people are often unused to having good attention and time for themselves.
- The story may be deeply moving and the client may need considerable reassurance to continue to tell it.
- Sometimes telling the story is sufficient for the person to gain either insight or understanding about their difficulty and further help may be unnecessary.
- Sometimes it is enough to share the difficulty knowing it is no nearer resolution.
- The client may believe telling their story won't change anything, (and, strictly speaking, they are right), but it will bring them up-to-date with their issue.

The practitioner needs to remember that the client is raising the lid on themselves. Questions are for the benefit of helping the client explore their world, not to feed the curiosity of the practitioner. The questions to hold in mind at this stage are:

- How does the person feel about what is happening to them and about themselves from inside their circumstances?
- What does it mean for this person to carry this issue in their life?

Where to Start: Near or Far?

A great deal of work may be needed to get here and if the clarifying stage encounters difficulties, then a return to the earlier stages of negotiating commitment and maintaining rapport may be necessary. The client, however, has by now learned something of what is happening and how the helping relationship works and what the conditions are in broad terms. They are now in the space with the time to begin but:

- 'How near to the present should I start?'
- 'How far back should I go?

For some, it is a matter of throwing themselves into the maelstrom of the present in the hope that you will know exactly who the characters are they are referring to. Others take themselves so far back into the mists of their own personal antiquity that the practitioner is left wondering just how this will ever fit together into something that makes sense of what is going on *now*. This is a very real dilemma for the client who believes that so much of what is happening to them *now* can only be understood if the practitioner knows what happened to them *then*.

So, getting the story is neither straightforward nor a matter of routine. Each of us comes at our own story, and how we tell it, in novel ways but the distinction drawn here between near and far is one that is very prevalent. In part, this is because some of us believe we *have* to tell you everything so that you can understand and so that you can tell me what I should have done then, or what I should do now.

The Need for an Answer

Most clients, at the early stages of the relationship, no matter what you have told them, will both hope and expect that you will give them *the* answer and do it rather quickly. Implicit is that you are the source of the answer and listening to the story is only the prelude for delivering a judgement on what needs to happen. Often the story is an elaborate self-justification. It is told in order for you to exonerate the teller for having indeed done all they could and agree that the world is full of bad people, nasty managers or difficult neighbours – whatever myth the story is designed to reinforce. It isn't that people necessarily start out telling their story for these reasons but they do hope to get answers, some kind of reassurance, or both. Rarely do they expect to get listened to deeply and inquired into more fully so that they begin to unravel what they really understand and feel about what has happened.

A caricature of this type of experience might go something like the following. They will recognise that you cannot give them *the solution* until they have told you sufficient about the problem for you to decide what the real problem is. Since it is only their life they are talking about, they would not presume to have any views of their own about what the real problem is, only an expert, such as *you*, could be expected to have an answer. 'So, will you please, now provide one? Because I have been a 'good person' and told you why it is like it is, and why it is all my fault, or definitely not my fault, or the fault of the stars on that particular Wednesday, when it all began'.

As we have already seen, blame is often a strong feature in the novice[60] client's story. Most of us have been trained throughout life to view problems as having a cause and the important thing is to find the cause, because once you have found the cause it is then someone's fault. When you have found out whose fault it is, you can blame them and then the problem goes away!

Entering a helping relationship turns that idea upside down from the outset. Most problems do not, in any useful sense, have a cause; they have many and it is not always beneficial or necessary to know even what the causes were in order to improve things *now*. And indeed, if what is important is to change, the question is not, 'How did this start?' but, 'Where do you want to be instead?'

---

[60] In contrast, an 'experienced' client is likely to be taking increasing responsibility for their own experience and what they can do to change it.

Yet without a dose of self-induced guilt and shame, or a blast of righteous indignation and accusation against the perpetrators of the damage to the client's self-image, progress may be impossible. I exaggerate only to make a point. The point being that so many of us are much more invested in finding out 'how it got to be the way it is' rather than what we might do from now on. We want to find someone to be responsible, as though it will then exonerate us from further effort.

The practitioner's job at this stage, so far as the client is concerned, is to recognise whatever childish view they bring. And childish view it will, in all likelihood, be since the client's adult functioning will be impaired and their emotional self will be under stress from the discomfort of whatever is causing their difficulty. So, naturally, they want you to listen, hear them out and then send them away with a solution that will bring the whole thing to an end.

In the beginning, they will not even mind that you ask questions to clarify and deepen your understanding – that will show that you are listening. It will also demonstrate how patient and wise you are, since everyone else they have spoken to will usually have interrupted them long before you do and told them what the solution is, or what a fool they are for putting up with it, or whatever other nostrum they have been given.

It may take a little while, even a few sessions, before the client catches on that however much they tell you the story and however much they insist on whose fault it is or what the 'right way' is to put things 'right', you still haven't come up with the answer or agreed with them that they are 'right'. Slowly they will become a little bemused and impatient and finally frustrated because the realisation will dawn (if they stay long enough) that you will not give them an answer and that you are not much interested in your own answers but very interested in theirs.

The reflective practitioner will resist temptations to offer solutions because they will know that, at this stage, even if a solution is all too apparent to the practitioner, it will not be *that* apparent to the client. Often, the practitioner cannot possibly know how it is for the client even when they tell you because they, the client, do not know what is really going on either – yet. If the practitioner is reasonably sure they know 'what is going on', it will not harm for keeping until later when the client may well be able to use it. If it is the client who is to live the solution, the more they generate it for themselves the more it will fit in with their overall circumstances and with their own internal make-up. So the key is to resist helping the client (rescuing) in favour of gathering a more complete description of the problem as they experience it.

> This is the stage of using *refraining* skills: refraining from offering opinion, solution and direction. This stage of helping is focused around assisting the client to gain coherence in their account of themselves.

The practitioner's role is to enable the client to inhabit more fully the life that is theirs, understand its interconnections and inter-relationships so that, as they move toward action, which comes later, the client will have a deep sense of what the implications are of what they are attempting. They will have given a good deal of consideration to the potential challenges and limitations that they might encounter. But all that is another stage. *This* is about 'getting the story': enabling the client to enter more fully into the richness of their own meanings, of their own experience, and to learn something about how it all fits together, and to enable you to have a real sense of understanding the client's frame of reference.

Taking 'Ownership'

This is often a transitional point both in the helping relationship and in the clarifying stage especially. At some point, the client has to begin to recognise internally, and not simply as a form of words, that this kind of help is about enabling them to work out *their own sense of what needs to be done or what needs to be tried.* This may be wholly revolutionary for them.

A lifetime of others deciding for the client, telling them what to do and who they are, may mean that being offered the chance to choose for themselves is more threatening than anything they originally needed help with. Because, of course, if they give themselves the permission to think for themselves about *this* matter, then they may have to start doing the same for other aspects of their life and that might lead anywhere.

At home, the partner who has been watching this process may well begin to feel reassured that this thing called 'counselling' (if that is what it is being termed) is at last losing its allure. After a time of the client being 'a pain and a nuisance' around the place, going on about their 'counselling' as though they have now found the elixir of life or discovered Nirvana and appear to be out of the mire in one step, they are now, thankfully, showing signs of disaffection with the practitioner, questioning the process and threatening to stop going. The partner is relieved; a bit of a crisis is passing and things will go back to 'normal'.

But many clients pass this point. For all they have not yet got a solution, they have received a deep listening. They have been heard. They have enquired into themselves and been enabled to find some of the elements and strands that link this present crisis to other moments in their life, to other events and to other figures.

They have begun to realise that life is not necessarily something that just happens to us but that, indeed, we do make choices, ignore options or disregard invitations and that they all contribute to the end result that is 'our life'. So, all the time the client is attending sessions, their life, their values and their beliefs are being thrown into further turmoil because *this* relationship, that was supposed to help them and make things better, is actually not doing that. It is making things potentially worse!

And then it changes.

The client begins to find the time and the effort worthwhile. Gradually, the process of unfolding themselves to themselves via your attentive listening and gentle questioning begins to help them form connections and raise themes. Although the confused strands and tangles of the story may well not be sorted in any practical or direct sense, this process does enable the client to begin to understand more, to consider further. It leads to changes of thinking, feeling or even acting in the present. It contributes to re-evaluating the way the past was and recognising that the past is no longer set in stone but that it is more of a 'flexible country', full of potential other meanings and interpretations, some of them more useful than others.

The client is beginning to get hooked on the process. They are moving. The work is *through a major threshold* and on its way. The insights gather from session to session and the client returns with enthusiasm and interest in the connections and thoughts. The 'presenting' problem, whilst perhaps little different from when the sessions began, is now in perspective and less a priority.

Working with the Story

The practitioner's task is to *facilitate that process* and gather a sense of how the client comes to have the difficulty they face at this *particular time*. As the story unfolds in the telling, the practitioner needs also to be alert to listen for any 'blind spots' the client has overlooked, and any *unexamined assumptions* they are making about themselves, others or their world. All these limit their freedom of action. It is important to be free to listen to the story as it unfolds and if you are not distracted, then you have time to think of how to respond and where to go next.

A story has a number of facets to it. Stories:

- Have a *content*: a series of events.
- Acquire a *meaning*.
- Have significance according to the *values* and understanding of the person narrating them.
- Have a *feeling tone*.

The importance of the story lies in the inter-relations of all these elements. The meaning a person has about the events that have taken place may be a good deal more primitive and simplified than the events themselves would suggest. The feelings about the events may be occluded or displaced elsewhere. The content may be so distorted, exaggerated or contrived to create a preordained meaning that it is hard to find how it all 'hangs' together.

What a person has in the beginning by way of recollections, feelings and understandings may, over a few sessions, become further elaborated, enriched and deepened until a quite complex inner world is revealed that is being managed with great courage by someone who is still saying, 'It's nothing really'.

As a person unfolds their story to themselves, it brings with it many gifts and the undoubted potential for revealing great learning. But that can only become available if the client is able to stand at a little distance from the immediacy of events, their judgements about them and have a little internal space not to become overwhelmed by the feelings that may well be re-stimulated as a result of a deep listening.

Applying the Skills

There are a number of ways of separating out the work of the practitioner, and several have been described already in *Section Five: The Core of Helping*. Relevant to this stage are:

Clarifying questions. Offering questions in ways that deepen the client's inquiry into their own experience (rather than to satisfy the practitioner's urge to know more) is a key skill.

Listening for themes. Some stories indicate a major theme is being enacted or a recurrent element is present and that this particular problem is a manifestation of a deeper current that is at work in the client's life.

Offering permission. The practitioner indicates the importance of the client managing themselves, as they need to. It may be that the client finds it embarrassing to cry or to become annoyed. The practitioner may well offer a little encouragement as a way of indicating that this is one place where such things are acceptable and the discharge of feeling is useful.

Identifying issues. Whilst the client is taking the time to assemble their narrative, session by session or in a single session, the practitioner concentrates upon listening for the issue underlying the obvious content; issues that will need further attention or areas of tension that will need more exploration at a later point.

Testing understanding. Before any movement to another stage of the work or within the clarification stage is attempted, frequent testing out of the understanding that the practitioner has gained against the client's story is crucial. Although we may have listened well and even have understood what has been said, the danger of interpreting what it means is all too easy. Before moving into the land of false understanding it is much better to check, 'This is what I have made of what you have said, is that how you experience it too?'

Identifying the impasse. At a later stage of the clarifying process, when the work needs to move beyond gaining more and more understanding of what is now well known, there will come a choice point that will move towards change. In order for that moment to be managed, the practitioner needs to have listened to gain a sense of where the impasse lies; where the block is held in the description and experience that the client relates, and which holds the key to progress.

The Transition from Clarifying

Whilst the benefits of the opportunity to explore and assess, consider and experience more fully the weight and significance of events and situations is inestimable for folk who have not had such a luxury in their lives, in the end, the need for movement and direction is likely to return. The period of clarifying itself may bring such a direction to the surface.

After a time spent working through the various aspects of a dilemma, such as whether to take a new job a hundred miles away and risk the relationship that they are in, the client knows a choice needs to be made. Time will not stand still nor will other people wait indefinitely. Sometimes, it is only the pressure from such external forces that brings the need for a choice to the fore.

Clarifying can be seductive to both practitioner and client because it is a time when they are most *aligned* together. Anything beyond this phase is likely to mean having to face pain and struggle and is likely to mean bringing action into the world – a much riskier phase of the helping relationship.

It might seem that once I have a strong sense of what I need to do then the next stage is the simple matter of making a plan and putting it into effect (managing change). This is far from the case. If a matter has been under review for any length of time, then approaching the idea of change, even when I know what it is, is likely to surface fears, anxieties and genuine risks. All these need to be taken into account if the client is not to practise making the kind of mistakes that we all have littering our past.

Beyond Learning to Acting in the World

At some point, too, there is often a sense that we have learned enough about *this* and need 'to do something' with what we have learned. This is the stage of transition: of moving beyond clarifying and into *challenging*. It is indicated when themes are well expressed or clearly identified; when the issues that are living inside the themes are evident and the need for movement becomes more apparent.

The practitioner must ensure they are *neither choosing for* the client, nor, when the client has chosen, pushing the client further into the work than the client wants to go. If the client has set the pace up to now, for a time the practitioner will take up the pace once the clarifying stage is left. Why should this be so?

As we shall see as we move into the following phase of *challenge*, the client cannot both understand their own process and change it simultaneously. Deciding to take up a challenge means they will become much more engaged with their own internal experience and the question of evaluating the implications of the changes they are contemplating. In order to do that the client will pass a greater measure of the control over to the practitioner. The practitioner will begin to set the pace of the change, work with the representations and descriptions that the client offers and become considerably more 'interventionist' than has been the case so far. This is one good reason why challenge is not something to approach early. It requires not only trust but also a real understanding by both client and practitioner of what they are setting about to change.

The Need for Summary

The importance of an *effective summary* at this point cannot be overemphasised. Only if the client and the practitioner truly feel they are aligned together in their joint understanding of things can the challenge stage hope to succeed. Hence the need for the practitioner to offer the opening to the challenge phase with something to the effect of, 'Let me give you a sense of what I make of all that we have been covering...'

In other words, the practitioner offers a rich summary that conveys the elements of the issues, the balance of forces and the sense of the way the client has described their experience of what the situation is like. It is offered, not as a means of displaying the practitioner's skills to the client, but of ensuring that the client not only feels understood and that the practitioner has been listening, *but understood in a way that is similar to their own view of things.*

It is not simply a matter of the content being accurate, but that the significance of the elements are accurately reflected and represented in the way the practitioner offers back the account. If the client finds that there is a relative match to their own view, then the chances are that they have travelled together. If the client considers it and amends or modifies the description, or changes it significantly, this is not necessarily to be taken as an indication that the practitioner 'got it wrong' so much as, having heard the summary of the story, the client now feels the balance and weight of meaning requires some new modification. Offering summaries of major pieces of a story creates opportunities for the client to weigh and consider the gathering meaning that they are expressing. It may, as a result, require them to shift an emphasis or give more prominence to other factors not previously recognised or accepted.

Twin Forces

If the summary is accurate then the shift can be considered. Summary leads to selection and selection leads to *re-contracting*. Realising that there are a number of strands to the matter that the client is seeking help with inevitably means there has to be some ordering of what gets tackled when; *prioritising* is a skilled activity. The practitioner offers the client a choice as to:

- Which of the issues to pick.
- Which of the themes to explore further.
- What aspect of the problem to go into in more detail.

These are major choice points and require the greatest skill and sensitivity on the part of the practitioner in how to manage their contribution and their role. If too trivial an aspect of the whole is taken up then the work will lose drive and energy. If too challenging a theme is attempted then the client will, in all likelihood, face the impossibility of the situation and stand on the threshold of potential failure.

A theme has to have both enough strength of interest in it and enough significance to make a useful difference to the overall circumstances of the client to be worth moving into. The practitioner can provide a useful sounding board to the client by checking, 'Is this really the issue you need to move into?' or 'Is this the most useful priority to select out of all those we have spoken about?' Offered in a non-defensive and enquiring way, the client is given another chance to reconsider before moving ahead. Once the selection has been made and both practitioner and client are clear that it is indeed the topic to be focused upon, then the work is about to enter a more provocative stage.

Stage Four: Challenging

Purposes

Identifying the impasse
Working with themes or patterns
Offering permission
Encouraging self-confrontation
Supporting through discharge
Holding the challenge
Developing new/latent strengths

Skills

Focusing
Defining
Confronting
Immediacy
'Tough loving'
Cathartic skills
Specificity

Constructing a 'Singular' World-View

Challenge is the point at which the person begins to remap their world. Exploring may be difficult – challenging, indeed, in its own way – but the challenge stage moves the forcefulness of understanding into more precise and particular places. It begins to make the patterns and the assumptions and how they operate within the client's world more apparent to the client in ways that are rarely welcome. None of us like to give up our illusions, however painful the cost of holding on to them. Few of us enjoy admitting that we are more complicit in what happens to us than we have believed and who wants to give up the chance of blaming others for the pain of facing that we are part of the problem or we wouldn't have the problem!

The clarifying stage is the beginning of the client developing what we might call, without any exaggeration, their own 'personal philosophy'. They are inquiring into the way they construe the world and their experience of it, subjecting their beliefs to some sort of sifting or sorting process in order to assess what is contributing to making things feel the way they do, and then considering and evaluating what they might do in relation to them. The following extract from an interview between Isaiah Berlin and Bryan Magee (1978) gives a clear insight into the issues involved.

> Berlin: … philosophical questions are interesting in themselves. They often deal with assumptions on which a great many normal beliefs rest. People don't want their assumptions examined over much – they begin to feel uncomfortable when they are made to look into what their beliefs really rest on – but in fact the presuppositions of a great many ordinary commonsense beliefs are matters for philosophical analysis. When examined critically, they sometimes turn out to be a great deal less secure, and their meaning and implications a good deal less clear than they seemed at first sight. Philosophers, by examining them, increase man's self knowledge.

> Magee: As you say, we are *all* of us made uncomfortable by having our presuppositions probed beyond a certain point, and beyond that point we all resist. Why are we like that?

Berlin: Partly, I suppose, because people don't like being over-analysed – having their roots laid bare and closely inspected – and partly because the need for action itself precludes this kind of thing. If you are actively engaged in some form of life, then it is inhibiting and, perhaps, even in the end paralysing if you are constantly being asked: 'Why do you do this?' 'Are you sure that the goals you are pursuing are true goals?' 'Are you certain that what you are doing does not in some way contravene the moral rules or principles or ideals which you would say that you believed in?' 'Are you sure that some of your values are not mutually incompatible, and that you are failing to admit this to yourself?' When you are involved in some kind of dilemma, are you not sometimes so nervous of looking it in the face that you avert your gaze and try to shift responsibility from your own to some broader back – state, or church, or class or some other association to which you belong – perhaps to the general moral code of ordinary, decent people – but shouldn't you think the problem through yourself? Too much of this daunts people or irritates them, undermines their confidence and naturally creates resistance.

Well, if such effort is difficult for philosophers who prepare themselves for such work, how much more so for the client who is beginning to construct their own world-view in front of this person in whom they may still only have a tentative trust.

The above is a good description of the problems and pitfalls of challenge, the task to hand as well as of the inquiry-based nature of the work. One of the secondary contributions of helping conversations of depth is the increasing sense of individuality as a distinct person in the world that the client experiences themselves becoming. There is greater awareness of having a personal view and a singular 'take' on aspects of life that derive from the understanding gained from the experiences that the client has lived through. That is something that we, as practitioners, may rejoice in because it is a journey we began a while ago but it is useful to remember just how risky it felt to express a very singular view that is distinctly our own, and which might have gone against the prevailing view of our social group, culture or network, at a similar point in our own progress.

Clarifying into Challenging

Following the clarification of the issue or difficulty, which helps the client reveal to themselves something of the understanding they have of their dilemma, the sessions and the work are poised to move forward. In the clarifying stage, the control over what happens next rests very much with the client; they can decide how far to go, just what they disclose and how they tell their story. Once a session moves on from examining the implications of the situations described into a more threatening and insecure phase of testing out possibilities for change, then the control and influence over the process moves away from the client and transfers across to the practitioner much more.

The practitioner now takes up the task of facilitating the client in moving forward and in doing so *challenges* the client. This can be done with sensitivity and skill to the point where the client barely notices it or it can be a very direct, confronting experience. However it is done, it needs to be done not only with the client's interests paramount but also with the client's permission. It is not an opportunity for the practitioner to demonstrate how well they know what the client has overlooked. This is not helping in order to ensure that the client has got the 'right message'.

Challenge is designed to assist the client to move forward, to liberate their own inner resources, skill and potential. It can only come about if the client has real ownership of the issue. The practitioner needs to look for points of leverage to alert the client to qualities they already possess but which they could exploit more successfully in their own lives. Challenge is offered to:

- Discover the impasse caused by rigidity in behaviour or fixed belief.
- Open a new perspective.
- Increase awareness.
- Widen options.
- Discharge feelings.

Understanding & Change

Whilst the clarifying stage is often an enormously revealing process, nothing is likely to *have to change* as a result, (however, very often a great deal does almost by unconscious rearrangement rather than considered plan). The amount of change that clarifying can generate is not to be minimised but that is not its primary purpose. The situation out in the world, the circumstances that the client is battling with, may have changed very little, not at all or may even be worse.

This is not something to have any great concern about since most of us take flight into activity all too readily and a period of enforced consideration would benefit many of us. However, there comes a point when the period of exploration yields less and less in the way of insights or new perceptions. For *now* and for *this* purpose, the client knows enough about themselves and the situation. The energy in the work needs to shift.

Change can only arise when there is some real *movement* and shift in the internal tension that has held the client up for so long. Occasionally, the reflection and exploration of the clarifying stage makes more and more apparent what needs to be said or done in the world and that may well produce change. Often, the *permission* to feel the extent of the confusion or ambivalence about a situation is enough for the client to recognise that they are not 'going mad', not 'weird' or suffering from any of the other fears that they have harboured. Similarly, probing and enquiring may have revealed a deeper commitment to some values than the client had ever expected to find, which then helps explain how come the situation is so much more difficult to manage than it appears on the surface. All these gains are real, important and substantial.

Next Steps

But often they are not the end of the work. There is usually more to do. If the client is to make further progress and to generate change then the internal conflicts and the discrepancies that have been highlighted need further work. Issues that express themselves as polarities, such as between how it is and how I want it to be, need to be resolved or transcended. This means there is a lot at stake in any course of action. The greater the risk, the more likely the client is to swing between polarised extremes of 'giving in', or of 'going for broke', only to retreat from doing anything by the time the next session arrives.

This cycling back and forth may be part of a productive testing out of 'what-would-happen-if', a kind of imaginative rehearsal and trial. It can just as easily get to a point where it is little more than the expression of frustration and an increasing sense of impotence at the feeling that there is no solution that can be lived with. So often we reach the point of potential change and then... some underlying belief or some irresistible limitation stands in our way and we know we cannot yet do what we want. Or the way ahead is clear but the cost to others or the steps involved are simply beyond what we believe we or others can bear, and so the longed for choice, the much prized change, is lost for now.

There is something near to unbearable about walking the journey with someone who moves nearer and nearer to their heart's deepest wish and then falters at this stage because of a lack of faith or trust. Sometimes the practitioner has to stand by and watch the client withdraw from a step that the practitioner is convinced is possible and desirable, even necessary, but then has to remember that the *work is for the client* and the client has to decide. The challenge stage in any relationship, therefore, is often a point of challenge for both parties:

- The client and their work.
- The practitioner and their ability to stay engaged but truly disinterested i.e. to remain unattached to a particular outcome or course of action.

Challenge & the Need for Freedom

The practitioner must remember to allow the client the freedom to choose for themselves even when it is not what the practitioner would choose for them. This tests out the strength of the relationship that has been built so far. It is a mark of the real detachment (not indifference) of the practitioner when they are faced with a client who makes a decision they would regard as not 'helpful' but the practitioner, nevertheless, stands by them honestly. In doing so, the practitioner neither becomes sentimental, attempting to 'make it better', nor subtly judging, indicating to the client that they are really 'letting the side down' or disparaging all the good work that has been done so far.

Real challenge is not simply about changing behaviour or adopting a new outlook to a difficulty; it goes deep and touches the foundations of our self-image and our self-concept. It reshapes our internal map of the world in which we find ourselves, the others with whom we share our world and the person we think we are. The ripple effects of challenge should never be underestimated. A small shift on the surface may be a volcanic expression rising to the surface. And all that said...

Working with the Impasse

...If the client is to move forward something has to give way; boundaries may have to move, action may be necessary. This is where the identification of unused resources, capitalising on unnoticed opportunities or hidden potential becomes crucial. All this involves risk and uncertainty and the consequences for self-image and self-esteem are likely to be high. The question for the practitioner is, 'Can we two people evaluate the issue so as to make the uncertainty manageable?' For a challenge to succeed, it is essential that the client 'owns the issue' i.e. takes responsibility for their part in whatever situation they are in. If a client is not able to take such responsibility, it is unlikely that any lasting or effective shifts will take place.

Finding ways to displace the problem away from oneself, to make-up excuses for, 'Why I can't change' or to play games with themselves in the hope that the problem will go away, all have to be surrendered if the client is to move forward. Energy spent avoiding the issue is energy needed to resolve the dilemma. In all this, the client needs to feel supported by the practitioner. This is the phase of 'tough loving' where attempts to 'rescue' the client from the potentially painful realisations they may have to face will only delay the inevitable and where false reassurance is more likely to be an attempt at the self-protection of the practitioner themselves.

In the end, we have to exchange blame (toward others or self) for the pain of realisation and a practitioner who must keep things 'nice' will help no one, not even themselves: just as a counsellor interested merely in pushing the client into seeing what they 'need to do' will only be counterproductive. If the client pushes themselves prematurely or does it to please the practitioner, where is the real learning? Often such premature efforts backfire and the client is left more demoralised than ever.

The Balance of Love & Power

The *challenge stage requires a balance between love and power* on the part of the practitioner.

> A sufficient degree of *compassion* to be present for the client, so that rather than see them 'get better', 'make a go of it' or any of the other rationalisations we might put forward, we are 'with them' through the pain.

> Enough *power* to hold the challenge effectively when the client's frightened, inner child wants to run away to the safety of keeping things the way they have always been.

Any anxiety or uncertainty on the part of the practitioner will only get in the way of offering a clear, non-defensive challenge. Unsolicited challenge, it is worth remembering, is hardly ever successful and that is why it is worth waiting until this point in a session or in a relationship to offer a challenge, when the relationship can bear the weight of the confrontation of the client with themselves.

Offering a challenge is not the opportunity to roll up one's sleeves, pull the gloves off and get on with it. It is about recognising that any breakthrough in behaviour, insight or understating is a deeply insecure experience through which to travel — especially if it is for the first time. Just as it requires enough interest in the client to hold them caringly through the difficulties, it is also requires enough steadfastness not to 'rescue' them either. But it certainly doesn't need to end up in a competition where the practitioner is arguing that client 'ought' to change and 'get on with it'. Such barely concealed parental behaviour will either produce a compliant client or one who fights back. Either way there is no real learning to be gained.

Approaching Challenge

When approaching challenge, it is important to consider all three components — thinking, feeling, acting (willing). Often, in the beginning, these aspects are experienced separately by the client. They might emphasise 'thinking' through the issue or they may focus primarily upon experiencing the feelings surrounding the issue. The client who wants to solve the problem by solely thinking it through, and not feeling the attached emotions, will not experience a lasting change; equally, nothing much will change for the client who simply stays in the morass of catharsis. Challenge, when managed sensitively and effectively, can break these limiting beliefs so that thinking and feeling can be integrated and the will can then be harnessed in order to move on. The practitioner has to enable the client to mobilise the will since, for many clients, the effective use of will is the least developed component.

The following approaches will enhance the likelihood of an effective challenge:

- **Be tentative:** It's my impression that...
- **Be tactful:** I've got a sense that...
- **Build upon success:** When did you last achieve this, or anything like it?
- **Be specific:** You have said how much you 'care' but each time you say it I've noticed your hand hitting your wrist. Are you sure you know how you feel?
- **Relate it to aspects of the client's behaviour that the client can undertake:**
  - What time could you find to work this out?
  - How much do you think you will have to give?
  - What would it take?
- **Challenge strengths to develop rather than point out failings.**

Working with Challenge

Described below are some of the essential elements that need to be borne in mind in preparing to develop the skills of challenge.

Self-challenge is the most potent form of challenge. Always allow the client the opportunity to challenge themselves, to discern the discrepancies and incongruities in their own account of themselves for themselves. This allows the client the opportunity to assume responsibility for taking themselves through this stage. That way they can take all the credit for themselves.

Identify the issue and stick to it. Sometimes the issue is not *the* issue and the client has to return to a further stage of clarifying. This will only happen if you hold the challenge firmly to let the client know where they are with themselves. Don't be distracted by irrelevant issues or smoke screens, including emotional outbursts of an exaggerated kind i.e. 'racket feelings'[61].

Use challenging questions. Get a full representation of the internal experience the client goes through by using focused questions. If possible, get the client to bring the problem into the room: to *demonstrate* just where and how they get stuck. This is an example of *immediacy*. That way you will see it and will not have to rely on their description. Be imaginative in finding ways to do this. Whilst the manner of the challenge offered by the practitioner needs to be tentative and tactful, it should also look to identify examples that highlight the client's potential to work with an issue.

Driver & the Impasse Within

Sometimes the conflict the client is struggling with lies not in the world, a relationship or situation but in an internal opposition between competing values or beliefs, such as the need for security versus the risk of trying something new. As the challenge approaches or as the client begins to work at the edge of the impasse, they may well begin to display an element of pursuing something that the client believes will change everything. Such irrational beliefs are often related to the patterns induced in early 'scripting' that the person may have little conscious awareness of influencing them at all. Such deep-seated impulses are literally beyond question and therefore 'not to be questioned'. They amount to 'no go' areas and are usually signalled by all kinds of non-verbal reactions out of proportion to where the conversation has reached: backing off, shifts of position and so on.

There is a whole series of polarities to which many issues become reduced. These are frequently related to self-limiting beliefs about one's own talent, potential or about oneself as a person, about moral constraints, or fixed ideas about personal identity. Conflicts can often be identified as a struggle between:

What I ought to do	v	What I want to do.
What I think	v	What I feel.
What I say	v	What I end up doing.
What I want for myself	v	What others expect of me.
What I think of myself	v	What I'd like to aspire to.

There can be an exaggerated need for:

- Approval
- Perfection
- Recognition
- Being right

[61] A 'racket feeling' is a 'here and now' expression of emotion that is not proportional to the actual situation. It is therefore a reminder of an earlier situation that is being evoked and re-stimulating the distress of that earlier situation. 'Racket feelings' are likely to be very much in evidence when people are moving through thresholds and something practitioners need to understand how to point out, work with and help clients move beyond.

There can also be exaggerated fears of:
- Rejection
- Sense of failing
- Condemnation
- Catastrophe

Which may have led in the past to:
- Repeatedly using self-defeating behaviour that reinforces the cycle.
- Evasion and avoidance.
- Playing games.
- Smoke-screening the real issues.
- Displacing responsibility and blaming others.

Beneath the impasse you will often find one, or all, of the following dynamics at work:

1. A sense of **helplessness:** 'I wouldn't know how to do that.'

2. A sense of **hopelessness:** 'People like me don't have any right to...'

3. A sense of **worthlessness:** 'I am just not worth anybody's trouble to put this right. It doesn't really matter anyway.'

Helping shift such deep-seated beliefs is not easy and a modest improvement is the aim.

The 'Drivers' & the Irrational

These beliefs are often displayed via the 'drivers' that derive from Transactional Analysis. The 'drivers' are five commonly held beliefs about how to act in the world that are counterproductive but plausible. They therefore give the impression to the holder as being a rational response to the situation. However, the underlying consequence is always to undermine their capacity for making an informed and adult decision about what is the most appropriate action in the circumstances.

The more driven the behaviour, the more likely we are to switch into being over-adaptive and compulsive and then the 'drivers' come into play and take over. This pushes the person into a way of behaving that may feel internally as though they are more mature or adult but, in reality, they are now 'trying hard' to act in that very fashion rather than actually 'being it'. 'Trying hard' is an adapted response. A good deal of behaviour under stress is an attempt to stay in one state or another (calm, confident or whatever) but these attempts are actually based upon early life efforts to comply in order to avoid something else (punishment, criticism, feeling foolish etc). They are usually maintained by a lot of 'internal dialogue'.

1. 'Be perfect': leads to people feeling guilt at the fact that they aren't (perfect) and yet they have to work hard to pretend they are. This leads to them making mistakes and getting caught out. Often they feel they are a fraud. The underlying message is that, 'It is not OK to be you unless you are perfect'.

Contradiction: 'It is OK to be who you are and to do things well or not at all. You can work out the standard you wish to meet.'

2. 'Be strong': leads to people pretending to be invulnerable, untouchable and utterly and unrealistically dependable until they flake out, drop dead or have a coronary. 'Be strong' is based on the fear that, 'Unless I act in this way I will not be appreciated for being who I am'. There is a fear of not being loved enough to find closeness and intimacy, so respect or even inspiring fear in others is better than nothing.

Contradiction: 'It is OK to be and get close to others (first deciding who you want to be close to) and it is OK to ask for things and receive them. Accept you're human like the rest of us, for goodness sake. And lighten up!' (Said humorously.)

3. 'Please me'. The underlying concern here is that, 'Unless I anticipate whatever anyone else needs before they need it, 'I won't be accepted'. There is a very strong need to be needed. This leads to people stepping into 'help' before it is required, this leads to creating further difficulties, finding ways to 'mess up' without realising it, that then have to be put right. This draws negative attention. 'Please me' is a mechanism to avoid humiliation, lack of acceptance or loneliness. The need to gain acceptance is so strong that the compulsion to 'help' is very strong – even when it is inappropriate. 'Please me' is based on the belief that unless I anticipate how to gain the approval of the others, i.e. please them, I am worthless.

Contradiction: 'It is OK to be you as you are. And you can please yourself without it meaning that you will be selfish and inconsiderate.'

4. 'Try hard'. The concern here is that success is not actually achievable (by me) but at least I can kill myself by making the effort to appear that I have tried my hardest to do 'it' – whatever that might be. This is a strong injunction given by parents on the grounds that, indeed, you may not be any good but you can flog yourself to death in 'trying hard' – a recipe for failure. It has a huge negative influence because it is so culturally reinforced and so apparently apt. 'If at first you don't succeed, try, try again….' is a pointless message for anyone. In effect the message is, 'If it doesn't work, keep on doing what doesn't work'. Of course, people don't access the real meaning of what it says, only the supposed meaning.

Contradiction: 'It is OK to decide to do it or not. If you do it, do it to your standard and enjoy it.' 'Try' implies failure in the English language – remove it from your vocabulary and the world will change overnight. What needs to happen is to stop and ask:

- Is it possible to do 'it'?
- Is it possible for me to do it?
- Is it possible to do it in the time available?
- Do I want to do it?

If the answer to all these questions is 'yes', then simply do it. This will transcend 'trying' and break the script pattern.

5. 'Hurry up'. The understanding here is, 'Given a limited amount of time, let's do so much that none of it is done effectively but at least we will have been busy. And then after it is all over we can be really critical at the mess we made of it and how we would have done better if only…' It is a recipe for being harried, unhappy and never accomplishing anything satisfactorily. It leads to never being with yourself or others either. People into 'hurry up' are no sooner 'here' (always arriving late) than they have to be somewhere else. They may even believe their appearance is vital to the events they barely touch and that only reinforces how much they need to 'get on to the next place'. They are deeply out of touch with themselves and what is going on inside them. 'Hurry up' prevents thinking and evaluating what is needed now. It creates panic and is not far short of a kind of madness. In the end, it leads to despair and even rage when nothing works and I am no happier.

Contradiction: 'It is OK to take your time and to do what you can in the time you have.'

Even practitioners have these kinds of 'drivers' working in their lives – and in their helping – so there is a good chance that when the client is getting into one of theirs the practitioner may be fielding one of their own to combat or compensate. Drivers are pernicious moment-by-moment interruptions to our 'here and now' aware choice about things and seem to offer such a plausible rationale for getting into them that they are irresistible. The more attentive we are to how they appear and contradict them by returning to our still centre of choice, the more we will observe them at work in our clients. The more, too, we will be able to see how they can enter into the helping work, especially at the impasse, either driving the client further into their difficulties (but appearing to offer a way out) or keeping them worrying around the issue that at other times the client knows they are able to tackle.

Rational Emotive Therapy

Rational Emotive Therapy (RET) works well in disputing irrationally held beliefs, but only when the client is prepared. Some of the characteristics of such beliefs are set out below:

Demanding: they often include elements of must, should or ought.
Self-fulfilling: because we have always failed in the past, we expect to in the future and we make sure we do – all without realising it.
Self-evaluating: we are highly judgemental of self – the opposite of self-forgiving and self-accepting.
Awfulness: there is usually a sense of heightened emotionality or crisis about events.
Mis-attribution: there are elements of the situation that claim exaggerated importance, and responsibility is shifted onto self or others, or away from self or others in unrealistic ways.
Repetition: we indoctrinate ourselves with other, related self-defeating ideas so they assume an often-unquestioned consistency.

There are five steps to challenge the consequences of such irrational beliefs (if the client is ready). These steps are drawn from the work of Albert Ellis, the founder of RET:

A: There is an a*ctivating* event.

B: This triggers the irrational *belief* that determines what the event must mean.

C: There is a set of predictable *consequences* that follow: a pay-off.

D: To change the pattern, there must be a successful challenge or *dispute* of the irrational belief.

E: Leading to a successful *effect*.

Challenging Questions

Challenging questions are not necessarily experienced as unpleasant or hostile, whilst many questions of clarification (at the early stage of a helping relationship) can be experienced as relatively challenging to the client because they are so unfamiliar with making explicit to themselves features of their own internal world. Challenge may be experienced at any point in a helping relationship, but the explicit use of challenging questions at this stage has three principal purposes:

1. To obtain more refined information: to encourage the client to give a more explicit account of their experience. Who? How? Where? What else? Whom? All these questions encourage the client to explore further into their own internal *representations* of their experience – where the information lies. They are thus more likely to give additional information they have not thought about or considered relevant but which actually has a substantial influence in generating the difficulties they are working with.

2. To elaborate distinctions with and between the experiences that are being worked with. One example might be to distinguish between anger, unpleasantness and irritation. The question, 'When you say you get "cross", just what happens to you?' will generate a lot more useful information than assuming 'cross' means 'mildly annoyed'. 'Cross' may well mean 'livid' or 'furious' but is just a 'nice' way of saying so. The precise experience of the client needs to be identified otherwise the practitioner is left assuming that they know what the client must mean. Such questions generate a more explicit description of what is happening to them in relation to the issues at hand.

3. To bring more specificity to the work. This is to gain detailed internal descriptions of the processes and sequences of internal responses that take place: a way of getting the client's account of what actually happens. Precise behavioural and emotional descriptions of an actual example are far more valuable than the client's opinion of the matter. For example, 'I tried it and it didn't work.' 'What did happen?' and 'At what point did it begin "not to work"?' are of crucial significance when working at the challenge stage. The answers help highlight the point in a process where the client's activities are in need of other forms of intervention and help. Where the motivation lies is often highlighted by how the client both answers such questions and where in their process they can track the breakdown.

This challenge process looks at similar issues to those involved in changing behaviours, as described in *Practitioner Resources,* but the focus here is on the practitioner enabling the client to go deeper, to move beyond current understanding or experience. Clients are often all too uninterested in their own experience and yet that is where the answer lies. Challenging questions are designed to *elicit* and *retrieve* the information that highlights how to move beyond the impasse. Examples of such challenging questions are:

What is the pay-off for things being like this? What is the emotional result i.e. the level of investment or pattern of feelings being reinforced?

What have you tried already? What attempts indicate what kind of motivation and resources the client has brought to the situation already?

What happened? Brings descriptions which highlight how far the client is aware of internal and external factors in the situation and illustrates what they omit.

What would happen if you did...? Checks where and what the restrictions are that the client is using to limit themselves. This may be an all too real and potentially accurate assessment of the risks. They may be internally generated: concerns about self-image and fantasised consequences etc.

What is the worst thing that could happen? Raises the same kind of material as above i.e. what is holding the client in thrall and how realistic those fears are.

What would you really like to do? Identifying the emotional energy, level of motivation and realism in the hoped-for answer gives a strong indication of where the client is in relation to the likely amount of work required in obtaining success.

What stops you? Identifies the limits, whether internal or external, to progress.

Who says you can/cannot? Where does the client assign the power that limits them; to internal process or external figures? How realistic are those assessments?

How do you know? What is the client using as the basis for making any assessments?

How do you feel about...? What is the feeling that is linked to this situation and how deep does it go? Does it begin long before the situation and simply become more acute as it proceeds?

Cautions for the Practitioner

- No one should challenge another without being willing to go through the same process themselves, albeit with someone else.
- Openness to challenge oneself offers a model that challenge is valuable and works.
- The relationship must have sufficient rapport. You have to be both interested and care enough.
- Your challenge should be open to being refused, 'I am not ready to deal with that yet,' or rejected, 'I think you got it wrong.' If you are really 'there for the client' you can always return to the subject at another time.
- Remain positive.
- Do not become over-invested.

Counter-productive Challenge

There is a series of interventions that can occur any time in a counselling/helping session which may hinder the client. In themselves they are often experienced as challenging in a threatening rather than a productive way. They rarely help. Amongst the most frequent are:

- **Commanding:** ordering or directing the client to change, however benignly expressed.
- **Warning:** pointing out, however gently, the unpleasant consequences of the client continuing as they are.
- **Moralising:** offering, however rationally, your own position as the one to adopt.
- **Advising:** offering a solution of your own to the client's supposed problem.
- **Lecturing:** using logically convincing explanations that are supposed to show the client the way.
- **Ridiculing:** belittling the client in any way.
- **Interrogating:** questioning the client to help them 'face up to what you know they are avoiding'.
- **Humouring:** distracting yourself and the client into letting yourselves off the hook.
- **Reassuring:** sympathising or consoling the client is not what you are there for.
- **Approving:** agreeing with the client is irrelevant to the task.

Summary

The challenging stage is likely to be the most emotional of all the phases of a helping relationship.

The two key reasons for this are:
- The client is meeting the limitations in themselves or the situation.
- The client is facing that, whatever they may wish, only certain things are possible.

It is a phase where growth is often linked to pain, to the shedding of illusions about others or oneself; of recognising that, given the way things are, then certain things do in fact follow and they have to be borne.

It is also a time when the client experiences the emotion of *breakthrough*. The elation of moving beyond a place in themselves that previously they were sure was going to limit them forever. It is a time when there is the excitement of attempting new actions in situations that have hitherto baffled or overpowered them. It is a time of satisfaction at the realisation that some long-held self-belief or sense of inadequacy is about to fall down and reveal the client to be far more capable of many things than they had ever considered.

Movement through challenge will frequently produce a discharge of pent-up feelings, either positive or negative. This is all too understandable when we remember that holding on to certain kinds of feeling out of fear or disapproval, fear of being overwhelmed or some other limiting belief, has usually been a strong part of the difficulty itself. As the client begins to make progress, the logjam of unexpressed emotion (locked up energy) begins to run free and that adds to the strength of movement in the challenge phase. Where the situation cannot be managed, it is often in the struggle, at an emotional level, where it is most noticeable. Whatever the client wants and says, the fact is that their emotional preparation is insufficient, and they are unwilling to allow themselves to enter into the feelings that accompany the step. This is to be recognised and not judged. The question for the practitioner is, 'What can the client attempt?'

Stage Five: Choosing

Purposes	**Skills**
Opening new perspectives	Re-contracting
Widening and considering options	Problem solving
Generating choice	Planning
Identifying resources	Dreaming
Anticipating consequences	Imagining
Helping move towards change	Testing out ideas

In the challenging stage we noted how control passed from client to practitioner: in the stage of choosing it now returns to the client. Following a successful challenge, there is a sense of renewed enthusiasm, a willingness to go forward and a more committed potential for change. However, the freeing of energy and the increase of insight needs to be managed so that the client moves forward at a pace and in a way that they can successfully maintain. Over-eagerness at this stage can throw the client into making ill-considered plans and taking hasty action that may sabotage or undermine the hard work that it has taken to get this far. No one needs to practise their mistakes!

Before we make any change there is the need to explore, consider, invent, design, play or create. It may be there is only one place we want to get to … but it won't harm to consider how many ways there are to get there. If there is one aspect of helping that seems to be widely neglected it is the element of 'homework', of making more connection between the work done in the session and the wider life of the client.

Nowhere is the opportunity more present to encourage the client to find out, to go and meet, to discuss with, to write, to draw, to go and practise, to test out, than at the choice stage. It is only through flexing the muscles of choice that they grow. It is a great opportunity for a person to learn not only to be more inventive about *this* change but also about life generally.

If what I want is straightforward then the elaborations that the choice stage offers may seem unnecessary. Nevertheless, the process is useful because we are helping people widen their options rather than simply going for the obvious. If helping has a sub-text it is to assist the client to become more inventive and creative about the *whole of their life* and not just when they have problems – and certainly not just about this problem. Ideally, there will be lots of work of this kind long before we get to this stage, but if not then it does play its part here because it enables the client to rehearse and prepare themselves for secondary influences and effects that the change will have upon their life and their network.

As the change process approaches it is not simply a question of 'Can I do it?' or of 'How do I do it?' but 'What effects will this have upon my connections with other people?' The secondary effects of any change begin to play an important role as it approaches and act as a drag factor. The choosing stage offers an opportunity to identify them as they come into view and to begin to plan how to tackle them. The effect of such practice is then to reduce their influence come the day when the change is introduced.

The 'True Third Alternative'

The choosing stage is akin to the earlier clarifying stage, but with an added dynamism. It enables the practitioner and the client to work together to take *stock of options, consider courses of action and play with possibilities.*

> *One choice is no choice, two choices only give a dilemma: real choice begins with three options.*

Helping the client to generate the *'true third alternative'* – the direction that offers a greater sense of freedom and responsibility – is the essence of the choosing stage. The original dilemma may have been expressed as a forced choice: a conflict between equally unappealing options such as, 'I feel like I want to do this, but I know I should do that'. Following the challenge stage, the client will have more awareness to see beyond the imprisoning restrictions of the two choices.

There may be many possibilities now. This itself may cause new problems. 'How do I choose when I have so many options before me?' For some clients it was better when they had no choice, because then they didn't have to take the responsibility that this stage inevitably requires. So often in a helping relationship, the client comes face to face with the realisation that it is not that the world does not offer them the potential to choose what would most suit their best interests, but that they lack any skilled practice in knowing how to choose wisely.

Choice without Consequences

In the choosing stage all this exploration of options and weighing of alternatives is, as yet, free of consequences. That is why it can be seen as a 'playtime' for both practitioner and client. Now is the time to dream: to open oneself imaginatively to what the options could be. Never mind, for a moment, what it costs or whether it is feasible. Simply offering the client permission to play with ideas can lead to novel ways of fulfilling the task. I may dream I would like to fly and I do know that human beings don't have wings, but there are many ways to reproduce the experience of flying, whether by going in a plane or taking an 'inner journey'. Good work at this stage can leave the client with a richer sense of their capabilities and resources for taking action and becoming more effective in the world. 'How many ways are there to...?' is the focus of the choosing stage.

When people speak of their fantasies, they have often discounted any possibility of their fulfilment because they tend to take them literally. What is important is not the literal expression but the *symbolic representation* that they are expressing. It is this that the practitioner needs to hear and extract the essence from. Often by doing so, what seems like a 'pipe dream' may well have elements or a particular form of expression that is all too possible.

Then the client has to decide if they *will* – another set of problems altogether. They may like their dream for its very impossibility. Knowing they could have what they have always wanted is, for many people, only the realisation that this is not a sufficient reason to have it, or to be grateful to you for helping them see that they could. Dreams sometimes serve to limit and enslave us rather than point the way ahead. We might not know which until we have played with them.

From such activities, the client may begin to recognise new elements that require consideration or to evaluate the potential effects of a planned change. This may lead to a further stage of clarifying – not of the original dilemma, but of the impact of the proposed change upon their network or their life circumstances.

Choice & Responsibility

Many of us have a history of knowing that what we choose often does not work out the way we hope and so we choose blindly or erratically. Others have a history of impulsive choosing and then waiting for the fall-out to occur. Still others choose with an indifference as to the costs involved or the impact on others and deny all responsibility for what is brought into being.

Choosing is perhaps the most surprising of the stages for the work of the client. All of us are making choices moment-by-moment about all manner of things, some serious, many less so. At one level, it may seem that we need little practice in making choices but most of the choices we make on a day-to-day basis are more like reinforcing habitual choices than making a steady appraisal of the likely effects of what we do.

So choosing has many ramifications for most clients when the issues they are working out are of any consequence. Learning about the implications of choice is frequently an integral part of the learning process for most of us. It often enables us to make more sense of how come we have been so stuck for so long, once we understand the consequence of any choice will not be easy.

All too often there is something to let go of, or something to face, no matter which choice is taken – something many of us wish were different. Realising that real life brings these costs to all choices can lead the client into an awareness of the need for action rather than allowing them to accumulate in the hope that someone else or something else will come along to prevent the choice being necessary.

Real choice consists of thinking, feeling and acting all functioning together in harmony. These elements need to be managed internally by the 'inner witness'. Rather like the conductor in an orchestra restraining and balancing the orchestral contributions, we need to develop that form of awareness that is able to draw upon and make use of our internal resources. The conductor (the inner self) stands in the centre integrating and balancing the separate players. If these elements are not in harmony, the conductor will not be in balance. In helping and therapy something changes; when people act out their own drama i.e. live out of their scripts, they will end up at the same dead-end all the time and nothing will change.

Choice of the kind indicated here, where we take full responsibility for what is brought about, can often be the beginning of a new stage of emotional maturity and personal responsibility for any client. Realising that it is indeed possible to give real consideration not only to what I want to do but also to what that will bring about and how I will manage those consequences, whilst sometimes intimidating and used as an excuse for maintaining the status quo, is more likely to herald a whole new stage of learning for the client.

Creativity, Choice & Change

Choice implies creativity and creativity is linked to imagination and freedom. Only when something in the situation has moved does the client have the freedom to move beyond the duality and polarities that the situation has previously represented – usually two unacceptable alternatives.

Creativity can be encouraged by journal keeping, colour work, reading, writing, dialogues between parts of the self in conflict, by making visits – by anything that enables the client to engage with themselves and their opportunities more fully. Not all help has to take place in sessions and here, more than at any stage, the client can get on with researching their own life and learning what levels and styles of creativity they actually possess.

Jourard (1968) points out a number of important features about creativity as part of our efforts to take up a place in the world. He notes that much effective creativity is fostered by the attitude of '*letting be*': the need to '*not try*'. What is important here is to have periods of non-possessive openness of attention – *reveries* – to let the unconscious pour through. We need to recognise how much of our effort is limited by our habitual perception; our efforts at reducing the world to the familiar and remember the great importance of holding a *real fascination and interest* in whatever activity is being pursued and in yourself as you do it. This is a quality that cannot be overestimated. Other features that are important to bear in mind include:

- Openness to remembrance: holding a non-anxious interest.
- The possession of a form of self-confidence that is realistic, adaptable, responsive and open to revision.
- The attachment to a symbolic image or allegiance to a higher order set of values that inspire or encourage effort.
- The willingness to be challenged and to meet obstacles positively.
- A willingness to pause and consider; to ponder, to contemplate – all from a place of minimal defensiveness. To cultivate 'need-free attention' and ask, 'What is this saying to me?'
- The importance and the meaning of the task attempted. There is the meaning in and for itself; there is the meaning in relation to other ends; the importance of it having a value.
- There is the question of commitment: values and meaning shape commitment – to release inner resources. A shared trait that connects all great achievers.

"...When one is so absorbed, all else is excluded from awareness, one '*opens up*' to the information[62] being disclosed by the problem, or task, and one lets one's problem solving apparatus work by itself." S Jourard, 1968.

---

[62] As one reader observed, "The issues of information – creativity – choice deserves a book of its own, particularly in today's small-print world where the Orwellian 'choice' means 'no-choice'". This is an important point and worth noting and our thanks go to Bill Berrett for pointing it out.

Frankl gives a clear vision of the value of creativity in an individual's life. Enabling someone to discover their own creativity, to own it, to value it and to live through it, is a wonderful part of the choosing stage.

"Man has the freedom and responsibility to pursue creative values, that is, to work, to make things, to use his energy and resources to produce wealth, or goods. He has the freedom and responsibility to pursue experiential values – the good things that life provides such as beauty, food, pleasure. When creative and experiential values can no longer be fulfilled, as occurs when one knows that he will soon die, then man has the freedom and responsibility to fulfil attitudinal value. This last term has reference to the attitude with which one faces the certainty of death, or extreme hardship. Ideally one will face the extremities responsibly, seeking to give the meaning, and seeking to address them at a human level of more responsible functioning." V. Frankl, in S. Jourard, 1968.

Stage Six: Changing

Purposes

Enabling the individual to take charge

Learning about the change process

Managing the change process

Monitoring and evaluating results

Bringing action into the world

Managing consequences

Skills

Goal-setting

Action planning

Rehearsing

Homework

Implementation

Revision

Change comes about through choice

Loss & Change

This is the stage where client and practitioner return to a more aligned relationship. The impasse has been overcome, the insight needed has been gained or the understanding explored sufficiently, the implications of the intended change considered and the client is ready to act.

The rehearsal and practice of choice, the opening of options and deepening of implications, which all precede implementation, mean that this stage requires precise and focused attention on the work to be done. This may be particular kinds of intervention, the development of a specific skill or the creation of a planned series of actions. We have explored personal problem solving in a number of places in this book, and here we outline the movement that takes place in the change process between client and practitioner particularly.

Each plays their complementary role in the overall effort to bring change to the world of the client. If it is true that change comes about through choice, then with change also come costs and sacrifices. As a result of the challenge stage, the client has realised that 'wish lists' and idealisations have to be surrendered in favour of a developing recognition of the 'realities of the situation'. They have begun to recognise that they can hold themselves internally upright as they travel through the process they need to initiate to get them where they want to be. With change we now find out the real consequences of our intentions, discover how far our resolve holds in the light of what we meet coming towards us, and acknowledge that all change has with it some accompanying loss.

> *There is no change without loss and no loss without change.*

Often we consider only one aspect of these two interlinked and interdependent forces rather than both together. For example, *if I change my job*, I am likely to focus upon the opportunities which lie ahead. If *I am made redundant*, I am likely to be all too well aware of the loss that it represents and helpful hints about the new opportunities which lie ahead are not likely to be welcomed. Those who are anxious about change are likely to anticipate the losses that will accompany any change and the temptation is to remain immobile for too long, finally finding some way to be 'pushed over' the threshold at the last moment.

On the other hand, those who cannot bear to wait for a change to happen might well propel themselves into the future and, only once there, begin to face the loss of what has been left behind. Either way, both have to deal with the effects of their personal way of managing the effects of movement; the loss and the change: the shedding of what has been left behind and the taking on of what we find in the new situation awaiting us. Following the *challenging* stage of the helping process, the potential for *choosing* and then *changing* occurs. The role of the practitioner is to enable the client to manage both sides of the process, at the pace and in the way that fits the client's own individual style.

There can be a mixture of feelings (often confusing) as well as responses within our reactions to the different aspects of the experience of loss. Three of the most common aspects are summarised below:

1. The inevitability of loss. Including a sense of losing control, experiencing a reduced sphere of personal influence and concentrating upon aspects of discomfort and difficulty – or denial of difficulty at all.

2. Substitutional loss. There is temporary discomfort, replacement of old, attachment with new and motivation to find positive aspects of the newly emerging situation.

3. Irreplaceable loss. There is no consolation to be found and the following reactions are common:

- Nothing can change it.
- There is no useful meaning to this.
- What could there possibly be to learn?
- How do I accept this?
- I want to feel this bad.

Types of Change

It is useful to consider the types of change we endure as falling under four main headings.

- There are those that are **voluntarily** sought: going on holiday or choosing to get married for example.
- There are events that happen, whether we want them to or not; events over which we have no choice. These are **involuntary:** being made redundant, for example.
- There are those events that we know will happen and which we can plan for, events that are **predictable:** citizenship through reaching voting age, for example.
- There are those events which are outside our awareness and which affect us without any forewarning; events which are **unpredictable**, such as accidents.

There are some changes that are to be expected given the culture and the times we live in. Some changes are much more idiosyncratic or at odds with what else is happening to people like ourselves. This can create difficulties for us in adjusting and understanding what has happened. *Our individual biography, or life script, will have a crucial influence upon the way we respond to what happens to us.*

Many people adopt an attitude to life that ensures that much of what happens to them is experienced as being **involuntary and unpredictable**. They take little initiative in finding out what is likely to happen and only face change when it is forced upon them. The more we take such a passive attitude to our lives, the more we are likely to feel we have little significant influence over our lives. Part of the counselling process is to enable the individual to develop an increasing awareness, and therefore more capacity to take charge of what happens to them, and to become an 'actor' in their lives rather than to feel a 'pawn'.

Traumatic change is usually experienced as involuntary and unpredictable.

	Voluntary (Choice)	Involuntary (Lack of Choice)
Predictable AWARE	Promotion Marriage Entering college Buying a car	Paying taxes Redundancy Retirement Ill-health Dying
Unpredictable UNAWARE	Moving house Changing jobs Holiday Computer dating Beginning a course	Sudden death: parent/child/friend Divorce/separation Accidents Robbery Rape

Some of the events in the figure above could appear in both the voluntary and involuntary 'sides'. Divorce, separation or retirement, for example, depending on the circumstances, might be voluntary and an aware decision or it might be a shock and be very unwelcome, i.e. involuntary. The aim is to push the window back further and further into the 'voluntary / aware' section. In this way we can see things coming and **choose** a response rather than endure effects we feel forced upon us.

Myths about Change

How we understand what is happening to us and those about us strongly influences what we decide we can or cannot do about it. *If we are using inappropriate ideas or have inadequate concepts, then the actions which flow from them will not resolve our dilemmas or further our development.* However, having the right answers is of no use if we cannot get people to make use of them. We often hold several ideas about change simultaneously, or move between different ones in rapid succession. They all have appeal at different times but they are all limited in their ability to enable us to move effectively through periods of rapid change, such as the times we are currently experiencing.

Some of the most commonly held ideas about the process of change include:

Incremental change: changes are linear and accumulate in sequence. One change doesn't much affect another until 'the straw that breaks the camel's back' happens – a painful way for anyone to realise that they have been dealing with too much change.

Disruptive change: change is an interruption to a predictable order or routine. It ought not to happen and 'If I wait long enough it will go away'.

'One-off' change: change is an interruption as a means of re-organisation, from one state to another.

Momentary change: there is a stable state to which we shall one day return. Paradise, as we all know, lies in the past!

Imposed change: external agents impose their ill-considered and unworkable ideas upon what was an already perfect system. This is another version of longing for a golden era that fades further into the past. It is used as a refusal to grapple with the present.

Interruptive change: changes are deviations from an ordered and coherent system which is never allowed to operate because of such interruptions. This is akin to the nuisance theory of change i.e. change should not take place unless it suits me.

Revolutionary change: the political realities in the situation have changed and another group is now imposing their will upon what will take place. It is all out of our hands. This leaves us victims once more, unable to contribute anything useful. This is a version of the 'lie down and die' approach to change.

Random change: 'no one knows much of anything about what is happening, so there is really no need to do any more than muddle on as before.'

Programmed change: this is only a 'blip' on the graph of progress that underlies everything that goes on. 'We are ever nearer the golden future so don't make life difficult. Learn to grin and bear it.'

These kinds of views of change, whilst useful for many experiences or events, break down under turbulent and structural change that tears up the existing framework without replacing it with a new one immediately. Such change is akin to living through a revolution and revolutions throughout history have usually cost lives. Whilst the context of change is revolutionary, individuals are still living their own lives with their own rhythms of change and development, their own experiences of life to accommodate to, and they are still making the journey from one stage or phase of their life into another. Such transitions can make the challenge of external change even more difficult to work with. It can, of course, help too.

The Effects of Change

The Chinese symbol for change carries the double meaning of both crisis and opportunity. Reactions to change vary enormously within the same individual as well as between different individuals. Ways in which many people respond to the challenge of change are given below. An awareness of these ideas is useful in extending our understanding of the change process and enables practitioners to be more effective.

Impairment of adaptive responses. The effort of responding to change lowers the individual's usual capacity to adapt to other, simultaneous changes.

Reduction of tolerance. This is the *straw that broke the camel's back* syndrome. Yet another change, even one of a minor kind, can be just too much for a person to take on. Many people live with chronic levels of stress and they are often amazed at how 'such a little thing' is the crunch point when they have been 'coping with a lot worse for years'.

Rigidity in thinking. Some people become obsessive, quite unable to let go, have a break and then return to the issue. Their thinking and behaviour become grimly determined and flexibility goes. This may lead to tunnel vision: the inability to look outside for new perspectives in a desperate search for any solution. It may also mean foreclosing on options, rather than tolerating uncertainty any longer – any answer will do, even the wrong one, since at least that way the waiting is over.

From chronic to acute levels of response. If a person is already operating at chronic levels of stress, as further changes become acute they may become erratic and unpredictable in mood or behaviour and thus difficult to cope with or help.

Anxiety and panic. Some changes throw people into anxiety attacks, panic reactions, or dramatic games, all of which are simply ways of temporarily avoiding dealing with the situation.

Displacement in order to ignore or deny what is happening. Some people become over-committed to another *safer* area of life, usually only to postpone matters.

The Tasks of Change & Transition

To acknowledge the reality and impact of the event. The client must be enabled to face up to and recognise the change with a realistic sense of its importance and influence. This may take some considerable time.

Experience the accompanying feelings. Major change brings about emotional turbulence as well as potential for growth. Failure to work through the feelings associated with a significant change may lead to blocks in development later.

Make adjustment to the change and transition. Change also challenges the individual's understanding of themselves, the world, their place and the contribution they can make. Opportunities to reconsider and evaluate the impact of change are important factors in enabling an individual to grow in personal awareness and self-understanding.

Put emotional energy into the emerging situation. Some changes are emotionally demanding and draining, leaving the client, for a time, unwilling to look outside the immediate situation or help themselves move on. Periods of recuperation, gathering energy and so on, can become a habit leading to passivity, if left to go unchallenged for too long.

Major Conditions for Effective Personal Change

Conviction and commitment. The first step in any successful attempt to bring about change is the *recognition of the need for change*. The person making the change has to be both convinced and committed to change within themselves. Without such commitment there may be attempts but there will never be success. It may take a good deal longer to obtain a genuine commitment for change than many practitioners realise. *Commitment is harder to obtain than conviction.* People may be convinced of the need to change all kinds of things about themselves, but they are not necessarily committed enough to do anything about it.

The need for risk and anxiety. There must be a sufficient level of turbulence or anxiety to make the risk of experimenting seem worthwhile. If it all seems too easy, it may be that something else needs to be changed.

Safety and support. There must be enough trust in the relationship to explore and test out the possibilities of any proposed change and enough reward to make it worthwhile. People may be able to do things with a practitioner or even on their own, but not feel safe in the situation where it actually matters. Helping to create the safety where it matters may be a long-term process. It usually means creating a security zone within the client's own sense of themselves, an internal resource state that will give enough confidence for the person to tackle the real life situation successfully.

A real meeting. Bringing about change has to matter to both people involved, not only to the client but to the practitioner too. To the client it may be that the change is what has to matter; to the practitioner it is a demonstration of them being effective. This is the point where however well-meaning you are, if you can't help the client get to where they want to go then the helping relationship is limited. If the practitioner is half-hearted about helping, then the client won't even be half-hearted.

Rehearsal. It helps most people to have a sense of what they are in for; how things might work and what might happen. This, however, is different from giving lectures, or holding someone's hand and doing it for them. It's more like offering a few clues at a sensitive point. The client can then build their own map.

Experimentation. *Talking about it won't do it.* In the end the client has, where possible, to try out any new programme or behaviour in a live situation; a situation, as far as possible, where mistakes can be managed safely and appropriately, before trying it in the most challenging of circumstances. Doing so minimises the possibility of the client attempting the most difficult of examples or tackling the most serious of issues at the first attempt. Graded practice is essential. *All of us have failed enough times. We don't need to keep practising!* The practitioner must seek ways to help the client build on success, however small.

Reflection. 'Now I can do it' is only one element in the successful resolution of a piece of change work. As the client gets closer to moving on, they need to develop the habit of reflection: '*What does this all tell me about myself?*' '*How does this affect the image I have of myself?*' and '*What impact will this have on my other relationships?*'

Transfer. *It won't work without practice.* Helping people find times and places to practice what they are learning and to consider how to transfer such learning from one situation to another helps integrate change.

Working with Change

Before a change is attempted, the person, the situation and the world in which the person and the situation exist, must be *aligned* enough for the person to manage what comes. For some, the change will be privately experienced: it does not amount to a great difference on the outside, but it may represent a thorough revision of an individual's self-image internally. For others, it is the social aspect of the change itself that marks the progress not only to themselves but also to those around. It may be making a statement to other people in the client's world that means they need to ensure they have some self-protection in order to manage and to hold on to the changes they wish to implement. The networks in which people live their lives get shaken and there are times when some people get left behind as a change begins to takes effect.

There are certain beliefs surrounding change that will affect both how the client responds to the idea of change and also how the practitioner themselves views change. If the practitioner is not convinced change is possible, for example, then this belief will be passed on, albeit unconsciously, to the client. Knowledge and understanding of these beliefs is important:

- People can do it.
- You don't always have to know why someone can't do something in order to help them learn how to do something.
- The client can always identify people who can do what they want to do, who can be used as a base for modelling what they would like to accomplish.
- People have more resources than they think.
- People always make the best choice and if they don't, you certainly can't do it for them.
- Some people find the idea of change and personal responsibility very threatening.
- The ability to change is influenced by age, class, ethnic origin and so on but it is not controlled by them.
- Powerlessness is a self-generating spiral, creating meaninglessness, depression, leading to a sense of pointlessness.
- You can't have anything you want, simply because you can always decide on things which are irrational and you can always sabotage yourself.
- However, most people can have what they want, the problem is they don't know how to get it.
- It is not that the world does not offer people most of what they would like, it is that they do not have useful ways of knowing how to go about getting it.

There are many further factors that the practitioner needs to take into account in the change process and these include:

- The *context* of the change.
- The client's *frame of reference* for this experience.
- The *weight* of the particular event itself. An event which is intense and short lasting can be de-stabilising, just as an event which is not acute but is prolonged, especially if linked to uncertainty about the outcome, can produce long-term distress.
- What else is going on in the *client's world?* Are there other events with which the individual is also attempting to cope?
- How far is this change related to the *life-stage* of the individual?
- How far has the individual a *zone of stability* in their personal life? If work is changing, how stable is the pattern of personal relationships, for example, as a way of compensating?
- The *emotional stress of the event and the strain of the process* need to be considered in developing strategies.
- The *cognitive readjustment*: the need to find sense-making elements within the process. The need for our experience to make sense is a vital element in what makes the change process so ambivalent and uncertain. *Even changes we wish for bring a disturbance to our world-view and sense of how things are.* This makes individuals vulnerable for a period.

The helping relationship enables the person work with the kinds of elements listed above. Over the period of the work, the client increases their zone of stability, develops better emotional functioning and improves their understanding, all of which help them to manage ambivalence and uncertainty more successfully. The purpose of the work is to create an ecology for change. Strategies to facilitate this process include:

- Filtering other experiences and reducing the workload.
- Queuing: listing things in priority order to give ourselves more flexibility and fewer demands.
- Reducing our usual standards of performance – where possible – to an OK enough standard, as a way of freeing up energy to manage the change itself.
- Withdrawal: sometimes taking time out can be useful, so long as we realise that we will have to return to the situation. This can, however, be a negative, when, for example, it leads to failure of nerve to return to deal with the situation at all.

It is important for the practitioner to remember, however, that nothing changes in the client's life until they begin to act[63]. It is not sufficient to have an insight or come to a decision for change to take place: it has to be *implemented*. At this stage, the client may well become nervous and anxious all over again at the prospect of what they now know they have committed themselves to.

Stages of Change & Transition for Client & Practitioner

The following framework describes the key points of each of the main stages that connect widely differing change events. It is drawn from a range of sources and is largely concerned with the typical or predictable changes of day-to-day life: changing job or location, moving house, leaving a relationship. It helps explain the overall features of important changes and will often be useful in thinking through the effects of traumatic change.

There are two aspects to this framework, that of the client and that of the practitioner. They are described side by side to enable the reader to gain greater insight into the two different perspectives and the stages and tasks involved in each.

> **Reaction cycle for the client.** Not everyone passes through these stages in a straightforward manner, nor do individuals spend equal amounts of time within each stage. Individual progress is typically erratic, with periods of progress, punctuated by regression and occasional periods of feeling stuck. Although the reaction cycle given below must only be thought of as a general guide, it can be useful in a wide variety of situations.

> **The practitioner's stages and tasks.** Despite having the best of intentions, it is all too easy for practitioners to bring the client to a temporary

---

[63] Personal problem solving is a pervasive aspect of the helping relationship and is examined in more detail in *Section 6: Practitioner Resources*.

halt by an over-hasty challenge or an over-supportive response. Challenge and support are both necessary and important facets of the practitioner's task, but identifying which is required and when it is needed is by no means simple. This framework outlines a series of pointers for the practitioner to bear in mind when working with someone moving through a transition.

Stage I	**Client: Immobilisation**	This is a phase of '*It cannot be happening to me*'. The event is either so unexpected or so grave in its implications that the individual rejects the possibility of it happening at all. This is a stage of *denial* and can be seen as a necessary breathing space whilst the person mobilises their internal resources to cope with the impending change. Some people refuse to move beyond this stage. This is the period when it may well be plain to everyone else that things cannot go on the way they are and everyone has recognised the gathering forces of change, but the actual client is still oblivious to it all.
	Practitioner: Pre-Awareness	Resist all temptation to point out just how hard the client is likely to fall. Do not give way to the temptation to say, 'I told you so', when they have fallen. Gather information. Watch how the person operates, so that you can help them learn how they get themselves into such situations, in order that they can develop early warning systems of their own for future use. If the person refuses to move beyond this stage, that is their right, and the practitioner will gain nothing by trying to force movement – even with the best intentions.

Stage 2	**Client: Minimisation and Depression**	There is often a following period of making little of the event, making light of the situation generally, or of reducing the full implications of the prospect ahead. This is a time when people often attempt, unrealistically, to see the virtue in the inevitable.

At this stage, events gather together and change becomes inevitable. The deadline for the job application, or for handing in the piece of work, cannot be denied any longer, but the client is still not ready to act. This is the stage of reluctant recognition that the issue will not go away, though the client may wish it would. In a positive change this would be the stage where someone starts to comb the paper looking for job advertisements, even though they have not yet decided that they definitely want a new job.

The full impact of an event is often signalled by a sense of depression and helplessness, if not outright hopelessness. False comfort is of no real help at this point. Depression signals the recognition that the individual is actually starting to face the situation and is about to begin to tackle it.

The realisation that all efforts so far have done nothing to forestall the inevitable is a necessary and depressing precondition for any forward movement. This may be a long-lasting phase that tries the patience of those intimately involved, because they too are likely to feel inadequate or feel that the whole thing has lasted '*too long*'. |
| | **Practitioner: Present Awareness**

Patience and support | The client may be hinting at their readiness to be helped but actually resist that help if offered. Their investment in the outcome is not yet sufficiently strong to be tested with serious challenge. Things may have to get worse before they can get better.

Practitioners need to treat this phase with caution. Do not explode the bubble – it is all part of trying to cope. It shows signs of acknowledgement, however distorted.

Suggestions to 'pull yourself together' are all too easy to make, but they are of no use, since the client will already be doing the best they can. Practitioners must recognise such frustration as their own and keep it to themselves. Neither is it helpful to tell the client that 'everything will be alright' or to give false platitudes or reassurance. It will not be helpful to exhort them to 'accept the inevitable' or 'to put up with it'.

The practitioner can be of greatest help by being there with the client, trusting the process of the client and supporting them in what may be a dark, depressing stage. |

Stage 3	**Client: Bargaining**	Bargaining, whilst unrealistic, is nevertheless a real sign of willingness to face things. The stage of saying '*If only … then everything would be all right*' is a beginning of mobilising efforts to tackle things and suggests the return of the energy needed to make real progress. There may be some unrealistic expectations. Job seekers, for example, often apply for far too many jobs for which they are unqualified or unsuitable, or else think of trying careers for which they have no skill or preparation. But energy is now returning. This is the stage where the client shows at least minimal efforts at a response. It is often a time of half-hearted and unrealistic levels of commitment. It is the stage at which the client wishes not to become over-invested in case the whole enterprise fails. It is still possible to withdraw gracefully and pretend it all doesn't really matter. Minimising one's chances or expectations is a feature of this stage. Students, for example, who will go on to do extremely well, will often say that they are not sure how they got on with an exam. This is a way of hedging one's bets.
	Practitioner: Initial Bargaining Gentle probing	This is the time when the practitioner can afford to become a little more active, probing the client's uncertainties and gently confronting any exaggerated claims with light observations. The practitioner can engage the individual in planning and deciding what strategy to implement. This is not the moment to burst the bubble either – however beneficial you may believe it will be in the long run. It is far better to allow the client to test out their own enthusiasm, or their growing suspicions that all may not be well.

Stage 4	**Client: Acceptance**	A more realistic level of recognition is finally required. A certain degree of commitment must be declared if the client is to make something of the opportunity or challenge ahead. Coming to terms with the actual conditions of, say, a new job may mean dropping some of the grand schemes the client has been talking about. This is a phase in which realism begins to enter the picture. Acceptance is not necessarily embraced positively. It is not always a recognition that the worst is over. Acceptance means facing up to the full implications and impact of the event. Now there is a readiness to assess the full measure of what has happened. Now, too, a perspective and a timescale from which to view events become available to the client. This may be the long period of enduring day-to-day reality of what it means to be alone, for example, after the drama of separation or divorce.
	Practitioner: Acknowledging Serious exploration	Now is the time that enough experience and commitment have been mobilised for the client to have concrete issues to face up to and to work with. Serious exploration and open-ended questioning which leave options on the table to think about are important. This is not a time to seek to offer some supposed solution. The client may need their doubts and uncertainties for some considerable time. This, however, does not mean that the process is going awry. Trust the client and trust the process. Keep your own anxieties to yourself and help the client deal with their own rather than those you wish they would deal with.
Stage 5	**Client: Search for Meaning**	Gradually the transition becomes part of the overall pattern of life. It is still important but no longer a pre-occupation. Other dimensions of life press for attention, after having been neglected. The client must begin to adjust to the implications of the situation that are now beginning to appear explicit. This is the period when the event is beginning to be placed in the context of the growing themes of the client's life. It is the start of their coming to terms with events and learning some of the lessons of the experience.
	Practitioner: Managing the Change Challenge and Support	This is the period when the practitioner can be most free in their response and offer whatever is needed. The client has enough experience behind them to find the lessons, to confront their own exaggerated expectations and recognise the opportunities that they may be overlooking. A strong relationship between client and practitioner can make an enormous difference at this stage.

Stage 6	**Client: Integration**	The change event begins to become integrated within the overall features of the client's life. A sense of its impact begins to grow. The wider opportunities within the situation, both taken and lost, can be more easily acknowledged. Serious re-ordering is no longer possible, though small adjustments may take place. The final stage of moving through a major transition is that of *making it mine*, of owning and clarifying the event, along with all its shortcomings and blessings. The person can now move on, the experience of this particular transition complete.	
	Practitioner: Integration and Reflection	This is the time to help the client review and assess where they stand; to begin to integrate where they may still go and what they may still wish to contribute by way of effort to the change event. It is important at this stage that the client recognises that further efforts can only have a limited influence on the overall pattern that has developed. It is also important for the client to begin to develop a realistic appraisal of what has been accomplished. This is much more valuable than feeding false hopes or idealised visions. To be life-changing, to be a permanent transformation, integration has to take place. The new situation, the new way of being **becomes** a part of the individual when integration has taken place.	

Stage 7	Client: Reflection and Evaluation	Only with the perspective of time, distance and the opportunity to reflect, can the client begin to evaluate the overall influence of the change within the events that make up their life. The job may now only be a job. The ending of the relationship may have brought important learning despite the accompanying hurt. The move to a new area may have brought problems not anticipated at the time, and so on.
	Practitioner: Evaluation	The practitioner can now assist the client to review the event more clearly, by holding up a mirror and supporting them as they take stock of what they see. The client must begin to make sense of what has taken place and what the consequences suggest for the way ahead. This final stage has to be worked with consciously. Only in rare cases will reflection and integration occur fully without support and encouragement. People have to spend time and effort to gather the lessons of experience to themselves. All too often other events overtake us, crowding out the time we would like to give to reflection on past events. The practitioner is able to encourage this reflection and give the client the opportunity to identify and own the changes, the consequences of those changes and to consider, 'Where next?'

Summary

This framework is an outline only. It is not linked to any particular change event and so may be used as a guideline for many situations and events. Again, it should be stressed that not everyone will pass through the stages given, nor will individuals spend equal time passing through each phase. However, it will be useful to bear these stages and pointers in mind whilst working with anyone who is moving through the change process.

Stage Seven: Closing

Purposes

Bringing the work and relationship to a close

Reviewing and evaluating the work

Parting and saying 'good-byes'

Skills

Managing endings

Disengagement

Letting go

There comes a point when the work must come to a close. Who senses it first or whether it is by prior agreement may vary. It might be that the 'contracted' number of sessions has been completed and closing now needs attention. It may be that a short-term piece of work with a client has always had the end point in mind. It may be that a long relationship, which has moved through many phases, is facing completion and both people are coming to recognise a gathering sense of finality.

Endings are about death, loss, bereavement; the whole issue of mortality. It may, on the one hand, be about recognising that it is time to move on and to look ahead but, at the same time and in the same moment, there are the tremors of the loss that is ever-present in human affairs. Since this is a place of awareness, it is likely to be an even stronger reminder of the fragility of relationships and connection that is common in everyday life.

It may or may not be a time of celebration or of thanksgiving for the work done, but it is certainly an acknowledgement that we have done what we came together to do. Therefore, some evaluation of what we have made of the time together is important for each of us as we move on into the rest of our lives.

How early to raise the issue of saying 'good-bye', then, is neither simple nor straightforward. Talking about endings a long time before they have to be faced can help prepare both people beforehand but broaching the subject requires tact and thoughtfulness. Even though the work has been done, the client may still be reluctant to contemplate saying goodbye. In this event, they may well find ways to postpone the inevitability of living without the security of the listening ear upon which they have come to depend – a dependency they may only just be recognising. Giving the client time enough to adjust and working out ways to mark the closing stages of the work can help prepare both people for the undoubted loss that is present if the work has gone well and the relationship has been strong.

However it arrives, when the client knows what they came to learn and the time has come for them to move on, even from you, the end is in sight. This is not an easy stage to manage or do well.

Both parties are likely to have a good deal invested in the work they have done together and in the relationship that has grown. A good helping relationship can become a messy one simply because the practitioner cannot find a good time to broach the ending or the client isn't sure if they are ready to leave yet.

Completion

Closing is about *completion*, of the work or the issue: a time to look back and make sure what the client is taking away of the journey they have taken. It is an opportunity for the practitioner to assist by pointing out landmarks they have also noticed and offering appropriate disclosures about the meaning the work has had for them too. It is about being real; and partings can be moving. There is no need to pretend you are unaffected in order to make it easy for the client.

Closing is an important stage in any relationship and never more so than in a helping relationship of any significance. Endings and closing are not something our culture manages well, so many people who have done good work and gained a great deal from a helping relationship often approach the ending with trepidation – both practitioner and client.

Closing means recognising what we have done together – good and not so good. It may also be a time to acknowledge that, although *this* 'issue' or piece of work is complete, the process of opening eyes, mind and heart that the helping relationship has enabled can continue. It means acknowledging that we are no longer going to be meeting like this. It means that we are to separate and go our own ways. For the client who has found a most dedicated listener and steadying presence in the practitioner, such a loss may be another burden to bear. It is with these thoughts in mind that it is important to remember that preparation for the end of the relationship may be as important as the work that has been done within it.

Some people point out that the way things end is often very reminiscent of how they started: a considered beginning matched by a thoughtful and prepared ending; a scrappy beginning matched by a messy end. An ending that is hastened and rushed may be no more than an echo of a relationship that began without any real clarity.

One of the great dilemmas posed by 'endings' is the resurrection of any unfinished business the client (or the practitioner for that matter) may have to do with unfinished relationships in their past, and who has not? We all have things to work out about how we end things, and both the practitioner and the client will often be facing their own reflections and assessments. To bring these into the relationship in an appropriate way is an important dimension of ending. Talking together in good time about the parting to come and thinking beyond the relationship's conclusion so that the client can plan their future beyond the end of this time together are all important aspects in the final closing of a good working alliance.

If left to the end or put off because of anxieties on the part of the practitioner, then the client is ill served. Leaving it to the client to manage the ending is an abdication of the role of the practitioner and one that may leave the good work accomplished throughout the time together under question or tarnished. Individuals need to identify their own fears and concerns about what endings represent to them, so that they are as free in their closing of relationships as is possible, and the client is left with the opportunity to make this one more important learning from the relationship.

The Value of Rituals

Rituals are a cultural means of stage-managing the disruption that comes with abrupt changes or transitions. Whether it be the ritual of marriage, (which is a loss as well as a change), or bereavement, societies the world over have developed rituals as a way of providing a route through major life transitions. Our own culture has lost a good many of those rituals, or the rituals have lost their potency to support and sustain us. In such circumstances, it may be that client and practitioner create one of their own, a way of marking what the significance of the work has meant for each.

Certainly for those who are working through major issues of loss or bereavement, major disruption or catastrophic change, the use of ritual, albeit on a small and almost incidental scale, can be an important measure of their progress away from the upset and crisis they have been facing. Without the use of such markers, there is little beyond 'the feelings' of the event to recall and time itself will not necessarily either make those go away or heal them – certainly not for a long time. Without pointers, stages of recognition and acknowledged signposts, the past can become a blur of events and the crisis lost in some fictional pretence that we are now 'over it'. The value of rituals is that we know where we are – however bad it still might be – because we remember, thanks to the ritual, how we felt then, just what we could or couldn't do then and where we are now.

This aspect of rituals can so easily be overlooked, but like the point made several times in this section, homework is what makes the work work. Similarly, it is by taking the work into life through rituals and signposts that the client has some indications of their progress with their own struggle. They have markers of success in moving beyond circumstances that might well once have seemed beyond their capacity ever to manage: a strong position from which to move on from this helping relationship.

Suggested Reading

Bandler, R & Grinder, J: *Reframing*. Real People Press, Utah, 1982.
Ellis, A: *The Practice of Rational Emotive Behavior Therapy*. Springer Publishing Company, 1977.
Haley, J: *Problem Solving Therapy*. Harper Row, 1981.
Dilts, R; Hallbom, T & Smith, S: Beliefs: *Pathways to Well-being*. Metamorphous Press, 1998.

SECTION VIII

DEEPER ISSUES

Chapter 24
Moving Towards Deeper Issues

This chapter is a brief summary of some of the key elements of helping that have been highlighted and explored throughout this book. It provides the background for moving into a discussion of the issues that arise as a result of beginning to work at greater depth with those seeking help.

The Importance of Relationship

All help requires some form of relationship in order for it to take place, none more so than emotionally laden work such as 'counselling'. Relationship lies at the centre of the endeavour and at the heart of the enterprise. Yet, if all help requires it, why make something so emphatic of it? And, if all help works through the relationship then why make a special claim for it? We are always in relation to something, someone. *There is always me, you and a context* and who knows which is the more important and influential upon our endeavours?

Often it is what we do not yet know that is influencing what is happening. The world of helping and counselling is changing rapidly. There are now a prodigious number of folk who are 'trained' as 'practitioners'. There are legions of therapists and cohorts of psychotherapists roaming the world claiming territorial rights to the client's psyche. The emotional world is under siege from an army of competing factions all determined they know best what others need.

'Who and what are we dealing with?' are primary concerns in any helping domain. Techniques, methods, approaches proliferate, all claiming cure – instantly. It was not always this way. There was a time when 'growth', 'development', 'change' and taking oneself seriously enough to work at the 'work' was an expected commitment for any lasting change to take hold.

A Different World

Human relationships are increasingly fragmented, difficult to sustain and under constant revision in our turbulent world. It is easier and less painful to work with specifics, complaints, difficulties, the ubiquitous 'problem', rather than reach into the client's world and be there with them for a time: that is arduous and soul searching work.

Much 'training' leaves this out and much counselling leaves it out too. Putting the relationship, the willingness to be there, to engage, to work out with the client how and what to work with, at the heart of the work is not to ignore method or technique, it is to give them their due place; their proper role. Three important dimensions within this broad humanistic perspective are:

- A recognition that we are all creators, actors and participants in the world in which we live. This is not the same things as saying we are all free to do as we like.

- An emphasis upon the positive potential for growth and change, which is seen to lie within the individual.
- A whole-person perspective, which regards the conventional mind/body split as largely artificial.

Most helping and counselling work, and certainly training, focuses upon the method, approach, technique, or framework that the helper uses. Most are concerned to ensure that the helper gets it 'right' within the paradigm of the training, or within the framework of the approach in which they have been 'schooled'. The client is seen more and more as a person with 'difficulties', or 'in difficulties' and it is 'the difficulties' that we are there to help with. This quickly leads to the client being little more than the 'site of operations' for the skilled practitioner to do their work if we are not careful.

In the beginning, practitioners do need to attend to the issues that arise for the client – they need, in other words, to be able to make a useful contribution in helping the client manage the problem. Later, the practitioner comes to recognise that the problem does not exist in isolation from the living network that makes up the client's life. Gradually, the practitioner begins to recognise how these forces shape the way the problem is perceived, managed and lived with. The practitioner begins to locate the problem *within* the person.

At a later, and more experienced stage of the practitioner's career, there is a firmer recognition that it is the client's process that is the common feature of all helping relationships and how to work with the client's process that is the challenge. Only by exploring these same aspects of the practitioner's own make-up does it become possible to work effectively and sensitively with others.

The Practitioner's Values & Beliefs

The practitioner brings with them, to any meeting, their own beliefs, attitudes and values regarding themselves, others and the world at large. They also bring with them a legitimate degree of human 'woundedness'. This 'ground' of values and beliefs is an important aspect of any helping activity. It is what the practitioner draws upon to inform the interventions they choose to offer out of those available to them and which they regard as possible and desirable.

In part, this is no more than 'a skilled performance'. In part, it is also a decision based upon expressing in action the underlying view of the person, the nature of their difficulties, and the purpose of the help that is being offered. A skilled practitioner not only knows what they do, but can also discuss it; they have some competent description that explains why they are choosing to do what they are doing in the way they are doing it, at the time and given the circumstances.

The practitioner, however, is more than an assembly of skills. In an important respect, the practitioner is the instrument through which their help is offered. An understanding and considerable experience of the process of personal development and growth is central to the formation of any effective practitioner. The core conditions of empathy, respect and genuineness find expression through the *behaviour* of the practitioner towards the client. The practitioner not only has to develop and extend the range of their capacity to enter the client's frame of reference, through the development of effective rapport, but has to be able to offer appropriate techniques and strategies that will facilitate the client's progress towards a more effective resolution to their dilemmas.

Training or Education?

If the aim of training is to enable the would-be practitioner to offer themselves as a valuable resource to their clients, it must provide a balance between the following aspects:

- **Personal awareness:** of motivation, values and beliefs.

- **A range of strategies and skills:** to promote effective development that stems from within the client.

- **Social context:** within a context of rapid change, some understanding of the major forces at work within our society is important.

- **Distortions in the helping process:** collusion, illusion and delusion are dangers inherent in the relationship formed between client and practitioner; attention must be drawn to such potential distortions.

Most students are presented with a number of theoretical views as part of their counselling training. These views, however different from one another, fulfil a normative purpose. They are largely orthodox, uncontroversial perspectives and some are profoundly incompatible with one another. In addition, a good deal of their training will draw attention to the guidelines and frameworks of practice put out by examining and accrediting bodies. What this amounts to, if we are not careful, is a stultifying conformity where people may or may not believe what they have been taught. They may also have their own thoughts and reservations about the theories they have been given, but few practitioners in training will have been able to develop an experiential, inquiry-based understanding of their own practice.

There are two important consequences of this. One is that the students know the orthodoxies, if you like, of the helping world – Rogerian, Psychodynamic, Integrative and so on – but, in the view of the author, they will lack a good deal in confidence in building and developing their own framework of understanding. This will be particularly true the more the practitioner takes a participatory, co-creative view. Just as we have noted, in earlier sections, some of the restrictive effects that have entered in helping training as a result of it becoming more strongly academic, so there has been a similar narrowing of experimentation and exploration outside the well-accepted conventions that are currently promoted.

If the end is to see human beings as collaborators in their relationships, then there are few places where practitioners can learn about helping where the educational process mirrors such a view – though there have been some very notable exceptions. If one of the principal aims of helping, as we have been advocating throughout this book, is the promotion of autonomy, client self-direction, choice and responsible action in relation to oneself, others and the planet, then a prerequisite in the preparation of practitioners is an educational process within which these very elements are lived out to the full. And it is for these reasons just outlined that we have things to say about the theory of practice in general terms before looking more closely at individual practice.

Chapter 25
Working at Depth

Soundings

The phrase 'working at depth', like the term 'personal problems' referred to earlier, appears useful only until you begin to work out what it means. In the early days of learning about helping, practitioners, of whatever type, are busy absorbing a way to manage themselves whilst remembering what 'not to do'. They have to adapt their learning about the work to the agency in which they have a place, the organisation in which they are working and the people they are now seeing. Whether they are 'clients', 'mentees', or whatever term the practitioner applies to those with whom they work, they, the clients, now become the focus of the effort.

'Working at depth' may mean working with people over a longer time period. It may mean working at deeper levels of distress that surround individual issues. It may mean working more deeply at what was once regarded as a straightforward 'problem' but which, given greater experience and more self-awareness, we now realise is far from the relatively simple matter of 'sorting it out' that we may well have once believed. It infers that we have more to offer than a rudimentary idea of how to 'be there' for someone; that we can work with some degree of equanimity in the face of a person in some significant distress.

It may mean any and all of these things, but depth can only come with experience; to gain experience we need to practise and to improve in our practice we need some way of improving our model of how we go about what we do. In the end, it relates strongly to our own commitment to how we understand the nature of what we do: how important it is to us; how far we are prepared to engage with the questions that it raises for us; the dilemmas we meet in handling ourselves with others and so on.

Depth is not usually the issue until we have a body of experience on which to draw and some deeper questions about the enterprise upon which we are engaged. 'Working at depth' starts to matter to those who are going to make the work they do as good as it can possibly become. And, before long, those in practice come face to face with the fact that, whilst it may be true that many of the personal difficulties individuals encounter are amenable to progress and change in a relatively short time, there are many that aren't!

Many of those things people arrive seeking help with may seem straightforward – to them. Even though they have not yet 'sorted out' whatever is 'getting in the way', many folk who finally seek help look upon the practitioner much in the way they do a dentist or other technician. 'You have the tools. You make the diagnosis; you operate on me. I go away "better"', seems the unspoken expectation influencing many people – in the beginning.

The idea that they themselves have to contribute more than the practitioner to gain the improvements they wish for can come as something of a surprise to the potential client. Frequently, they expect it to require only a small matter of their time and yours before they will go away satisfied. It doesn't take long before the individual practitioner realises this is simply not the way human beings are put together, nor how 'help' works either.

Many things look straightforward – say the matter of being unable to manage a new situation – yet, likely as not, it will turn out not to be so simple. On the surface there may appear some obvious limitations and the need for some 'strategies' to alleviate the anxieties. 'Problem management', which seemed so modest an ambition when learning the trade in the safety of a diploma course, is often much more difficult to 'pull off' in practice. The kind of complex responses people have to the ordinary stresses of life, compounded by a real lack of educational understanding about themselves, others, and the way feelings operate, can make even a straightforward problem more complex than the time available allows.

Many practitioners find that all those claims for 'brief counselling', which appeal to those seeking some way forward, especially those involved in short-term work, don't actually apply directly to many of the people seeking their help. This is not to say that the techniques offered don't work – all too often they do – but they only apply to certain kinds of conditions, certain kinds of people and at certain points in their development. Many of those coming forward for help are not bringing simply one difficulty for resolution but, rather, they are presenting just one aspect of a well-constructed part of a whole miasma of internal uncertainties, doubts, insecurities or false notions of what is real and what is not. And, as someone remarked, 'that's just the practitioners!'

To the surprise of many new practitioners, they soon come to the realisation that most clients are not like those people they have been practising with and who attended the programmes where they have been learning the art of the work. Most people who seek help from agencies, to take only one example, often have a long history of difficulty, compounded by issues that cover a wider range of concerns than the focus of the agency itself.

Someone with an 'alcohol problem', for example, may well have relationship issues, problems about maintaining employment and a desperate personal history that goes back to their early childhood. In the face of this complexity of suffering what does the practitioner do? No matter what the agency may wish the practitioner to do, no matter how well prepared they have been, when such a person stands before them they have to make some effective and appropriate responses to the person and not simply to the difficulty that the agency is prepared to do something about.

The world of many clients is a lot more turbulent and uncertain than that of many of those people who seek to become practitioners. It is all very well learning how to be less judgemental of your peers on a training programme, but just how do you manage it when you meet some people who have values that are intolerant, exploitative and crudely manipulative and who show no sign of concern that they do?

How do you hold yourself through some of the deeply distressing sessions that may come your way when you illustrate to someone in difficulty that you are prepared to listen deeply to their story only to find it, the story, is bigger than expected? It is not always easy to maintain that sense of presence and detachment in the face of the complexities of human suffering and its entanglements.

'Working at depth' is the alternative to 'being out of your depth' – and most of us find ourselves out of our depth before we know it. It is often only through the realities of practice and good support that we begin to gain a real sense of the dimensions of the work that we have decided to take on. Then we begin to learn how better to manage some of those uncertainties, those irreconcilable elements to the human condition in the time we have, and how to stay involved with the client without becoming overwhelmed by them.

This is frequently how the issue of 'working at depth' arrives. As we gain experience and meet different situations, we are required to give more, to engage more, to wrestle with the work more, to learn more about ourselves. Suddenly we realise that even though the techniques are 'out there' somewhere, they are not to be found in anything like the time or the quantity needed. However, we always have *ourselves* and greater understanding of how we operate, how we work, could make the 'being with' the client a more productive exchange.

Many people certainly have an accumulation of experience but they don't take up the reflective opportunities to explore what those experiences might mean. Many people do indeed have 'clinical supervision' about the work they do with clients, However, they are so well protected and supported 'professionally' that questions which might well appear about their own development in the work are obscured or remain focused on the technical end of practice. 'Working at depth' is not something that automatically arises given sufficient time and experience.

It usually depends upon how far you are prepared to go in meeting yourself and working out more and more of your own blind spots, limiting beliefs and operating assumptions and how they are playing their part in your own contribution – matters that don't usually get surfaced easily. All this can be thought of as working with the 'shadow'. Without that willingness to keep on meeting what we find in ourselves and working with that too, our model of how we do what we do will be limited. This is an implicit part of the approach to working with others described here and is, therefore, a thread throughout the book.

The model may well be coherent and sophisticated, but it will lack the congruence that comes with knowing more about who we are and how we operate – and that often means having to face the fact that we are not altogether the person we like to project we are or would have others believe we are.

Models

All of us have a model of what we do for just about anything, and help is no exception. A model is simply 'a description of the processes and procedures that guide our way of doing the thing we call help' – in this case. We have a model for meeting strangers; we have a model of how to drive; how to eat in a restaurant; how to repair a plug. Anything you can do requires that you have a model in order to go about it i.e. some internal arrangement of information that guides the sequence in which you undertake the task in order to gain the desired result.

You often only realise you have a model when you find yourself out of your depth and not knowing what to do. Such an experience is an indication that the model you have has been 'unconscious' but has, nevertheless, been guiding your actions and that you have now reached the limit of the model's capability of guiding what you do from here on. When people 'feel out of their depth', they are experiencing having an inadequate model to guide their potential actions. This results in confusion and the fear that they may do something that they cannot foresee which will undermine themselves or make them appear foolish. Indeed, these kinds of feelings are often the indication that you are without a model for the situation that you're facing.

The problem of all models, however, is that they save time and therefore they discourage people from paying attention to what happens. This may sound paradoxical but it is the case. A good model saves you time: it works, you know it works and you apply it without thinking.

Models also are time limited. The flat earth model was fine until Columbus discovered the 'New World' and then a lot of things had to change. In some aspects of social life, for example, there used to be one agreed model of how it should be – one man, one wife and... Now there are a plethora of models about what is possible; some of them overlap and some of them compete and a lot of them are possible ways of doing, in this case, the thing called 'having a relationship'.

Models also only apply to some situations and not to all; that is their beauty and their strength. You want a model that works for what you are doing, not one that will cover a limitless range of situations or it will be so generalised that it will be of little assistance in the specifics of any situation. Similarly, you want a model that applies to what you are doing and not one that applies to *nearly* what you are doing or it could bring you hilarious – or dangerous – results.

All models have limitations of this kind. Having the 'right' model for the activity in question is one of the great talents to get on in the world. (The word 'right' here meaning 'useful' for the purposes you intend, not 'right' as in 'best'.) You can take a model and see if it works elsewhere, but you will then have to use the model as a basis for an 'inquiry'. Applying a model without paying attention to the results and effects is a little like throwing the contents of the cupboard into a wok and expecting a good stir-fry to be the result. You may have all the right ingredients and they may be in the right quantity, but in the wrong order or cooked for too long and the result is a disaster.

This balance between general principles and working with the specifics gives the whole question of having a model of practice its critical importance. If I have a model that works for interviewing but not for appraising then I am restricted. If I have a model that covers all interpersonal encounters then it is likely to be of little use in the nuances of any one particular form. Having a model that does what we want it to do is what we are looking for in any form of practice.

One of the major shifts in the 'person-centred' approach is the change from the 'problem – solution' model to the 'process – review' type of model i.e. the change from the study of model methods to the study of the nature of models.

Theories

If models show you *how*, theories tell you *why*. *How* you do something may or may not be related to *why you want to do it*. You might really want to know 'why it rains' but it won't stop you getting wet in a downpour. Why are there four seasons? Why do birds migrate? Why do we see seven colours in the rainbow? *Why* questions relate to:

- How come things are the way they are?
- What are the reasons that make this so?

These are *theoretical* questions and, of course, theoretical answers are not 'better' or 'worse': they are either more comprehensive and sophisticated or less, depending upon how much research has been done on trying to find out the answers to the questions. You want a model that works and the theories give some guidance about what works but they don't create a model of how to do what works. However, if it is a good theory it will suggest some things that would follow pretty inevitably from the information the theory has gathered: a theory of the weather will give some information about whether it might rain or not and therefore whether to take your raincoat with you.

However, theories are not always accurate: they change and the conclusions do not always appear obvious from the data. And there are usually any number of people who differ in their interpretations of what the data should mean and therefore what should be done about it, even if they agree on the data itself! Yet the appeal of theory is that it cannot be disputed in the way practice can

Theory is what you use to *guide you in practice*: it's akin to a road map. When it comes to practice-based activities *theories are meant to be useful*. 'Useful for what?' is the important question. What constitutes a useful theory is more complex when it comes to human activities, especially those involving human relationships and such questions as:

- What it means to be human.
- What it means to be in relationship.
- How and how far these influence one another.
- What procedures are legitimate within a given theoretical view?

Road maps can be of very different scales and, depending upon the length of journey and the detail you need, you have to make your choice. Similarly, theories can be very broad-based and open-ended or they can be very confining.

Theories about people are often partial. They refer to specific areas of conduct, behaviour, activity and so on. They have an *instrumental* use but they don't necessarily go very far in questioning the nature and the basis of the very activities themselves. We are also living through times when the 'givens' themselves are under question, and so thinkers and writers are asking themselves some very fundamental questions about the *way it could be*. When theories are developed simply to serve instrumental purposes, the implications of the ideas and the long-term consequences are often disguised and those adopting them ask no more than, 'Do they explain what we need to know?'

Many views of human beings begin with a flawed and damaged starting point – that we are already condemned to be less than we might be and therefore all we can do is make the best of it. Other views regard humanity as an unfinished project – capable of change, modification, and development. Each point of view can take examples from the history of humanity to find ample evidence to support their view. What each also has to incorporate is the findings from the natural sciences about such things as the process of ageing and the effects of diet and nutrition upon that process, as well as taking into account a wide range of other influences (social, political, economic etc).

Another major limitation about most theories when applied to people is that they provide an explanation that requires those so described to develop little motivation for challenging the description they are given about themselves. Yet we are increasingly confronted with people who actually defy the descriptions that have been given them, whether it is of physical limitations, illness, disease or distress. Time and again, people do not conform to the theory and demonstrate instead that human beings are not reducible to anyone's theory.

Psychology & Theory

Psychological theories would seem to be a promising area to look for some explanations about human relations but psychology as a discipline has limitations when it comes to providing useful guidance about live human relations. As one writer put it:

> "Psychology has attempted to achieve scientific status not by looking closely at its own phenomenon and developing rigorous methods or revealing the characteristics peculiar to this domain, but by mimicking the natural sciences. It has thereby not only placed itself at an insurmountable distance from human reality, but has itself fallen guilty of the dehumanising objectification of man."
> Wortz in M. Friedman, 1992.

We stand in danger of mistrusting our own experience and requiring experts on hand to tell us what our experience actually is and what significance it is supposed to hold. The arrival of the psychologist-as-spokesperson is increasingly a sign that some reassuring mechanical explanation for some dynamic process is about to be provided. The triumph of behavioural and mechanical descriptions of what it means to be who we are is a small wonder of our times and we should not forget that:

> "... to the extent that psychologists illumine human existence to bring it under the deliberate control of someone other than the person himself, to that extent they are helping to undermine some person's freedom in order to enlarge the freedom of someone else." S. Jourard, 1968.

Much contemporary psychological research and theory has little to offer those who are looking for tools to learn more about how we experience ourselves, others and the world; how to explore it, how to work out useful questions, gain new direction from it and what pitfalls to look out for.

It regards the *subject* as just that, as a 'thing' (an object in fact) to be observed, not a participant to share in the experience. It regards the findings as 'results', rather than as provisional data to be included in our joint exploration, and it sets out to discover things that, by and large, the subject knows little about and is encouraged to remain ignorant of. Such a paradigm runs counter to everything about a way of learning from experience together.

> "Over the years, theorists have conceptualised man as a machine; as an organism comparable to rats, pigeons, and monkeys; as a communication system; as an hydraulic system; as a servo-mechanism; as a computer – in short, he has been viewed by psychologists as an analogue of everything but what he is: a person. Man is, indeed, like all those things; but first of all he is a free, intentional subject. " S. Jourard, 1968.

At the same time, however, there is an increasing plethora of books and self-help manuals that are more commonly available and more widely referred to and these are often cited as examples of 'giving psychology away', of making the insights available more widely. We live at a time when we are the most explained we have ever been, the most transparent and the most understood, and yet we are in fear and ignorance of all we do not know of ourselves and one another.

> "Psychologists face a choice. We may elect to continue to treat our Ss[64] as objects of study for the benefit of some elite; or we may chose to learn about determiners of the human condition in order to discover ways to overcome or subvert them, so as to enlarge the S's – that is Everyman's – freedom. If we opt for the latter, our path is clear. Our ways of conducting psychological research will have to be altered. Our definition of the purpose of psychology will have to change. And our ways of reporting our findings, as well as the audiences to whom the reports are directed have to change. We shall have to state openly whether we are psychologists-for-institutions or psychologists-for-persons." S. Jourard, 1968.

[64] An S is the standard term for 'subject' in psychological discussion.

Combs, in his small and excellent book, A *Theory of Therapy*, addresses the problem for those engaged in human relations work and in the search for a theory and a theoretical stance that does justice to the humanness of the subjects. Perhaps more important than the final elegance of the theory, the 'scientific' accuracy of its account or its statistical correlations, the theory informing a practitioner's work must be 'owned', articulate and consistent. It must also apply to the kinds of work that the practitioner is involved in and it must draw upon relevant material from sources that are applicable to the setting and the contextual influences at work there.

Another way of saying this is that practitioners may find all kinds of help from all kinds of theories rather than have a single monolithic, total explanation. The most important thing by far is that they have thought through those influences, know their strengths and limitations as well as their use and extent, and that they are engaged in making themselves 'aware' of the way their theoretical influences inform their practice.

Along with this goes a recognition that no theory of human beings will be comprehensive or the final word on the subject. It must leave scope for new questions to arise out of the practitioner's work. Those new questions then engage them further as they gain more experience and develop a deeper perception of the ways human beings act alone, together and within the systemic forces that shape their choices.

Theory & Experience

People have their own theories that they employ when they do things just as they have models of how they do things. They have an espoused theory – what they say they believe. They have a *theory in use* – what they actually do in practice and what we can infer, given the practice we see. These two elements are often deeply at odds with one another, as those who did the research on this intriguing phenomenon quickly discovered.

Donald Schon and his contemporaries[65] went about looking at this phenomenon of 'theory in use' and noted just how professionals, particularly, diverged from their espoused theories when it came to making difficult choices about practice matters. So, for example, they would proclaim the importance of 'working for the client' but, in practice, when there were some difficult choices to be faced, the professional would often 'steer the client' to make the choice the professional preferred.

Here we enter the land of beliefs where both models and theories have some overlap and interconnection. Science may be a guide but it does not have the answer to our search for how to work at depth. It is important to note here that, in the view of the author, both theory and practice are relevant; there should be a spectrum and not polarities.

---

[65] The work in this field was undertaken by Donald Schon and Chris Argyris and is recorded in a book entitled *Theory in Use* and, later, Schon's book *Educating the Reflective Practitioner*. Books of great insight and commitment to transparent practice. The latter especially is a classic text that relates to many of these matters of applied and practice-based activities and the theories that inform them.

Theories need to arise out of experience or, at the very least, help us examine our experience further. Only such a type of theory can help inform *my method*; for my method is what comes after my experience has been refined by my growing theoretical understanding, my tentative hypotheses and continual reflective generalisations.

As a result of my experience, I reflect, consider, argue, discuss, reflect some more, have more experience and so on – in short, I remain engaged in assessing the significance of what my experience brings to me. From it all, I sift and assess, draw tentative conclusions. *I theorise* – propose the significance of what I have learned with the help and influence of other sources.

This is no argument for pioneering theory entirely alone or of relating to no one else's previous experience and observations. It is a warning against the uncritical adoption of theoretical positions developed by other people at other times to fit other situations and climates. The theory and approach of Carl Rogers is perhaps a good example of the way a theory from one time and place, as a response to one set of conditions, then becomes distorted[66] by others in a different time and place.

The Contribution of Carl Rogers

To propose a client-centred approach in the fifties and through the sixties, as Rogers did, was to be at the leading edge of challenge to the prevailing authoritarian ethos, the institutional and hierarchical organisation, which pervaded 'helping' work of all kinds. Rogers fought a brave and prolonged struggle to gain recognition for the subject of that help. He helped to restore the importance of the subject's experience as the centre upon which the helping process was founded – at no small cost to Rogers himself, both in professional recognition and in academic acceptance. In times like ours, when even the banks will listen to you, it is neither hard nor strenuous to proclaim yourself as 'person-centred' and it can often amount to little more than a deep unwillingness either to reveal yourself or express your authentic presence in the relationship at all for fear of influencing the client.

Anyone who has seen Rogers on film or read him knows that he was deeply present and engaged in his work – he was 'in it'. Anyone who is 'in it' is having an effect. It was the way he was 'in it' that had the effect it had. Many people adopting Rogers's views or their interpretation of them regard it as tantamount to commanding the client if the practitioner indicates the least involvement in the client's experience. Effacement rather than involvement becomes the aim.

Rogers was a deeply critical thinker challenging much of the orthodoxy of his day (and he would no doubt be doing the same still), however, many of his followers are in

---

[66] I realise I am on very shaky ground here. There are many variations of Rogers' way of working and many claim to be advances upon his foundational work. Some of it may be that, but to my mind, Rogers was nothing so much as himself and made the object of his work helping others to become themselves. He believed that given the 'right' conditions, just about anybody could make progress in that direction. His theory is an account of his developing understanding of that process and many who have gone on to develop it select aspects of the theory that miss this underlying commitment to what it means to be a person in relation to others, and emphasise other features of his theoretical account over that essential element.

danger of finding an accommodation to the world as it is. They use his radical tools as little more than a justification for focusing only on the person, leaving it up to the person to find their own way through the difficulties that they have sought help with. At the same time, they evade the political and leave the social context out altogether – something Rogers himself didn't do. He saw the interrelationship of those realms, and whilst his theoretical work and his observations make clear that person-centred work was his focus, it was done within a clear recognition of the social and political forces at work and a need for the practitioner to be engaged with those too.

'Living' Theory

Sometimes your theory takes you to places you'd rather not go. Sometimes theory requires you to extend your experience into domains that are uncomfortable. Because if it's *your* theory and *your* attempt to make sense of how come your practice and experience are raising issues that have to be thought through, then your theory can start to influence your practice in a living way.

Theory, then, is no mental exercise, not a post-operative means of providing an explanation and justification for why things worked out the way they did. Theory is an active force bringing the mental and emotional together (because a theory can arise out of passion and conviction as well as needing the coolness of thought and assessment). Your theory can also, crucially, arise out of insight, intuition, imagination, creativity.

I don't want a theory so comprehensive and complete that it excludes or discourages me from continuing to ask new questions. Nor do I want a theory which so foreshortens the questions that they are of the, 'What happens if you move your head three inches to the right?' variety and then the next three years is spent setting up a controlled experiment to discover the obvious – that 'not a lot happens'. This can be the way some research and theory develops (but not always and when it does it is actually indicative of poor research).

I want my theory to be capable of informing me and the work I do in ways that are useful to what we are attempting to accomplish i.e. to learn more about the nature of the questions we face; the decisions we have to make together; the implications of the choices that we are assessing and so on – to learn more of what it means to be who we are, where we are conjointly doing what we are doing *together*. At best, a theory for such affairs is going to be tentative, however comprehensive its references, in the sense that it is always open to modification and development. I want it to be able to *involve* us and our experience of what we do in what is a shared enterprise. My theory needs to take account of that. I want a theory to *inform* what I do, not *determine* what I do and I want a theory that is imaginative, that has possibilities for the future.

"Humanistic psychology is a goal, not a doctrine. It owes its renaissance to the growing conviction that current and past approaches to the study of man have reached their limits in elucidating man's behaviour and his 'essence'. It is a growing corpus of knowledge relating to the questions, 'What is a human being?' and 'What might man become? Thus, humanistic psychology can be regarded in analogy with industrial psychology or the psychology of mental health or of advertising. These specialities are systems of knowledge bearing on particular families of questions: e.g. what variables affect morale, or the output of workers, or the maintenance of wellness, or the purchasing behaviour of potential customers. Humanistic psychology asks, 'What are the possibilities of man?' and from among these possibilities, 'What is *optimum man*, and what conditions most probably account for his attainment and maintenance of these optimums?'" S. Jourard, 1968.

Theoretical Perspectives in Helping

Combs gave a number of headings about theories that can give further insight into the nature and use of theories in helping situations. Since Combs had therapeutic help as his focus he understandably begins there. For our purposes we might add the term 'practice' to the word 'help'. The practitioner has to understand something about the nature of when, and when not, the work is possible. The practitioner has to have a sense of when, and when not, interventions are capable of bringing a positive outcome and under what circumstances matters should be left alone.

Practice must be defined as to what it includes and what it excludes i.e. the 'domain' of the activity and the 'range' that the practice is to cover. In part this gives a practice its legitimisation; it is its claim to a territory.

Comprehensive. A theoretical perspective must be comprehensive, not necessarily exhaustive but certainly capable of encompassing a wide range of the phenomena that it is setting out to account for. The difficulty with a comprehensive explanation is that it may be superficial and of limited value in particular circumstances, just as an explanation that is highly specific may not travel to many situations.

Accurate. Clearly no set of guiding ideas and overall explanations is useful if they are without any validity or accuracy. The ideas upon which you draw must have a fit with the realities with which you are grappling. As we've already observed in human relations, this is nothing like as easy as it sounds since human beings disagree widely over what the data is, what it means and how it should be used. So 'accuracy' is no simple concept but at the very least it needs to be accurate and consistent with the assumptions of the theory being proposed. It needs to explain what is happening or how events unfold from within the system of presuppositions it has adopted.

Operationally adequate and yet simple. Any practitioner-based activity needs a theory that is usable, that can help the practitioner get on with the practice, that can wrestle with the issues as they appear not as they are hypothesised or idealised in order to make interesting theoretical points.

This is the 'swampy ground' of the world of Donald Schon where the real problems exist, which often defies the theoretical models that the practitioner has been fed through programmes of study. A theoretical perspective that is over-elaborated may well mean that it doesn't fit into the conditions of the 'swamp' at all well. One that is overly simple ends up offering little in the way of insight to make progress. A way of explaining the phenomenon and releasing meaning that is accurate and useful is what is needed. The more theory is hatched away from the realities of practice, the more it stands in danger of being plausible but ultimately difficult, if not impossible, to use on the ground.

Consistent. The theory needs to be coherent in its explanatory power. It has to hang together within the range of situations that have been identified. It is no good having a theory that only works for a very confined number of examples if your work is going to take you into a diverse range.

It is no good, either, having a global explanation if your 'arena' of practice is very, very specific. Consistency here is as much about internal consistency and applicability of your theory to the actual world of *your* practice. A theoretical perspective doesn't have to be universally consistent: indeed one of the values of knowing the source of your theoretical influences is knowing where they will travel to in a useful way and at what point they cease to have a valid or useful explanatory power.

Appropriate for the issues. As well as being appropriate to the view of human beings and human activities that you hold, a theoretical perspective needs to have *relevance* and *regard* for the issues that are under consideration. Whilst it may be useful, for example, to have behavioural explanations for how individuals respond under the stress of conflict, it is also useful to understand something of how their *values* impinge upon their behaviour if you are interested in helping people learn more effective ways of resolving conflict. (It's not that the one explanation is inadequate or inconsistent nor that it isn't appropriate, it isn't however *comprehensive* enough for the issues. Its appropriateness is too limited.) Appropriateness of theoretical views needs to take into account not only the issue itself but also its context and dimensions.

Able to incorporate new data. Theoreticians may seek to chase the grail of a total explanation, and may even be given time and sufficient funds for the search, but most practitioners in any aspect of human relations are unlikely to find themselves in such a position. They need enough theory to get the show on the road – to begin to practise with a sense of 'safety' or 'competence'. They also need a fair idea of what is happening, just as they need to know when they are beyond their understanding; in other words, when they are out of their depth and the swamp is about to come over their 'wellies'.

Most practitioners, if they have any interest in developing themselves, will soon learn that what they start out knowing is only the beginning and that as they practise, issues will arise in and of themselves. In addition, there will be dilemmas that appear in practice itself. There will be conflicts and choices that are far from simple to resolve and through which the individual practitioner may gain stature in their work if they are willing to engage with the discomfort and the ambiguity that is involved. *All these provide motivating forces for the continuous revision of understanding.*

New data here is not simply reading the latest research reports (though they can often be helpful) so much as reflecting upon what practice is asking of ourselves; of recognising how our perception and engagement with issues is changing. No one – certainly no one who is going to be effective in human relations – knows enough about anything not to need to enquire further into their experience and reflect upon their practice. In that way, if no other, new data in the form of reactions, responses and results need to be encouraged to take up their place in the ever-deepening understanding that the practitioner is seeking to develop.

Motive for intervention. Since practice is about 'doing' – about *application* – a theory needs to guide what the practitioner does when and how. It needs to inform practice and it needs to help the practitioner understand something of the limits to practise in the moment.[67] The exploration of motives for interventions is a good deal more complex than is often acknowledged.

In training, practitioners are often introduced to the rationale for an intervention, the justification that underlies a range of action, on the basis of the conditions that pertain. But many practice-based interventions rely upon the practitioner as part of the equation. In other words, the decision to 'do this now in this way' is not value free, nor based entirely upon the information that lies in the context, the participants or the situation, but is a good deal dependent upon the 'interpretations' of all this information made by the practitioner themselves.

Indeed, one of the distinguishing features of any good practitioner is that they can bring to their work a flair and a poise that creates an opportunity to work with talent and 'grace' out of even the most mundane and unprepossessing of situations. Similarly, what often makes a situation beyond rescue, is the overzealous commitment of the practitioner to a particular course of action that has less and less suitability to the circumstances pertaining. Motive for intervention needs to take into account:

- The individual psychology of the practitioner.
- Their own preferences, investments and value systems.
- How these interact and how they are understood and sensed.

The more participatory the practice, the more this is absolutely required.

---

[67] Practice is legitimised by claims about the range and the domain of the activity. Establishing the warrant to practise is the usual way an activity seeks to gain recognition as a distinct occupation or profession. But also, any applied activity has to have a way of legitimising its moment by moment conduct, of establishing the 'appropriateness' of what is done according to the needs of the situation, the people involved and the circumstances faced. The influences from theory and reflection about what informs a practitioner when they seek to do 'this' 'then' is part of the growing corpus of experience upon which the identity of the individual practitioner is built.

Change as Learning

An applied activity needs a theory to help shape its activities and help inform the goals it regards as important to pursue. Just as there is a need for legitimising the domain and the range and to claim a warrant for the activity itself, so there needs to be some statement about the nature of the endeavour and what it is to accomplish, if only so that we can begin to learn what happened when we don't get there and end up somewhere else! Was this an over-ambitious claim or did some new feature enter into the activity that diverted our efforts and energy to produce a new result? Theories often begin to reveal their inadequacy when the goals being pursued are not much connected to the theory that is supposed to inform it.

No one can learn without changing and no change can happen without people learning, even if all they learn is a reinforcement of what they already know. For an experience to be perceptibly *different*, then a recognition has to take hold that makes us look into the events more closely to find out what else is there. If this does not occur, we risk 'foreclosing', seeking to reduce the new experience to nothing more than a repetition of the old, therefore leaving us with nothing to learn. Human beings have the capability to 'screen out' what they *could* learn just as they have the opportunity to see new patterns in familiar experiences. Understanding how the change process works within individuals, between them and within systems, is an important feature of theoretical concern for anyone involved in human relations work since many of the experiences that individuals, groups and organisations have to manage are as a direct result of the accelerating pace of change.

Chapter 26
The Self as Instrument

The Image of the Person

This is the heart of the matter. In the end, what the practitioner regards as the nature of people, their image of the person, how they view the ultimate purpose of human relationships and their social and planetary role, determines all else. This will imbue practice and may be a much more difficult matter to tease out than many of us realise.

Given the opportunity, most of us can trot out the right kind of platitudes about what we think we think about these things. Given a little more thought, we also know that there are some situations that are beyond our present scope of understanding. There are also some that we 'feel' we know what to do but, thankfully, we are not there having to make the decision because we wouldn't know how we would cope if we did act in a certain way. (The complexity of the *War on Terror* is perhaps an obvious example of the way most of us would be uncertain to know how best to act or which values to promote.)

In many practice situations, values are often in conflict and, sometimes, even incompatible. This makes the usual notions we hold about the nature of people, the role of human relations, and the ultimate purpose of our role, not something that remains stable and unchanging (unless we adopt a fundamentalist view and surrender our right to self-direction, self-consciousness and personal responsibility for the values we hold). The image of the person we hold, what emerges from our practice, and how far we strive to work from a base that does justice to our views, is an important aspect of the development of any practitioner.

What we believe makes us the way we are, in large measure, influences and informs what we do and what purposes we pursue. All the following will have a decisive influence upon the stance to practise any one of us takes:

- Deciding the legitimate limits to our influence.

- Deciding how far we use knowledge gained in one situation in others.

- Knowing how far we can make use of our understanding of the way people react and behave.

- Knowing how far we need to include the other in our considerations.

The more we wish to be viewed as an 'expert', the more we will cling to our separate knowledge and our training – those things which distinguish us and keep us apart in order to maintain the role distance required to hold the sense of being *other than* and *apart from* that is the basis of many professionals' practice. The more collaborative and participatory we intend to be, the more willing we will be to share how we are developing our rationales for action, and the more open we will be to enter into early discussions about potential options and likely consequences.

An equally important influence upon how practitioners relate to others is the image they hold of their own place in the world. This raises many questions:

- How do we understand ourselves in the world?
- How do we understand the process of being?
- How do the parts of the person fit together?
- Do we have a mechanical and reductionist view of the person, seeing them as an assembly of bits and pieces that operate in relation to one another, or do we conceive the person with many facets and aspects but essentially as a whole person?
- What place do we give to the personality? Is that all we are?
- Is there more, perhaps something more intangible: a soul that informs our life and helps give expression to that personality which is formed by having to take up a place, first in our family of origin and then in the wider world?

This is an area of exploration which has far reaching consequences upon how the practitioner not only looks at things but how they decide to act and at what level of depth they offer themselves in relation to the other.

> "Many humanistic psychologists nowadays are actively involved in researching the importance of transcendent, mystical, or 'trans-personal' experiences. Such research leads them to confront metaphysical questions and realities; and an acquaintance with that level of experience makes it all the more obvious how insufficient older theories of personalities have been." Arroyo, 1975.

A Working Theory

Theories aren't neutral. It is evident from all that has gone before that they are generated or arise out of moral stances, positions and beliefs. Some theories are more aligned than others with our values and beliefs and it is only natural that we are going to look for theories to sustain us in our practice. Nevertheless, we should pay attention to alternative explanations in order to keep our practice alive to the issues of the times in which we live. The theory we hold – if it guides practice – will influence what we do. If the theory we hold is one of which we are unaware and it remains unarticulated it will still influence practice. The work of Schon, once again, highlighted many of these points.

Practice-based professionals often have an 'espoused' set of motives and an espoused theory which they become all too willing to forgo when it comes to dealing with the messiness of the 'swamp'. What we say we *would* do then starts to give way to an altogether more 'pragmatic' set of actions and an altogether more expedient range of decisions if we aren't careful. And they are all justified in the name of being 'helpful' or of acting in the 'customer's best interests'.

Theory is meant to increase the intentionality of practice but those who have not explored the fit between their theory and themselves, their own values, the values of the profession and the system in which they operate, may find themselves acting in ways that are at odds with their own views without knowing quite how. They may find themselves being left with little more than a vague sense of troubling disquiet.

All too often at such times, theory is resorted to as a way of explaining *why things had to be the way they were*, largely because the practitioner has not thought through what other options (ones that might lie outside the theory that is proving inadequate) there might be. In that sense we can be imprisoned within our theoretical ideas as any others.

How does all this work out in practice and what does a practitioner need to take account of? Since theories can be explored endlessly and are certainly more reassuringly stable than the swamp, how do we get off the high ground and down there in amongst the mess and the beauty of human relations?

What does a working theory involve? I suggest there is one key area of concern in human relations as we move into practice: the **self as instrument**. The concept of 'self as helper' was briefly addressed in *Section Four: The Helping Conversation*, and we will now look at it in more depth.

In human relations, the practitioner is the instrument through which their contribution is offered. How far they are alert, aware, engaged has a direct impact upon the calibre of the work and what it achieves. The tools alone aren't sufficient and the person who is committed can often accomplish more than the technically experienced but casual practitioner. There is no escaping this aspect to the work. Who you are and how you are matter every bit as much as what you have to offer, and the more the outcome matters to the folk involved, the more this will be true. Just as children don't learn from teachers they don't like[68], so adults will not respond well to someone who demonstrates low commitment or indifference to the difficulties faced by those with whom they are collaborating. The self-as-instrument concept involves three main features:

- Self-awareness.
- Emotional competence.
- Self-direction and accountability.

The key is the ability to apply knowledge sensitively and appropriately to facilitate an individual or group toward the resolution of their dilemma as they describe it, own it, and choose to change in relation to it. *Consequently, a practitioner's main resource for their work is themselves.*

Self-awareness

The more they understand about themselves, the greater self-awareness they possess, the less likely it is that they will become subject to many of the pitfalls that can limit effective helping. *Self-awareness* is an all-embracing term to describe a group of inter-related aspects of self-other understanding. There appears from research (Avila, Combs and Purkey, 1977) to be six major elements of self-awareness that contribute towards making an effective practitioner and in developing one's own resource strength.

---

[68] A survey in the seventies went to considerable trouble to demonstrate this link: that learning and who you learned from, and especially how you 'felt' about them, was an important aspect to the rate and the significance of the learning achieved by young people.

I. Knowledge. Practitioners need to have a sound understanding of the underpinning rationale for whatever kind of help they are offering. 'Intuition' and 'playing hunches' can sometimes be a potent source of assistance but are not a sufficient basis for offering systematic, purposeful and aware help to others.

For individuals coming into a helping role without prior preparation, acquiring a sound understanding of the effective limits to their helping role can take a considerable time and cause much uncertainty and anxiety. It is important for practitioners to take time to discuss their views and increase their understanding of how they can help, what help they can legitimately provide and, perhaps most importantly, why they are being seen as a helper in the first place. Experience in such matters is no alternative to training. Opportunities to share issues and concerns with others in a similar role are essential for developing a sound understanding of what they are there to do.

At a time when the helping world is undergoing so many changes itself, it is crucial for practitioners and agencies to remain alert to the modification and developments of the context in which they work and live and which, therefore, influence changes (however slight) in how they approach the work they do.

2. Frame of reference. All people in a helping role act upon some basic assumptions they have acquired, often unconsciously, about the nature of the world in which they live, the rights and responsibilities of people, and how they regard helping as an activity. This forms their frame of reference. An individual's frame of reference is often not easy to identify, least of all for the person themselves, yet it influences all that they think and do. It provides people with their ready-made view of the world, which they bring to any situation in which they find themselves.

How people behave at any particular moment is a result of how things seem to them. Helping people achieve more satisfying ways of living and being is therefore a matter of facilitating change in what people think and believe about themselves and their world. To do this well, effective practitioners need to understand the nature of personal meaning and how the individual's view of the world can be widened and enriched.

Over time, and with experience, the practitioner develops themes of interest, preferences for certain issues or certain kinds of clients; they may lose interest with areas of the work and find their commitment engaged elsewhere. None of this implies they will not be doing a valuable and effective job, but the way they perceive what that job is and how it is best done will vary. This is something that is to be welcomed because it is one way of enriching the work over time.

3. Views of what people are like. Practitioners are influenced by their views of what they think people are really like. If a practitioner's view is based upon a need for control and direction for the client's 'own good', then this will find its way into the practitioner's way of responding. On the other hand, an attitude towards others in difficulty that respects the dilemmas they face and offers support without taking over the problem will communicate itself to the individuals seeking help. The beliefs that underpin such an attitude are that:

- People are essentially worthy of dignity and respect.
- People can resolve their own predicaments, given support of the right kind, and will do it better than others since they got themselves into the predicament to start with.
- People can work together positively.
- People have an inherent capacity to work, learn, grow and mature.

There are days when most of us find all these too hard to embrace with the wholehearted commitment we know we would like. The problem with having views about 'people' is that the views change according to the people we have in mind. And it is all very well believing these things about people in general (or, more often, 'people like me') but when it comes to my clients then...

Many of those seeking help from helping agencies are not necessarily well educated, able to evaluate options, or even recount their own story with any degree of real understanding. The more restricted and limited the individual, the more they may try the patience of the overworked practitioner. If such a practitioner is not careful, they may well subscribe to the non-judgemental views expressed above, in theory, but in practice operate with quite another set of beliefs.

Such views as those above are not 'official statements' but the living expression of the worth of the other that the practitioner actually embraces, however much it is a struggle. Surfacing discrepancies and confronting one's limitations to an all-embracing tolerance and all accepting saintliness is difficult. This is especially so in the company of others because we tend to believe that other people are better at it than we are.

4. Practitioner's self-concept. An individual's self-concept is not a 'thing', but an original set of ideas, perceptions and values that attach to an individual's sense of self. It extends to cover one's loved ones and possessions, such as when my friend becomes upset when I thoughtlessly put aside a piece of 'junk' which he later tells me he created at his art class.

Our sense of self becomes invested in our relationships with others, so that we come to feel keenly the distresses they experience and the satisfactions that accompany their achievement. Self-concept represents what people perceive themselves to be and what they believe themselves to be.

For the practitioner, it is especially important to investigate and understand their own self-concept in order to increase their awareness of the motivations and beliefs influencing them in offering help to others. If the practitioner has a self-concept that is categorised by low self-esteem – for example, if they believe themselves to have little to offer – then they may be in the helping business to earn the gratitude of those they help.

People who are seeking help are often at their most vulnerable and have to overcome the embarrassment and insecurity of admitting they need outside assistance. This may make them easily dependent on the practitioner and may lead them to see the practitioner as some kind of wise and all-powerful mother or father-figure able to make things right. A practitioner who is looking to earn gratitude from their clients may easily succumb to such appeals. They might then run round doing things and putting the client's world right in order to secure the praise clients can readily give, never realising, until too late, that such activity only fosters the dependency of the client upon the practitioner.

A practitioner's self-concept will influence considerably how far they set out to encourage a client to move toward a genuine independence, autonomy and freedom of choice, and so will affect how successful they are as a practitioner. Individuals who have examined themselves, who have seen something of the discrepancies between how they would like to think they are and how they really are, and who can accept themselves with all their imperfections, are likely to be more effective in encouraging others who are struggling with the same process.

The more the practitioner learns to accept themselves, the more, it seems, they are able to accept others, and the more able those people are to accept themselves. Self-acceptance is a strenuous form of self-assessment: it is not an over-anxious concern with presentation or an indifference to the views of others. Self-acceptance is more an ideal to work towards than a state to be attained. As practitioners gain stature through their ability to face themselves and manage the resulting turbulence, they gain not only insight and understanding but self-acceptance.

5. Purpose. The practitioner must take account of their activity in relation to:

- The purpose they set for themselves.
- The purpose of the setting in which they find themselves.
- The time available and the wider purpose of the society in which they exist.
- The purposes the client may have.

These can be difficult issues to integrate harmoniously. Many practitioners have to learn to live with high levels of ambiguity about what they do and how far the limits of their involvement should extend. This is an issue that can be particularly acute. A willingness to 'do one's best' to help another may well begin to reveal dimensions of difficulty that the practitioner is ill-equipped to deal with and that the organisation is unprepared to accept, with too little time to handle any of it constructively. The results can be distressing, or worse, for all concerned.

Development programmes, where such issues can be explored in the company of others facing similar issues, can help inexperienced practitioners begin to understand the complexities of their dilemmas and to learn that there are no simple answers. In acute cases where the purposes of the organisation and the purposes of the practitioner are too wide, the practitioner may well need to leave to seek a setting that is more in keeping with their own values and beliefs.

6. Helping methods & techniques. Gerard Egan (1975) says that ineffective help is not something neutral; it can have deeply damaging effects. It may reinforce the individual's belief that no one will really listen and therefore lead them to avoid looking for help elsewhere. Or it may help precipitate an avoidable crisis.

The practitioner, therefore, needs to have a repertoire of methods, techniques and skills at their command and be able to use them with deliberate and aware choice. It is not possible to know the effects of interventions before they are made, but it is important to recognise the likely areas of inquiry which certain skills will open for examination. Skills to help others can be acquired with development, practice and review.

This is the domain of training and education but as a general observation here, it is worth noting that many practitioners have an abundance of techniques and skills, but often lack a broad approach to the helping relationship or, alternatively, they have a well-worked out approach but are at odds with the application of specific techniques. Finding the blend between relationship and technique is an important aspect of any practitioner's path of progress to finding an individual way of offering themselves to others.[69]

No one achieves an end state to these areas of exploration: it is a *path of continuous learning*. We are all becoming more or less competent in the way we handle these dimensions of personal development. Sometimes we are entering new terrain and beginning to be willing to meet new aspects of powerful emotions or to encounter situations charged with powerful emotions for the first time. These are not the kind of situations and circumstances that we learn how to manage ourselves well as a rule when we are growing up. Indeed, many of us are 'taught', or certainly learn in our growing up, that some situations are to be avoided because of the unpleasant feelings involved. It is often learning of this kind (to avoid situations rather than learn to overcome them) that creates such a handicap for people in their adult life, especially in their personal relationships and in the work setting.

---

[69] See *The Art of Brief Counselling: Technique or Relationship?* Bryce Taylor, Oasis Press 1997.

Overcoming such resistance and fear, and learning to meet difficult feelings, is a much-neglected domain of our educational system and all the more necessary for the human relations practitioner to explore and experience. The disturbance such emotions cause to the clear, aware functioning that is required to meet unexpected and unmanaged emotional reactions often takes away any sense of the practitioner being in charge of the situation or of being able to have any realistic sense of what is needed. At such a critical moment, the practitioner finds themselves preoccupied with managing their own performance. And, of course, time spent managing one's own emotional state is time and energy taken away from working out what is happening in the situation itself and, more importantly, how to contribute to it effectively.

Emotional Competence

Emotional competence and personal awareness are very closely linked. The more occluded my emotions, the more 'out of awareness' my reactions (due to the repressed or well-defended reactions that I may have), the less is my present awareness able to operate with clarity and appropriateness.

If I have strong reactions to some situations that are a result of unconscious or unacknowledged experiences from the past, I will not only be in ignorance of what is needed now, but I will also be spending a part of my time keeping myself away from the openness necessary to realising what is provoking the reaction that I find so discomforting. Awareness operates on the calm waters of emotional steadiness. If I don't have that then the awareness will be disturbed and my functioning will correspondingly be limited.

The levels of distress for the great mass of human kind are of disabling proportions. Large numbers of our fellow beings live in want of the basics: food, shelter, and security. Many, many millions more live in insecure political, economic and social arrangements, and those of us who live in the more materially secure (for the present) societies of the developed world have uncovered massive forms of emotional exploitation and abuse. Distress on such a scale might easily lead some to view the human being as an unfinished project – therefore capable of developing in unexpected and altogether creative and glorious ways – but the result so far leaves little to inspire one to any great hope. However, emotional competence lies at the root of much of the change that is needed to create the kinds of conditions for us all to flourish – rather than for some to live at the expense of others.

Of the distress condition of humans on the planet, John Heron (1992) writes:

> "This is a vast social pathology, a vast malaise. It cannot be regarded as a therapeutic problem, other than in the short-term individual case. It is an educational issue. We need concepts of child-raising and of education at all levels that foster the progressive development of emotional competence, in the same way that at present we foster the development of intellectual competence."

Emotional competence begins with the capacity of the individual to be able to identify, take responsibility for and accept emotions of all kinds, along with the accompanying ability to switch and redirect emotional states with some elegance and awareness. At an everyday level, emotional competence means being able to spot the restimulation of old emotional pain and to interrupt its displacement before it is let loose into forms of distorted behaviour that is then acted out upon others or internalised upon oneself. Such 'pattern interruption' begins to remove old hurt-laden agendas so they are no longer 'projected' out onto others, nor are they 'transferred' onto current situations inappropriately. Such a view is based on the general insight that early traumatic experiences have a major influence on adult behaviour.

The implications of developing an emotionally competent culture would go a long way beyond the claims made for most forms of emotional management or self-control that are increasingly popularised. It would mean being able to spot institutionalised and professionalised forms of displacement, and finding ways of replacing them with more rational, flexible and adaptive behaviours.

> "This is a cry-ing need in all the helping professions. So the doctor abandons the repeat prescriptions of psychotropic drugs and cultivates an ability to handle psychosocial disorders. The academic relinquishes sixty-minute lectures and develops more skill in facilitating self-directed learning. The priest stops preaching sin and acquires competence in enhancing spiritual self-esteem.
>
> It means being able supportively to confront other people who are unawarely acting out their denied distress in negative and disruptive forms of behaviour. The confrontation does not shirk the behavioural issue: it deals with it straight and true. At the same time it does not attack, invalidate or abuse the person who is being confronted about the issue. The uncompromising feedback is fundamentally respectful." J. Heron, 1992.

'Emotional competence' means many things and is, in the author's view, a richer concept than that of 'emotional intelligence' which suggests that emotions have an intelligence rather than that persons have intelligent ways of managing their feeling life, and that 'emoting' is only one way of expressing feeling.

Emotional competence recognises that an event can give rise to either positive or distress-laden emotions for the person at the centre of that event. It also acknowledges that one person may experience positive emotions whilst another experiences distress-laded emotions from the same event. The response is not determined by the event itself but by the individual's own internal processing.

Emotional competence also recognises the importance of *catharsis* and the release of distress emotion as "evidence of self-healing, not as evidence of breakdown". It also differentiates the originating distress induced from the later distorted forms it acquires once it has been repressed and denied. The emotionally competent person is someone who knows the difference between "the catharsis of distress, which occurs when repression is dismantled, and the displacement or acting out of distress, which is the result of repression still being in place". They can also distinguish between "catharsis as such and dramatisation or pseudo-catharsis, which is the last vestige of acting out as repression falls away".

Emotional competence also means enjoying and expressing positive emotions, as well as noticing when these are clouded by distress to such an extent that we need to take time-out to release it. Along with this goes a strong enhancement of positive and affirmative forms of celebration and the promotion of positive self-esteem as a foundational element of emotional life.

In broad terms, there are four distinctive elements to any mapping of emotional competence. They are:

1. The management of emotion through creative expression.

2. The ability to suppress and manage feelings of all kinds in an aware way when appropriate,

3. The ability to discharge distress via a variety of cathartic skills at appropriate times and places,

4. The ability to transmute aspects of distress emotion rather than suppress or repress them.

Self-direction & Accountability

Self-direction and accountability rely upon my being able to have some predictability over my conduct, of being able to have a confident sense of delivering what I say in the time I claim. Self-direction allows me opportunity to continue to increase my sense of personal authority, my understanding of the realities acting upon me, and the deepening sense of what potential I can call upon to help me. Accountability is its corollary.

If I develop my capacity to be more self-directing, to become more autonomous, I am also more capable of taking responsibility for my actions and thoughts. I am more able to know what is realistic for me to commit to and to be willing to be accountable for the result. Such accountability is a long way from simply having to 'carry the can'; it is a much more engaged commitment to myself and my learning, a willingness and a wish to stand by what I do so that I am able to learn.

Accountability is an important element to any body of practice that works in relation to third parties. If I hire you to provide me with practitioners for my staff, then I have every right to expect that you will give some assurances about just who those people will be and what their level of competence will be.

Accountability is part of the managerial culture we have adopted for many endeavours; education, public service, as well as commercial operations. This 'one model suits all' approach does helping work few favours. Whilst no one would promote a lack of accountability as the norm, if accountability is no more than a mantra for surveillance

– for one group of 'licensed' people to oversee another with little dialogue about how those to be monitored will be evaluated and what they are accountable for in ways that bear a clear and direct relationship to the work being attempted – then it may be little more than a form of smoke screen to appear to be doing things that actually get in the way of what does need doing.

The public sector is full of people who can give descriptions of how their autonomy as practitioners is undermined by the relentless prescription of targets they have to meet, leaving them few opportunities to make decisions about their own practice. Helping work is no exception to all this. However, helping, if it is be effective, has to get out from under such a stranglehold and ask itself a number of questions about the forms of accountability that suit the various types of help. And the starting place, in my view, is with self-direction.

It was once a premise that the purpose of counselling was to promote the self-direction of the client; the client is in charge of their own lives, has opted to enter into the relationship to change it, can withdraw if they don't like it, and challenge the work if they feel it is not suited to their needs. They can, in short, vote with their feet. However, if the client is cajoled into attending, and if a system is determined people will have counselling (that is little short of benign disciplinary exhortation) then it undermines the principle of self-direction altogether.

If the practitioners who are operating within such a system themselves come from a form of training where self-direction is more of a concept than a fundamental requirement of the preparation, then they are likely to adopt the norms of the system in which they serve. Everyone is then perpetuating a deception.

Client self-direction is based on the degree to which the practitioner has embraced that idea for themselves in their own life and work – and that includes their preparation. I cannot be much use in helping someone explore their 'real options' if I don't believe I have any myself – for how would I recognise what a 'real one' was as opposed to the fixed choices that face me? If I don't employ self-direction in a convincing way to my own circumstances then how would I be of use to someone else in the same matter? If I believe that it is important for people to make sense of their own experience (with help) but then find myself trained in a way that requires me to reproduce the answers the course requires, where do I get the experience of what that it is like?

Self-direction lies at the heart of helping. I cannot decide for you and I cannot help you decide for yourself if I have no serious experience of what that entails. I then become drawn to offering normative solutions that may or may not be dressed up as choices, but essentially I am providing you with time and space to come up with one of the options that we both know are expected.

The preparation of practitioners to explore, understand and begin to grapple with the concept and practice of self-direction seems to me to be the fundamental bedrock upon which this thing called 'helping' rests. Without it there has to be some appeal at some point to some external authority to prescribe what needs to happen.

Accountability can either be a piece of the managerial superstructure, externally imposed and normatively enforced, or it can be a strenuous exploration of the internal sense of what it means for me to be accountable to myself and to you (and those other parties that have an interest in what we do). Self-direction determines the capacity for accountability. If I am not willing to make my own credo for the work I do review it, revise it, develop it, modify it, throw it away when it fails, then by what claim do I come to stand before you to be your practitioner?

If, as I expressed at an earlier point in this book, the practitioner is committed to helping the client take up the life that is theirs, it first and finally depends upon the degree to which I am prepared to do that also – prior to meeting you.

I cannot expect of you that which I don't expect of myself. I have found this to my cost time and time again when spending time with someone and realising, 'If we go over this edge of yours together, then my commitment to self-direction will require me, too, to make changes in my life'.

It seems to me after over twenty years in this work of helping that it isn't possible or likely that all the changes that self-direction might require me to make will occur before I meet the client who is making them too. There have been significant occasions when the answer a client has found for themselves has been the impetus for me to return to my own life and make major changes there too. Not because the client expected it of me or because it would have been hypocritical not to, but more because the relationship we had developed together had opened up insights, supposedly for the client but equally for me, that could not be confined to the work room.

Helping is like that: if you do it with a conviction that human beings are capable of self-direction, it changes you in ways you never knew were possible and, at times, in ways you would not have ever expected. It also brings pain and hardship, in my experience, yet it brings glories of an altogether wonderful kind that make all the pain and anguish of development and growth more than worth it.

Suggested Reading

Argyris, C & Schon D A: *Theory in Practice: Increasing Professional Effectiveness.* Jossey Bass, 1987.

Combs, A W: *A Theory of Therapy: Guidelines for Counselling Practice.* Sage, 1989.

Frankl, V E: *Psychotherapy and Existentialism.* Penguin. 1967.

Friedman, M: *Dialogue and the Human Image.* Sage 1992.

Harre, R & Gillet, G: *The Discursive Mind.* Sage, 1994.

Jourard, S: *Disclosing Man to Himself.* Van Nostrand, 1968.

Schon, D: *Educating the Reflective Practitioner.* Jossey Bass, San Francisco 1984.

Steiner, C: *Scripts People Live.* Bantam, 1979.

References & Bibliography

Argyris, C & Schon D A: *Theory in Practice: Increasing Professional Effectiveness.* Jossey Bass, 1987.

Arroyo, S: Astrology, *Psychology and the Four Elements.* CRCS Publications, California, 1975.

Assaglioli, R: *Transpersonal Development: The Dimension beyond Psychosynthesis.* Crucible, 1991.

Avila, D L, Combs, A W & Purkey, W L: *The Helping Relationship Source Book,* Volumes I & II Boston. Mass. Allyn & Bacon, 1977.

Bandler, L C: *Solutions.* Future Pace, San Rafael, 1985.

Bandler, R: *Using your Brain for a Change.* Real People Press, Utah, 1992.

Bandler, R & Grinder, J: *Reframing.* Real People Press, Utah, 1982.

Bauman, Z: *Life in Fragments.* Blackwell, 1988.

Bauman, Z: *Postmodern Ethics.* Blackwell, 1993.

Becker, C S: *Living and Relating.* Sage, 1992.

Berne, E: *Beyond Games and Scripts.* Grove Press, 1976.

Berne, E: *Games People Play.* Penguin, 1976.

Berne, E: *What do you say after you say hello?* New York, Grove Press, 1975.

Brammer, L M: *Helping Relationships.* Allyn & Bacon, 1988.

Buber, M: *I and Thou.* Scribener, New York, 1987.

Carkhuff, R R: *The Development of Human Resources.* New York, Holt Rinehart, 1971.

Combs, A W: *Studies in the Helping Professions.* Florida, 1969.

Combs, A W: *A Theory of Therapy: Guidelines for Counselling Practice.* Sage, 1989.

Daloz, L A: *Effective Teaching and Mentoring.* Jossey Bass, 1986.

Dass, R & Gorman, P: *How Can I Help?* Rider,1985.

Dilts, R; Hallbom, T & Smith, S: Beliefs: *Pathways to Well-being.* Metamorphous Press, 1998.

Edelwich, J & Brodsky, A: *Burn Out: Stages of Disillusionment in the Helping Professions.* Human Sciences Press, 1980.

Egan, G: *The Skilled Helper: A Model for Systematic Helping and Interpersonal Relating.* Wandsworth, 1975.

Ellis, A: *The Practice of Rational Emotive Behavior Therapy.* Springer Publishing Company, 1977.

Ferrucci, P: *What we May Be.* Turnstone Press Ltd, 1982.

Fielder, F E: *The Concept of the Ideal Therapeutic Relationship.* Journal of Consulting Psychology, Volume 14 (p 239-245), 1950.

Fisch, R; Weakland, J H & Segal, L: *The Tactics of Change.* Jossey Bass, 1992.

Frankl, V E: *Psychotherapy and Existentialism.* Penguin. 1967.

Friedman, M: *Dialogue and the Human Image.* Sage 1992.

Grinder, J & Bandler, R: *Frogs into Princes.* Real People Press, 1976.

Grinder, J & Bandler, R: *The Structure of Magic,* Volumes I & II Palo Alto, Science and Behaviour Books, 1976.

Haley, J: *Problem Solving Therapy.* Harper Row, 1981.

Harre, R & Gillet, G: *The Discursive Mind.* Sage, 1994.

Halmos, P: *The Faith of the Counsellors.* London, Constable, 1978.

Harris, T A: *I'm OK – You're OK.* Pan Books, 1969.

Hay, J: *Transformational Mentoring.* Sherwood Publishing, 1999.

Heron, J: *The Complete Facilitator's Handbook.* HPRP, Guildford, Surrey, 1977.

Heron, J: *Feeling and Personhood.* Sage Publications, London, 1992.

Heron, J: *Co-operative Inquiry.* Sage Publications, London, 1996.

Heron, J: *Helping the Client.* Sage Publications, London, 2001.

Hillman, J: *Egalitarian Typologies versus the Perception of the Unique.* Eranos Lectures, 1980.

Hillman, J: *The Soul's Code*. Bantam Books, 1997.

Hillman, J & Ventura, M: *We've had a Hundred Years of Psychotherapy: and the world's getting worse*. Harper San Francisco, 1993.

Jongeward & James: *Born to Win: Transactional Analysis with Gestalt Experiments*. Addison-Wesley, 1976.

Jourard, S: *Disclosing Man to Himself*. Van Nostrand, 1968.

Jourard, S: *The Transparent Self*. Princeton. New Jersey: Van Nostrand, 1971.

Kahler, T: *Transactional Analysis Revisited*. Little Rock, Human Development Publications, 1978.

Keen, S: *The Passionate Life*. Gateway Books, 1975.

Kegan, R: *The Evolving Self*. Harvard, 1982.

Kopp, S: *If you Meet the Buddha on the Road. Kill Him!* London, Sheldon Press, 1974.

Kopp, S: *Who am I … Really?* Jeremy P Tarcher, 1987.

Lefebure, M & Schauder, M: *Conversations on Counselling: between a Doctor and a Priest* (3rd edition). T & T Clark, 1990.

Magee, B: *Talking Philosophy*. Oxford University Press, 1978.

Marris, P: *Loss and Change*. Routledge and Kegan, 1986.

Maslow, A H: *Towards a Psychology of Being* (2nd edition). Van Nostrand Reinhold, New York, 1968.

Maslow, A H: *Farther Reaches of Human Nature*. Penguin, 1977.

Miller, J C: *Tutoring*. London: Further Education Curriculum Review and Development Unit, 1982.

O'Neill, O: *A Matter of Trust*. The BBC Reith Lectures, 2002. Cambridge University Press, 2002.

Parker, I et al: *Deconstructing Psychopathology*. Sage 1995 in Self and Society Vol. 25, No 1, March 1997.

Scott Peck, M: *The Road Less Travelled*. London, Arrow, 1990.

Pietrofesa, J J; Hoffman, A; Spekte, H J & Pinto, D V: *Counselling: Theory, Research and Practice*. Chicago, Rand McNally, 1978.

Reason, P & Rowan, J: *Human Inquiry*. Wiley, London, 1981.

Rogers, C R: *On Becoming a Person*. Boston, Houghton Mifflin, 1961.

Rogers, C: *A Way of Being*. Boston, Houghton Mifflin, 1980.

Rowan, J: *The Reality Game*. Routledge Kegan Paul, 1983.

Rowan, J: *Ordinary Ecstasy*. Routledge, 1988.

Schon, D: *Educating the Reflective Practitioner*. Jossey Bass, San Francisco 1984.

Schutz, W: *Elements of Encounter*. Joy Press, California, 1973.

Schutz, W: *Profound Simplicity*. Bantam Books, 1986.

Schutz, W: *The Human Element*. Jossey Bass, 1994.

Steiner, C: *Scripts People Live*. Bantam Books, 1979.

Stewart, I: *Transactional Analysis Counselling in Action*. Sage, London, 1989.

Stewart, I & Joines, V: *TA Today*. Lifespace Publishing, 1993.

Taylor, B: *Helping People Change*. Oasis Press, 1995.

Taylor, B: *The Art of Brief Counselling: Technique or Relationship?* Oasis Press, 1997.

Taylor, B: *Forging the Future Together*. Oasis Press, 2003.

Truax, C B & Carkhuff, R R: *Toward Effective Counselling and Psychotherapy*. Chicago, Aldine, 1967.

Vaughan, F: *The Inward Arc: Healing and Wholeness in Psychotherapy and Spirituality*. London, Shambhala, 1985.

Wolinsky, S: *Trances People Live*. The Bramble Company, 1991.

Woollams, S & Huige, K: *Transactional Analysis*. Dexter, Huron Valley Institute, 1978.

Index

A

accountability 16, 251, 333, 340, 341, 342
advising 46, 48, 51, 56, 70, 80, 285
advocacy 34, 37, 44, 46, 48, 51, 54, 55, 56
authenticity 135, 136, 161, 165, 166, 168

C

challenging 10, 12, 60, 81, 97, 122, 133, 142, 180, 182, 184, 188, 189, 190, 201, 217, 223, 237, 241, 244, 257, 259, 272, 273, 279, 283, 284, 285, 287, 293, 298, 322, 325
changing 16, 18, 19, 28, 43, 74, 95, 102, 116, 123, 128, 181, 207, 219, 230, 237, 240, 241, 242, 255, 276, 284, 292, 293, 294, 299, 300, 305, 313, 329, 330
choosing 9, 108, 131, 237, 240, 241, 265, 268, 271, 273, 274, 275, 279, 283, 287, 288, 289, 291, 293, 314
clarifying 186, 189, 202, 217, 221, 239, 241, 242, 243, 244, 246, 258, 264, 265, 268, 270, 271, 273, 274, 279, 283, 288, 289, 305
closing 237, 241, 242, 307, 308
collaborative endeavour 19, 21, 134, 241
confidentiality 209, 222
contacting 237, 240, 241, 242, 244, 246, 249
contracting 68, 171, 206, 207, 208, 209, 217, 237, 240, 241, 242, 244, 246, 250, 251, 252, 253, 254, 255, 257, 272, 287
core conditions 3, 122, 123, 129, 135, 144, 150, 161, 162, 168, 169, 172, 314
counselling 2, 3, 14, 16, 37, 38, 41, 43, 44, 45, 46, 47, 48, 54, 66, 69, 75, 76, 77, 78, 80, 81, 91, 94, 95, 96, 97, 98, 99, 119, 120, 121, 122, 123, 124, 125, 126, 127, 128, 130, 131, 134, 136, 161, 189, 200, 201, 209, 213, 214, 216, 218, 219, 227, 239, 240, 241, 243, 255, 258, 268, 285, 294, 313, 314, 315, 337, 341, 342, 343, 344
creativity 261, 263, 290, 291, 326

D

drivers 105, 279, 280, 282

E

emotional competence 333, 338, 339, 340
empathy 129, 135, 161, 168, 169, 170, 171, 172, 178, 183, 193, 203, 314

F

facilitating learning 46, 48, 58, 68
feedback 60, 115, 188, 190, 191, 232, 239
frame of reference 129, 154, 156, 169, 170, 178, 247, 248, 259, 268, 299, 315, 334

G

genuineness 129, 135, 161, 165, 166, 167, 168, 172, 193, 315
guidance 3, 41, 44, 45, 47, 48, 58, 59, 60, 61, 62, 63, 64, 65, 68, 69, 70, 71, 73, 74, 75, 76, 77, 80, 123, 185, 210, 214, 220, 321, 322

H

helping agencies 14, 18, 28, 30, 33, 37, 94, 102, 335
humanistic psychology 326, 327

I

image of the person 130, 136, 331
informing 46, 48, 58, 68, 70, 210, 261, 324, 326

L

listening 2, 3, 46, 60, 74, 77, 78, 81, 139, 141, 142, 144, 145, 146, 149, 150, 155, 156, 157, 159, 160, 164, 171, 172, 175, 187, 191, 197, 198, 224, 237, 246, 248, 258, 260, 262, 263, 266, 267, 268, 269, 270, 272, 307

N

narrative 154, 219, 238, 242, 259, 260, 270
negotiating systems 46, 48, 58, 68, 72

O

ordinary caring 3, 9, 10, 11, 220
outcomes 64, 74, 201, 218, 220, 222, 230, 249

P

persecutor 205, 206
personal myths 109, 110
politics 22, 62, 87, 93, 126, 129
practitioner myths 111, 231
problem solving 45, 49, 64, 68, 177, 184, 189, 229, 230, 233, 237, 243, 261, 287, 290, 292, 300, 309
professionalisation 35, 37, 91, 92, 97, 98, 120

Q

question open/closed 183, 186

R

rapport 3, 46, 48, 129, 145, 154, 162, 172, 173, 174, 175, 176, 177, 178, 184, 207, 217, 232, 237, 246, 248, 265, 285, 315
rescuer 25, 205, 206
respect 29, 55, 58, 65, 105, 126, 129, 135, 136, 141, 157, 161, 163, 164, 165, 166, 172, 192, 193, 205, 227, 232, 233, 281, 314, 315, 335

S

self as helper 130, 131, 333,
self as instrument 331, 333
self direction 2, 21, 49, 50, 70, 93, 121, 125, 186, 316, 331, 333, 340, 341, 342
support systems 115, 125, 315
supporting 34, 46, 48, 75, 76, 80, 81, 82, 83, 126, 237, 256, 273, 302, 306
survival strategies 113

T

taking action 43, 46, 48, 51, 54, 69, 210, 288
theory in use 324

V

victim 15, 87, 106, 108, 110 205, 206

W

working alliance 21, 134, 135, 162, 169, 221, 237, 241, 244, 246, 249, 251, 255, 308